D1074332

STANDING AGAINST DRAGONS

STANDING AGAINST DRAGONS THREE SOUTHERN LAWYERS IN AN ERA OF FEAR

Sarah Hart Brown

LOUISIANA STATE UNIVERSITY PRESS
Baton Rouge

Copyright © 1998 by Louisiana State University Press

All rights reserved

Manufactured in the United States of America

First printing

07 06 05 04 03 02 01 00 99 98   5 4 3 2 1

Designer: Glynnis Weston

Typeface: text: Sabon 10.5/14; display: Copperplate 32 BC

Typesetter: Wilsted & Taylor

Library of Congress Cataloging-in-Publication Data:

Brown, Sarah Hart, 1938–

    Standing against dragons : three southern lawyers in an era of
fear / Sarah Hart Brown.

        p.   cm.

    Includes bibliographical references and index.

    ISBN 0-8071-2207-6 (cloth : alk. paper)

    1. Coe, John Moreno. 2. Durr, Clifford J. (Clifford Judkins),
1899– . 3. Smith, Benjamin Eugene. 4. Lawyers—Southern States—
Biography. 5. Civil rights movements—Southern States—History.
I. Title.

KF372.B76   1998

340'.092'2—dc21   98-24110
                                                    CIP

COME NOT BETWEEN THE DRAGON AND HIS WRATH.
—Shakespeare, *King Lear*

for
Marjorie Mackey Hart / *mother, mentor, friend*
and
for Sandy, *always*

CONTENTS

ILLUSTRATIONS

Several years ago I began reading through John Moreno Coe's personal papers and case files, which had been recently acquired by Emory University's Special Collections Department. I thought I knew something about John Coe, or Moreno Coe, as he was always called in Pensacola. He had lived in my hometown while I grew up, and local gossip reported that "everybody knew he was a Communist" who had resigned from the ABA and "joined the Negro lawyers association." Though I tended to view him sympathetically, as an interesting nonconformist in difficult times, I still entered upon the project as something of a voyeur and skeptic. He was not, after all, one of the well-known civil rights lawyers mentioned often by southern historians. The pages that follow are evidence of changes in my homegrown attitudes, and of my search for answers to the many questions that arose from reading his papers: What forces drove Coe to become, by conservative local standards, a "radical" lawyer by the late 1930s and 1940s? What were the roots of his unconventional political ideas? Why did he, a native southerner, join suspected "outsiders" in denouncing the cold war and opposing the rising tide of anti-Communism and massive resistance after World War II? Why did the FBI track his career for many years? What did it mean to be called "subversive" in the postwar South? Were there similar lawyers of his era, white southerners who might be described as civil libertarian, integrationist, politically progressive—advocates for alleged Communists and militant civil rights workers long before such advocacy became acceptable? If so, how important or influential was their work, in the long run?

The career of Alabamian Clifford Judkins Durr, about Coe's age though better known than Coe among those who study the modern South, had to be taken into account first. Durr already had been the subject of an approving biography, and he had not been as consistently scorned by moderate contemporaries as John Coe. But his work was simply too significant, and in broad outline too similar, to leave out of a story about southern lawyers and southern antiradicalism between 1945 and 1965. Other practicing lawyers who fit the parameters surely lived but were not found—among white southerners born at the turn of the century, they all seemed to have escaped to the federal bench or the law schools. But one younger man, Benjamin Eugene Smith of Louisiana, had by the mid-1950s defended clients in both civil liberties and civil rights suits, and he reflected attitudes toward politics and the law similar to those espoused by his older colleagues. By his thirtieth birthday he had attracted almost as much government surveillance as had Coe and Durr at fifty; and as with them his FBI files reflect that, despite repeated efforts, the bureau never justified its surveillance by proving him to be a criminal or a Communist. Smith worked with both older men on various occasions; he admired them, and they him.

Other southerners, black and white, fought against segregation and disfranchisement. Coe, Durr, and Smith exhibited broad civil libertarianism and political progressivism that included, but was not limited to, civil rights matters. In general these lawyers reflect the attitudes of New Deal–era liberalism, when coalitions of leftists and liberals joined to effect reform. Although the "popular front" as designed by the Communist Party in the 1930s was short-lived, the energy and openness of that period inspired many non-Communist liberals.

After the war, the cold war hardened and both *liberal* and *popular front* became fighting words in many quarters, but a few organizations continued to act like popular front groups. They worked for social and economic change or civil liberties and, most importantly in the view of those who castigated them, did not reject supporters because of past or present political affiliations. Enlistment in the cause at hand—civil liberties in the face of anti-Communism, civil rights during the era of massive resistance, redistribution of political or economic power in the South, and so on—became their primary litmus test. Sometimes historians call this perspective "popular front liberalism" to distinguish it from the pointedly anti-Communist "vital center" creed that captured the Democratic Party during the postwar period. Despite the appellation, however, especially after 1948 or 1949 the level of participation by Communists or former Communists in many of these groups is problematic—sometimes nonexistent, unknown, or insignificant except to enemies intent on using anti-Communism as a weapon against them. And though they made some singular and valuable contributions, the "popular front" groups were neither large nor profoundly influential in the Truman and Eisenhower years. Nevertheless, such organizations—among them several that influenced or benefited from the work of Coe, Durr, or Smith—became early, easy, and frequent targets of federal and state anti-Communists. Prominent support of the National Lawyers Guild, the Southern Conference for Human Welfare, the Progressive Citizens of America, the Highlander Folk School, or the Southern Conference Education Fund, to name a few of the best-known, was disdained not only by right-wing conservatives but by center (or "cold war") liberals as well. Congressional committees produced documents accusing them and made broad assumptions about the loyalty of American citizens based on affiliation with them, whether as "members" or as legal advocates. Attorney Joseph Welsh's famous plaint in the army-McCarthy hearings ("At long last, sir . . . have you left no sense of decency?") protested McCarthy's linking a young lawyer in his firm to the National Lawyers Guild. And like the senator from Wisconsin, his southern white supremacist imitators attached the hurtful label "subversive" to such Americans with abandon.

As will be seen concerning the three lawyers under consideration here, the designation often arose from the prejudices of the beholder rather than from fact. The reader will become acquainted with some ideas, organizations, and institutions that touched the lives and work of these unusual southern lawyers in Chapter 1, which offers a brief overview centering on American political opinions in the postwar period. The story of their careers begins in earnest in Chapter 2.

My work began at the Emory University Library and the Martin Luther King Center in Atlanta, and continued at the Historical Society of Wisconsin in Madison, the Meiklejohn Civil Liberties Institute in Berkeley, the Amistad Center and Tulane University Library in New Orleans, the Alabama Department of Archives and History in Montgomery, and the Florida State Archives in Tallahassee. Archivists, I think, must be required to take special courses in good manners. In every place I visited they were uniformly helpful, patient with my questions, and attentive to my many requests. I cannot let the subject pass without saying a special thanks to Dr. Linda Matthews, whose efforts in obtaining John Coe's papers for Emory was the beginning of this book, and to Ann Fagan Ginger—lawyer, activist, archivist, writer—who greatly increased my understanding of antiradicalism and forced me to rethink and rewrite many of my pages. Her unstinting devotion to the Meiklejohn Institute has saved a small but superior collection for American historians, a collection that deserves our attention and support.

I am also indebted to many people who agreed to talk to me about John Coe, Cliff Durr, or Ben Smith—some of them, in fact, named Coe, Durr, or Smith. Though too ill to read the final product, Virginia Durr graciously submitted to two interviews and commented on the first draft of my manuscript. Her daughters read later versions. I am especially grateful to Ann Durr Lyon, both for her thoughtful criticism and for her substantive additions. Jim and Ellen Coe and Evalyn Coe Grubbs shared not only their thoughts but also letters and papers they hold privately, as did Patrick Smith, who took me to the best restaurant in Ruston, Louisiana, after a long morning of questions. Penny Smith Jones let me use her own articles about her father, and she and her uncle, Bill Massimini, gave me insights into his personality I could never have obtained elsewhere. Durr and Coe left behind voluminous files and many long letters, but Smith wrote fewer letters and many of his files were lost. In his case, interviews formed the basis of the research, and I could not have known him without the help of his former law partners, clerks, colleagues, family, and friends. Among these, Jack Peebles and Corinne Barnwell were crucial. They shared important papers and ideas as well as valuable interview time, and retained an interest in the book over the long haul.

John Matthews of Georgia State University read this manuscript many more times than he wanted to. He inspired me, guided me, and was a thorn in my flesh for several years. He is one of my favorite southern historians. Gary Fink's kind but perspicacious comments frequently made me rethink my purposes, keeping me focused on a few primary ideas. And Merl Reed's flying red pencil really did make my writing better. I am grateful for other friends at Georgia State as well. Ed Gorsuch, Cynthia Schwenck, David McCreery, Kay Kemp, and other fellow (time) travelers taught me what it means to be a historian. Ray Mohl of Florida Atlantic University (now at the University of Alabama, Birmingham) read the manuscript twice and suggested important changes; I am deeply indebted to him for his help in getting the book into its final form.

Finally, one has to thank one's family and friends for putting up with it all. A few friends have kept me going, occasionally even laughing. These wonders know who they are, and how important they have been during this process. My extended family is unbeatable—uncles and aunts, cousins and in-laws—everybody supported my work and wondered why it took so long. My brothers are southern lawyers of whom I am very proud; their industry and integrity inspired me. While I composed these chapters, my sons began promising careers and established families; their love and encouragement sustained me. The book is dedicated to my mother, who believed in this endeavor and forced me to see it through, and to my husband, who cared for me and kept me sane during the process. If there is anything of value here they deserve most of the credit.

STANDING AGAINST DRAGONS

CHAPTER ONE

The Problemed Peace:
Civil Libertarianism, Antilibertarianism, and Cold War Doctrine

By the end of World War II, the United States had become the world's most powerful and influential nation, but perplexing American problems, new and old, awaited solution. None of these seemed more pressing than the nation's sole ownership of the atomic bomb, the challenge of Communist ideology, or the persistence of racial segregation in the face of the nation's heralded democratic ideals. As the country faced these important challenges, the American people gradually adjusted to the political and economic changes engendered by the New Deal and the war. The liberal agenda of the 1930s, which had ushered in the era of big government and welfare capitalism, did not enjoy universal admiration. Franklin Roosevelt's charismatic leadership held together a fragile but diminishing liberal consensus through the war years; after his death, under pressure from a conservative resurgence, liberals began to reevaluate that consensus.

Since the turn of the twentieth century, disparate groups had identified themselves as liberal: Progressives who battled monopoly and poverty, racial moderates in the South, the emerging black bourgeoisie, moderates and radicals from the labor movement, and Marxists of various sorts. On the far left the Communist Party in the United States (CPUSA) functioned as a legitimate, if small and often factionalized, American political party from the 1920s until the 1950s.

John Patrick Diggins has written that during the 1930s the collapse of capitalism "sensitized intellectuals to life at the lower levels" of American society. At the same time, "Russia's highly propagandized economic progress" gained attention "not only [among] the small American communist Left but the larger liberal Center as well." One unique element of liberal politics during this period involved the respectability of "popular front" alliances, associations of liberals of the center and the left constituted to accomplish common goals. The Communists invented the term in the mid-1930s to indicate their willingness to cooperate with Socialists and others in the fight against Fascism, but over time "popular front" came to signify any collaboration that included both liberals and leftists or radicals. In spite of the complexity of policy formation within the party, after 1935 the CPUSA generally supported the New Deal; and the party always advocated legal equality and social justice in the South, as did most center liberals. Although they were often very fragile unions, popular front alliances presented a public facade of left-liberal harmony in the 1930s. Though some writers have tended to overstate left-wing strength by labeling this the "Red Decade," Mary S. McAuliffe and others have pointed out that "the left was more unified and exercised more influence over American politics than ever before" during the depression and New Deal years.[1]

American liberalism defied precise definition even during the 1930s. A vague but ardent belief in "Jeffersonianism"—in particular, ideas pertaining to democracy, human freedom, and civil liberties—may have been the only tenet around which Americans of the left ever coalesced. So-called "liberal" opposition to the business- and national security–centered conservative right traditionally represented by the Republican Party ranged from a majority who wanted to regulate capitalism to the CPUSA and others who demanded its eventual overthrow. But when the Communists retreated from anti-Fascism as a result of the 1939 Nazi-Soviet nonaggression pact they began to lose the confidence of the larger American left and, despite the renewed unity of the war years, drift toward disgrace. "The CPUSA's successes," Harvey Klehr wrote, "were always hostage to Soviet foreign policy." Both during and, especially, after World War II, broad popular front coalitions became discredited, and conspicuous divisions developed within American liberalism. Always tenuous, most alliances of Marxists and non-Marxist liberals perished by the 1940s.[2]

1. John Patrick Diggins, *The Rise and Fall of the American Left* (1973; rpr. New York, 1992), 148–54, quotes on 148 and 150–51; Mary Sperling McAuliffe, *Crisis on the Left: Cold War Politics and American Liberals, 1947–1954* (Amherst, 1978), 1; Harvey Klehr, John Earl Haynes, and Fridrikh Igorevich Firsov, *The Secret World of American Communism* (New Haven, 1995), 9–10.

2. Klehr, Haynes, and Firsov, *Secret World,* 10.

Two liberal groups established in January, 1947, exemplify the split within American liberalism. One, a left-liberal alliance called the Progressive Citizens of America (PCA), formed to support Henry Wallace, Roosevelt's secretary of agriculture, vice-president, and secretary of commerce, in a bid for the presidency in 1948. Wallace was never a Communist but he accepted a variety of leftists into his party, and his movement has come to represent a final burst of popular front liberalism. The PCA kept alive the idea of rapprochement and cooperation with the Soviet Union that had been the hope of most liberals in the 1930s. Wallace condemned the Truman administration harshly for its anti-Soviet foreign-policy initiatives and its anti-Communist efforts on the domestic front. He finished a poor fourth in the 1948 race.

The other group, created only a week after the formation of the PCA, was the Americans for Democratic Action (ADA). While most leaders of the PCA professed non-Communist liberalism, the ADA's members pointedly denounced Communism and especially the CPUSA. Supported by liberal luminaries such as Reinhold Niebuhr, Arthur M. Schlesinger, Jr., John Kenneth Galbraith, and many former New Dealers, the ADA proclaimed its liberalism, anti-Communism, and support of Truman's drive to contain the expansion of the Soviet Union in Europe. It redefined the New Deal in cold war terms. Members of the ADA and other liberals who shunned radical connections in the 1940s and 1950s have been called "vital center" or "cold war" liberals. They viewed themselves as realists, contrasting their realism to the idealism of the popular front left. The "vital center," according to Schlesinger, became the logical home for liberalism, a center point between the totalitarian extremes, Fascism and Communism. Both popular front and cold war liberals took pride in the accomplishments of the New Deal, but they had different views about the dangers of international Communism, and "thus they differed on the issue of the united left."[3]

The schemes of cold war liberals like Schlesinger positioned traditional conservatives to the right of center, but right-wing political ideas were also somewhat ameliorated by the repercussions of World War II. In foreign affairs the historic isolationism of most American conservatives had been preempted by bipartisan support of postwar internationalism. America's business and

---

3. Arthur M. Schlesinger, Jr., *The Vital Center: The Politics of Freedom* (Boston, 1949); McAuliffe, *Crisis on the Left,* 7, 63–74, quote on 7.

military establishments perceived fresh opportunities and new missions and responsibilities in war-torn Europe and Asia. Conservatives and cold war liberals alike looked with pride on what *Time* publisher Henry Luce called the "American Century." This concept unfolded with the Truman Doctrine and the Marshall Plan, efforts to check Communist advances and rebuild Western Europe in the American image as a bastion of democratic capitalism. The new internationalism contained some elements of the old isolationism, such as a fear of losing control of commercial and military prerogatives, the desire to create simple militarized perimeters, and naive expectations about benefits of American individualism and ingenuity for the rest of the world. But it also represented a new and expansive kind of Americanism, more preoccupied with defining and protecting the "Free World," less with shielding "America First."

The old isolationism found its real postwar expression in the drive to purify America internally, to rid her of elements that might subvert her mission. Americans were weary from nearly two decades of depression, economic experimentation, and war, and uneasy about Soviet expansion in Eastern Europe. Many could be persuaded by conservative rhetoric that the menace of international Communism and the treachery of its "fellow travelers" in the United States constituted the nation's most pressing problem. External power and alien doctrine, not internal inequity, seemed the source of instability in American society. By the end of the 1940s, right-wing politicians of both parties had channeled the nation's energies either into the search for subversives or into cold war initiatives, thereby avoiding elemental, politically risky domestic problems that troubled liberals but seemed almost incapable of solution. Both reactionaries and business conservatives used anti-Communism skillfully to further their own ends, resolutely steering the nation away from the liberal activism of the Roosevelt years. Fear of subversion became the primary rationalization for a conservative resurgence that swept the nation, splintering American liberalism and nearly obliterating its left wing.[4]

The activities of the first House Un-American Activities Committee (HUAC) foreshadowed the antisubversive endeavors of the postwar era. The committee began its work in 1938 with conservative Texan Martin Dies at

---

4. McAuliffe, *Crisis on the Left*, 63–74.

its helm, and promoted the passage of the first peacetime sedition act since 1798, the Alien Registration Act of 1940, popularly called by the name of another southerner, Congressman Howard Smith of Virginia. The Smith Act differs from the Espionage and Sedition Acts of 1917–1918 in that it applies in peacetime as well as wartime and is not confined to advocacy directed at interfering with the armed forces. The earlier acts condemned verbal attacks on the American form of government, but the Smith Act banned only advocacy of acts of violence or force, that is, joining, endorsing, organizing, or publishing or using the mails to distribute material supporting "any society, group or assembly of persons who teach, advocate or encourage . . . the overthrow of the government of the United States." It provided for ten-year sentences and fines up to $10,000 for those convicted. Like HUAC's investigations and hearings, this legislation aimed originally, if fleetingly, at Nazi subversion.[5]

Over the next thirty years many southern congressmen sat on HUAC's panels, none more dedicated than John Rankin of Mississippi, who in 1945 offered the bill making this the only permanent investigating subcommittee in the House and giving it extraordinary powers of subpoena. Like Dies, Rankin passionately hated the New Deal and considered it "Communistic"; he also regularly expressed approval of the Ku Klux Klan. He proposed a corollary to the Smith Act that would have made American teachers subject to the penalties of that act if they conveyed even "the impression of sympathy with . . . Communist ideology."[6]

Perhaps even more important, the Federal Bureau of Investigation, under Director J. Edgar Hoover, developed a zealous anti-Communist counterintelligence force that underwent considerable growth in size and influence during the 1940s. The bureau marched hand in hand with congressional investigations, each the perfect complement for the other. Hoover held disapproving congressmen in thrall to his power; FBI surveillance and Hoover's files became a fact of political life few liberal politicians could escape. A

5. Congress repealed the harsh 1918 Sedition Act in 1921, though the advocacy provisions of the original 1917 act remain largely in force today. Joseph Celinni, ed., *Digest of the Public Record of Communism in the United States* (1955; rpr. New York, 1977), 188–205.

6. David Caute, *The Great Fear: The Anti-Communist Purge Under Truman and Eisenhower* (New York, 1978), 89–90.

participant in the brutal but brief Red scare that followed World War I, Hoover as a staunch conservative believed that it was impossible for a leftist, much less a member of the CPUSA, to be a loyal American. "Hoover became a state within a state," noted David Caute in *The Great Fear;* "politically sacrosanct, he made the FBI his own private army, modeled according to his own passions and prejudices, dedicated to the cult of his personality." The FBI's authority for political surveillance originated in vague presidential directives in 1936 and 1939 and in Hoover's interpretation of antisubversive laws of 1939–1941, primarily the Smith Act.[7] One of the bureau's self-appointed tasks involved the provision of information about subversion, sometimes mere conjecture, to government agencies and committees. These bodies usually used FBI information without questioning its accuracy.

As the wartime romance with the Soviet Union cooled after 1945, legislative hearings about nuclear spying and loyalty of government employees captured the front pages of American newspapers along with stories about Communist expansion in Europe and Asia. In the lexicon of postwar conservatives, the pejorative term "fellow traveler" eventually encompassed almost all social and economic reformers, regardless of political affiliations. Suspect liberal organizations such as the National Association for the Advancement of Colored People (NAACP) and the American Civil Liberties Union (ACLU), which claimed the Bill of Rights to be its "only client," tried to disassociate themselves from persons or groups denounced by the anti-Communist committees. Stung by a Dies committee accusation and prodded by liberal and Socialist board members, the ACLU in 1940 passed an anti-Communist resolution and expelled one of its founders, longtime Communist Elizabeth Gurley Flynn. After the war, the ACLU board strengthened the resolution and made it a part of the organization's constitution. In the late 1940s and early 1950s the NAACP, led by the determined anti-Communist Walter White, satisfied contributors by firing research director W. E. B. Du Bois, "a popular front liberal who supported Wallace," and purging suspected subversives from its branches. During the same period, Communist-dominated unions faced expulsion from the Congress of Industrial Organizations (CIO).

---

7. Ibid., 111–16, quote on 113; Percival R. Baily, "The Case of the National Lawyers Guild, 1939–1958," in *Beyond the Hiss Case: The FBI, Congress, and the Cold War,* ed. Athan G. Theoharis (Philadelphia, 1982), 133.

The cold war became as much a drive for domestic conformity as a war of propaganda and nerves against the Soviet Union, and in the former effort it succeeded, at least in the short run.[8]

Conservatives in both the major parties wanted to control change and limit social disruption. Particularly, they would discontinue what they saw as the leftward, antibusiness trend of domestic policy in the Roosevelt years. From its beginning, postwar anti-Communism sought to discredit New Deal innovations and liberal groups trying to expand on them as much as to search for saboteurs. Extremists in the FBI and on congressional committees conveniently blurred distinctions between Communists and liberals. Attempting to establish their loyalty in an increasingly repressive climate, liberals who had welcomed allies of all political persuasions before the war began to judge radicals or leftists expendable. Popular front associations were simply no longer worth the risk.

In the South, many established politicians endorsed the Red scare primarily to discourage the disturbing social ideas that emanated from the New Deal and the war against Fascism. Although New Deal programs had not undermined southern segregation, blacks perceived the general concern of the Roosevelt administration about the inequities of southern society through such signs as appointments of prominent blacks to federal positions and scattered economic improvements resulting from the work of New Deal agencies. During and after the war, both blacks and southern liberals compared the evils of Fascism to the oppression of African Americans in the United States. And European allies welcomed black soldiers despite segregation within the U.S. armed forces, underscoring white America's indifference to southern racial mores. As they returned from Europe or the Pacific, black GIs were naturally reluctant to reassume lower-caste positions in a segregated society.

On the other hand, white supremacists regarded all agitation against segregation as Communist-inspired and used this notion to gain acceptance for their positions. Perhaps because civil rights progress had long been supported by the CPUSA, "in the heyday of red baiting after World War II, these tactics worked."[9] While still nominally faithful to the party of Franklin Roosevelt,

8. McAuliffe, *Crisis on the Left,* 57–62, 90–91; Numan V. Bartley, *The New South, 1945–1980: The Story of the South's Modernization* (Baton Rouge, 1995), 42–46, 68–69, quote on 68.

9. Harvard Sitkoff, *The Struggle for Black Equality, 1954–1980* (New York, 1981), 17.

most white southerners perceived the liberal agenda to be toxic to "the southern way of life." Clinging to the popular misconception that regional problems originated somewhere outside the South, they identified themselves with the conservative agenda and anti-Communism.

Nevertheless, beginning with Supreme Court cases mandating integration of graduate schools in the late 1930s and with *Smith* v. *Allwright*,[10] which ended all-white Democratic primary elections in the South in 1944, blacks began to reclaim their American citizenship. Black political power was becoming a force to be reckoned with in southern cities, where over 80 percent of black voters resided. By 1950 about 12 percent, and by 1960 about 20 percent, of the African-American population of the South had registered to vote. The New Deal had brought public housing for blacks to a few southern cities, and in other towns black voters improved living conditions in their neighborhoods by supporting progressive candidates.[11]

Outsiders like the NAACP and the CIO often received blame for "race troubles" in the South in the 1940s. Blacks' access to decent education at any level proceeded at a snail's pace, but by 1947 the northern-based NAACP Legal Defense and Education Fund had begun the process that concluded with *Brown* v. *Board of Education*[12] and destroyed the legal basis of southern segregation. As a result of New Deal labor legislation, northern union organizers redoubled their efforts in southern mills. Union efforts culminated in "Operation Dixie," the massive CIO drive to organize southern textile workers that began in 1946 and ended in almost complete failure in 1950. But although these challenges to the southern status quo would have been impossible without the sponsorship of northern-based groups, internal phenomena germinated change in the South as well.

The war itself made the South richer and more urban than ever before. Southerners had been moving off their farms for twenty-five years, but the advent of work in defense plants vastly increased the flow from country to city. Returning veterans, black and white, often stayed in the cities or moved

10. 321 U.S. 649 (1944).
11. David R. Goldfield, *Black, White, and Southern: Race Relations and Southern Culture, 1940 to the Present* (Baton Rouge, 1990), 45–47, 55–62.
12. 347 U.S. 483 (1954); 349 U.S. 294 (1955).

north rather than coming back to rural areas of the South. More than 750,000 blacks and thousands of whites as well migrated from rural to urban areas of the South between 1940 and 1955.[13]

New, younger politicians emerged in the southern Democratic Party in the 1940s through political campaigns remarkable most of all for their lack of race-baiting. Some of them, such as Senators Estes Kefauver and Albert Gore of Tennessee, Frank Graham of North Carolina, and Claude Pepper of Florida, were racial moderates. Kefauver and Pepper advocated legislation to end the poll tax and provide federal penalties for lynching in the early 1940s. But these senators constituted a distinct minority as they took their place alongside such entrenched segregationists as Senators James O. Eastland of Mississippi and Richard Russell of Georgia. And on the local and state levels, while aggressive new leaders sought to improve living conditions and provide jobs, a direct assault on legal segregation did not become a part of the political agenda. Racial tensions actually increased in the years just after the war, when many outbreaks of racial violence erupted, most intended to discipline returning black GIs who had acquired ideas about racial equality during the fight against Fascism. Before Frank Graham went to the Senate in 1948 he helped to author the Truman administration's civil rights declaration, *To Secure These Rights,* a document reluctantly sponsored by the administration after the spate of southern lynchings in 1945 and 1946.[14]

Segregation, the President's Committee on Civil Rights declared, "had become a bottleneck to the South's progress." Truman sent a legislative proposal based on the report to Congress, where southern conservatives blocked its implementation into law. Most of its sponsors understood at the outset, given the antiliberal political climate, that it was a legislative impossibility. As the anti-Communist movement gained force it became increasingly common, in Congress and elsewhere, to combine race-baiting with Red-baiting. Segregationists who saw little qualitative difference between a threat to democratic capitalism and a threat to southern social stability considered it inconsequential whether the "outside agitators" who pushed for integration were in reality anti-Communists, like the NAACP and the southern leadership

13. Goldfield, *Black, White, and Southern,* 47.
14. Ibid., 45–62; Bartley, *New South,* 76–78.

of the CIO, or cooperated with Communists, as did some early organizers of Operation Dixie. One kind of leveling seemed as dangerous as the other.[15]

"Communism and integration are inseparable and . . . integration is the southern expression of the communist movement," said a leading member of the Louisiana legislature in the mid-1950s. J. Edgar Hoover echoed this view, at one point describing civil rights advocates as subversives at an Eisenhower cabinet meeting. He assisted conservative southern politicians in their relentless stalking of southern integrationists. The FBI kept detailed records about liberal southerners and provided undercover informers and professional ex-Communist witnesses for committee investigations that linked southern civil rights activism to Communism and sedition. In other parts of the country, as well, "black reds" and their white allies became subjects of witch-hunts. "Of course the fact that a person believes in racial equality doesn't *prove* that he's a communist," said one loyalty board chairman in Washington, "but it makes you look twice, doesn't it?" In the postwar period it became de rigueur for conservative newspaper columnists, often employing information "leaked" from the FBI, to label integrationists "Communist" with the same equanimity used to identify other targets of government investigations. Many states passed "little Smith Acts" and other legislation to restrict or bar Communist or popular front activities. Southern legislatures and law enforcement officials used these laws to discipline integrationists more often than Communists or fellow travelers.[16]

The "100 percent Americanism" of white supremacy combined with the defensive mentality of the lost cause to create a southern regional creed that owed much more to fear of social change than to any understanding of Marxism or domestic subversion. Though the South became predominantly

15. Bartley, *New South*, 41–46; Linda Reed, *Simple Decency and Common Sense: The Southern Conference Movement, 1938–1963* (Bloomington, Ind., 1991), 130–31.

16. Jack Peebles, "Subversion and the Southern Conference Educational Fund" (M.A. thesis, Louisiana State University at New Orleans, 1970), 33; Taylor Branch, *Parting the Waters: America in the King Years, 1954–1963* (New York, 1988), 182; Caute, *Great Fear,* 166–68, quote on 168; Celinni, ed., *Digest of Communism,* Part 2, "State Statutes and Decisions," 241–455. See also Don E. Carleton, *Red Scare! Right Wing Hysteria, Fifties Fanaticism, and Their Legacy in Texas* (Austin, 1985). Texas, where right-wing hysteria aimed as much at unions as at integration, may be the exception to the statement that state witch-hunts in the South were directed mainly toward civil rights advocates.

urban, built roads with federal money, and sought northern industry during these years, a deep suspicion of modern, "foreign," and egalitarian ideas remained. Entrenched southern politicians encouraged and built on these fears in the 1940s and 1950s to keep themselves in power, characterizing liberals who championed constitutional rights or suggested the redistribution of economic or political power as threats to national security. Southerners who deplored the hopelessness of lost cause rationalizations or found southern race relations morally indefensible often faced isolation as traitors not only to the South but to the nation as well.

On the other hand, some southern moderates demonstrated patriotic Americanism and at the same time argued for a gradual end to the old patterns of segregation and disfranchisement. Vital center liberals walked a very thin line in the South, but the cold war and the search for subversives offered some protection. Strident anti-Communism became a way for centrist liberals to assert their patriotism and remain on the safe side of the witch-hunters. Nationally, groups like the NAACP, the ACLU, and the ADA followed this course, and in other parts of the country the distinction between these cold war liberals and liberals who still advocated popular front relationships helped to shelter anti-Communist liberals. The NAACP, the ACLU, and the ADA, however, remained anathema in the South. In a 1955 speech titled "The Ugly Truth About the N.A.A.C.P.," Georgia attorney general Eugene Cook assured state policemen that the civil rights organization promoted "communist inspired doctrine" and that white southern liberals "aided and abetted" its agitation. For southern conservatives, differences among leftist and liberal ideologies blurred before the transcendent power of white supremacy.[17]

Nonetheless, a few southerners, like newspaper columnists Ralph McGill of the Atlanta *Constitution,* Harry Ashmore of Little Rock's *Arkansas Gazette,* and Hodding Carter of the Greenville, Mississippi, *Delta Democrat-Times,* voiced racial tolerance but simultaneously condemned Communists with great vigor. They also reproached popular front liberals who, they surmised, might be innocent themselves but naively cooperated with left-wingers to accomplish common goals. Members of this dominant wing of southern liberalism usually supported the Southern Regional Council's efforts to bring

17. Quote from the *Southern Patriot,* November, 1955, 1.

gradual improvement in race relations. The council, formed in 1944, began pushing for solutions to southern race problems by the late 1940s, took a formal stand in favor of ending southern segregation in 1951, and became a stalwart supporter of school desegregation after the 1954 *Brown* decision. Although the prevailing view held it impossible to be both a good southerner and an integrationist, conservative southerners could agree with cold war liberals about the evils of Communism and the perils of cooperation with nonconformist outsiders such as left-wing labor organizers or the supporters of Henry Wallace in 1948. Southern historian Anthony Dunbar called this phenomenon "progressivism shorn of its economic critique and absolutely unmarked by the radical protest of the past decade." Or, to paraphrase Numan V. Bartley, as segregation began to be perceived nationally as a moral issue and a diplomatic embarrassment rather than as part of a complex regional economic quagmire, the integration movement gained respectability among a broad coalition of moderate reformers. These reformers centered on ending de jure segregation and disfranchisement and often opposed any fur- ther redistribution of the South's political and economic resources.[18] Though hated by white supremacists, these mainstream liberals eluded the worst excesses of the Red scare in the South as elsewhere in the nation. In most cases they avoided complete isolation in their local communities and escaped the nets of state and federal investigatory agencies.

Southern liberals who saw de jure segregation as only the most visible of the South's several fundamental problems, and who also refused to take refuge in anti-Communist rhetoric, remained rare and easily identified by witch- hunters. Until dying in a flurry of suspicion, the Southern Conference for Human Welfare (SCHW) represented this strain of southern liberalism. SCHW typified a politically tolerant popular front approach. New Dealers and other liberals formed SCHW after the Roosevelt administration's *Report on the Economic Conditions of the South,* which listed serious inadequacies in education, housing conditions, and health and other services in southern states and cited the region's dependent "colonial" economy as the main culprit. SCHW organized state committees and a regional staff to work to- ward liberalizing and modernizing the South along the lines outlined in the

18. Anthony Dunbar, *Against the Grain: Southern Radicals and Prophets, 1929–1959* (Charlottesville, 1981), 221; Bartley, *New South,* 69.

report; a few SCHW volunteers were Communists. Despite a promising beginning in 1938 and support from the Roosevelt administration, the organization collapsed only ten years later, during the 1948 presidential campaign. SCHW's support for federal intervention to end racial discrimination certainly contributed to its early death. But the organization's internal divisions, including both staff disagreements and a split among its supporters into center and popular front factions, became the most crucial element in its demise. Active participation of several important SCHW board members in Wallace's 1948 presidential campaign increased segregationists' accusations that SCHW was controlled by Communists and stopped vital grants and union donations.[19]

The Southern Conference Educational Fund (SCEF), SCHW's tax-exempt wing, survived the parent organization and continued to publish the liberal periodical *Southern Patriot*. Based in New Orleans during most of its history, SCEF's staff and board members were by charter all southerners, though the organization frequently mounted fund-raising drives in the Northeast and West and solicited money from northern foundations. Its leadership and most board members remained non-Communist, but like SCHW and the PCA, SCEF eschewed political tests for membership even at the height of the Red scare. No other group combined SCEF's southern leadership and militancy about the need to revolutionize race relations with a willingness to accept all volunteers who shared similar goals, whatever their associations or political bent. A small but tenacious remnant of the popular front era, it would provide one link between the collaborative left of the 1930s and the many-faceted New Left radicalism of the 1960s. From 1948 through the mid-1960s, SCEF was the only white-led southern organization devoted single-mindedly to ending segregation and disfranchisement.[20]

19. Bartley, *New South*, 1–3, 27; Reed, *Simple Decency*, 126–28.

20. SCEF's longtime president, Aubrey Williams (1948–61), and executive directors, James A. Dombrowski (1946–65) and Carl and Anne Braden (1965–74), were white. The Bradens worked for SCEF as field secretaries and edited the *Southern Patriot* beginning in 1957. However, after Williams' resignation he was replaced by two blacks, first Bishop Edgar A. Love of the Methodist Church (1961–63) and then Rev. Fred A. Shuttlesworth (1963–74), prominent member of the Southern Christian Leadership Conference and a Baptist minister in Birmingham and Cincinnati. In addition, there were through the years many black board members, including such luminaries as Benjamin Mays (who resigned in 1954) and Mary McLeod Bethune. "Officers of

In a letter printed in the first issue of the *Southern Patriot* after SCEF's incorporation as SCHW's propaganda arm in 1946, Senator Theodore G. Bilbo of Mississippi called the organization an "un-American, negro social equality, communistic, mongrel outfit."[21] While this letter, a response to SCHW's support for abolition of poll taxes, exhibited Bilbo's singular tastelessness, it is roughly typical of criticism leveled at SCHW and SCEF by southern politicians over the next twenty years.

The repeated branding of SCEF as subversive and un-American by politicians, compounded by the national fear of Communism and SCEF's inflexibility on discrimination issues at least five years before the Southern Regional Council endorsed gradual integration, created a wall between SCEF and southern liberals of the center. The southern liberal coalition of the 1930s and 1940s, "both real and potential," according to Bartley, "manifested more than its share of internal contradictions" because its members often "shared little beyond opposition to the policies and practices of the old regime."[22] Even after most moderates accepted integration as inevitable, and in spite of the fact that some SCEF activists, including its longtime president Aubrey Williams, enjoyed wide respect, all but the most zealous southern liberals avoided identification with SCEF. Scarcely a mainstream cultural force, southern liberalism divided along regionally distinctive lines that paralleled the divisions affecting the wider American left. Estrangement from centrist liberalism isolated SCEF and diminished its influence as a civil rights organization.

Throughout its history, many SCEF supporters also endorsed the Highlander Folk School of Monteagle, Tennessee. In 1932 the school began working with labor unions to bring social justice in the South, and soon thereafter it joined the fight for integration; like SCEF, it was never Communist-controlled but suffered repeated attacks from southern anti-Communists. James Dombrowski, who served as SCEF's executive director from 1948 until 1965,

---

the Southern Conference For Human Welfare which later became The Southern Conference Educational Fund (SCEF)," in Box 11, Folder 13, James A. Dombrowski Papers, Archives Division, State Historical Society of Wisconsin, Madison [hereinafter cited as Dombrowski Papers]. See also Peebles, "Subversion and SCEF," iii.

21. Quote from the *Southern Patriot,* January, 1956, p. 1.

22. Bartley, *New South,* 28–30, quote on 28.

came to SCHW in 1943 from a position at Highlander. Dombrowski shared many of the philosophical and religious ideas of Highlander's principal founder, Myles Horton, and other backers, such as Dr. Alva Taylor of Vanderbilt University's School of Religion and his disciples Don West, Claude Williams, Ward Rodgers, and Howard Kester. Their brand of southern liberalism has been described as "a 'radical gospel' movement, which conceived that the world might be redeemed not through good works but through the rising up of the poor." Dombrowski, an ordained Methodist minister from Florida, graduated from Atlanta's Emory University and then obtained a Ph.D. under Harry Ward and Reinhold Niebuhr at Columbia University, where he became a member of the Socialist Party. Dombrowski organized a group that later became the Fellowship of Southern Churchmen as his first assignment at Highlander; one of his fellow workers, Howard Kester, was rejected for membership on the NAACP board of directors in 1934 because "Walter White believed he was 'too radical.'"[23]

Kester's rejection is an early example of the way suspicion affected popular front southerners. Another illustration involving the NAACP's White comes from the autobiography of southern liberal Virginia Durr, who tells of joining an SCHW committee organized by Jim Dombrowski to protest what amounted to a pogrom against the black community of Columbia, Tennessee, in 1946. Police arrested about one hundred persons when they tried to prevent the lynching of a black soldier. The Columbia blacks were held incommunicado, denied counsel, and beaten, and two were killed by officers. Both SCHW and the NAACP set up committees to help the twenty-five men finally charged. Durr had already met with Dombrowski and his committee when she received a call from White, who urged her to join his group instead: "Mrs. Durr, if you join *that* committee, you are going to be sorry. It has communists in it." A founder of the Southern Conference movement, native Alabamian Durr stayed with her original choice; and ultimately SCHW, the NAACP, and other liberal groups combined to address the Columbia situation. The NAACP provided counsel, including Thurgood Marshall, for those accused in Columbia and joined an umbrella defense committee spearheaded by

23. Dunbar, *Against the Grain*, 62–73, quotes on 63 and 73. See also Peebles, "Subversion and SCEF," 9, and Frank Adams, *James A. Dombrowski: An American Heretic, 1897–1983* (Knoxville, 1992).

SCHW and headed by Eleanor Roosevelt and Dr. Channing Tobias of the YMCA. Dombrowski, who published a searing propaganda piece called "The Truth About the Columbia, Tennessee Cases" for SCHW, later became a target of a federal grand jury's investigation into the case.[24]

If the NAACP's leader suspected SCHW, his reservations paled beside those of retired army major Monroe Schaff, chairman of the American Legion's Americanism Committee. In a speech to the Kiwanis Club of Columbia, Schaff called Dombrowski "a seasoned, well trained agitator for the Communist Party" who duped unsuspecting southerners by faking his group's intentions to "uplift living conditions of the South." People like Dombrowski, "who support the FEPC, e.g., SCHW, CIO-PAC and others," were "as guilty of treason as was Benedict Arnold."[25] Labeling supporters of the Fair Employment Practices Committee "Benedict Arnolds"—that is, equating Roosevelt-era liberalism with Communism—had become a commonplace in patriotic associations like the American Legion.

This contagious malady, since the 1950s commonly called "McCarthyism" after its best-known champion, Republican senator Joseph R. McCarthy of Wisconsin, infected not only government but millions of Americans and hundreds of organizations all over the nation. The Veterans of Foreign Wars and the Daughters of the American Revolution, for example, became intensely anti-Communist. But other groups which at first glance seem much less susceptible to reactionary rhetoric were profoundly affected as well. Universities, schools, churches, fraternal orders, men's service organizations, women's clubs, and professional associations all joined in the ostensibly patriotic crusade. "The American Bar Association and the American Medical Association (seized by a fear of socialized medicine) were in competition for the Purple Heart of anti-communism," noted David Caute. Jerold Auerbach claims that "from [the ABA's] vantage point the New Deal was institutionalized subversion." Often confusing "corporate capitalism and patriotism with legalism," the association "equated reform with revolution and economic regulation with dictatorship, warning lawyers against 'rash experiments with American

24. Hollinger F. Barnard, ed., *Outside the Magic Circle: The Autobiography of Virginia Foster Durr* (Tuscaloosa, 1985), 186. See Box 16, Folder 11, Dombrowski Papers, and Adams, *James Dombrowski,* 158–62.

25. Nashville *Banner,* July 19, 1946, in Box 15, Folder 3, Dombrowski Papers.

ideals.'" This reaction to New Deal liberalism seemed to forecast the legal establishment's enthusiastic response to the anti-Communist crusade a decade later.[26]

No professional associations became more involved in the postwar pursuit of conformity than those of American lawyers. Challenges to the government's search for subversives by attorneys brandishing such national icons as the First, Fifth, and Sixth Amendments were not suffered lightly. The ABA made every effort to purge radicals from its ranks, and "in one state after another bench and bar mobilized an array of professional weapons: contempt citations, disbarment, exclusion, and subtler forms of coercive socialization."[27] Government lawyers and legal or quasi-legal processes operated at the center of postwar anti-Communism, and the movement enjoyed the sanction, even the encouragement, of the legal establishment. Professional groups applauded lawyer-legislators, prosecutors, and judges who ignored the First and Sixth Amendments in their search for Communists in the federal government.

By the same token, southern lawyers and judges who defied efforts to reinvigorate the Fourteenth and Fifteenth Amendments enjoyed the respect and approval of their fellows. "Liberal" politician-lawyers like Senators Lister Hill and John Sparkman of Alabama found it necessary to swear allegiance to both white supremacy and anti-Communism in order to be elected. With very few exceptions, federal legislators who could be tarred with a leftist or integrationist brush, like Frank Graham and Claude Pepper, faced defeat. While a few southern moderates in politics and law firms survived, white lawyers who could be labeled "leftist," "radical," "activist," or even "liberal" or "civil libertarian" were exceedingly rare before 1965.

Nonetheless, there is in American legal parlance an area of concern called "the independence of the bar." The phrase refers to the function of lawyers as autonomous officers of the court, advocates whose independence is as critical to the equity of the legal system as the detachment of the judge or the impartiality of the jury. An independent lawyer chooses clients freely, for personal, political, or business reasons, without fear of being discredited by

---

26. Caute, *Great Fear*, 403; Jerold S. Auerbach, *Unequal Justice: Lawyers and Social Change in Modern America* (New York, 1976), 191.

27. Auerbach, *Unequal Justice*, 240.

the press or rejected by the bar because of the crimes, ideas, or caste of those he represents. The criminal and the dissident, in this view, are entitled to competent and committed legal advice; attorneys who defend the unpopular or champion the oppressed uphold constitutional democracy. It is one of the ideals upon which American justice is based, but it is an elusive ideal.

"The independence of the bar," in the words of one radical lawyer, "is a fragile commodity inordinately dependent on community mood and judicial tolerance."[28] The American justice system, particularly on the local level, is inherently conservative and has only rarely encouraged diversity, much less dissidence, among members of the bar. Since the labor battles of the 1890s, the natural tendency of the judiciary, and of Americans generally, has been to distrust lawyers who represent unpopular classes of people or divergent political views. This pressure from professional and public opinion has been one check on the independence of the bar. Another force curbing independent advocacy has been the suppression of subversion—real, invented, or imagined—by local, state, and national governmental agencies.

Nowhere have such forces prevailed more deeply than in local, state, and national bar associations, all of which have restricted or attempted to control their memberships using racial, ethnic, economic, or political tests. In 1939 the ABA rejected black federal judge William Hastie's application for membership. In the early 1940s the ABA "discovered" that it had admitted a black lawyer by mistake in the same year that it rejected two blacks who openly challenged the bar's racial discrimination. Although only a handful of black lawyers struggled to make a living below the Potomac before the 1950s, southern ABA members complained vehemently. The ABA remained virtually an all-white organization until the 1960s, while local southern bar associations functioned largely as exclusive clubs regulated by the professional elite.[29]

The ABA Canon of Ethics promulgated in the early 1900s emphasized dignity, decorum, and reputation—that is, the professionalization of the bar. ABA rules attempted to limit membership to those whose training and behavior conformed to an accepted norm. The canons discouraged so-called

28. Ann Fagan Ginger and Eugene M. Tobin, eds., *The National Lawyers Guild: From Roosevelt Through Reagan* (Philadelphia, 1988), 26.

29. Auerbach, *Unequal Justice,* 216; Walter J. Leonard, *Black Lawyers: Training and Results, Then and Now* (Boston, 1977), 266.

"ambulance chasers"—lawyers paid by contingency fees in personal injury cases or similar work—and successful lawyers denounced them as immoral. In effect, according to Auerbach, the canons and the profession "ostracized plaintiff's lawyers who, representing outsiders to the legal system, solicited certain types of business." They also discouraged all but the most stalwart from making labor unions, the poor, blacks, or immigrants the center of their practices, since these lawyers often supplemented their unprofitable cases with personal injury litigation. Of these, the practice of labor law alone benefited substantially from New Deal legislation. During most of the twentieth century, typical American lawyers have had roots, personally and professionally, in small-town business interests, corporate board rooms, or a bureaucracy; bar associations and their rules have instinctively reflected this base. Atypical lawyers, whose backgrounds and/or clients were working-class, ethnic or racial minorities, or off-center politically, and whose ability to collect fees often rested on their skill in winning settlements from prominent business and professional men, were routinely isolated from professional connections.[30]

In 1948 the Georgia Bar Association refused admission to William George, a Washington, D.C., native who came south with the National Labor Relations Board (NLRB) and then attended Emory Law School. An early organizer for the ACLU in Georgia, George, along with his wife, Lavinia, published a labor newspaper in Macon; members of the bar anonymously accused him of being a Communist. Interestingly, his wife joined fifty other southerners who met at Monticello, Virginia, in November, 1948, to sign the "Declaration of Civil Rights" which announced the establishment of SCEF as an independent educational organization dedicated to racial justice. A graduate of Agnes Scott College in Decatur, Georgia, she later attended Emory Law School and became her husband's law partner. With the assistance of two corporate lawyers who knew him through his NLRB work, George prevailed and gained admission to the bar, but his case serves as an example of the "exclusive club" ambiance and the strident anti-Communism of southern bar associations at this time.[31]

30. Auerbach, *Unequal Justice,* 40–50, quote on 49.

31. William George, interview by author, tape recording, Atlanta, June 11, 1990; "A Declaration of Rights," November 20, 1948, in Box 17, Folder 3, Dombrowski Papers.

Other liberal lawyers in the South, especially labor lawyers, felt the sting of ostracism, rumor, or worse. Despite the fact that his father sat on the U.S. Supreme Court, in the 1950s Hugo Black, Jr., could not play tennis after Birmingham closed its recreational facilities to avoid desegregation, "since the two country clubs wouldn't let a labor lawyer join." The Atlanta Lawyers Club refused admission to Morgan Stanford, a white attorney from an old Atlanta family who represented CIO unions. A black lawyer of an equally illustrious local ancestry, future Atlanta mayor Maynard Jackson, received similar treatment.[32]

In Texas, Houston labor lawyers Herman Wright, Arthur Mandell, and Ben Ramey were suspended for ninety days by the state's bar association in 1957, allegedly because of "solicitation of clients for personal injury suits." Although the three decided not to appeal, they denied the charges. Wright attributed the bar's action to their political activities, their longtime representation of leftist unions, and their success as personal injury lawyers. Like Lavinia George, Mandell signed SCEF's 1948 "Declaration of Civil Rights." In addition, in 1956 Wright had become a vice-president of the National Lawyers Guild (NLG), a left-liberal lawyers association assailed by both the ABA and the government's anti-Communist apparatus. SCEF and NLG member Leo Sheiner, who invoked the Fifth Amendment when questioned by Senator Eastland about his past associations, suffered disbarment in 1955 as a direct result of his testimony before Eastland's committee. Sheiner spent more than five years in litigation before regaining his license to practice law in Florida. In addition to being charged with using unsavory methods, such lawyers were assumed (sometimes correctly) to share their clients' political views.[33]

Associations formed by liberal and leftist lawyers faced quarantine and denunciation both from the ABA and from representatives of the legal profession within the government, that is, judges, attorneys general and their

32. Roger K. Newman, *Hugo Black: A Biography* (New York, 1994), 538; Morgan Stanford, interview by author, tape recording, Atlanta, April 24, 1990.

33. Herman Wright, interview by author, tape recording, Houston, September 11, 1991; Carleton, *Red Scare,* 290–91; Ginger and Tobin, eds., *NLG,* 144–45. For details on the Sheiner case see also Boxes 53 and 54, John Moreno Coe Papers, Collection No. 628, Special Collections Department, Robert W. Woodruff Library, Emory University, Atlanta [hereinafter cited as Coe Papers], and Chapter 5 in this text.

subordinates, and other bureaucratic lawyers. Although it is true that civil libertarian organizations of any kind were in jeopardy by the late 1940s and 1950s, minority or left-wing legal movements were especially vulnerable to cold war pressures. In the 1950s, ABA resolutions specifically condemned attorneys who took refuge in the Fifth Amendment in congressional hearings, recommended the disbarment of lawyers who "advocated 'Marxism-Leninism,'" voted to bar from ABA membership any lawyer who was "sympathetic to world communism," and asked for periodic loyalty oaths for lawyers.[34] These resolutions were aimed at lawyers who belonged to the National Lawyers Guild, some of whom had connections to the Communist Party. Like SCHW, the guild had been organized in the heyday of popular front liberalism.

The NLG, a racially and ethnically diverse "national bar association" founded by New Deal supporters in 1937, formally protested the extralegal methods of the FBI, congressional investigating committees, and executive-branch loyalty boards. It almost perished in the 1950s under pressure from these government agencies and the ABA. The guild's early membership included representatives from the ACLU, the NAACP, unions, law schools, government agencies, and the judiciary. The distinguished liberal lawyer Frank P. Walsh served as its first president, and Justice John P. Devaney of the Minnesota Supreme Court as its second. Other founding members included Governor Philip F. LaFollette of Wisconsin, Senator Homer J. Bone of Washington, a future Supreme Court justice, Solicitor General Robert H. Jackson, future federal district judge William H. Hastie, and Charles Hamilton Houston of the Howard Law School and the NAACP. New Deal lawyers like Abe Fortas and Jerome Frank responded to the call for a liberal bar association, as did leftist labor lawyers like Lee Pressman and Maurice Sugar, law professors Karl Llewellyn, Thomas Emerson, and Walter Gellhorn, and civil libertarian lawyers of all stripes.[35]

By the mid-1950s only a few stalwarts among these founding members remained, primarily as a result of a lengthy series of attacks by HUAC, the FBI, and finally, the attorney general's office. When New York district judge

34. Ginger and Tobin, eds., *NLG*, 136–40, quotes on 139.
35. Baily, "The Case of the NLG," in *Beyond the Hiss Case,* ed. Theoharis, 162–63; Ginger and Tobin, eds., *NLG*, 9.

Harold R. Medina sentenced five defense attorneys to jail for contempt after the highly publicized trial of eleven Communist leaders charged under the Smith Act in 1949, all five were identified as members of the NLG. Two of them were subsequently disbarred. The publicity added force to cases already being constructed by the guild's enemies.

In 1977, through the Freedom of Information Act, the guild retrieved more than 300,000 pages of FBI documents covering a period beginning in 1941. The FBI had used wiretaps, both private law firm and NLG office break-ins, and over a thousand informants, some of them FBI plants on NLG boards; had surreptitiously worked to defeat guild members when they ran for public office; and had "released derogatory and misleading information about the Guild to judges, the media and the public." After the guild published a lengthy report illuminating and criticizing FBI methods in 1950, HUAC issued a hastily devised response entitled "The National Lawyers Guild: Legal Bulwark of the Communist Party." This frequently cited government report recommended that the NLG be placed on the Justice Department's list of subversive organizations, that NLG members be barred from federal employment, and that the ABA study the NLG with a view toward relieving NLG members of their ABA affiliations. The guild's membership dropped from a high of some five thousand in the mid-1940s to an all-time low of just over five hundred in 1955.[36]

"The cold war against lawyers had begun," said Yale law professor and NLG president Thomas I. Emerson. When Attorney General Herbert Brownell announced in an address to the ABA in 1953 that he had ordered the NLG to "show cause why it should not be designated on the Attorney General's list [of subversive organizations]," almost seven hundred members resigned within two weeks, fearing loss of clients or even disbarment. The NLG challenged the attorney general in court, and after eight years of harassment and intermittent litigation the attorney general's office abandoned the case. The NLG survived, but by the middle of the 1950s its center liberal members had departed.[37]

Centered in eastern and midwestern cities and California, the NLG at-

36. Ginger and Tobin, eds., *NLG,* 336.
37. Baily, "The Case of the NLG," in *Beyond the Hiss Case,* ed. Theoharis, Emerson quote on 175, n. 92; Ginger and Tobin, eds., *NLG,* 11, 114, quote on 136.

tracted only a sprinkling of southern members in the 1940s and 1950s, though it welcomed black attorneys and made sincere attempts to attract liberal southerners. Another lawyers organization, the National Bar Association (NBA), had the potential for developing a cadre of black activist lawyers but failed to do so. Formed in 1925 to serve and encourage the growth of the black bar, the NBA for several reasons did not have a measurable impact on the larger American bar in the 1940s and 1950s. In the first place, the pool from which it drew members was very small. In 1940 only .06 percent of American lawyers (1,925) were black; by 1960 more than 10 percent of the country's population, but still less than 1 percent of its lawyers, were black. Only a very small fraction of these African-American lawyers practiced in the South.[38] Second, until the 1960s the NBA remained primarily a self-help organization, usually conservative or apolitical. Finally, the very existence of the NBA abetted white rationalization of the ABA's unofficial ban on black membership, a peculiar and extreme application of "separate but equal" doctrine. In any case, both the NBA and the NLG were distant voices for most lawyers in southern cities and towns. Except in a few cities like Atlanta and New Orleans where local black bar associations developed, black lawyers, like the few white liberal lawyers in the South before the mid-1960s, generally functioned without the support of sympathetic professional friendships and associations.

The editors of the institutional history of the NLG noted that by 1960 "veteran Guild members knew something about the legal system in the South from the very small band of delegates to the national conventions—John Coe of Florida, Clifford Durr of Alabama (late of Washington, D.C.), Herman Wright and Arthur Mandell of Texas, Professors Mitchell Franklin and Laurent Frantz of several cities, and Ben Smith of New Orleans."[39] Neither Mandell, who migrated to the United States from Romania in the 1930s, nor Franklin, who returned to New York after a long tenure at Tulane Law School, was a native southerner. A radical intellectual active in student politics at the University of North Carolina and then in early labor wars in Birmingham and elsewhere, Frantz became an "expatriate" by moving to California early in his career. Herman Wright, who retired from a long and successful

---

38. Leonard, *Black Lawyers,* 121; Auerbach, *Unequal Justice,* 266.
39. Ginger and Tobin, eds., *NLG,* 178.

labor law practice in Houston in the late 1980s, was a native of Amarillo, as much a westerner as a southerner. As noted above, he and Mandell, his longtime partner, suffered as advocates for left-wing labor unions during Texas' virulent Red scare. This study considers the careers of the three remaining lawyers mentioned in the passage from the NLG history. They were all natives of the Deep South who, despite considerable familial, professional, and societal pressure, practiced civil liberties and civil rights law in their native region.

John Moreno Coe of Pensacola, Florida, Clifford Judkins Durr of Montgomery, Alabama, and Benjamin Eugene Smith of New Orleans, Louisiana, stand out not simply because they affiliated with the guild but because they consistently took risks to represent proscribed clients, black and white. They were also exceptional because, like the southerners who worked for SCEF and Highlander Folk School, they represented a last flowering of popular front liberalism in the South. "The popular front liberals," Bartley has said, "were the heirs to the New Deal and the proponents of detente with the Soviet Union." None of these lawyers ever considered becoming Communist, and each disparaged the doctrinaire pro-Soviet stance of the CPUSA. But they were among the "ideological opponents of the Cold War liberals within the Democratic party" not only in the late 1940s but through the 1960s. Except for Coe's and Smith's deviation to join the Progressive movement of 1948, all three men were lifelong—though usually minority and sometimes abstaining—members of the Democratic Party.[40]

Clifford Durr never served as a SCEF board member and had loose ties to the NLG after his term as guild president ended in 1950. Nevertheless, he maintained close personal and professional relationships with left-liberals like SCEF president Aubrey Williams; Myles Horton and others at Highlander; Clark Foreman, Leonard Boudin, and Corliss Lamont of the Emergency Civil Liberties Committee (ECLC);[41] and Yale law professor Thomas

---

40. Bartley, *New South*, 457.

41. The ECLC, founded in 1951 by Lamont, Harvey O'Connor, and other disgruntled former ACLU board members, asserted that the First Amendment, rather than the Fifth, should be the refuge of victims of HUAC and other government investigatory bodies. A very effective liberal defense organization, the ECLC was hounded and disparaged but never listed by the attorney general or the Subversive Activities Control Board.

Emerson. Emerson, Boudin, and several other longtime Durr associates and financial supporters maintained active membership in the NLG. Coe and Smith became board members and officers of both SCEF and the NLG in the 1950s. All three men served as cooperating ACLU attorneys, tried important civil liberties cases, faced harassment from legislative committees and the FBI, and resigned from the ABA.

These attorneys frequently characterized themselves, even when defending black civil rights workers, not as "civil rights lawyers" but as "civil liberties" advocates. Their liberalism began in the classic sense, with commitment to individual liberties and a fear of oppressive government. In 1945 Coe said in response to questions about defending clients challenging Florida's white primary law that "the proscription of minorities within the state is the mark of Fascism and a dishonor to Democracy." If rights can be denied to blacks, he reasoned, why not to other racial and religious minorities? "As long as any man is oppressed . . . the liberties of all are imperiled." Deeply involved by 1957 in "civil rights" cases in Montgomery, Durr wrote to columnist Drew Pearson that "in the center of the hurricane over integration, I find myself still thinking in terms of civil *liberties* rather than civil *rights*." He worried most about "the repression of the right to think and talk" that consumed public life and private freedoms in the South. "We are lawyers in the great tradition," Ben Smith declared in an address to the NLG in 1965; "what started as a revolution for Negro rights cannot remain only that. It is the first, small opening that leads to a truly constitutional society."[42]

In a book tracing the history of freedom of speech in the United States, NLG lawyer David Kairys discussed the vigilante citizens committees and the statutes created to suppress suspicious antislavery opinions a century before the Red- and race-baiting of the 1940s and 1950s. "It became common," he wrote, "to repudiate the notion of 'natural rights' and the Declaration of Independence, which were both seen as based on Jefferson's 'radicalism.'"[43]

42. J. M. Coe to Walter P. Fuller, January 26, 1945, in Box 27, Folder 1, Coe Papers; Clifford J. Durr to Drew Pearson, October 18, 1957, in Box 38, Folder 1, Clifford J. Durr Papers, LPR No. 25, Alabama Department of Archives and History, Montgomery [hereinafter cited as C. J. Durr Papers]; *Guild Practitioner*, XXIV (Fall, 1965), 96–99, quote on 96.

43. David Kairys, "Freedom of Speech," in *The Politics of Law: A Progressive Critique*, ed. Kairys (New York, 1982), 149.

An antilibertarian wave reappeared in the South a hundred years later as part of the effort to contain the incipient movement toward racial change. As these three lawyers confronted the repressive antiliberalism of the postwar period it was as disciples of Jefferson, most of all, that they could be classified as "radical." Although as southerners they felt deeply about the oppression of black Americans, their efforts concentrated not so much on the rights of particular classes of people as on the equal and unqualified application of the Bill of Rights.

These three lawyers faced ostracism in their conservative local communities and in their professional associations, yet each man remained in and of the South all his life. A disillusioned Smith returned after a year in Philadelphia near the end of his life to the safety of New Orleans' Garden District. Similarly, Durr decided after an unhappy year in Denver that he would never live anywhere outside Alabama again, claiming that he and his wife were "both southerners to the core, and this is where we belong." He found "a quality of personal loyalty which gives health to the political and moral climate" in the South, despite its many problems. In a letter to New Yorker Leo Sheiner, John Coe described a delightful Florida morning when he and Mrs. Coe caught "a couple of big Spanish mackerel . . . so big that the two of us could only eat one for breakfast." Another letter testifies that "after I finished with your file last night, I went down to the end of the wharf and threw my cast net [for mullet] several times in the dark. . . . This is a nice life; I wish you and yours could enjoy the like." Such self-satisfied southern fish stories pepper angler Coe's correspondence.[44]

All three men had deep southern roots and long family histories in the places they loved, and each exhibited an extravagant pride in family tradition and accomplishment. And like southern liberals before them, while their "southernness" did not prevent criticism of the South, it sometimes made them her defenders, too. Regardless of contemporary public perceptions, Coe, Durr, and Smith remained both devoted southerners and loyal Americans. To classify them as "radical" or "left-wing" without considering their time and place would be, at best, misleading. They lived their lives as southern liberals and southern lawyers.

44. C. J. Durr to Justice James H. Wolfe, Utah Supreme Court, April 24, 1953, in Box 2, Folder 5, C. J. Durr Papers; John M. Coe to Leo Sheiner, August 12, 1957, in Box 53, Folder 41, and August 23, 1958, in Box 54, Folder 1, Coe Papers.

Nevertheless they were unusual, even within the small company of south-ern liberal lawyers. Like other liberals, they rejected segregation and disfran-chisement of African Americans and worked diligently toward ending both. But they also saw deeper, older divisions in southern society; and they rejected the rising tide of postwar antiradicalism, advocating both international co-operation and First and Fifth Amendment freedoms at a time when both were suspect. While each formally rejected Communism, they were "non-Com-munist" rather than "anti-Communist," defending freedom of expression and association in almost every instance. They rejected individualism in favor of the common good but feared the oppression of unbridled government. This political creed, which flourished in the New Deal years, lost favor in the prosperity and cynicism of the postwar period. The liberalism of the postwar left, often demeaned by anti-Communist liberals of the vital center, eventually became a bridge to the civil rights and free speech movements of the 1960s and 1970s. Among the members of local bar associations in Montgomery, Pensacola, or New Orleans, supporters of such ideas were not only unusual, but often very unpopular as well.

CHAPTER TWO

On Becoming Southern Liberals:
Prelude to 1948

Although the work of Coe, Durr, and Smith is distinctive, other southern lawyers sometimes upheld professional ethics by representing clients accused of subversive activities in the 1940s and 1950s. When state legislators called Georgia social worker Loretta Chappell a Communist in 1951 largely because she invited a black fellow worker to lunch in her home, state representative and Decatur lawyer James A. Mackay "rose up to defend her," according to the Atlanta *Constitution*.[1] Because similar stories abound, it would be preposterous to imply that no other white attorneys held moderate or liberal positions on racial issues during these years.

Labor lawyers, some of them native southerners like Texan Herman Wright, CIO lawyer Morgan Stanford and AFL attorney Joseph Jacobs of Atlanta, or William Mitch and Hugo Black, Jr., of Birmingham, multiplied in the South, as in other parts of the country, in the late 1940s. Stanford represented the leftist United Packinghouse Workers of America (UPWA) in Georgia and Herman Wright's Houston firm had both the Packinghouse Workers and the National Maritime Union (NMU) as clients, but few southern labor lawyers volunteered to represent such left-wing unions. The UPWA and the NMU both backed Henry Wallace, and in 1948 Wright represented local Communists fighting against the NMU's national leadership for control of the Houston local. Though the top national leadership of both these unions remained non-Communist, both were deeply involved in the CIO purges of the late 1940s, and the Packinghouse Workers strongly supported integration. Through such clients, labor lawyers, like some in general practice, sometimes became coincidentally involved in civil liberties cases, but they seldom directly challenged segregation laws.[2]

---

1. Atlanta *Constitution*, May 11, 1990, Sec. E, p. 1.

2. Stanford and Wright interviews; see also Harvey A. Levenstein, *Communism, Anti-Communism, and the CIO* (Westport, Conn., 1981), 50, 69, 227, 253–260; Numan V. Bartley, *The Rise of Massive Resistance* (Baton Rouge, 1969), 306; and Carleton, *Red Scare*, 38–51.

On the other hand, in cities like Birmingham, Atlanta, and New Orleans, black attorneys, among them veterans Arthur Shores, Austin T. Walden, and Alexander P. Tureaud, had been working with the NAACP since the 1930s. Although they began to multiply after World War II, their numbers were very small. Twelve African-American attorneys practiced in Atlanta and fourteen in all of Louisiana in 1951, nine in Alabama in 1958, perhaps as many as forty-five in Florida in 1962, but only four in Mississippi as late as 1964. By the early 1960s a few young white lawyers, men like William Higgs and Leonard Rosenthal in Jackson, Charles Morgan in Birmingham, Tobias Simon in Miami, or Smith's young law partners in New Orleans, cooperated with the new black attorneys. New Orleanian Jack Nelson, a dedicated liberal Catholic and professor at Loyola University Law School, joined a young black lawyer to represent two students in the suit that finally desegregated Smith's alma mater, Tulane, in 1963. By 1963 and 1964 northern liberal groups were mobilizing hundreds of attorneys, black and white, who committed themselves to temporary stints in southern locales supporting civil rights activities. But most of these lawyers of the 1960s became more concerned with the Fourteenth and Fifteenth Amendments than with the First and Fifth. They were preoccupied with the inequities of southern society produced by segregation and disfranchisement. These were *civil rights* lawyers.[3]

John Coe, Cliff Durr, and even the younger Ben Smith might be described as precursors of the movement lawyers of the 1960s and 1970s. They hated discrimination and wanted to overthrow the existing segregationist order in the South, but would accomplish this by ending repressive government practices everywhere. If federal bureaucrats or the southern states denied civil liberties, civil rights existed only at government's whim. Fearing the devel-

---

3. J. L. Chestnut, Jr., and Julia Cass, *Black in Selma: The Uncommon Life of J. L. Chestnut, Jr.—Politics and Power in a Small American Town* (New York, 1990), 88–89; Jack Oppenheim, "The Abdication of the Southern Bar," in *Southern Justice*, ed. Leon Friedman (New York, 1965), 127–28; Donald Hollowell, interview by author, tape recording, Atlanta, May 22, 1990; John M. Coe to George Crockett, April 12, 1962, in Box 4, Folder 25, Coe Papers; Bruce Waltzer, interview by author, tape recording, New Orleans, September 6, 1990; John P. Nelson, Jr., interview by author, tape recording, New Orleans, September 5, 1990. Later, Charles Morgan served as a director of the ACLU in both regional and national capacities.

opment of a police state, they stood with other "radicals" who paradoxically fought not to overthrow the democracy but for the rehabilitation of ancient constitutional principles. In the absence of unlawful acts, they judged restraints on freedom of belief, opinion, expression, assembly, or petition unconstitutional. As lawyers they understood the practical limits placed on freedom of expression by the state, prohibitions against libel, espionage, or inciting mobs to violence or panic; but social or political motives, even most "national security" agendas, were insufficient basis for abrogation of the First Amendment. Thus they were in the vanguard—perhaps at the base—of the freedom movement, devoted to civil rights but not as narrowly absorbed by racial discrimination cases as were the civil rights attorneys who followed or worked with them.

In addition, circumstances of time and place affected their work with the civil rights movement. Coe fought intolerance and repression for fifty years but because of failing health never became deeply involved with the new black civil rights organizations of the 1960s. Though Coe and Durr were of the same generation, because Durr worked in Washington for almost two decades his liberal southern practice began about the same time as Smith's professional tenure. Durr defended alleged Communists and militant integrationists with equal grace. However, he retired in 1964 and was never considered a "movement lawyer," as were the peripatetic younger black and white lawyers of the civil rights era. Smith, seemingly born a generation too late to be a McCarthy-era civil liberties attorney, nevertheless as a very young lawyer countered anti-Communist persecutions, echoing Coe and Durr. Ultimately, as an attorney for the Student Non-Violent Coordinating Committee and the Mississippi Freedom Democratic Party, Smith became known as a "radical" civil rights lawyer. While their work was dissimilar, Coe and Durr both came early to the civil liberties struggle; Smith joined them midway, and seems to complete their story. Thus for primarily chronological reasons, Smith's story almost exclusively occupies the final chapter of this narrative.

Whatever their unofficial credentials may have been, the three men had backgrounds strikingly different from their northern counterparts. Brooklyn native Bruce Waltzer, a "movement lawyer" who became Benjamin Smith's law partner in 1962, contrasted his "very liberal" northern Jewish family's long involvement in New York's leftist politics with Smith's "traditional southern family."[4] Coe and Durr grew up in similar circumstances. All three men came from well-established Protestant families in very conservative southern towns. As they left home, learned the law, and married well-bred young southern women, their families could expect that they would become prosperous southern lawyers. They might have made places for themselves as respectable moderates in the changing region. Instead they almost instinctively adopted liberal causes and defended unpopular people, without prolonged soul-searching or expectation of acclaim or reward. Their communities labeled them crusaders, idealists, civil libertarians, sometimes eccentrics or radicals; and their enemies called them Communist sympathizers or worse. A consideration of the families and early professional lives of these three lawyers sheds light on the incongruities between their histories and their uncommon careers.

The youngest child of a comfortable, socially prominent Montgomery family, Clifford Judkins Durr exhibited the kind of easy self-confidence engendered by a happy and stable childhood. Born in 1899 and educated in local private schools, he was president of his class at the University of Alabama and a Rhodes scholar in the years just after graduation. An Oxford law degree and an early position in a Birmingham corporate law firm gave him a natural entrée into Alabama's legal establishment. Steady, scholarly, good looking and well liked, he had the air of a friendly law professor or an enlightened Presbyterian cleric. Presbyterianism, in fact, played an important part in his life. Reared in a faithful and devout family, Durr remained a member of the First Presbyterian Church of Montgomery until leaving in anguish over the integration issue in the 1960s.

Cliff Durr, a man of great personal integrity who could be a tenacious adversary when aroused by matters of principle, was not drawn to competition, argument, or intrigue for its own sake. When a problem existed, he tried to face it straight on and get it over with as quickly as possible. In her autobiography, his wife, Virginia Foster Durr, says her husband "just did what came naturally. If it was wrong, it was wrong. If it was right, it was right." She thought this resulted from "the tradition of the principled, honorable southern gentleman." His family, and especially his beloved grandfa-

4. Waltzer interview.

ther James Henry Judkins, had driven "the idea of honor and truth" into Cliff Durr as a boy.[5]

That same beloved maternal grandfather, a former Confederate captain, displayed a flair for independent thinking unusual among southerners of his generation. He had been a part of the failed experiment by ex-Confederates to re-create the plantation South in Brazil. He also publicly humiliated his solidly Democratic Alabama family by announcing support for Republican Theodore Roosevelt in the presidential race of 1904. Perhaps this forebear instilled something of his rebel spirit in Cliff Durr, who spent happy boyhood summers at the Judkins farm in Wetumpka, a place he would inherit and call home in retirement. Certainly this was a deep and important relationship that added strength to Durr's character. The fact that his grandfather was a lawyer must have influenced Durr's decision to study for the bar.[6]

Nevertheless, in the years before he joined the Roosevelt administration's team of New Deal lawyers, Durr had little interest in Alabama politics, even the 1932 Senate campaign of his brother-in-law Hugo Black.[7] Although he became deeply and energetically committed to the New Deal and later to other liberal causes, he was never political in the sense that he enjoyed party politics or participated actively in particular campaigns. Not a "joiner," Durr told the Nashville ACLU in 1967 that he remained a member of only two organizations, the Presbyterian Church and Sigma Alpha Epsilon (his college fraternity). The former membership he thought was "maybe a mistake," the latter one he retained because when he "took the vows of brotherhood" they told him that only expulsion or death could end the affiliation, and neither path seemed worth the effort.[8] By choice he was not a member of many organizations, nor was he wealthy enough during his active years to be a substantial contributor to causes. Clifford Durr's name, unlike the names of many other prominent liberals of his generation, is not one that can be identified by its repeated presence on letterheads or in organization newsletters.

Nevertheless, Durr was neither provincial nor apolitical, even as a young

5. Barnard, ed., *Outside the Magic Circle*, 216–17.

6. John A. Salmond, *The Conscience of a Lawyer: Clifford J. Durr and American Civil Liberties, 1899–1975* (Tuscaloosa, 1990), 3.

7. Virginia Durr, interview by author, tape recording, Montgomery, September 23, 1991.

8. Speech, "The Sin of Silence," May 11, 1967, in Box 14, Folder 7, C. J. Durr Papers.

man. After beginning his legal career in Montgomery, he practiced law in Milwaukee for another year (1923–1924) before joining the Birmingham law firm of Martin, Thompson, Foster, and Turner, whose impressive list of corporate clients included the Alabama Power Company. More important, he left Birmingham in 1933 to spend seventeen years in Washington, D.C., seven of them as an activist member of the Federal Communications Commission. When his government service ended he stayed in the capital for two more years, establishing a private law practice that consisted almost entirely of civil liberties cases. By the time he returned to Alabama in 1951, after a few unhappy months in Denver with the National Farmers Union, he would have found it difficult to conform to the conservative style and constituency of the Birmingham firm he left as a full partner in 1933. The New Deal years changed Cliff Durr.

The Reconstruction Finance Corporation (RFC), headed by Texan Jesse H. Jones, provided Durr's early Washington jobs. The RFC was created during the Hoover presidency to provide loans to banks, railroads, and other distressed businesses, and although Congress broadened its authority in 1933, it remained one of the most conservative New Deal agencies. First the agency's banking section and later its litigation section benefited from Durr's experience as a corporate lawyer. His biographer, John Salmond, noted Durr's reputation for "diligence, attention to detail, and legal skill" while at the RFC.[9]

This position offered Durr a view of the whole country during the depression and a chance to develop associations with many other young lawyers who had come to work in Washington. It was a good spot in which to begin the transition from representative of the Alabama Power Company to representative of the public interest. During his years at the RFC, Durr reevaluated his ideas about big government and confronted the conditions of life in his native South squarely.

He became a leading member of the committee of southern New Dealers which in 1938 produced the *Report on the Economic Conditions of the South,* urging fundamental economic and political changes in the region and providing the impetus for the formation of the Southern Conference for Human

---

9. Salmond, *Conscience of a Lawyer,* 52–53. Correspondence, letters, and subject files relating to Durr's service in the RFC are found in Boxes 27, 28, and 29, C. J. Durr Papers.

Welfare that same year. The committee met and drafted most of the document in the Durrs' living room in Alexandria, Virginia. Atlantan Clark Howell Foreman, who served Interior Secretary Harold Ickes as adviser on African-American affairs, first recommended to Roosevelt that the report should be written. Foreman became a close friend of Durr's, as did two other southerners, fellow Alabamian Aubrey Willis Williams of the Works Progress Administration (WPA) and National Youth Administration (NYA) and Williams' former colleague in the NYA, Texas congressman Lyndon Baines Johnson. The four southern families, all convinced New Dealers, gathered often at the Durrs' home on Seminary Hill near the Virginia Episcopal Seminary and established important, lifelong friendships. These early Washington years were heady times for the Durrs and others who came to serve in New Deal agencies; never again would their lives be as exciting and romantic or their opinions so challenged and changed. The ardor of the recent convert infected this group of southerners as their worlds broadened and they saw their society from new perspectives. Cliff Durr, blessed with a logical and discerning mind and afflicted by a Presbyterian conscience, began to view with healthy skepticism not only the business community but American justice and southern racial mores.[10]

Virginia Durr, a southern gentlewoman and daughter of a conservative Presbyterian minister, also became an outspoken liberal during her years in Washington. As her interest in political matters blossomed during the 1930s and early 1940s she became active in the SCHW, especially its anti–poll tax committee, and developed friendships with a wide variety of liberals in unions and government. Virginia had the distinction of being the first Durr denounced on the floor of the U.S. Senate. During a 1941 filibuster against the poll tax bill, Senator Kenneth D. McKellar of Tennessee "I think called me a communist, a nigger loving communist," she said.[11] Cliff Durr and his intel-

10. Salmond, *Conscience of a Lawyer*, 55–58; Barnard, ed., *Outside the Magic Circle*, 99–122.

11. Barnard, ed., *Outside the Magic Circle*, 152–70, quote on 163. The bill to abolish the poll tax was introduced in 1941 and annually thereafter throughout the 1940s by SCHW ally Claude Pepper. Pepper's state, Florida, and Tennessee, the home of Estes Kefauver, the single other southern senator who supported the bill, had abolished the poll tax by state law. Abolition was widely supported by liberals as a way to democratize the electoral process, but was repeatedly stymied by southern filibusters.

ligent, compassionate, strong-willed wife were an impressive match. Hugo Black, the family member who had first convinced Durr to come to Washington, became another important influence on Durr's ideas. Black's liberalism and growing commitment to civil liberties had a profound influence on Durr's own developing civil libertarianism. Both men read deeply and both were self-reliant, independent thinkers. The brothers-in-law (both married to the Rev. Foster's daughters) always expressed a deep respect for each other. "We were," Durr said, "like brothers"; and Black called him "one of the best men I have ever known." The Durrs were exceedingly proud when Roosevelt appointed Black to the Supreme Court in 1937, and later of Justice Black's liberal opinions as a member of the high court.[12]

Cliff Durr arrived in Washington as a lawyer used to considering the prerogatives of banks, companies, and investors. By the late 1930s he thought in terms of protecting the rights of depositors. His new role as protector of the public interest became evident in 1940 and 1941 as he fought to free a new subsidiary of the RFC, the Defense Plant Corporation (DPC), from business control. Jesse Jones (by then federal loan administrator), William S. Knudsen of General Motors, and several other business leaders fought tooth and nail with Durr, RFC attorney Hans J. Klagsbrunn, and other New Deal lawyers, trying to deny the government's authority to manage defense contracts. In the end the DPC operated mostly within the parameters defined by Klagsbrunn and by Durr, who became the DPC's general counsel and later one of its directors. Durr had, however, made an enemy of the powerful, egotistical man nicknamed "Jesus H. Jones" by President Roosevelt. Jones took personal credit for the agency's creation and avoided mentioning Clifford Durr when writing the story of the DPC in *Fifty Billion Dollars: My Thirteen Years with the RFC*. According to Virginia Durr, "Jesse emerged as the hero for preparing the country for war, when he didn't do a damn thing but stand in the way and block it." Jones had been so irritated and embarrassed by Durr's defense of the government's priorities, she added, that he tried to lure Durr away from the DPC to a high-paying job on Wall Street.[13]

12. Newman, *Hugo Black*, 381–82; Salmond, *Conscience of a Lawyer*, 58; Clifford Durr, "Hugo L. Black: A Personal Appraisal," *Georgia Law Review*, VI (1971): 1–16.

13. Barnard, ed., *Outside the Magic Circle*, 145. Correspondence, subject files, and leases and contracts relating to Durr's service with the DPC are found in Box 27, Folder 6, through

Durr refused the Wall Street post in 1941 and instead, at the instigation of Senator Lister Hill, accepted appointment by President Roosevelt to a seven-year term on the Federal Communications Commission (FCC). In this position his concerns about the relationship between business and the public interest crystallized, and he increasingly became a public figure. Though Durr often enjoyed public speaking, when asked by Jim Dombrowski to join a panel with Frank Graham, Arthur Raper, David Lilienthal, Lucy Randolph Mason, and other liberals at SCHW's third national conference in Nashville, he demurred. In a witty but cynical reply, he told Dombrowski he had "thought about the matter a lot but have about decided that this is not the time to tempt Providence. . . . As you know, you and my wife are dangerous people, and the less I have to do with you the better."[14] After less than a year on the FCC, Durr acknowledged that he had become controversial and should protect his image as an impartial commissioner.

The press became interested in Durr in the early years of his FCC service for several reasons. In the first place, the FCC itself became a newsworthy agency during the early 1940s under the leadership of James Lawrence Fly. During the period of Fly's chairmanship, the commission aggressively projected itself as the guardian of the airwaves, protecting the public's ownership of radio frequencies from monopoly ownership and commercial dominance. In the process the agency ruffled powerful feathers in the business world. Second, Durr not only agreed with Fly but earnestly undertook to spread the message, becoming through a series of speeches and public dissents a champion of the public interest and a proponent of more rigorous regulation of the broadcasting business. Durr saw civil liberties issues, particularly freedom of speech and religion, as central to the business he encountered as a member of the FCC. He sought to curb such practices as single ownership of multiple media outlets in a city or excessive advertising which could control programming. Third, Durr authored a report for the FCC in 1946 called "Public Service Responsibility of Broadcast Licensees," usually known as the "Blue

Box 29, Folder 8, C. J. Durr Papers. See also Salmond, *Conscience of a Lawyer,* 60–71; Carleton, *Red Scare,* 77–82; and Gerald T. White, *Billions for Defense: Government Financing by the Defense Plant Corporation During World War II* (Tuscaloosa, 1980).

14. Clifford J. Durr to James A. Dombrowski, March 20, 1942, in Box 1, Folder 5, C. J. Durr Papers.

Book." This publication outlined standards for granting licenses and renewals and caused an outcry against Commissioner Durr in parts of the broadcasting industry, though Durr himself always expressed pride in the activity. Finally, and perhaps most consequentially, Durr was the FCC spokesman in a series of unpleasant encounters with the FBI, HUAC, and powerful members of Congress.[15]

Almost immediately after his appointment, Durr became involved in a controversy over Dr. Goodwin Watson, a liberal agency analyst. The FCC appointed Durr to investigate Dies committee (HUAC) charges of disloyalty against Watson. After a thorough examination of Watson's background and writings, the fledgling commissioner found the charges of subversive activity to be ridiculous. When Durr informed his colleagues that some of the allegedly "subversive" organizations Watson belonged to had "a most interesting collection of 'party liners' as members, including Chief Justice Hughes, Secretaries Stimson and Knox, and even Senator Carter Glass,"[16] they voted to keep Watson.

Congress responded by amending the FCC appropriation bill to exclude Watson from receiving a salary. Determined to defeat the rider, Durr arduously pressed his case with members of Congress, and he succeeded in 1942. But the following year a similar rider passed, this time incorporating the names of FCC employee William Dodd and the secretary-general of the Virgin Islands, Robert Morss Lovett. In a speech supporting the rider, Martin Dies denounced all three men, along with thirty-six others, as Communists and "irresponsible, unrepresentative, crackpot bureaucrats."[17] Reflecting on this legislation a few years later, Durr wrote that "because their beliefs happened to differ materially from the beliefs of certain members of Congress, they were, by legislative enactment, declared disloyal to their country."[18] In 1946 the accused government employees finally achieved vindication in *United*

15. Correspondence, clippings, articles, subject files, and other materials relating to Durr's service as FCC commissioner are found in Folder 9, Box 29, through Folder 5, Box 36, ibid. See also Salmond, *Conscience of a Lawyer*, 72–97.

16. Clifford J. Durr to Douglas Arant, February 5, 1943, in Box 1, Folder 5, C. J. Durr Papers.

17. *Congressional Record*, 76th Cong., 1st Sess., 479–86.

18. Clifford J. Durr, "Freedom and Fear," Birmingham *Age-Herald*, September 13, 1947, in Box 11, Folder 8, C. J. Durr Papers; see also Salmond, *Conscience of a Lawyer*, 98–103.

States v. *Lovett, Watson and Dodd,*[19] in which the Supreme Court judged the act used in their prosecution an unconstitutional bill of attainder.

Durr estimated in mid-1942 that "Mr. Dies' prestige is definitely on the wane,"[20] and Dies himself suffered defeat in the 1944 election. But his committee, HUAC, actually gained potency in the mid-1940s, encouraged and supported by the anti-Red obsession of the FBI under J. Edgar Hoover. As a result of the Watson-Dodd affair, the bureau investigated Clifford Durr for the first time. Durr believed the Dies committee initiated this activity at the instigation of its vice-chairman, Joe Starnes, who came from Anniston in Durr's home state.

The Birmingham *News* ran an article in 1942 quoting Starnes's claim that 1,123 federal employees or former employees, including North Carolina editor Jonathan Daniels, price administrator Leon Henderson, Milo Perkins of the Board of Economic Warfare, FCC general counsel Telford Taylor, Goodwin Watson, and Clifford Durr, had been documented by HUAC as members of suspect organizations. Anniston *Star* editor Harry M. Ayers replied with a scathing editorial called "Flogging a Dead Horse," scolding both Dies and Starnes. Both he and Durr, who wrote thanking Ayers for his support, thought the Dies committee hampered the war effort and that its wild allegations caused ordinary Americans who had little understanding of Communism to believe, falsely, that subversion riddled the federal government. Durr's subsequent letter to Starnes displayed his indignation over the committee's methods and criticized its abuse of its congressional mandate.[21]

Not Starnes, however, but another southerner, Eugene E. Cox of Georgia, became Durr's most notable congressional nemesis in 1942 and 1943. When FCC investigators completing a routine relicensing check discovered that an Albany, Georgia, radio station paid Representative Cox $2,500 for help in obtaining its original license, the FCC submitted the matter to the attorney general for possible prosecution. Infuriated, Cox launched a counterattack,

19. 328 U.S. 303 (1946).
20. Clifford J. Durr to Robert O. Kevin, July 1, 1942, in Box 1, Folder 5, C. J. Durr Papers.
21. "Jonathan Daniels Reported Investigated as Subversive: Representative Starnes Predicts the Witch Hunt Will Bring 'A Beautiful Coat of Calamine,'" Birmingham *News*, n.d., in Box 11, Folder 4, "Flogging a Dead Horse," Anniston *Star*, July 9, 1942, and Clifford J. Durr to Harry M. Ayers, July 18, 1942, in Box 1, Folder 5, all in C. J. Durr Papers; Salmond, *Conscience of a Lawyer*, 104.

naming the FCC with metaphoric abandon first a "gestapo" and then "a nest of reds."[22]

Congress promptly named the unrepentant Cox chairman of a Select Committee to Investigate the FCC. When this committee asked all seven commissioners for details of their personal finances in January, 1943, Durr alone refused to comply. Unless the investigation involved bribery, he said, they had no right to his records. In an open letter the following May he petitioned Speaker Sam Rayburn to remove Cox from the committee for cause, citing the chairman's bias against the FCC and documenting the FCC's original charges against him. "It happens," wrote Durr, "that there is a criminal statute dealing with the matter of Congressmen accepting compensation for services before government agencies." In September, prodded by publicity in the Washington *Post,* an embarrassed Rayburn finally persuaded his friend Cox to step down.[23]

The Birmingham *News,* also friendly to Durr, carried an editorial and an article extolling his boldness captioned "The Dogged Durr" and "Clifford J. Durr Fast Becoming One of Best Known Capital Figures: FCC Member, Alabamian, Wins Recognition for Courageous Stands." And when James Fly resigned from the FCC chairmanship in 1944, the Macon *News* in Cox's home state recalled Durr's "courageous stand" and urged that Durr be pressed into service as Fly's successor.[24] But regardless of these plaudits and the obvious absurdity of Cox's position, Durr had raised the ire of congressional conservatives at a time of their growing influence. Unfortunately, it would not be the last time he came to their attention.

In 1946 the commissioners faced the loyalty issue from another angle when FBI director Hoover sent them unsolicited dossiers on investors in the Hollywood Community Radio Group, Inc., an applicant for a radio license in California. The dossiers contained lists of the investors' relationships, show-

22. Resolution of Eugene E. Cox, House of Representatives, January 6, 1943, quoted in Salmond, *Conscience of a Lawyer,* 106.

23. Clifford J. Durr to Martin P. Knowlton, June 25, 1943, in Box 1, Folder 5, Washington *Post,* April 25, 29, May 14, 1943, in Box 11, Folder 4, and Washington *Post,* July 9, 1943, St. Louis *Star-Times,* September 28, 1943, New York *Times,* October 1, 1943, in Box 11, Folder 5, all in C. J. Durr Papers. See also Salmond, *Conscience of a Lawyer,* 105–10.

24. Birmingham *News,* September 30, October 4, 1943, and Macon *News,* November 13, 1944, in Box 11, Folder 5, C. J. Durr Papers.

ing various connections to left-liberal persons and organizations, but revealed no evidence of violations of the Smith Act or the Espionage Act of 1917. Finding in the FBI reports no basis on which to deny the Hollywood group's application, but careful to protect itself, the FCC's majority voted to conduct its own investigation, also inconclusive. Cliff Durr pushed to grant the license, but the commission simply tabled the application, deciding that the safest path lay in taking no action.

Durr exposed the matter publicly in a speech to the National Association of Educational Broadcasters, criticizing the FBI's shady methods and anonymous informers. Liberal newspapermen like Marquis Childs, I. F. Stone, and Jennings Perry praised the speech, but it brought additional unhappy consequences for Durr. Other FCC commissioners repudiated his criticism of the FBI, and Durr endured a vicious attack by Senator Homer Capehart of Indiana on the floor of the Senate. Capehart called Durr one of the "Communists and their New Deal fellow travelers . . . being harbored" in the federal government, "where they can sabotage our Nation's policies."[25]

Even before this public chastisement, Durr had been singled out by conservatives in the media. In an editorial titled "Durr's Slurs," one of many critical articles, *Broadcasting* magazine called him "the latest crusader" among the "radical fringe, who choose to call themselves 'liberals.'" This imaginative editor titled another editorial "Durrmocracy," insisting that Durr did not support the law that established the FCC as a servant of the industry, but simply pursued censorship of programming. By 1945 Durr had become known for his dissents from FCC decisions. According to one Washington broadcaster, "You can't convince people that Durr is not for government ownership and operation of radio." Durr sought no government ownership. Nevertheless, he did want time left free from advertising and commercial programming for community use, the reservation of some FM channels for newcomers, the breakup of media monopolies, and the end of absentee ownership. He also objected to the skyrocketing prices of radio stations, insisting that only the businesses themselves, not radio frequencies, could be bought and sold.[26]

25. Speech to National Association of Educational Broadcasters, Chicago, October 26, 1947, in Box 13, Folder 6, and Washington *Post*, November 19, 1947, in Box 12, Folder 8, both ibid.; Salmond, *Conscience of a Lawyer*, 113–16, quote on 115.

26. "Durr's Slurs," *Broadcasting*, May 14, 1944, in Box 11, Folder 5, "Durrmocracy," June

There was a chance in early 1945 that Durr might leave the FCC for a new job as federal loan administrator. When Roosevelt died, however, President Truman appointed John Snyder, Durr's former colleague at the RFC, and Durr remained at the FCC until his term ended in 1948. He became identified more and more as a civil libertarian in his last years on the FCC, both because of his dissents and for his frequent statements in public forums. Executive Order No. 9835, Truman's order requiring loyalty oaths and investigations of persons employed or seeking employment in the federal government and sanctioning denial of employment based on "reasonable grounds," particularly concerned Durr. Responding to questions put by Virgil M. Hancher of the University of Iowa, he adjudged one of the most important questions of the day to be "How do we preserve civil liberties in the face of government encroachment?"[27] In 1948 Durr refused Truman's offer of reappointment and resigned from government service to protest the loyalty oath order. Although resisting pressure to follow his wife, Virginia, into the Progressive Party of Henry Wallace, he remained a vocal critic of the Truman administration.

John Moreno Coe, born in Pensacola in 1896, like Durr traced his chronological roots to the last decade of the nineteenth century. He could also claim an illustrious local ancestry, and reaffirmed throughout his life an affection for his past. "My people" held slaves and fought for the Confederacy, he said. His paternal great-grandfather served with Andrew Jackson at New Orleans, and John Quincy Adams appointed his maternal great-grandfather marshal of West Florida. Several of his ancestors named Dorr, members of a Massachusetts mercantile family who migrated to Pensacola in the early nineteenth century, served in the American Revolution. Coe's Landing on the Apalachicola River is near the site of a cotton plantation owned by John Moreno

---

4, 1945, "Dissent by Durr," *Tide,* November 1, 1945, "FCC Reaches New 'Low': People's Air Rights Tossed to Big Interests," *Labor,* September 15, 1945, Lowell Mellett column "On the Other Hand," Washington *Evening Star,* September 22, 1945, "Is Radio Freedom Endangered?" *Radio Craft and Popular Electronics,* July, 1944, all in Box 11, Folder 6, and "Durr Again Makes Scorching Protest on Ruling by FCC," *Labor,* March 16, 1946, in Box 11, Folder 7, all in C. J. Durr Papers.

27. Clifford J. Durr to Virgil M. Hancher, August 26, 1947, in Box 1, Folder 6, ibid.

Coe's grandfather, and Moreno, a name from his mother's family, indicates descent from Don Francisco Moreno, a prominent Spanish diplomat. His aunt, Angela Moreno, married U.S. senator and Confederate secretary of the navy Stephen R. Mallory.[28]

Coe's difficult youth, burdened by his immediate family's financial misfortunes and his father's confinement in a mental institution, may have engendered his combative antiestablishment attitudes as well as an insatiable intellectual curiosity and an enormous capacity for work. His self-guided education left gaps and undoubtedly reinforced natural predilections and prejudices.[29] But in the law, his chosen field, he drove himself until reaching almost flawless technical knowledge and skill. One of the youngest lawyers ever admitted to the Florida bar, he began practicing law in 1917 when only twenty years old. He educated himself for the bar by reading the law in the office of a distant cousin. According to his daughter, he worked during the day for another cousin in the sawmill and building business and read the law at night, often aloud to his adoring mother. She was "quite a southern woman" who "filled him with ideas that a man . . . stood up for his country and his ideas and that was that."[30]

Like Durr, Coe had an air of courtliness and a sense of honor and responsibility that reflected his genteel southern roots and turn-of-the-century beginnings, but there the similarities of personality ended. Unlike Durr, Coe was a joiner, active in civic and professional organizations from the early 1920s and an enthusiastic supporter of progressive causes and candidates. He signed petitions, gave generous contributions, and thoroughly enjoyed the rough-and-tumble of party politics. During the years when the Durrs lived in Birmingham and Washington, John Coe participated actively in Demo-

28. John Coe to Ralph E. Shikes, July 5, 1948, in Box 1, Folder 54, Coe Papers; James Mansfield Coe and Evalyn Coe-Grubbs, interview by author, tape recording, Pensacola, February 13, 1988. See also Sarah Hart Brown, "Pensacola Progressive: John Moreno Coe and the Campaign of 1948," *Florida Historical Quarterly*, LXVIII (July, 1989), 1–26.

29. Coe himself disagreed with this. Attempting to sell his services to the army judge advocate general's office at the beginning of World War II, he claimed that "I have endeavored to avoid that lack of balance which often characterizes the self-educated, and believe I have done so." John Coe to Judge Advocate General, application blank, 1941, in Box 18, Folder 27, Coe Papers.

30. Coe-Grubbs interview.

cratic Party politics in north Florida. While Durr made speeches as a member of the FCC, Coe traveled around the state supporting candidates in the party's primaries.

In 1924 Governor John W. Martin appointed Coe to fill the unexpired state senate term of a Pensacola lawyer who migrated to Miami only weeks after his election to take advantage of the Florida boom. Coe had campaigned for Governor Martin, a "business progressive," and he agreed with many of the new official's plans for Florida. While Martin made road building his first priority, Coe entered the legislature with proposals to help his county collect back taxes, reform the local judiciary, and assist Pensacola's commercial fishing industry.

Early evidence of Coe's nascent civil libertarianism appeared in his sponsorship of the judicial reform measure and also in his vehement opposition to two other bills. One, a "Bible bill," would have required the reading of the King James version of the Bible in Florida classrooms every day; the other, a "search and seizure" bill, sought greater latitude for police enforcing prohibition statutes. Both bills received open support from the active north Florida Ku Klux Klan and strong opposition from Coe's large Catholic constituency and other Pensacola non-Protestants. Neither bill passed, but Coe's role in their defeat fueled his opposition during the reelection campaign in 1926, and he lost a close race.[31]

Coe had enjoyed his years in the legislature and became bitter over the loss. It helped to solidify his developing dislike for the reactionary elements that he found destructive of progress in Florida and the rest of the Deep South. Combined with the depression and collapse of the Florida boom, his defeat kindled both his identification with the victims of the Klan and his distrust of the southern establishment. Nonetheless, in the late 1920s and 1930s, Coe, by then in partnership with another young attorney, became a very successful small-town lawyer. He cultivated a broad general practice, and one of his specialties, admiralty and maritime law, led him to practice often in federal courts. Known as a meticulous and unrelenting advocate, he seldom lost cases. Reportedly, one Pensacola shipping business kept him on retainer just so he would refrain from suing them, though another firm handled most of their

31. Bills, correspondence, and other papers relating to Coe's senate term are found in Box 1, Folders 2 through 28, Coe Papers.

legal affairs. A few years later fellow attorneys called him "brilliant" and "a keen thinker" whom they believed to be "loyal to the Government" despite the fact that he had "gotten off on a political tangent." They informed the FBI that Coe had long enjoyed a "high standing at the Bar" and the "prestige that comes with holding such official positions as secretary to the United States District Judge, Assistant United States Attorney, State Senator, and committee assignments of the Florida State Bar Association."[32]

Even as a young attorney, Coe had a penchant for accepting clients and causes unpopular with the conservative local establishment. In 1936 he stood before a meeting of the Pensacola chapter of the Florida Bar Association and asked the shocked lawyers to sign a petition asking for clemency in the deportation hearing of CPUSA leader Earl Browder. On the other hand, a colleague recalled his energy and industry as one of Escambia County's earliest "plaintiff's lawyers." When the attorneys gathered in front of the courthouse at the beginning of each term waiting to file their cases, he always filed more than any other lawyer, mostly damage suits. Though these were not his only profitable cases, Coe, like liberal lawyers in other parts of the country, discovered early in his career that personal injury cases could supplement and often support his progressive practice. His ability to combine a successful local practice with civil liberties and civil rights work proved to be one of the fascinating elements of his career. He sometimes felt that his controversial clients affected his general practice, and he suffered personal stings repeatedly, but he was always a good businessman in spite of his politics.[33]

Nevertheless, by 1940 his political opinions had become flagrantly radical by conservative local standards. After 1929, Coe said years later, he became "particularly interested in defending cases of Negroes who were subject to discrimination and oppression." He litigated peonage cases originating in turpentine camps in Pineapple, Alabama, and Franklin County, Florida. These cases later appeared as evidence in a United Nations document compiled by Stetson Kennedy, another north Florida liberal with whom Coe

32. Coe-Grubbs interview; Department of Justice, Federal Bureau of Investigation, File 100-358684, Section 1, Subject: John Moreno Coe, Report, June 6, 1949, pp. 13–14 (file obtained by author under Freedom of Information Act, August, 1995) [hereinafter cited as Coe FBI File].

33. Report, September 12, 1949, p. 8, in Coe FBI File, Section 1; E. Dixie Beggs, interview by author, tape recording, Pensacola, February 14, 1988.

corresponded for many years. Unfortunately, most of his papers from the 1930s and the early 1940s no longer exist, though his children have many memories of early civil liberties and criminal cases handled by their father. Although they disagree on exact dates, they remember that he represented black clients in cases involving segregation rules on Pensacola city buses, a jim crow ordinance requiring black citizens to defer to whites on city sidewalks, and many instances of negotiation between members of Pensacola's black community and the city police. No black lawyers practiced in Pensacola until 1952, when Coe wrote his National Lawyers Guild friend George Crockett that "a Negro lawyer has made his debut in town for the first time in about 40 years." Indeed, for years the city's black community affectionately called him "Lawyer Coe."[34]

In 1939, accepting a small retainer from the Pensacola NAACP chapter, Coe appealed a case to the Florida Supreme Court involving a black man sentenced for shooting a policeman. This unsuccessful effort, predicated on the victory won by the International Labor Defense in *Norris* v. *Alabama*,[35] asked for reversal of the circuit court decision because the exclusion of black names from jury lists in Escambia County violated the defendant's constitutional rights. Three years later Coe won a similar appeal involving Will Lewis, a black man convicted of rape. In 1944, soon after *Smith* v. *Allwright*, Coe received statewide publicity when he successfully appealed two suits brought to register blacks as Democrats in Escambia County. Seeking a legal precedent that would have permanent force in Florida, he carefully covered all bases by filing both suits, one the petition of R. A. Cromwell, who sought to register for the first time in a city precinct, the other the application of Esau Chavis, who wanted to change his registration in a county precinct from Republican to Democratic.[36]

As a result of these cases the Coe family received telephone threats and a rock crashed through their living room window wrapped in a note announc-

34. John M. Coe to Louis Touby, September 30, 1948, in Box 1, Folder 56, John M. Coe to Stetson Kennedy, June 14, 1957, in Box 3, Folder 67, and John M. Coe to George Crockett, September 15, 1952, in Box 2, Folder 63, all in Coe Papers; Coe-Grubbs interview.

35. In *Norris* v. *Alabama*, 294 U.S. 587 (1935), the U.S. Supreme Court reversed a "Scottsboro" verdict because blacks had been systematically excluded from Alabama juries.

36. *State of Florida* v. *Ben Davis*, in Box 14, Folder 11, and *State* v. *Will Lewis* and *State ex rel.* v. *Ben L. Davis* (the Cromwell and Chavis cases), in Box 27, Folder 1, both in Coe Papers.

ing "Beware!" Although the Pensacola press barely reported the appeal, other Florida newspapers publicized the Supreme Court hearings and Coe's name appeared prominently in many of the stories. Answering a Tampa newspaper man's request for information about the registration cases, he proclaimed that despite his descent from West Florida "slave owners" he still bore "a consciousness of human rights." During the war against Fascism and racism abroad, he believed "we should make a special effort to root out from our own society discrimination and injustice."[37] His local image suffered and he lost a few clients, but Coe expressed pride in his part in changing the Florida white primary law.

Perhaps as a result of the publicity surrounding the registration cases, Coe resigned under pressure from the local post of the American Legion in 1945. During the same period he began carrying a pistol in his automobile.[38] On the other hand, in response to a congratulatory letter from Arthur Garfield Hays, he became a cooperating ACLU attorney, an unusual appointment for a member of the Escambia County Bar Association in the 1940s. "This is a matter of honor, not profit," he said in a letter to his son, "but I am deeply interested in their type of work." Coe spoke of his pleasure in joining the ACLU's brief challenging the Florida law mandating licensing of union organizers.[39]

The registration cases indirectly provoked Coe to become a regular subscriber to the *Daily Worker*. Having received a copy of the New York–based Communist newspaper sent anonymously, he found topics covered therein never reported in the Pensacola *News-Journal,* and the paper's leftist spirit piqued his curiosity. He informed the *Worker* about the *Chavis* and *Cromwell* cases and also asked for a subscription. Coe read the publication faithfully until 1956, when the Florida Supreme Court amended its grounds for disbarment to include membership in the CPUSA or "any of its various 'fronts.'" Coe and others argued against the new rules and were able to force a few

37. John M. Coe to Walter Fuller, January 1, 1945 [misdated 1944], in Box 27, Folder 1, ibid.

38. W. Raymond Chesser, Jr., Adjutant, Frank Marston Post, American Legion, to John Moreno Coe, June 14, 1945, in Box 27, Folder 1, ibid.; Coe-Grubbs interview.

39. Arthur Garfield Hays to J. M. Coe, February 28, 1945, in Box 27, Folder 57, and Coe to Charlie (Charles Coe), March 21, 1945, in Box 22, Folder 20, both in Coe Papers.

changes, such as "doing away with the use of the Fifth Amendment or its State equivalent as automatic grounds for disbarment," but he still feared persecution because of his "subversive" subscription. "Continuing as a subscriber to your paper imperils one's continuance at the bar," he wrote the paper's editors. "I have always stayed free of associational entanglements which might impair my own freedom of thought or action; but I am regretfully compelled to request that you take my name off your mailing list, and permit my subscription to lapse."[40] Although it may be imprudent to draw other conclusions from this letter, the missive does suggest the value Coe put on his profession. He did nothing that might put his ability to practice law in jeopardy.

John Coe loved being a lawyer. In a particularly exhilarated letter to one of his sons, he exulted about how much he had enjoyed a "vicious and bitter trial" in which he "blistered" the prosecution. The opposition likened his final speech to being "burnt by nitric acid," Coe boasted. "The jury stayed out six and one-half minutes and acquitted. I was very happy, and proud because right had been done." Never tiring of extolling the joys of litigation, he savored each success, whether or not the case had great significance.[41]

He also enjoyed politics. Coe attended the four national Democratic conventions that nominated Franklin Roosevelt as a Florida delegate, an ardent admirer of Roosevelt, and an early and convinced New Dealer. In 1944 he fought on the convention floor with Senator Claude Pepper for Henry Wallace's retention as vice-president. Like Pepper and Durr, Coe expressed little enthusiasm for Harry Truman. After Roosevelt's death he worried about the future of the Democratic Party, predicting correctly a division between liberals and conservatives in 1948. In an optimistic but rather polemical letter to his son in mid-1945, he voiced both his fear of a temporary conservative victory and his belief that in the end liberals would triumph: "The pendulum will swing back, and we may enjoy a more or less pink, or even a slightly red administration." With the Fascists beaten, modern men would rise up against injustice and refuse to be oppressed, and "these things add up to the inevitable

40. John Moreno Coe to the *Daily Worker,* July 31, 1945, in Box 27, Folder 1, and July 23, 1956, in Box 3, Folder 60, both ibid.
41. John M. Coe to "Mansy" (James Mansfield Coe), September 2, 1946, in Box 14, Folder 2487, ibid.

achievement of social justice."[42] In 1948 he and his wife, Evalyn, always his most sympathetic supporter, left the Democratic Party to support Wallace for president.

Unlike Coe and Durr, whose families lived less than two hundred miles apart on the coastal plains of Alabama and west Florida, Benjamin Eugene Smith came from the piney hills of northern Louisiana and southern Arkansas. A full generation also separated Smith from the older men. The oldest of three children of a hard-working family, Smith was born in El Dorado, Arkansas, in 1927. His mother, Jo, daughter of a country doctor, grew up in Arkansas. Family legend notes that a hot-water bottle kept Ben Smith alive because he weighed only two pounds at birth, an apparent overstatement since in the 1920s such a small baby would probably have either died or suffered permanent damage. Nevertheless, much effort went into young Ben's survival; perhaps as a result his mother always acted as his protector, and he remained her favorite. Because his father worked for various oil companies, he grew up in towns in Arkansas, Texas, and Louisiana. Smith had begun high school when his family returned to settle permanently in Ruston, Louisiana, where the grandfather whose first name he had received operated successfully as a land speculator, money lender, and rural landlord.

During the depression the family sometimes approached destitution when Louis Smith, an unassertive, soft-spoken gentleman, unlike Ben Smith or his grandfather, faced unemployment. At one point Louis bought and managed a bakery in Acadia, Louisiana, but lost it when larger businesses entered the local market. After the rest of the family returned to Ruston, Louis Smith worked for several years in Tullos, Louisiana, while Jo Smith performed secretarial duties for a local judge. Eventually he returned to Ruston, entering his father's "hip-pocket" but thriving small loan and land management business. The family rented a home on Ruston's main street next door to the sister of future Louisiana governor Earl Long.[43]

The area around Ruston, sometimes called "Earl Long country," was rougher country than the older parts of the South in which the Durrs and the

42. John M. Coe to Charles Coe, April 21, 1945, in Box 22, Folder 20, ibid.

43. Patrick Smith, interview by author, tape recording, Ruston, Louisiana, October 1, 1991; Penny Smith Jones, interview by author, tape recording, Phoenix, January 30, 1992.

Coes lived. Although a college town, Ruston, founded in 1884, was a smaller, poorer, younger, and more provincial place than either Pensacola or Mont- gomery in the 1940s. Perhaps this is one reason why Ben Smith migrated to more cosmopolitan southern Louisiana soon after graduating from college.

During his years in Ruston, however, Smith seemed happy, adored by an ebullient and affluent grandfather who lived "in the big house on the hill." In the summers he and brother Patrick enjoyed working visits to their grand- father's properties in Texas and Louisiana. The younger Pat "idolized" Ben. In the summers the two boys sometimes worked as field hands on Smith landholdings in east Texas, and they hunted together around Ruston. Throughout Ben Smith's lifetime he valued the skills of the southern out- doorsman learned as a young man. He kept guns, loved to hunt and fish, and was a proficient horseback rider and boatman.[44]

The family was always "fairly liberal," meaning that they avoided "racial troubles" and voted for Franklin Roosevelt. Churchgoing Methodists, their religious practice endured more as a civic and social responsibility than as the spiritual center of their lives. An Eagle Scout and a cheerleader in high school, Smith, like Clifford Durr, wore a Phi Beta Kappa key in college. Educated in the local college, now Louisiana Tech University, and at Tulane Law School after World War II, he became, unlike Durr or Coe, a liberal political activist and "true believer" from his undergraduate years.[45]

Both Coe and Durr entered the U.S. Army in 1918 to fight in World War I, though neither saw combat. Smith suffered the same fate at the end of World War II, although according to some reports he had tried his best to enlist earlier, when still under age. Like the overage John Coe, who tried desperately to enlist in the war effort in 1941, Smith wanted to fight the Fascists. He underwent navy flight training in Iowa and later told his family he once ditched his plane after an accident in a training mission over Kansas, and he apparently flew a few missions in the Caribbean after the war ended. The FBI reported that he "started flight training but was dropped from same on January 26, 1947 because of high blood pressure." Smith's military career, though brief, had at least two permanent effects: flying remained a personal passion, and he developed a love of military history. Like Coe and Durr,

44. Smith interview.
45. Ibid.

Smith read voraciously; his favorite books included Samuel Eliot Morison's thirteen-volume set on World War II naval history. His friends in the antiwar movement of the late 1960s and 1970s must have found his fondness for military history bewildering.[46]

Ben Smith, only twenty years old when leaving the navy in 1947, had by this time, according to his family, become a "liberal" by local standards. The navy sent him to Rice University in Houston for a semester in 1946, but after his discharge he returned to Ruston and finished a degree in engineering. He joined a fraternity and became a college cheerleader, but he also began to invite some "unusual people" to the family home. One of these, a "radical" professor of English literature and "spellbinder" named H. S. Sachs, is the person the family credited with having the greatest influence on Ben's early liberal thinking. Sachs may have been the one who convinced him that the law could be a vehicle for the application of his liberalism. Unable to recall any specific ideas advanced by Professor Sachs, Patrick Smith imagined them to have been similar to Marxism. Sachs remained Ben Smith's close friend and confidant until his death, perhaps the only white citizen of Ruston, excepting a few family members, who openly accepted Smith's later work. Jo Smith, steadfast and supportive, defended her eldest son even when the rest of the family disavowed his left-wing ideas. A Tulane friend, Leonard Dreyfus, found Smith's father and brother very conservative in later years and credited his mother with keeping the family together through the controversy surrounding his work as a liberal lawyer.[47]

Later, some believed that the nature of his father's business had a lasting effect on Smith's feelings toward oppressed people. Louis Smith supervised the collection of rents and personal loans from a fairly large number of sharecroppers and other debtors. He knew each family owing money, many of them customers inherited from his own father, and treated with paternal kindness the procession of borrowers who came to a table in the Smith's

46. Ibid.; Department of Justice, Federal Bureau of Investigation, File 100-408581, Subject: Benjamin E. Smith, Report No. 100-13805, May 29, 1954, p. 3 (file obtained by author under Freedom of Information Act, October 6, 1994) [hereinafter cited as Smith FBI File]; Jack Peebles, attorney, interview by author, tape recording, New Orleans, September 4, 1990.

47. Smith interview; Corinne Barnwell, interview by author, tape recording, New Orleans, September 6, 1990; Leonard Dreyfus, telephone interview by author, tape recording, Charlottesville, Virginia, July 17, 1991.

backyard on Fridays to satisfy their obligations. Ben Smith was keenly aware of the circumstances under which most of these unfortunate people lived and, despite the benevolent attitude of his father, may have been troubled by the fact that he profited from the labor of poor and subjugated workers. In any case, he was able to view the economic deprivation and social divisions of the rural South at close range, perhaps much more intimately than either Clifford Durr or John Coe. His first wife and her brother thought such concerns became "pivotal" in the formation of Smith's liberalism.[48] Possibly youthful idealism, an energetic search for answers to universal questions, and ambivalent feelings about his father's business combined to lead him to examine his society critically and, like Coe and Durr, to find it tragically flawed.

Soon after enrolling at Tulane, Smith met his first wife, Lillian Massimini, a Sophie Newcomb College student and New Orleans native who worked in the university library. That summer he visited her at summer school in Austin, Texas, then joined a migrant crew following the wheat harvest, working in fields from northern Texas to Canada before school reopened in September. His former brother-in-law, then a Tulane undergraduate, remembered wondering why Smith chose such a difficult way to earn college funds. But it typified Smith's outlook and personality. Exuberant, physically robust, and strong, he was a very appealing person and always something of a ladies' man. He and Lillian married during his second year in law school.[49]

Smith encountered another liberal teacher at Tulane Law School in New Orleans, Hegelian scholar Mitchell Franklin. Franklin's lectures about Hegel's dialectic, especially the notion of struggle and change as necessary for the realization of freedom, influenced Smith and his fellow students immediately after World War II to think about the meaning of freedom and the uses of struggle in twentieth-century America. A 1948 report from the FBI's file on NLG activities in New Orleans called Professor Franklin a "misguided intellectual," "the only active member of the Guild in New Orleans," and "one of the leaders of the Henry Wallace movement in the vicinity." Like Sachs, Franklin became Smith's lifelong friend. An amusing tale about their early relationship comes from Smith's FBI file. "[Franklin] was regarded to

48. Jones interview; William A. Massimini, interview by author, tape recording, Slidell, Louisiana, April 9, 1992.

49. Jones interview; Jones to author, letter, April 19, 1992.

be so pro-Communist by his class that on one occasion the entire male component of the class showed up with red neck ties." The informant cited Smith's
refusal "to go along with the gag" as evidence of his "pro-Communist
views."[50]

Much published and well known in leftist legal circles and in academia,
Franklin was one of the "southern" professors mentioned by the editors of
the NLG's history. But though he taught at Tulane for more than thirty years,
he was a native Canadian educated at Harvard whose legal experience outside
the classroom took place in Massachusetts and New York. A longtime NLG
board member, Franklin frequently spoke at guild conventions during the
late 1940s and early 1950s about the "fiasco" of Truman's foreign policy
and the relationship of the Atlantic Pact to the United Nations. Also a constitutional scholar, Franklin became known just a few years later for articles
exposing the fallacy of interposition, the reinvented southern strategy for
circumventing *Brown* v. *Board of Education*. In 1958 he entitled his NLG
convention talk "The Supreme Court, the Constitution, and Integration."
One of Smith's law partners said Ben Smith was "really hung up on the First
Amendment." Perhaps Franklin's tutelage or the reading he encouraged influenced this propensity.[51]

Through Franklin, Ben Smith became a student leader of Henry Wallace's
small Louisiana Progressive Party in 1948, an activity that caused his family
in northern Louisiana much distress. Through the Progressive movement he
began to make contacts with others leftists whose ideas influenced him as he
entered the legal profession in 1951. By that time he had also become a
member of the National Lawyer's Guild.[52]

Smith's dedication to his profession sprang largely from his conviction that
the law could be an agent for change, and he thrived on contacts with like-
minded individuals, especially liberal lawyers. He enjoyed the NLG primarily

50. Memo to SAC from Russell T. Coon, SA, Re: National Lawyers Guild, March 18, 1948,
in FBI files for New Orleans chapter, National Lawyers Guild (copies, gift of Mary E. Howell,
attorney); Report, July 20, 1954, p. 13, Smith FBI File.

51. Peebles interview; *New York Guild Lawyer*, VII (March, 1949), in Box 90, National
Lawyers Guild Papers, Martin Luther King Library and Archives, The Martin Luther King, Jr.,
Center for Non-Violent Social Change, Atlanta [hereinafter cited as NLG Papers, King Center];
Lawyers Guild Review, XVIII (Winter, 1958), 1.

52. Peebles interview.

for this reason. In later years he knew John Coe through SCEF and NLG business, and was pleased when Cliff Durr asked him to cooperate in an important Montgomery case in 1961. Judge John Minor Wisdom of the Fifth Circuit Court of Appeals also became his friend in the 1960s. A law partner says Smith was "never happier" than when he returned to the office after a long discussion of substance in Judge Wisdom's chambers. A liberal southern Republican, Wisdom in retrospect found allegations that Smith was a Communist to be "ridiculous." Indeed, Wisdom's influence may have somewhat moderated Smith's youthful liberalism and helped him to clarify his political motives. Wisdom viewed him as an idealist but a "good lawyer . . . trustworthy, competent, and diligent." Smith, whose respect for constitutional values matched those of the judge, venerated Wisdom as a man of great courage and intelligence.[53]

If Smith had a quiet, contemplative side as he matured, it could be seen in his artistic talent. Like Jim Dombrowski, who became his close friend, his avocation was oil painting. A brother-in-law still enjoys a group of Smith's "peaceful pictures," all landscape paintings, that hangs in his home. The same man also remembered Smith's success as a young scoutmaster, his adeptness at teaching outdoor skills, and the delight this volunteer activity brought.[54] Nevertheless, while a much more expansive, informal, and charismatic public person than either Coe or Durr, Smith failed to balance his professional mission with the obligations of his personal life. He earned a reputation for commitment, enthusiastic advocacy, and great success as a litigator, but his three marriages, legendary drinking habits, and an unhappy break with his brother suggest his stressful personal lifestyle, a handicap avoided by his older colleagues.

A disease exacerbated by his drinking led to Smith's untimely death at age forty-nine. Coe and Durr both lived into their mid-seventies, best remembered for work done after their fiftieth year. Personally conservative, almost old-fashioned men, they contrasted sharply with Ben Smith, who remained an extravagant individualist, always young and spontaneous. Yet though the three lawyers differed greatly in style, their professional goals coincided, they

53. John Minor Wisdom to author, letter, June 5, 1991; Waltzer interview; Arthur Kinoy, *Rights on Trial: The Odyssey of a Peoples' Lawyer* (Cambridge, 1983), 226.

54. William A. Massimini, telephone interview by author, notes, April 22, 1992.

knew and respected each other, and their careers echoed and complemented one another.

These lawyers might have been routinely called "radical" by a hostile southern press or local bar associations, but that word should be used here very cautiously. Their legal work was deeply informed by politics and principles, but all three men remained committed to legal processes to accomplish their goals. Neither fanatics nor revolutionaries, they cherished the precepts embodied in the United States Constitution. NLG lawyer and Rutgers law professor Arthur Kinoy, Benjamin Smith's good friend, suggested that instead of "radical" they be called "progressive" lawyers, a word with perhaps less worrisome overtones. Numan Bartley has pointed out that by the late 1940s "the very word *liberal* disappeared from the southern political lexicon, except as a term of opprobrium."[55]

Regardless of our imperfect labeling, however, all three clearly revered Thomas Jefferson's ideals and the Bill of Rights. As the political climate changed in the years just after the war, it became clear that such attorneys and their nonconformist clients faced formidable opposition from a growing antiradical consensus, North and South. Cliff Durr, John Coe, and Ben Smith persevered, each struggling against the conservative majority in his own distinctive way. These southern lawyers recognized and mourned the glaring contradictions between the promises of the Constitution and the repressive, invasive bureaucracies that imperiled dissent and frustrated reform in postwar America.

55. Arthur Kinoy, interview by author, notes, Atlanta, November 2, 1990; Bartley, *New South*, 71.

CHAPTER THREE

Crossroads:
Progressive Politics and
Other Pipe Dreams, 1948–1950

The author of a book called *The Road to Daulis*[1] depicts an ancient story as a parable about the causes and consequences of decisions. Driven to a journey by a confusing oracle and by his own conscience, Oedipus, scion of an illustrious Greek family, came to a place where three roads met. Impulsively he killed the arrogant stranger blocking one road, an anonymous king, actually the monarch of Thebes and his own biological father. After this altercation, instead of following the obvious road to Daulis, Oedipus proceeded to Thebes to begin a life at the center of the struggle between good and evil. Most English translations of the myth indicate that the choice was predestined and that his heroic character equipped Oedipus to pay its price; and as moderns we are unduly influenced by Freud's cumbersome interpretation of the story. But the decision was also, Robert Eisner points out, unplanned and unnecessary if one looks at the story as the ancient Greeks tended to do, on a human scale. Oedipus chose instinctively, perhaps, but voluntarily and with a tinge of hubris. He could have calmly stepped aside or solicited advice from the dead king's retinue, which included an old shepherd who knew his identity. The road to Daulis might have led him to an obscure and easy life; Oedipus chose Thebes.

By the early 1950s, each of the southern lawyers highlighted here had purposely if somewhat imprudently invoked an expatriate's future in his own country. No efforts undertaken by Cliff Durr or John Coe before 1948 shook their conservative southern moorings as vigorously as did their activities during that turbulent election year and the paths chosen in their professional lives between 1948 and the end of the decade. Ben Smith as well began in

---

1. Robert Eisner, *The Road to Daulis: Psychoanalysis, Psychology, and Classical Mythology* (Syracuse, 1987), see esp. 9–15.

1948 the process that would make him a political outsider. Like the legendary Oedipus, none of the three aspired to or enjoyed the social or professional isolation resulting from their decisions, but once taken, their roads led directly to that end.

The bungled, ill-fated Wallace campaign affected each of the three differently but marked them all. As a law student Smith joined the Progressive Party enthusiastically, securing his reputation by organizing the Louisiana "Young Progressives" and speaking on Wallace's behalf at Tulane and in other settings around the state. Durr stood clear of the campaign, but the press chronicled his wife's involvement and often speculated on his views. Even more important, his resignation from government service on civil liberties grounds and his subsequent well-publicized representation of alleged Communist clients had personal and professional repercussions. Coe became state chairman of the Florida Progressives. This, coupled with his increasingly suspicious clientele, brought him notoriety and the mistrust of acquaintances and professional colleagues. All three men had established a relationship with the National Lawyers Guild by 1950, when Durr served as that organization's president.

For good or ill, decisions made in the late 1940s molded their professional lives in the years to come. Consequences of these decisions—FBI surveillance, congressional investigation, and professional ostracism—drew Coe, Durr, and Smith deeper into the fight for civil liberties. By 1950, barring an inconceivable change of character in each case, they were headed down difficult paths that led to steadily expanding personal convictions about the applications of civil liberties law and toward encounters with southern racial mores that would finally cut them off from many old and treasured associations.

For Cliff Durr, rejection of the liberal Democratic establishment really began with President Truman's Executive Order No. 9835. "We are going to fight communism employing the methods upon which we profess to base our abhorrence of communism," he wrote in response to the loyalty program's debut in March, 1947. A few weeks later, in a speech reported as "the first open criticism" of President Truman's loyalty order, Durr compared the present to the period of the post–World War I Red scare. "Having no vision of the future, we feared it and sought safety in clinging to the things with which we were familiar," he said, and "[we] came close to losing our liberties by the very methods we employed to defend them." If a man shows by his actions that he is disloyal to his country, he said, of course he should not be the country's agent. But if no action shows disloyalty, how "can we avoid confusing loyalty to particular economic, social, or even religious institutions, or political parties or factions, with loyalty to country?"[2] In these speeches and other public pronouncements, Durr challenged secret police investigations, the use of associations and affiliations as proof of disloyalty, and the anonymity granted to accusers in loyalty hearings.

After an address to the Washington chapter of the Southern Conference for Human Welfare centered around the dangers of restraining speech, Durr was called "the outspoken stormy petrel of the FCC" by the Washington *Post*. A few days later, commenting on a speech Durr presented to the National Citizens Conference on Civil Liberties (described as a meeting of "150 national civil rights leaders"), the *Post* labeled him "among the foremost critics of the government's loyalty program." *Variety* presented Durr with its award for excellence in 1947, calling him "the 'Great Dissenter' . . . guardian of the American people's stake in the air they nominally own." Clifford Durr had become the lonely voice of protest against Executive Order No. 9835 among top-level administrators in the Truman government.[3]

Durr's year of government employment after the instigation of the loyalty program (March, 1947–June, 1948) turned into a disturbing evolutionary period in foreign as well as domestic affairs. The debate over the Truman Doctrine, then the Marshall Plan, the Communist coup in Czechoslovakia, and the Berlin blockade pushed concern over Communist expansion to the front pages of American newspapers and helped to justify both increased anxiety and political posturing about subversive activity in the United States. The introduction of Truman's ambitious civil rights report and the president's unsuccessful veto of the Taft-Hartley Act also occurred in 1947, as did the germination of mutiny against the Democratic incumbency from left, right, and center.

2. Undated, untitled speech, in Box 12, Folder 8, Speech titled "Freedom and Fear," April 22, 1947, in Box 13, Folder 6, Speech before the National Conference for Civil Liberties, April 21, 1948, in Box 11, Folder 9, Birmingham *News*, April 21, 1947, in Box 11, Folder 8, and Washington *Post*, April 15, 1948, in Box 11, Folder 9, all in C. J. Durr Papers.

3. Washington *Post*, April 8, 15, 1948, in Box 11, Folder 9, and *Variety*, May 12, 1947, in Box 11, Folder 8, both ibid.

Before the 1948 convention, three groups fomented agitation against Truman's nomination. Opponents of his foreign policy and loyalty measures, mostly followers of Henry Wallace, attacked the president from the left; members of Americans for Democratic Action and other cold war liberals of the vital center supported other challengers, especially that great unknown quantity, Dwight D. Eisenhower; and many Democrats on the right championed the southern status quo and feared Truman's civil rights agenda. Arrows aimed at the president from the sophisticated Northeast, the liberal Midwest, and the conservative South.[4] From such a vulnerable position, it seemed unlikely that the president would choose to reappoint a vocal critic like Commissioner Durr when his term expired in 1948.

Perhaps a more important problem for Truman's political advisers, with Clifford Durr's opinion of Henry Wallace generally unknown, was his wife's declared support of Wallace. The Progressive Party attracted not only non-Communist liberals like Virginia Durr and the Durrs' good friends C. B. Baldwin and SCHW board president Clark Foreman, but also members of the CPUSA and other radicals. Even before Wallace announced as a candidate for the presidential race, many of his followers vigorously opposed the administration's anti-Soviet moves in Europe. Virginia Durr also remained a member of the suspected SCHW (and of the Southern Conference Education Fund's board until 1950), and while Durr himself never held a position in the organization, he addressed SCHW meetings on several occasions in 1947 and 1948 and attended SCHW social functions throughout the 1940s.[5]

By 1947 SCHW had lost both members and political clout to the anti-Communist crusade. In April of that year James Dombrowski wrote a moving letter entreating Eleanor Roosevelt, who had quietly withdrawn her support from SCHW in 1946, to reconsider her position. He assured her that no member of the SCHW board was then or had ever been a Communist. Dombrowski listed Clark Foreman, Lucy Randolph Mason, Frank Graham, and

4. See McAuliffe, *Crisis on the Left,* Chapter 2, "Liberals and the Cold War," and Chapter 3, "Defeat for the Popular Front," for a thorough description of the diverse forces within the Democratic Party in 1947 and 1948.

5. Virginia Durr said, "I was the only one in the entire family who was for Henry Wallace. I was mighty lonesome, I'm telling you" (Barnard, ed., *Outside the Magic Circle,* 196); Reed, *Simple Decency,* 130.

Aubrey Williams, members with whom she had been friendly in the past, as persons who "would not have continued to serve on the board if they thought this was a communist-dominated organization." His failure to convince Roosevelt underscores the organization's loss of broad support in the liberal center.[6]

The Southern Conference became the subject of a scathing HUAC report published in June, 1947. Although the committee refused to give SCHW board members a chance to speak at its hearings, their investigators concluded that SCHW's supposed interest in southern social and economic problems "deviously camouflaged" a "Communist-front organization." The report came just days before an announced Henry Wallace speech at a Washington gathering sponsored by SCHW. While Wallace proclaimed his presidential aspirations, HUAC investigators recorded the names of government employees in attendance. Clearly, HUAC meant to paint both Wallace and the integration movement with a red brush, and several articles in southern newspapers made this connection in the weeks after the report appeared.[7]

The following October, Columbia University law professor Walter Gellhorn published "A Report on a Report of HUAC" in the *Harvard Law Review,* concluding, in part, that "the committee has either been intolerably incompetent or designedly intent on publishing misinformation." Many liberal newspaper editors and columnists seconded Gellhorn's conclusions.[8] But conservative reaction to the report also surfaced. In New Orleans, where SCHW had recently moved its offices, the New Orleans *States* published a

6. James Dombrowski to Mrs. Franklin D. Roosevelt, April 23, 1947, in Box 17, Folder 3, Dombrowski Papers. After SCHW folded in 1948, Mrs. Roosevelt remained friendly with Aubrey Williams and Dombrowski (neither of whom joined the Wallace movement) and sponsored New York fund-raising efforts for SCEF through the early 1960s.

7. U.S. Congress, House Un-American Activities Committee, *Report on the Southern Conference for Human Welfare,* 80th Cong., 1st Sess., June 6, 1947, H. Rept. 592, quotes on 13 and 17; Peebles, "Subversion and SCEF," 21–25; Collection of notes and clippings re: SCHW and Henry Wallace, in Box 17, Folders 2 and 3, Dombrowski Papers.

8. Walter Gellhorn, "A Report on a Report of the House Committee on Un-American Activities," *Harvard Law Review,* LX (October, 1947), 1193–1234, quote on 1233. See also Walter Goodman, *The Committee: The Extraordinary Career of the House Committee on Un-American Activities* (New York, 1968), 201; and Morton Sosna, *In Search of the Silent South: Southern Liberals and the Race Issue* (New York, 1977), 145–48.

series of articles blasting SCHW, SCEF, and Dombrowski, and after the "Americanism Committee" of the New Orleans Young Men's Business Club started an anti-Communist campaign the *Times-Picayune* began to echo a similar refrain. The public's perception of SCHW became anchored to the committee's report, which southern politicians used repeatedly over the next twenty years to prove that these integrationists and their successors in SCEF were Communists. Already in financial trouble because the CIO, reacting to accusations of Communist control, had discontinued its contributions in late 1946, and deeply divided internally over the public involvement of some of its leaders in the Wallace movement, SCHW was mortally wounded by the HUAC report. In November, 1948, the Southern Conference for Human Welfare formally dissolved.[9]

Regardless of Durr's antiadministration pronouncements or suspected associations, however, Truman invited him to the White House in April, 1948, offered him reappointment, and guaranteed the commissioner that he would "go to bat" for him during the Senate's confirmation process. This assurance must have been important to Durr, who knew about his controversial status and his enemies among powerful legislators. Earlier he had watched in dismay as southern conservatives in the Senate smeared the reputation of fellow Alabamian Aubrey Williams and denied his appointment to head the Rural Electrification Administration. Support for Durr appeared in the liberal press, and the new FCC chairman, Wayne Coy, urged Truman to reappoint him. But others agreed with the *Public Utilities Fortnightly* that "the withdrawal of Durr relieves the Truman administration of several embarrassing situations."[10]

When Durr announced his retirement in April, 1948, almost every news-

9. Collection of clippings from New Orleans *States* and *Times-Picayune,* June, July, August, 1948, in Box 17, Folders 2 and 3, Dombrowski Papers; Numan V. Bartley, "The Southern Conference and the Shaping of Post–World War II Southern Politics," in *Developing Dixie: Modernization in a Traditional Society,* ed. Winfred B. Moore, Jr., Joseph F. Tripp, and Lyon G. Tyler, Jr. (Westport, Conn., 1988), 185–87; Sosna, *In Search of the Silent South,* 145–48.

10. C. J. Durr to James Durr, April 15, 1948, in Box 1, Folder 7, *Billboard,* April 17, 1948, *Variety,* April 28, 1948, and Washington *Post,* April 15, 1948, in Box 11, Folder 9, Washington *Times-Herald,* December 18, 1947, in Box 11, Folder 8, and *Public Utilities Fortnightly,* May 20, 1948, in Box 12, Folder 1, all in C. J. Durr Papers.

paper account, both friendly and unfriendly, suggested that Virginia Durr's participation in the Wallace campaign concerned Truman or caused Durr to refuse reappointment.[11] Considering the heat of the Democratic nomination race and the campaign strategies of Truman's advisers, which included Red-baiting Wallace's followers, Truman seems to have displayed noteworthy tolerance and respect for Durr in making the reappointment. In later years, as Durr's reputation as a civil rights advocate became widely known in the South, segregationist opponents often implied that he had been "fired" by President Truman. Truman himself denied this insinuation both in public statements in 1948 and years later in correspondence with Hugo Black. Durr declined reappointment because he could not in good conscience administer the president's loyalty program. After he left government service, this prin-cipled stand would profoundly limit his professional options.[12]

As his retirement date approached, Washington rumors suggested that Durr might accept an academic post. Good friends on faculties of law and political science at Yale, Princeton, and Wisconsin encouraged him to pursue this course, and the idea appealed to Durr. If he could find an academic job that would support his family, he confided to his brother James, he would take it; otherwise he "always [had] the law to fall back on." It was not that Durr did not love and respect the law; he simply enjoyed thinking and talking about law more than practicing it day-to-day. After the busy, controversial FCC years he found himself ready for a respite. Earlier he had turned down

11. Virginia Durr disputes this idea in her autobiography, saying, "You can see how lightly everybody took my supporting the Progressive Party by the fact that Harry Truman decided to reappoint Cliff to the FCC in 1948" (Barnard, ed., *Outside the Magic Circle*, 201). But see also numerous articles in Box 12, Folder 9, C. J. Durr Papers, including these headlines: "FCC Member's Wife Takes Wallace Post" (Washington *Times Herald*), "White House Denies Durr Visit Is Linked to Wallace Drive" (Washington *Star*), "Durr Resigns Job with FCC: Husband of Wallace Backer Blames Poor Pay for Past Action" (Tulsa *World*), "Durr of FCC Resigns: Wife Backs Wallace" (Washington *Post*), "Durr Resigns: Wife Backs Wallace" (New York *Times*), "Durr Center of New 'Incident': Wife's Backing of Wallace Brings Crisis" (*Billboard*), and "Liberal Durr to Leave FCC" (*Public Utilities Fortnightly*).

12. Martin Bauml Duberman, *Paul Robeson* (New York, 1988), 324; Washington *Star*, April 22, 1948, in Box 11, Folder 9, New York *Times*, February 5, 1948, in Box 12, Folder 1, C. J. Durr to Ervin James, January 1, 1950, in Box 1, Folder 12, and Harry S Truman to Hugo Black, March 24, 1966, in Box 4, Folder 2, all in C. J. Durr Papers.

a chance to teach at Yale Law School because he felt obligated to complete his term on the FCC. He hoped that offer would be renewed.[13]

Several columnists expected him to declare for Wallace after his June retirement. Like Jim Dombrowski and Aubrey Williams, however, he remained detached from the Progressive Party and generally aloof from the 1948 election, despite his wife's Progressive candidacy for the U.S. Senate from Virginia.[14] In October, 1948, as a member of the Alabama bar, he assisted the Democratic National Committee and its counsel, the firm of Arnold, Fortas and Porter, in bringing Governor James Folsom's unsuccessful suit to replace the Dixiecrat ticket with the national Democratic ticket on Alabama's ballot.[15]

In any event, although a university job remained illusory, the summer before the 1948 election took shape as an exciting time. As Durr left office, admiring groups feted him on several occasions and praise for his courage came from the FCC, the Institute for Education by Radio at Ohio State University, the New York Radio Critics Circle, the National Lawyers Guild, *Time, Newsweek, Variety,* the New York *Times,* and many other newspapers. He had delivered a stirring defense of free speech and the people's right to control the airwaves as a guest speaker at the Eighth Annual Convention of the NLG in Chicago the previous February, and the guild honored him with a luncheon at the Astor Hotel in New York in June. Thurman Arnold served as toastmaster at this event, which featured testimonials to Durr's accomplishments by Hugo Black and Claude Pepper and a laudatory address by FCC chairman Coy.[16]

In July the sponsors of the One World Award invited the Durrs to attend a conference of World Intellectuals for Peace being held in Poland. In place of the ailing original delegate, Fiorello LaGuardia, the Durrs would accompany a small group of distinguished Americans to the meeting. Though the

13. C. J. Durr to James Durr, April 15, 1948, in Box 1, Folder 7, C. J. Durr Papers; Barnard, ed., *Outside the Magic Circle,* 219. Box 11, Folder 9, and Box 12, Folder 1, C. J. Durr Papers, contain clippings pertaining to Durr's resignation.

14. Durr interview.

15. *James E. Folsom* v. *Albritton et al.,* in Box 39, Folder 1, C. J. Durr Papers.

16. Speech, "The Voice of Democracy," February 21, 1948, in Box 11, Folder 9, and Washington *Post,* June 20, 1948, *Variety,* June 23, 1948, and *Broadcasting,* June 28, 1948, in Box 12, Folder 1, all ibid.

conference itself accomplished little, the Durrs enjoyed the trip, especially stopovers in Prague, Paris, and Rome. They reacted with dismay, however, to the rudeness and anti-Americanism of both the Russian Communists they met in Wrocław and French Communists in Paris, including the influential writer Jacques Duclos. In a confrontation with Virginia Durr, Duclos railed about the impotency of American liberalism. Cliff Durr brought home a new sensitivity to European attitudes toward the United States and a deepened concern about the efficacy of the Truman administration's efforts to contain Communism.[17]

When they returned to Washington in September, Tom Emerson, Durr's friend since early New Deal days, told the Durrs that the hoped-for job at Yale Law School would not materialize. Yale reportedly declined to employ Durr because board member Dean Acheson and law school dean W. W. Rostow took offense at his objections to the Truman Doctrine and the loyalty program. The academic career turned out to be a pipe dream, and Durr reluctantly opened a solo law practice. He wrote to several former New Deal colleagues about his difficult but necessary adjustment. A few years earlier his Seminary Hill neighbor, Thurman Arnold, had asked him to join in creating a new firm, but by late 1948 Arnold, Fortas and Porter functioned productively without him and the offer was not renewed. A few Wall Street law firms sought to take advantage of Durr's FCC experience, but he conscientiously refused to represent the communications giants he had fought so long. Years later he commented that he "did not like the idea of hiring myself out to undo all that I had tried to do while working for the government." Having represented large corporations before his government service, he "had observed that if big enough, such corporations are often inclined to expect more from their lawyers than strictly legal services." They wanted, the Durrs concluded, to buy "Cliff's reputation for being a man of integrity," and he turned them down.[18]

17. Durr's notes on this trip are in Box 7, Folder 4, ibid.; Barnard, ed., *Outside the Magic Circle,* 196–97; Salmond, *Conscience of a Lawyer,* 123–26.

18. Durr interview; C. J. Durr to Wayne Coy, November 4, 1948, and to Milo Perkins, October 26, 1948, in Box 36, Folder 7, and C. J. Durr, draft of book review of *The Superlawyers* (by Joseph Goulden) for the *Alabama Law Review,* Box 25, Folder 1, all in C. J. Durr Papers; Barnard, ed., *Outside the Magic Circle,* 218.

With Virginia campaigning for Henry Wallace and Cliff opening his new office, the Durr household buzzed with activity in the fall of 1948. Another Wallace supporter, Ben Smith, also kept busy, making travel arrangements for Wallace, vice-presidential candidate Glenn Taylor, and black opera singer Paul Robeson while attending classes at Tulane Law School. Smith managed to escape, according to an FBI report, when police arrested "sixty-four Progressive Party, Young Progressives, and Communist party members . . . at an interracial affair" in the French Quarter. Agents noted that Smith delivered the opening address at the state convention of the Louisiana Progressive Party, a detail that may say as much about the size and strength of the group as it does about the prominence of the zealous young speaker. When Wallace planned a visit to northern Louisiana, Smith asked his father and brother to welcome the candidate in Monroe, where a barrage of tomatoes and rotten eggs greeted the Wallace party. A similar display by local toughs occurred at a rally in Ruston. Perhaps Louisiana newspapers had carried stories about Wallace's recent refusals to speak before segregated audiences in Georgia and Alabama. Smith also convinced some old family friends to provide Wallace with overnight lodging in Shreveport. The Shreveport couple, who had little knowledge of Wallace's current notoriety, spent a sleepless night listening for gunfire from the men who patrolled the street in front of their house. Virginia Durr, John Coe, and attorney Herman Wright, who headed the Progressive Party in Texas, told similar stories about Wallace's southern campaign.[19]

For both Smith and Coe, the 1948 campaign brought important new relationships with other white liberals. Smith began a lifelong friendship with Jim Dombrowski. Dombrowski, eager to protect SCEF's tax-exempt status, took no part in the presidential race and actually endorsed Truman's civil rights plan. But he was arrested with Wallace's running mate, Senator Glenn Taylor, when both were speakers at a conference of the Southern Negro Youth Congress in Bull Connor's Birmingham in May, 1948; and before Wallace declared for the presidency, Dombrowski, under SCHW's auspices, had helped to organized his 1947 southern tour. So the SCEF leader had much in common with New Orleans Progressives despite his decision not to take part

19. Dreyfus, Smith, and Wright interviews; Memorandum SAC, New Orleans, to Director, FBI, February 24, 1954, p. 1, and Report, April 16, 1954, p. 4, both in Smith FBI File; Barnard, ed., *Outside the Magic Circle,* 197–98.

in the campaign, and he met them on social occasions. The warmhearted, scholarly, conscientious Dombrowski became the perfect foil for Smith's energy and enthusiasm. They established a close and enduring association sustained by shared concerns, personal admiration, and intellectual compatibility. After Smith's admission to the bar in 1951, he served as Dombrowski's personal attorney and often acted as SCEF's lawyer.[20]

Other accounts of disrupted Progressive meetings and similar predicaments come from Florida. Press stories published during the Progressive campaign ensured John Coe's enduring local reputation as a leftist. In the aftermath of a Tampa meeting chaired by Coe and featuring Paul Robeson and Clark Foreman as principal speakers, a local businessman and party executive committee member endured vilification. He and his wife entertained Foreman and Robeson as their houseguests after the party gathering, and the St. Petersburg *Evening Independent* published a picture of Robeson entering their home. As a result of segregationist publicity, other investors forced the businessman to sell his share of the local Kaiser-Fraser dealership, his wife lost her position as PTA president at their child's school, and the family suffered a prolonged period of harassing phone calls and threatening notes. A few weeks after the Tampa incident, an outdoor speech by Senator Taylor in Jacksonville nearly ended in a riot when a mob began lobbing eggs at the speaker and those around him, including Coe.[21]

Although hostility toward Florida Progressives seemed aimed at their integrationism, Coe worried that the party was taking "the path of least resistance" by spending most of its time and energy trying to generate black votes and getting little in return for such efforts. In this first presidential election since the end of the all-white primary, Coe felt that most blacks would be too protective of their new registration as Democrats to abandon Truman, and

20. Jack Peebles, "Reminiscences of the 1960s Civil Rights Movement in New Orleans and Mississippi," unpublished manuscript in possession of author (1990), 19–20. For a moving description of the Smith-Dombrowski friendship see eulogy, "Benjamin E. Smith Memorial Service, Unitarian Church," February 14, 1976, in Box 11, Folder 21, Dombrowski Papers. Similar descriptions of Dombrowski come from many sources, including Durr interview and Anne Braden, telephone interview by author, tape recording, Louisville, August 28, 1991. Both called him "a saint."

21. Brown, "Pensacola Progressive," 21. It should be noted that the St. Petersburg *Times*, that city's leading newspaper, was more sympathetic to Progressive aims.

he was right. However, he conceded that he found "a certain masochistic pleasure in confessing in public" his party's integrationist platform "and in purging from our hearts under the fire of public criticism the remnants of old prejudices."[22] Through such statements he exposed the conscience of an archetypal southern liberal, and perhaps the audacity of a dedicated nonconformist as well.

Florida Progressives hoped in vain that liberal Democrats who admired Claude Pepper would join the Wallace movement in spite of Pepper's refusal to leave the old party. Pepper had participated in an ADA-sponsored coup to draft Eisenhower before the convention, but afterwards affected a reconciliation of sorts with Truman. Coe saw the failure to attract white liberals mostly as a result of the Red-baiting publicity surrounding the Progressives' integrated meetings. But Pepper's campaigning, the Progressive position against the popular European Recovery Plan, and both Truman's civil rights stand and his support for repeal of the Taft-Hartley Act also contributed to keeping liberal Floridians in the Democratic fold. Cuban Cigar Workers and several small CIO groups in central and south Florida supported Wallace, but Coe judged most Florida unions "A.F.L. and . . . reactionary." Unable to secure a sizable labor, black, or liberal Democratic following, Progressives remained virtually "marooned in left field."[23]

As chairman of the Progressive Party in Florida, Coe traveled the length of the state meeting with liberals and leftists interested in the third-party movement. Although the party collapsed in the early 1950s, Coe, like Ben Smith, forged relationships during 1948 that deeply influenced his thinking and in large part determined the direction of his professional life for the next twenty-five years. One of these was Miami lawyer Leo Sheiner, a New York native and graduate of Cornell Law School who served on the Progressive Party's executive committee.

Sheiner had also been chairman of SCHW's Fourth District (Florida) Committee. In May, 1948, in the absence of Clark Foreman, he presided at one of the last SCHW board meetings. Although the disposition of SCHW's considerable debt awaited a final conclave in Richmond five months later,

22. J. M. Coe to Marjorie Haynes, October 10, 1948, in Box 1, Folder 47, Coe Papers.
23. Ibid.; John Egerton, *Speak Now Against the Day: The Generation Before the Civil Rights Movement in the South* (Chapel Hill, 1995), 479; Brown, "Pensacola Progressive," 22.

the organization effectively ceased to do business after this Atlanta gathering. Dombrowski remained as SCEF executive director and editor of the *Southern Patriot,* Aubrey Williams agreed to become SCEF's president, and SCEF assumed the lease on the parent organization's New Orleans office and closed SCHW's telephone and telegraph accounts. In 1954 Sheiner's association with SCHW, SCEF, the NLG, and the Progressive Party attracted the attention of James Eastland and the Senate Internal Security Subcommittee. As a result he eventually became John Coe's client in an important Florida civil liberties case involving both the Fifth Amendment and the independence of the bar.[24]

Coe's first case challenging allegations of subversion, however, concerned not Leo Sheiner but another New York native living in Miami, a former garment worker named Leah Adler Benemovsky. In February, 1948, Elizabeth Gurley Flynn and Pennsylvania Communist leader Steve Nelson spoke at a meeting of Communist Party regulars in Miami Beach. Benemovsky wrote notes to various people inviting them to attend. In the aftermath of the meeting she was caught in a "dragnet" designed, according to the Florida Supreme Court's final opinion, to catch "criminal communists." Florida officials charged her under the state's "little Smith Act," actually a series of antisubversive measures passed by the 1941 legislature. When questioned about party membership, names of other Communists, or participants in the meeting, first by HUAC and then by the Dade County solicitor, Benemovsky took refuge in the Fifth Amendment of the U.S. Constitution, or in the corresponding section of Florida's constitution. Denying her right to refuse to testify, a Dade County judge found her guilty of contempt and sentenced her to jail for ninety days. After her case was remanded to Dade County by the Florida Circuit Court, she faced imprisonment without bail. Alabama Communist leaders Sam Hall and his wife, Sylvia, traveled from Birmingham to visit her in jail. Sylvia (Hall) Thompson described Benemovsky as a shy, self-effacing person, the daughter of immigrants, a dedicated party worker of the "old school."[25]

Coe probably came to the attention of Benemovsky's friends in Miami

24. "Minutes of the Board of Representatives, Southern Conference for Human Welfare," Atlanta, May 22, 1948, in Box 17, Folder 3, Dombrowski Papers.

25. *State of Florida ex. rel. Benemovsky* v. *Sullivan, Sheriff,* 37 So. 2nd 798, 907 (1948); Sylvia Thompson, telephone interview by author, New York, tape recording, December 18, 1991.

because of his ACLU membership and Progressive Party leadership; his name also appeared on the NLG's referral list for 1948.[26] By late April he was writing Progressive Party friends about "running around like a cat shot with salt in connection to the case of Leah Adler Benemovsky" and "sweating a good deal of blood trying to defend even a remnant of freedom in Miami." Coe first convinced the Florida Supreme Court to require the lower court to set bail and then, after a second high court argument, saw the bail reduced from $100,000 to $500, an amount that the imprisoned woman could raise.[27]

In October the court heard substantive arguments in the case, and again Coe succeeded in Tallahassee. "The courts make a clear distinction," reads the majority opinion published in December, "between a Communist Party and a criminal Communist Party or one engaged in criminal communism." The Communist Party had not been outlawed in the United States, reasoned Justice William Glenn Terrell, only subversive activity that aimed to overthrow the government. The judge classified Benemovsky as a political Communist, not a criminal one. She had a right to refuse to answer the county solicitor who attempted to link her with "criminal communism."[28] This interesting decision came only a few months before the Smith Act convictions of eleven Communist leaders in New York, and Coe remained very proud of the victory. A grateful Leah Benemovsky for many years thereafter sent him a gift of her homemade sausage at Christmas.

An ideal client because she let her attorney choose the path of her defense, Benemovsky wanted to escape the clutches of the criminal justice system rather than to make a propaganda statement. Her defense was practical, not ideological, quite different from the defense of the Communist eleven in the Foley Square trial. Coe saw her as a victim of government excess and argued civil liberties law instead of economic or political theory. Propaganda, he believed, "should be left to extra legal agencies." Wary of extralegal maneu-

26. "National Lawyers Guild, Lawyers Referral List, 1948–1949," in Box 92, NLG Papers, King Center. The FBI reported in 1949 that Coe had been a member of the guild since 1940, though Coe's records do not show contributions that early. Memo to Director, FBI, from Guy Hottel, June 29, 1949, Coe FBI File, Section 1. The NLG submitted an amicus brief to the Florida Supreme Court in *Benemovsky* v. *Sullivan*.

27. John Coe to Marjorie Haynes, April 30, 1948, in Box 1, Folder 47, and to Max E. Bear, April 30, 1948, in Box 1, Folder 42, Coe Papers.

28. *Benemovsky* v. *Sullivan*.

vers and reluctant to endow legal matters with political overtones unless it became absolutely clear that no other strategy would work, he never lost sight of his primary objective, winning the case at hand.[29]

In the midst of the presidential campaign and the Benemovsky case, Coe gave advice to Progressives in Tampa who wanted to protest press treatment of blacks accused in a series of rapes and perhaps to become parties in the case. He urged them to allow the NAACP to handle the matter rather than commit the party to any action. They should participate "only if [they saw a] clearly established wrong and oppression capable of becoming a cause celebre. . . . Cases like those of Sacco and Vanzetti demand public attention, but there are not many like them." Coe's clients would not always be as willing as Benemovsky and the Tampa Progressives to accept their lawyer's counsel, and this invariably created difficulties for him. Ten years later, when SCEF staff member Carl Braden, standing on principle, refused to acquiesce to similar practical advice from Coe and New York lawyer Leonard Boudin, their appeal of his contempt conviction failed.[30]

Surely the rhetoric of Coe's frequent letters to Florida editors during the campaign and his speeches at campaign rallies appealed to leftists such as the Miami Communists and the enthusiastic Progressives in Tampa. Early in 1948, for example, he chided the Pensacola *News-Journal*'s attempt to "brand as subversive" public servants like Wallace, "who speak out against the poison of race prejudice [and] anti-labor propaganda. . . . Only those who hate Democracy," he wrote, "seek to stifle it with poll taxes and loyalty oaths." In an official party press release from Miami, he declared that the nation needed Wallace to "take up the mantle" of Roosevelt and change the focus of what had become "a campaign of privilege against labor" in the years since FDR's death. After the Progressive convention in Philadelphia he wrote several letters quoting his favorite funny slogan from the convention, the Missouri delegation's rhyme: "Rocking chair's ready—Piano's in tune— We want our Harry—Send him back soon!" Other articles in the party newsletter hailed Coe's participation in the defeat of a convention "red-baiting" proposal related to the approaching Foley Square Smith Act trials.[31]

29. Report, November 13, 1953, p. 3, Section 4, Coe FBI File.

30. Marian Mix to J. M. Coe, August 30, 1948, and Coe to Mix, August 31, 1948, in Box 1, Folder 49, Coe Papers; *U.S.* v. *Braden,* 2 U.S.C. 192 (1961).

31. J. M. Coe to Editor, Pensacola *News-Journal,* February 3, 1948, in Box 1, Folder 50,

After the election, Coe surmised that the people wanted domestic policy like Roosevelt's and thought they would get that from Truman. But they "didn't give a damn about foreign policy, and were unimpressed by the risk of war, or they were sold on the anti-Russian propaganda, and regarded Wallace somewhat as the Federalists did Jefferson at the time of the French Revolution." Wallace, who won no electoral votes at all, attracted pitifully meager support in the South. Truman won Florida with 281,988 votes, followed by Dewey's 194,780, Dixiecrat nominee Strom Thurmond's 89,750, and Wallace's 11,620. North Carolinians gave Wallace 3,650 votes, and about 2,000 Georgians voted for him; elsewhere in the South, Progressive totals fell even lower. Coe rejoiced that Florida had the highest percentage of Wallace votes in the region but credited the northerners in south Florida and "the blessed Spaniards in Tampa," not native southerners like himself. He was a renegade, and he knew it.[32]

Nevertheless, he wrote his sons in July that he had been "trying cases hand over fist," and in November he reported that "[the] law practice is active, the month of October was excellent." With the fervor of a true Progressive, moderated, perhaps inconsistently, by the shrewdness of a savvy business-man, he continued: "The purchasers have defaulted on the house, and I am going to foreclose and get about $3,600 out of the government guarantee, if all goes well. This is one bunch of cash they won't piss away on Greece and China." The Coes had recently built a new home in Gulf Breeze on Pensacola Bay; the foreclosure related to the family's former homestead in town. Despite his unusual leftist associations, he could still claim to be "quite successful in a material way" as a lawyer in a small and very conservative southern city. Amazingly, he also retained some very prosaic hometown affiliations, such as membership in the Kiwanis Club, which he had served as a state governor in the early 1940s. Though his own attendance was infrequent, his wife and five children retained active membership in the First Presbyterian Church.[33]

Pensacola *News,* February 16, 1948, p. 4, and Coe to Charlie and Mansy (Charles Coe and James Mansfield Coe), April 7, 1948, in Box 22, Folder 20, all in Coe Papers.

32. Brown, "Pensacola Progressive," 22; J. M. Coe to Charlie and Mansy, November 11, 1948, in Box 22, Folder 20, ibid.

33. J. M. Coe to Charlie and Mansy, July 30, November 11, 1948, in Box 22, Folder 20, and to Marjorie Haynes, August 2, 1949, in Box 2, Folder 7, ibid.

Besides his general practice, Coe continued to take controversial local cases he felt needed representation. He bragged a little to a Progressive associate about the case of a black teacher with a master's degree from Columbia University. She taught in the Escambia County system for twenty-eight years, but "they fired her cold out of caprice," he said, and he rejoiced that "she had the nerve to fight." He won her reinstatement despite the best efforts of a formidable foe on the school board whom he described in classic southern style as "the grandson of Admiral Raphael Semmes who commanded the *Alabama*." The matter "got a good deal of local publicity," Coe wrote, "and has, I think, had a mighty good effect." Coe seemed to get a special satisfaction from trouncing the Pensacola establishment. "You can imagine how happy they were," he chortled, but teachers seemed pleased, though most white educators feared to say anything.[34]

Other fights brought less satisfaction. In 1949 Coe found himself uncomfortably pitted against practicing Communists and former Communists, such as members of the Cigar Workers Union in Tampa. "You know these super leftists are hard to deal with," he wrote a Progressive friend in mid-1949, "because when you do not go all the way with them you lay yourself open to suspicion of being a little chicken hearted or rightist in attitude." In late 1948 HUAC had held two days of hearings in Miami. As a result, at the instigation of U.S. attorney general Tom Clark, a federal grand jury was impaneled in March, 1949, to consider possible indictments of Dade County "subversives." As this specter approached, Coe told Progressive Party members to rely on the *Benemovsky* precedent, take the Fifth, and refrain from making propaganda statements or disrupting the hearings. But the party became involved in internal squabbles, and sometimes his advice fell on deaf ears. The Florida Progressive Party remained a legal entity until 1952, but its unity already strained over how to react to such challenges.[35]

Certainly John Coe himself was neither "chicken hearted or rightist," as his subsequent legislative testimony against a bill outlawing the Communist Party in Florida proved. He stood out as one of the few witnesses in the Tallahassee hearings about the bill who did not hold membership in the CPUSA. The law, he declared, "is aimed at the Progressive Party . . . and can

34. J. M. Coe to Ralph E. Shikes, July 5, 1948, in Box 1, Folder 54, ibid.
35. J. M. Coe to Marjorie Haynes, August 2, 1949, in Box 2, Folder 7, ibid.

be used against any democratic group." He pointed out to the legislature the Klan's open existence in Florida, "without one suggestion of registration or even identification . . . yet when a group speaks up for the Negro people it is immediately singled out for attack" by state government. After the measure passed in April, Coe became "convinced that there are forces at work which can and will destroy the liberties of our country. . . . Every man or woman who does not lift his hand or raise his voice, neglects his duty." When a vicious anti-Communist purge began at the University of Tampa, he fired off a dissenting missive to the Tampa *Tribune*. He also explained the legal consequences of different courses of action to targeted individuals, many of them Progressive Party members. Coe counseled them to answer all of the legislative committee's questions except "the $64 question" because it remained "outside the scope of legitimate inquiry" and protected by the Fifth Amendment.[36]

At the beginning of 1949, Coe agreed to represent six African Americans applying for admission to the University of Florida. A liberal coalition including both Progressives and members of the NAACP and the ADA backed the suit. In the inevitable struggle between these popular front and vital center liberals, the Florida ADA characterized John Coe and the Progressives as Communists. In the end the group replaced Coe with Alex Akerman, a lawyer and rare Republican member of the Florida legislature from Orlando. After the denial of this original application Akerman decided against appeal, but he undertook another case, that of an applicant to the law school, Virgil Hawkins, that ultimately reached the U.S. Supreme Court.[37]

Coe's practice between 1948 and 1950 varied from routine personal injury,

36. Report, June 1, 1949, p. 10, Section 1, Coe FBI File; J. M. Coe to Bertha Davis, April 30, 1949, in Box 2, Folder 4, to Frederick Miller, May 7, 23, 1949, in Box 2, Folder 9, to Miriam Arons, May 14, 21, 1949, in Box 2, Folder 1, and to Editor, Tampa *Tribune*, in Box 2, Folder 8, all in Coe Papers.

37. Paul H. Cootner and Jim Crown to J. M. Coe, March 21, 1949, Coe to The Committee on Equal Education, March 23, 1949, Crown to Coe, May 11, 1949, and Coe to Crown, May 18, 1949, all in Box 2, Folder 3, Coe Papers; "Six Negroes Denied UF Entrance—Republican Lawmaker Applicants' Counsel," Pensacola *News-Journal*, February 2, 1950, p. 1. On March 12, 1956, the U.S. Supreme Court ordered Hawkins' immediate acceptance, but the university simultaneously raised its admissions standards and refused him admission on that basis. Finally in September, 1958, George H. Starke, a graduate of Morehouse College, applied and gained admission to the law school without incident.

maritime, probate, divorce, and other civil matters that fed his family to the more notorious litigation that increased as a result of his Progressive Party associations. Because he had first established a stable local practice, he could risk taking the civil liberties and civil rights cases that engrossed him intellectually. Cliff Durr, on the other hand, did not have a well-established practice or a secure client base, and he worked in a much more competitive political environment. When he opened his office in 1948, his celebrity status limited his capacity to develop a successful general practice. Unhappily, at least from the point of view of his declining financial stability, Durr found himself involved almost exclusively in civil liberties cases from the first day his Washington office opened. The practice began with a loyalty oath case and continued to attract clients in trouble with investigatory committees and loyalty boards, but few others.

Durr began his career as a corporate lawyer in Birmingham, and most of the work he did at the RFC and FCC honed the skills he brought with him to Washington, adding the communications industry as an area of special proficiency. Many lawyers in his position, before and since, have sought practices that use contacts and expertise gained in government service to the advantage of private clients. Even if he disdained the networks, for instance, it would have been logical for Durr to accept radio and television stations as clients or to pursue his attachment to educational television. But he had made numerous public pronouncements criticizing the president's loyalty order, and he also wrote an article for the *Chicago Law Review* that stimulated his reputation as a legal expert on the issue.[38] Though his best chance for lucrative practice lay in the communications field, after he rejected reappointment to the FCC on controversial grounds his chances of attracting radio or television stations as clients evaporated.

In the 1930s and 1940s, Durr became a committed civil libertarian, an eloquent speaker, and a fair and able administrator, but he had never practiced civil rights or civil liberties law, handled criminal litigation, or competed in the difficult process of "client development." Although certainly not penniless, for the first time he found himself self-employed, with thorny adjustments to make, personal and pecuniary. The former commissioner would

38. Clifford J. Durr, "The Loyalty Order's Challenge to the Constitution," *University of Chicago Law Review,* XVI (Winter, 1949), 298–306.

never again have a travel budget, a large staff, or easy access to the corridors of power. "We had no inkling at the time Cliff turned down reappointment to the FCC that the next years were going to be as hard as they turned out to be," wrote Virginia Durr.[39] As his fiftieth birthday approached, Clifford Durr launched a challenging but perplexing new career.

He became one of very few lawyers in Washington who took cases of self-confessed ex-Communists. Many scholars of this era note that most liberal defense lawyers served only those who established their political purity. Successful firms rarely risked "guilt by association" with radical clients. Though they often defended former New Dealers falsely accused in loyalty cases, Arnold, Fortas and Porter sent cases involving past or present party members to Durr. According to David Caute, the mere fact that one "well known and very liberal Washington lawyer" represented a client "was a signal to the judges that the client was 'all right.'" This judicial attitude surely handicapped the few lawyers who, out of a sense of public duty, defended those less zealous about anti-Communism. Attorneys for alleged subversives who employed the Fifth Amendment as a defense often faced suspicion and ridicule from bench and bar.[40]

Between 1947 and 1951, the Civil Service Commission and the FBI investigated more than three million government employees, caused the resignation of several thousand, and asked for the dismissal of 212 as security risks. Not one federal employee was indicted for espionage or treason. Durr's first case, that of Labor Department statistician Roy Patterson, typifies these sad proceedings, and has been discussed at some length by Durr's biographer as a good example of the cases he handled between 1948 and 1950. The department accused and dismissed Patterson, a much-decorated veteran of World War II, on the basis of anonymous allegations. Even the loyalty board that reviewed the case claimed ignorance of the accusation's source. Although Patterson denied several of the incriminating associations, the board refused to tell him whether they believed, or ever investigated, his denials.[41]

In an article in the *Nation,* Durr outlined the loyalty board's questions,

39. Barnard, ed., *Outside the Magic Circle,* 219.

40. Ibid., 222; Auerbach, *Unequal Justice,* 255–56, Caute, *Great Fear,* 197.

41. David McCullough, *Truman* (New York, 1992), 552; Salmond, *Conscience of a Lawyer,* 127–28.

noting its refusal to inform Patterson or his counsel whether he had given "the right answer." Patterson admitted, for instance, having received the assignment to read the *Daily Worker* as part of his job as an investigator at the Labor Department. He also acknowledged being associated briefly with two suspect groups, the Washington Committee for Democratic Action and the Washington Bookshop Association. But he had not seen a copy of the *Daily Worker* since he left the job to join the army, and he had resigned both affiliations early in 1941. Accusing Patterson only of belonging to "front" groups, not of membership in the Communist Party, the board questioned his ideas more than his possible participation in subversive activities.

The questions themselves communicate persuasively the board's antiliberal bias and the difficulty of disproving its allegations of disloyalty. Durr listed them in his article:

> What were your views on the Spanish revolution?
> Were you always for China in its war against Japan?
> Do you favor the present draft?
> Do you recall if you had any ideas about European aid prior to 1939?
> What distinction do you draw between the terms "communism" and "fascism," if you see any, and if so what is it?
> What was your government bond-buying record from the beginning?
> I am interested to know when you became really interested in the question of non-segregation because it is rather unusual you will have to admit, for persons born and raised in Texas to feel that would be a reason to join the Washington Bookshop, for instance, because he could there attend unsegregated meetings. I would like to get your thinking on that.[42]

Opposition to Franco during the "dress rehearsal for World War II" indicated, in the prevailing view, a pro-Communist bias before the war (or, as one writer quipped, "premature antifascism"); unquestioning support for

42. Clifford J. Durr, "How to Measure Loyalty," *Nation*, April 23, 1949, p. 472.

Chiang Kai-shek proved true anti-Communism; and advocates of the peace-time draft revealed their agreement with the policy of containment and thereby their Americanism. On the other hand, champions of war against Germany before the Nazi-Soviet pact had followed the lead of international Communism; and in 1949 real patriots perceived Communism as analogous to Fascism in 1941, a new (or reborn) totalitarian menace. Centrist liberals as well as conservatives declared the indivisibility of totalitarianism. A 1948 HUAC pamphlet asked the question, "What is the difference between a Communist and a Fascist?" and answered resolutely, "None worth noticing."[43] The board's last question demonstrates the prevalence of the conviction that integrationism equaled subversion, especially if advocated by a white southerner. In the logic of southern anti-Communism, at least, the Communist Party's advocacy of racial equality colored any "unsegregated meeting" red.

Loyalty boards often defined subversion in broad, vague, and very subjective terms. Durr characterized these panels along with congressional inquiries as "strange new courts unknown to our Constitution" created "to try men for offenses unknown to our laws."[44] What American citizen would have believed in 1941 that the regularity with which he purchased war bonds might be used publicly to judge his loyalty? he asked. In the *Nation,* Durr despaired that although "democratic process" purportedly guided loyalty hearings, "certain men are empowered, in secret hearings, to render judgment against others" and thereby to divest them of employment, reputation, and friends arbitrarily, without explanation. "Is the issue of our time really democracy versus communism?" How, he asked, can we call this the era of the "Fair Deal"?[45]

Appalled by Patterson's dismissal on flimsy evidence without due process, after two departmental hearings Durr appealed the case to the Loyalty Review Board. He asked them to hold open hearings in order to expose the case to public scrutiny. Though they refused to hold open hearings, in the end the

43. Quotes from Sam Sills, "The Abraham Lincoln Brigade," in *Encyclopedia of the American Left,* ed. Mari Jo Buhle, Paul Buhle, and Dan Georgakas (Urbana, Ill., 1992), 3; and "100 Things You Should Know About Communism in the U.S.A.," in Caute, *Great Fear,* 101.

44. Unidentified Montgomery, Alabama, newspaper story based on Associated Press release, dateline Washington (n.d.), "New Blast Loosened by Retiring FCC Chief," in Box 12, Folder 1, C. J. Durr Papers.

45. Durr, "How to Measure Loyalty," 473.

review panel reversed the Labor Department loyalty board's decision.[46] A dismal footnote to such procedures comes from an interview with one of Truman's most influential political advisers, Clark Clifford, by journalist Carl Bernstein, whose parents suffered in loyalty board hearings. The loyalty order, Clifford said, simply answered a political need in 1948. "The president didn't attach fundamental significance to the so-called Communist scare. He thought it was a lot of baloney." The administration did not "believe there was a real problem," but created the program to satisfy a problem "manufactured" by anti-Communist Republicans who questioned Democratic patriotism. So the administration sacrificed Patterson, along with hundreds of other liberal federal workers, to the political needs of the moment.[47]

In 1949 and 1950 Durr handled about a dozen other matters similar to Patterson's, appearing before HUAC and SISS as well as executive-branch loyalty boards. Frank Oppenheimer, a University of Minnesota physicist and the brother of J. Robert Oppenheimer, and Philip O. Keeney, a former government librarian, and his wife, Mary Jane, a United Nations employee, became targets of congressional investigations. As in most similar cases, anonymous FBI informants identified these witnesses as Communists. Like Coe, Durr advised such clients to rely on the Fifth Amendment when questioned about political associates. Although tragic personal and professional consequences still ensued, Frank Oppenheimer and his wife managed to escape contempt charges and prison. HUAC released the Keeneys in 1949, but SISS cited them for contempt the following year. Found guilty in their first trial, they ultimately achieved exoneration in 1955, though by then represented by another lawyer.[48]

Like the Keeneys and the Oppenheimers, another Durr client, Robert Oppenheimer protégé David Bohm, had flirted with Communism in California in the 1930s. Bohm insisted that his attorney place in the record his First Amendment objections to HUAC's investigation. That move angered the committee, especially the young congressman from California, Richard M.

46. Salmond, *Conscience of a Lawyer*, 127–29.

47. McCullough, *Truman*, 553.

48. Celinni, ed., *Digest of Communism*, 223; Caute, *Great Fear*, 328–29; Washington *Post*, June 10, July 26, 1949, and Washington *Star*, June 9, July 25, 1949, all in Box 39, Folder 6, C. J. Durr Papers.

Nixon, and in the end Bohm employed the Fifth Amendment as well as the First. Regardless, Congress cited him for contempt and he endured a trial before being acquitted of all charges. Subsequently the president of Princeton, like Frank Oppenheimer's supervisor at the University of Minnesota, decided to let Bohm's contract lapse. After accepting a new position in Brazil, he lost his U.S. passport as well. Eventually Bohm settled in England, accepting a full professorship at the University of London. Frank Oppenheimer, a close friend of the Durrs, became a sheep rancher in Colorado, then a high school physics teacher. Finally, in 1959, he reentered his profession as an assistant professor in the physics department of the University of Colorado.[49]

Two other cases, based on even more uncertain evidence, illustrated again HUAC's total lack of objectivity and the humiliation inflicted upon its victims. In late 1949 the committee launched a probe of Communist activity in the District of Columbia. Two of those questioned—Bella Rodman, the wife of a Washington contractor, and Rose Anderson, owner of a business facetiously labeled "The Subversive Drugstore" by the *Nation*—came to Durr for assistance. Both women had joined the Progressive Party in 1948, and Rodman admitted having supported SCHW with gifts of "several thousand dollars." Mrs. Anderson, Russian by birth, answered questions about her first husband, a State Department employee, and her current husband, a labor organizer. On Durr's advice, both relied on the Fifth Amendment when asked if they had ever been Communists. The *Nation* surmised that while this caused the press to brand them "as party members," it nevertheless provided some protection from charges of perjury or contempt as HUAC debated whether they or their accusers seemed more believable. HUAC never brought charges, but both women suffered from the publicity surrounding the hearings. Mrs. Anderson lost the successful business she had owned for twenty-two years.[50]

The case of Dr. Karl F. Heiser, a psychologist who worked with the Allied occupation forces in Europe, further illustrates the frustrations of appealing

49. Salmond, *Conscience of a Lawyer*, 131–34; Ellen W. Schrecker, *No Ivory Tower: McCarthyism and the Universities* (New York, 1986), 143; Philip M. Stern, *The Oppenheimer Case: Security on Trial* (New York, 1969), 445–48.

50. Washington *Star*, June 28, 1949, in Box 12, Folder 1, and unidentified newspaper story, "In the Wake of Red Probe," ca. September 28, 1949, in Box 39, Folder 8, and Malcolm Hobbs, "The Subversive Drugstore," *Nation*, November 26, 1949, in Box 1, Folder 11, all in C. J. Durr Papers; Salmond, *Conscience of a Lawyer*, 135.

loyalty board decrees. Found disloyal for reasons never explained, Heiser was barred from government jobs when he returned to the United States. In one hearing the chairman stated that he simply disagreed with Heiser's "basic philosophy": "Let's get this clear. The point which I am disturbed about is that while you would neither advocate communism nor do anything consciously to implement it, nevertheless, you would go to the limit in defending the right of other peoples, or groups of peoples to advocate communism, through political parties or otherwise."[51] Three loyalty boards told him that, though not accusing him of being a Communist, they worried about his broad interpretation of the First Amendment. "Subversion" had taken a very anti-Jeffersonian turn. In a no-win position, Heiser gave up trying to prove his loyalty and fitness for government employment. The case depressed and disheartened Durr. He protested in a letter to White House assistant David Lloyd that Heiser had been found disloyal for supporting "an interpretation of the First Amendment made by a unanimous Supreme Court in an opinion written by Mr. Justice Holmes," the well-known "clear and present danger" test of *Schenck* v. *U.S.*[52]

Besides his civil liberties practice, Durr also did some part-time teaching and writing between 1948 and 1950, but by mid-1950 his hopes had dimmed for a profitable Washington practice or a permanent academic position. He felt morally impelled to accept cases of those in trouble with the government's anti-Communist apparatus, but these cases damaged his professional reputation and provided meager financial rewards. Many of his clients could pay very little for his services.

Cliff Durr's antipathy toward arbitrary power and abusive government ripened during this brief period as a struggling civil liberties lawyer in Washington. His understanding of the fear that drove human beings to cringe when threatened by such forces also grew. Perhaps this empathy later helped him tolerate the "good people" of the South who were afraid to take action. While

51. Quoted from C. J. Durr to Harry B. Mitchell, Chairman, Civil Service Commission, August 18, 1950, in Box 39, Folder 3, C. J. Durr Papers.

52. C. J. Durr to David D. Lloyd, February 1, 1951, in Box 39, Folder 3, ibid. In *Schenck* v. *U.S.*, 249 U.S. 47 (1919), the most famous precedent established under the Espionage Act, Justice Oliver Wendell Holmes first stated this test for speech the Court would consider protected by the First Amendment.

losing respect for timorous southerners, he always understood them. The loyalty oath battle, one of the crowning efforts of his career, constituted a moral and intellectual accomplishment almost overlooked in later years. Nevertheless, it seemed highly suggestive of both his character and the direction his career would take after 1950.[53]

Some of Durr's other notable contributions to the civil liberties struggle during this period resulted from his presidency of the National Lawyers Guild. Not a member of the guild until a short time before his election in February, 1949, and inactive soon after he left office, Durr nonetheless labored diligently for the NLG. He used his position in a crusade against abusive government. Although he never accepted the pro-Russian positions of far-left members of the NLG, he agreed with its majority about the dangers of a confrontational foreign policy and appreciated having a company of allies opposing the domestic anti-Communist movement.[54]

As happened to Coe with his chairmanship of the Florida Progressive Party in 1948, Cliff Durr found that the NLG affiliation marked him as a radical in public eyes. When Coe led the NLG at the end of the 1950s, his reputation as a nonconformist had already been established. Durr, on the other hand, accepted the position only a few months after resigning from the FCC. Though considered a leading liberal voice, he had thus far avoided official persecution by anti-Communists in the government, and in most quarters his reputation as a judicious and responsible government official remained intact. The NLG presidency, especially when combined with the loyalty oath controversy and his willingness to defend ex-Communists, distanced him from some old friends and acquaintances of New Deal days who had become cold war liberals. It also brought him to the attention of congressional committees.

The NLG convention that elected Durr president gave its annual "FDR Award" to federal district judge J. Waties Waring of South Carolina. This aristocratic iconoclast had shocked his neighbors by thwarting South Carolina's efforts to circumvent *Smith* v. *Allwright* and writing a stirring dissent in the *Briggs* case.[55] Durr's presentation speech paid proud and eloquent

53. Durr interview.
54. Ibid.
55. *Briggs* v. *Elliott*, 98 F. Supp. 529, 349 U.S. 249 (1955), combined with three other cases to create *Brown* v. *Board*.

tribute to a fellow southern liberal, one who displayed courage in the face of a disapproving society and who faced ostracism and loneliness. An NLG meeting provided an unlikely setting for a southerner to "without apology" defend his native region. "The South is a part of me and always will be," he said. He understood southern weaknesses, but claimed that "the spirit which gave us the Declaration of Independence, the United States Constitution and the Bill of Rights, came preponderantly from the South." That spirit "still lives. . . . I know that it will emerge again." Some of the radical members of the guild must have cringed in response to their new leader's list of the virtues of a region they saw as almost beyond redemption.[56]

During the eighteen months of his NLG presidency, Durr appeared in scores of settings, over radio programs, at religious conferences, and on college campuses, always reiterating a similar message. At Cornell he spoke on "America's Freedom and Responsibilities in the Contemporary Crisis," at Columbia about "Loyalty Probes and Due Process," and to the New York Teacher's Union on "The Fight for Free Schools." He debated HUAC star Richard Nixon in a Disciples of Christ panel discussion on "Security and Freedom in America Today," and at a meeting of the Princeton Liberal Union he joined a panel that included Erich Fromm, A. B. Hollingshead, Richard Hofstadter, C. Wright Mills, and his friend Hugh Wilson to discuss "The Problem of Power in a Democratic Society." The NLG provided Cliff Durr a platform to continue the civil liberties activity begun at the FCC.[57]

Still, a letter from his friend and former colleague Dallas Smythe of Ohio State University explained that "our Rockefeller financed seminar on educational radio" had shunned Durr because "somebody was afraid" to invite him. Smythe indicated that some participants criticized the omission of one of the earliest and most vigorous proponents of educational radio from the

56. "Remarks of C. J. Durr Before Lawyers Guild Dinner," February 20, 1949, in Box 13, Folder 9, C. J. Durr Papers.

57. These speeches and others from this period are found ibid. Various letters pertaining to radio programs on which Durr appeared are in Box 2, Folder 1, "Symposium of Power" program is in Box 1, Folder 11, "The Fears That May Ruin Us, Speech Before the Episcopal League for Social Action," St. Louis *Post-Dispatch,* October 21, 1949, is in Box 12, Folder 1, and C. J. Durr to Walter Sikes, February 10, 1949, is in Box 1, Folder 8, all in C. J. Durr Papers.

program, but this rejection demonstrated Durr's standing with conservatives in the media.[58]

President Durr's other NLG duties included taking a public stand against efforts to censure liberal lawyers, especially those attorneys who defended "hated men." An article in the August 25, 1949, issue of *Look* magazine, written by Attorney General Tom Clark as he left the executive branch for a seat on the Supreme Court, caused particular consternation in liberal ranks. Clark made sweeping statements about subversion in the legal profession, described a "fitness survey" for lawyers he claimed to have instituted in the Justice Department, and declared that the department had considered seriously whether the federal government should discipline lawyers "who act like communists." He also wondered if the department should encourage the ABA to expand its efforts against leftist lawyers, and, if so, what "direct action" might be required. Durr led a delegation of troubled NLG lawyers to discuss Clarke's article with the new attorney general, Howard McGrath, in September.[59]

The NLG delegation, composed of Durr, Charles Hamilton Houston, Martin Popper, Herbert S. Thatcher, and Belford Dawson, also voiced its objection to a 1948 resolution of the ABA Board of Governors, supported by Clark, that would deny admittance to guild members. Durr reported the meeting with McGrath to be "as satisfactory as could be expected." The attorney general, though unwilling to be critical of his predecessor, agreed with the NLG delegation that the prerogative for disciplining lawyers belonged to local courts and bar associations. Regardless of the article's claims, McGrath disavowed the Justice Department's "fitness survey" as a means of determining the suitability of lawyers for their profession.[60]

The most important activity during Durr's tenure as president involved a report on FBI methods published by the guild. An NLG committee including Durr, Professor Thomas Emerson, and civil liberties lawyers O. John Rogge

58. Dallas Smythe to C. J. Durr, September 7, 1949, in Box 1, Folder 10, ibid.

59. "Statement of the Delegation of Lawyers Who Conferred with the Attorney General September 26, 1949, Regarding the Survey Instituted by Tom Clark of the Fitness of Certain Attorneys to Practice Law," ibid.

60. C. J. Durr to Thomas H. Eliot, October 4, 1949, ibid.

and Joseph Forer based the trenchant faultfinding report largely on transcripts of the Judith Coplon espionage trial. "The practices and policies of the FBI violate our laws, infringe our liberties, and threaten our democracy," warned the report, which called for an independent citizen audit of FBI "programs, practices, policies, and personnel." The trial transcripts revealed, and the NLG recounted, unauthorized breaking and entering, opening of mail without search warrants, and extensive wiretapping including taping of privileged attorney-client conversations.[61]

J. Edgar Hoover routinely and ruthlessly stifled criticism of his agency. Since the guild's Washington office had long been the subject of an FBI wiretapping operation, the bureau surreptitiously obtained copies of the NLG report in advance and preempted newspaper reports of Durr's press conference introducing the NLG's "Report on Alleged Practices of the FBI." The Washington *Post* reported Durr's complaint that in a "maneuver to distract attention from the issue," HUAC member Richard Nixon asked the committee to investigate the guild less than twenty-four hours before the report was made public. Indeed, in the week before the report's release, columnists friendly to the FBI published several articles condemning the NLG as a "communist front." After bureau leaks and these press stories, the Associated Press headlined its article announcing the report "House Committee Urged to Probe Lawyers Guild."[62]

The report appeared at an inopportune time. The NLG distributed the full document on Monday, January 23, 1950, one week before the announcement of lawyer Alger Hiss's conviction on two perjury counts. Just a few months earlier, NLG president Durr appeared before the Senate Foreign Relations Committee in opposition to ratification of the North Atlantic Treaty, the Chinese Communists defeated Chiang Kai-shek, the Soviets exploded the atomic bomb, and Judge Harold R. Medina charged five NLG lawyers with contempt in the Smith Act trial of Communist leaders. As Percival Baily noted

61. "Guild Special Committee Reports on FBI Practices," *New York Guild Lawyer,* VII (November, 1949), 7–8, in Box 90, NLG Papers, King Center.

62. Ibid.; Washington *Post* and New York *Times,* January 20, 1950, and St. Louis *Post-Dispatch,* January 23, 1950, in Box 17, Folder 15, C. J. Durr Papers; Baily, "The Case of the NLG," in *Beyond the Hiss Case,* ed. Theoharis, 133–42.

in his essay detailing FBI persecution of the NLG, "under these circumstances it would have been surprising had the American press highlighted the claims of a heretical lawyers' organization that the FBI endangered civil liberties."[63]

At Hoover's insistence, HUAC began an investigation of the guild, and in September, 1950, the committee issued its conclusions in the report that named the National Lawyers Guild the "Legal Bulwark of the Communist Party." The committee held no hearings and based the report almost verbatim upon questionable FBI documents, but it had a devastating effect on the NLG. Thomas Emerson, who followed Durr to the NLG presidency, in a vain attempt to counteract the damage, branded the HUAC report an attempt "to intimidate or eliminate the only lawyers who have had the courage to defend those at the whipping post." The report, he said, branded as disloyal lawyers who upheld the ABA's own code of ethics, which called for lawyers to defend the unpopular, and the Constitution, which guaranteed the right to counsel.[64]

In addition to precipitating a decline in NLG membership, the report caused a reaction in the ABA, which stepped up its efforts to exclude radical lawyers. Meanwhile, the attorney general's office announced an investigation pursuant to placing the guild on its list of subversive organizations. Hoover had been pushing the Justice Department to list the guild since the passage of the Smith Act in 1940, despite the attorney general's repeated admonitions that insufficient evidence existed to take this action. When Attorney General Herbert Brownell finally issued a "show cause order" to the guild in 1953, the organization challenged the proposed listing in court. This fruitless effort of the Justice Department continued to drain guild resources until it was dropped in 1958, during the presidency of John Coe.[65]

Although a member of the NLG during the time of Durr's presidency, Coe did not attend a national meeting until 1951. Confiding to his friend Bella Abzug, Coe wrote of the pleasure he and his wife found in associating with others who shared "beliefs and opinions which in Pensacola are regarded as

63. Baily, "The Case of the NLG," in *Beyond the Hiss Case,* ed. Theoharis, quote on 142. Durr had known Alger Hiss since early New Deal days. The day the NLG report was issued, he wrote a poignant note that began: "Dear Alger: I am writing to tell you that I am sorry. I am sorry for my country." C. J. Durr to Alger Hiss, January 23, 1950, in Box 1, Folder 12, C. J. Durr Papers.

64. Baily, "The Case of the NLG," in *Beyond the Hiss Case,* ed. Theoharis, 146.

65. Ibid., 146–49.

exotic, not to say 'screwy.'" In 1949 and 1950 Coe still held together the struggling Progressive Party in Florida, and he attended several national party meetings during those years. In 1949 he became a regular contributor to SCEF and reworked and signed SCEF's amicus brief in *Sweatt* v. *Painter*,[66] the Supreme Court case that mandated the integration of the law school of the University of Texas in 1950.[67]

At home Coe's associations proved less secure. His "distinguished brethren of the Kiwanis Club of Pensacola . . . tried me for impure thoughts and expelled me therefrom," he wrote to an old friend. "We had a hell of a trial. I plead with the boys . . . for an intelligent understanding of things democratic and American and free." Claude Pepper suffered less dramatic but roughly similar treatment from the Downtown Kiwanis Club of Miami when he moved there after his Senate defeat in 1950. Like John Coe, whom he knew through club business as well as politics, Pepper had been a Kiwanian for over twenty-five years and served as a state officer. Exactly what lay behind Coe's dismissal remained unclear, but his public statement opposing the Korean War and a local case "to stop the widespread practice of arresting, and persecuting people, mostly negroes, for not giving information," which he won on appeal from the Pensacola Municipal Court, surely inflamed old enemies. He probably clinched his fate when he told the club's board of directors he thought the governments of South Korea and Nationalist China were "rotten and corrupt" and proclaimed that "he had a right to free speech and a right to think as he pleased." When asked about party membership, he said "I am not a Communist and I won't join the Communist Party because I won't put that yoke around my neck," but he did agree with "a lot of their policies" so he thought they might call him a "fellow traveler." At about the same time, Coe's law partner fled, though their longtime practice seemed to be thriving. Typically caustic, Coe complained that his partner "got feathers on his legs"; but he had given his squeamish colleague abundant reason to move on. The FBI, meanwhile, prudently collected the license numbers of all the cars visiting Coe's bay-front home.[68]

66. 339 U.S. 629 (1950).

67. J. M. Coe to Bella Abzug, November 19, 1951, in Box 2, Folder 48, James Dombrowski to Coe, December 12, 20, 1949, and Coe to Dombrowski, December 31, 1949, in Box 2, Folder 13, all in Coe Papers.

68. Brown, "Pensacola Progressive," 25; John M. Coe to "Sis" (Ruth Coe), October 18,

By 1950, John Coe and Cliff Durr had committed themselves to lives "outside the magic circle" of southern society, to quote the title of Virginia Durr's autobiography. Like Oedipus, they had rejected the easy road to Daulis. After Durr returned to Montgomery in 1951, he would be drawn more and more to local injustices, defending the rights of Alabama's black minority. Long involved in cases seeking racial justice in Pensacola, Coe's practice in the 1950s reached out past Florida to new endeavors generated by his associations with left-liberal organizations. When Ben Smith graduated from law school in 1951, already a member of the NLG and committed to liberal causes, he adopted leftist unions as early clients. His family and the prosperous New Orleanian relatives of his new wife surely hoped that his youthful fling with radicalism would be moderated by the practice of law in a conservative city, but they hoped in vain.[69] In the early 1950s his career began to parallel Coe's and Durr's in elemental ways.

The three men would not meet until 1954, when each of them, by that time with reputations firmly established, represented witnesses called to testify at New Orleans hearings of the Senate Internal Security Subcommittee chaired by Senator Eastland of Mississippi. But they seem in retrospect to have been destined for that meeting by the late 1940s, and in the intervening years the prospect only became more likely.

1950, in Box 22, Folder 20, and to Rebecca Standfield, August 26, 1950, in Box 2, Folder 29, Coe Papers; Report—"MO 100–199," September 13, 1950, pp. 11–14, Section 1, Coe FBI File.

69. Jones interview.

Clifford Judkins Durr, ca. 1950
Alabama Department of Archives and History

John Moreno Coe, ca. 1950
Courtesy of Evalyn Coe Grubbs

Federal courthouse in Atlanta, January 21, 1959, during Carl Braden's trial for contempt of HUAC. Left to right: Aubrey Williams, AME bishop C. Ewbank Tucker, Leonard B. Boudin, Braden, John Coe, and Jim Dombrowski.
Special Collections Department, Robert W. Woodruff Library, Emory University

Carl and Ann Braden and their children, May, 1960
Special Collections Department, Woodruff Library

At the "Conference on Freedom and the First Amendment" sponsored by SCEF in Chapel Hill, North Carolina, October 27, 1961. Left to right: Clifford Durr, Wyatt T. Walker of the SCLC, an unidentified participant, and Ben Smith.
Alabama Department of Archives and History

IN THE CRIMINAL DISTRICT COURT
PARISH OF ORLEANS
STATE OF LOUISIANA

N.O.P.D. ITEM NO.

APPLICATION FOR AND SWORN PROOF OF PROBABLE CAUSE FOR THE ISSUANCE OF

A SEARCH WARRANT HEREIN

PERSONALLY CAME AND APPEARED BEFORE ME, the undersigned Judge
of the Criminal District Court, Parish of Orleans, State of Louisiana,

Major Russell R. Willie, Louisiana State Police ~~of the New Orleans Department of Police~~, who, upon being by me duly sworn, depose(s) and say(s):

THAT A SEARCH WARRANT SHOULD ISSUE FOR THE SEARCH OF... that suite
of rooms located at 1006 Baronne Building, 305 Baronne Street, New Orleans,
Louisiana, occupied by Benjamin E. Smith, Attorney at Law, and his associates.
...FOR THE PURPOSE OF SEIZING THE FOLLOWING DESCRIBED PROPERTY... books
records and files of the Southern Conference Educational Fund, Inc. and James
A. Dombrowski plus any Communist Political Propaganda and Communist Party
records.
...FOR THE FOLLOWING REASONS: Benjamin E. Smith is openly acting as the
treasurer of the Southern Conference Educational Fund, Inc., an identified
communist front and a subversive organization as defined in RS14:358 et seq. He
has signed correspondence as such officer as recently as July 1963. He is listed
in various publications of the organization as its treasurer. Our informants have
seen and identified him acting openly and illegally in the management of this
organization. He is reported to us by informants to maintain certain files and
records of said organization in his office which are actual management functions of
the organization rather than files on legal representation. Smith has been seen and
identified on many occasions in the company of identified communists. He makes
no attempt to hide the fact that he is assisting in the management of the SCEF. His
office is located in the premises described above as are part of his files kept as
part of said management.

FILED
10/25   19 63
Ben J. Kelly
MINUTE CLERK

Russell R. Willie   Badge No.: 9

NEW ORLEANS DEPARTMENT OF POLICE

SWORN TO AND SUBSCRIBED BEFORE ME

THIS _2nd_ DAY OF _October_ , 196_3_ .

Hon. M. Brahney
JUDGE OF SECTION _D_ ,Criminal District
Court, Parish of Orleans, State of Louisiana

Search warrant for SCEF raid in New Orleans, October 2, 1963.
Specifically named are Ben Smith and Jim Dombrowski, and SCEF is called
"an identified communist front and a subversive organization."
Special Collections Department, Woodruff Library

Supreme Court of the United States

October Term, 1963

No. 941

JAMES A. DOMBROWSKI and SOUTHERN CONFERENCE
EDUCATIONAL FUND, INC.,

Plaintiffs-Appellants,

BENJAMIN E. SMITH and BRUCE WALTZER,

Intervenors-Appellants,

against

JAMES H. PFISTER, individually and as Chairman of the Joint Legislative
Committee on Un-American Activities of the Louisiana Legislature,
RUSSELL R. WILLIE, individually and as Major of the Louisiana State
Police Department, JIMMIE H. DAVIS, individually and as Governor
of the State of Louisiana, JACK P. F. GREMILLION, individually and
as Attorney General of the State of Louisiana, COLONEL THOMAS
D. BURBANK, individually and as Commanding Officer of the Division
of Louisiana State Police, and JIM GARRISON, individually and as
District Attorney for the Parish of Orleans, State of Louisiana,

Defendants-Appellees.

ON APPEAL FROM THE UNITED STATES DISTRICT COURT FOR
THE EASTERN DISTRICT OF LOUISIANA, NEW ORLEANS
DIVISION

APPELLANTS' RESPONSE TO MOTION TO
DISMISS OR AFFIRM

ARTHUR KINOY,
WILLIAM M. KUNSTLER,
MICHAEL J. KUNSTLER,
    511 Fifth Avenue,
        New York, N. Y.,

MILTON E. BRENER,
    1304 National Bank of Commerce Bldg.,
        New Orleans, Louisiana,

A. P. TUREAUD,
    1821 Orleans Avenue,
        New Orleans, Louisiana,

Attorneys for Appellants.

LEON HUBERT,
EDWARD BALDWIN,
ROBERT ZIBILICH,
    300 Oil & Gas Bldg.,
        1100 Tulane Avenue,
            New Orleans, Louisiana,

Attorneys for Appellants-Intervenors.

Of Counsel:
    ARTHUR KINOY,
    WILLIAM M. KUNSTLER.

Front page of appellants' brief in *Dombrowski* v. *Pfister,* in which the
Supreme Court ruled unconstitutional Louisiana laws that had been
used against Jim Dombrowski, Ben Smith, Bruce Waltzer, and SCEF.

State Historical Society of Wisconsin

Typical "Communist front" hate literature against the ACLU, 1960s.
The office was almost certainly the organization's New Orleans branch.
Special Collections, Howard-Tilton Memorial Library, Tulane University

Benjamin Eugene Smith, ca. 1970
Courtesy of Corinne Barnwell

CHAPTER FOUR

"Comes Now Willie McGee":
Communist Causes in
Southern Context, 1950–1954

Just as conservative national politicians merged their anti-Communism with anti–New Deal sentiment, leaders of the southern establishment derided and feared the potential of Roosevelt-era ideas in the postwar period. The Dixiecrats of 1948, though defeated except in those southern states where they managed to commandeer the Democratic Party's place on the ballot, retained great influence after the election. Their defiant positions mirrored commonplace, deeply rooted southern concerns about troubling currents in national life. By 1950, as it became apparent that legal segregation faced definitive challenges, Dixiecrat notions had attained a widespread acceptance that belied their inability to mobilize southern moderates in 1948. Not only softness on the race issue, but also allegations of "Trumanism, communism and labor bossism" infused the rhetoric of George Smathers and Willis Smith in their successful efforts to unseat the South's most liberal senators, Claude Pepper and Frank Graham.[1]

On the other hand, three U.S. Supreme Court decisions handed down on June 5, 1950, reinforced the view that *Plessy* v. *Ferguson,* the 1896 "separate but equal" decision, would soon be abandoned by the Court. *Sweatt* v. *Painter,* probably the broadest of the three, found Texas' "jim crow" law school clearly inferior to the law school at the University of Texas. It ordered the university to admit the plaintiff, Herman Sweatt. In *McLaurin* v. *Oklahoma State Regents for Higher Education* the Court mandated that a black graduate student be seated in the same classroom and enjoy the same cafeteria and library privileges as his white classmates, and in *Henderson* v. *U.S.* the

---

1. Bartley, *Rise of Massive Resistance,* 28–46, quote on 39. As a result of Pepper's participation in the attempt to replace Truman as the party's nominee before the 1948 convention, center liberals from the Truman administration also opposed Pepper.

Court ordered integration of railway dining cars.[2] The Virgil Hawkins case in Florida and a suit to integrate graduate schools at Louisiana State University, both similar to *Sweatt,* by 1950 also wended their way toward Supreme Court review, as did *Brown* v. *Board of Education of Topeka.*

If Supreme Court decisions seemed to grow more liberal, however, the same could not be said of the Truman administration, the Congress, state legislatures, or the lower federal courts. In June, 1950, with little debate and the overwhelming support of congressional liberals and conservatives, the administration negotiated United Nations support for an anti-Communist war in Korea and then proceeded to fight the North Koreans almost single-handedly. At the same time, over Truman's veto, Congress passed the McCarran Internal Security Act requiring Communist organizations to register with the government and publish their records. Then in 1952 the McCarran Immigration and Nationality Act tightened rules for exclusion and deportation of aliens and even naturalized citizens. Many state legislatures north and south enacted or reinforced laws against sedition, treason, "misprision (innocent knowledge) of treason," and related crimes.[3] In early 1950, British physicist Karl Fuchs confessed to spying for the Russians. As his testimony led to the eventual conviction and execution of Ethel and Julius Rosenberg, Republican senator Joseph McCarthy of Wisconsin captured and personified the American mood.

Two revisionist historians of the late 1960s, Michael Paul Rogin and Athan Theoharis, have suggested that McCarthy emerged not as a product of a dangerous right-wing populism, as consensus liberal scholars of the 1950s portrayed him, "but rather [as] a product of routine conservative politics." They see McCarthyism as the climax of the postwar collaboration between

2. *Plessy* v. *Ferguson,* 163 U.S. 537; *Sweatt* v. *Painter,* 339 U.S. 629; *McLaurin* v. *Oklahoma State Regents,* 339 U.S. 637; *Henderson* v. *U.S.,* 339 U.S. 816. In *Missouri ex rel. Gaines* v. *Canada,* 305 U.S. 337 (1938), and *Sipuel* v. *Board of Regents,* 332 U.S. 631 (1948), the Court had required either admission to state law schools or provision of "separate but equal" facilities. NAACP lawyers litigated all of these cases; however, the Communist-connected Civil Rights Congress also publicly supported Herman Sweatt. See Gerald Horne, *Communist Front? The Civil Rights Congress, 1946–1956* (Rutherford, N.J., 1988), 315.

3. Celinni, ed., *Digest of Communism,* 117–87, 241–455. The Communist Party was not outlawed under federal law until passage of the Communists Control Act of 1954 (ibid., 695–700).

business conservatives and vital center liberals. Both factions, they pointed out, applauded the foreign-policy initiatives of an activist presidency and rarely questioned anti-Communism as a sufficient motivating force for national strategies.[4]

According to this interpretation, both vital center liberals and postwar conservatives were elitists who distrusted the democratic tendencies of the old popular front left. Centrist liberals might question McCarthy's methods or his particular targets, but they seldom doubted the logic of his basic mission, purging Communists from American institutions. The Truman administration, according to Theoharis, had already "legitimized red-baiting at home" through its loyalty program, the attorney general's list, and "its public quest for total internal security." McCarthyism simply constituted "the crows coming home to roost" for the ruling Democrats, who had conceded the ideological advantage to the party of Taft and Hoover. Conservatives, on the other hand, valued McCarthy for his adroit exploitation of the "communists in government" issue, through which the Democrats and the New Deal could be attacked with impunity.[5]

This view of McCarthyism differs little from that voiced by John Coe, Cliff Durr, or Ben Smith in the 1950s. They, too, saw the senator's mischief not as evidence of a popular uprising against either Communism or the policies of the New Deal but as a consequence of flawed postwar politics. They also observed southern anti-Communism's resourceful blending of McCarthyism, a federally sponsored agenda that implicated "outsiders" as well as liberals, with the regional definition of radicalism. At one point Coe called southern McCarthyism "hydra-headed and amorphous," and Durr commented that life in the South in the early 1950s could be pleasant only "if one takes a firm stand in opposition to the boll-weevil and in favor of white face cattle and crimson clover and avoids the petty issues of domestic and international politics." As insiders who understood the southern psyche, they perceived

4. Athan Theoharis, "The Politics of Scholarship: Liberals, Anti-Communism, and McCarthyism," in *The Specter: Original Essays on the Cold War and the Origins of McCarthyism,* ed. Robert Griffith and Athan Theoharis (New York, 1974), 264–80, quote on 265; see also Michael Paul Rogin, *The Intellectuals and McCarthy: The Radical Specter* (Cambridge, Mass., 1967), Chapter 8, pp. 216–60.

5. Theoharis, "Politics of Scholarship," 279, 280.

very clearly McCarthyism's usefulness for southern politicians as the old social order strained and crumbled.[6]

McCarthy himself was widely admired in many parts of the South, and adjusted for regional differences and breadth of influence, many southern politicians seemed to replicate him. Georgia historian Numan Bartley says Governor Herman Talmadge "tended to confuse nationalism with orthodoxy and nonconformity with communism." Others who often misconstrued dissent as subversion included Strom Thurmond of South Carolina, Fielding Wright of Mississippi, and longtime Texas politician W. Lee "Pappy" O'Daniel. Senators such as Harry Flood Byrd of Virginia approached McCarthy's influence, but no southern politician venerated or imitated McCarthy more completely than the Communist-hunter from Mississippi, James O. Eastland. According to Bartley, Eastland "embodied neobourbon militancy." Though none of these politicians reached McCarthy's heights of flamboyance, they understood where to touch a southern nerve and how to capitalize on southern fears. Consequently their constituents, like McCarthy's, usually forgot or forgave their indiscretions and inadequacies.[7]

Anti-Communism fit the purposes of "neobourbon" segregationists perfectly, blending so well into their strategies that one fight became indistinguishable from the other. In a June, 1950, Senate speech, Eastland suggested that the South would play an absolutely critical role in fighting the Communist menace, because "the future greatness of America depends upon racial purity and maintenance of Anglo-Saxon institutions, which still flourish in full flower in the South." He called states' rights, protected jealously in the South, the only block to a Communist takeover of the country. Eastland's fervent, nationalistic Americanism survived discordantly alongside his dogmatic belief in the right of states to defy or ignore the Constitution or unacceptable American laws.[8]

Nothing could have been more loathsome or incomprehensible to such "neobourbons" or their antialien supporters in the national government than the professional activities of southern lawyers Coe, Durr, and Smith. In the

---

6. J. M. Coe to Bella Abzug, November 16, 1953, in Box 3, Folder 5, Coe Papers; C. J. Durr to John Kenneth Galbraith, July 2, 1952, in Box 2, Folder 4, C. J. Durr Papers.

7. Bartley, *Rise of Massive Resistance*, 43, 117–18.

8. Ibid., 32–46, quote on 118–19.

early 1950s as a Washington attorney, Durr defended alleged and former Communists and joined the staff of a liberal farmers union. Smith initiated contacts with radical labor unions and defended a controversial Tulane professor, not only an alleged Communist but an active integrationist. Coe took highly charged cases sponsored by northern radicals and tried his best to integrate Pensacola's vocational schools.

Coe's most challenging new cases in 1950 and 1951 came through his association with the Civil Rights Congress (CRC), a New York–based legal defense organization whose causes "were invariably the Party's causes." Successor to the International Labor Defense (ILD), which had defended the "Scottsboro boys" in the 1930s, the CRC functioned under siege from 1946 until 1956, when the Subversive Activities Control Board finally forced its dissolution. Its major cases involved either the defense of Communists or the defense of blacks indicted under questionable circumstances, especially rape cases. Three lawyers headed the CRC during the early 1950s: William Patterson, the grandson of a slave and her white master, a Communist, and an ILD activist who had been involved in left-wing causes since World War I; Ralph Powe, a Tuskegee and Howard Law School graduate and the son of black sharecroppers from Cheraw, South Carolina; and Aubrey Grossman, a Jewish Communist from San Francisco. Fund-raising efforts by well-known leftists Dashiell Hammett, Lillian Hellman, Frederick Field, Paul Robeson, Vito Marcantonio, Lee Pressman, and Harry F. Ward sustained the organization.[9]

Coe's first two CRC cases overlapped and involved almost identical local ordinances in Birmingham, Alabama, and Jacksonville, Florida. He sued successfully to invalidate city ordinances that made it illegal for Communists to reside within their city limits.[10] Though the Jacksonville ordinance copied Birmingham's law, Coe litigated the Jacksonville case first.

After the passage of the Jacksonville ordinance, a Jacksonville *Journal* reporter, unable to identify any local Communists, began combing Duval County's registration records. On August 24 the paper published a story headlined "Lone Registrant as Red in Duval County Has No Comment."

9. Caute, *Great Fear,* 178–79; Horne, *Communist Front,* 32–35.

10. Communists were given forty-eight hours to leave town or suffer both a $100 fine and 180 days in jail. Celinni, ed., *Digest of Communism,* 458–61; Caute, *Great Fear,* 568–69.

Five days later the Jacksonville *Times-Union* followed with "First Arrest Made Under Red Statute—Alexander W. Trainor, 54, Detained by Police." Trainor's friends wrote to Coe about the arrested man—a fragile person, mentally distraught, who feared for his life. He registered as a Communist in 1947 but had since quit any political activity. He said he had simply forgotten that he needed to change his registration. Coe notified Ralph Powe, legal director of the CRC, that since the Birmingham case had been continued he would go to Jacksonville. With added assistance from the ACLU office in Miami he made this trip twice, first to get Trainor out of jail on a writ of habeas corpus, then to argue the case in circuit court.[11]

Coe's brief cited the Florida Supreme Court decision in *Benemovsky* v. *Sullivan* as well as the First and Fourteenth Amendments as grounds for asserting the unconstitutionality of the ordinance. The court concurred with his argument. Trainor, alleged the prosecution, had once served as "the Secretary of the Communist Party in Florida." In response, Coe "accused the municipality's lawyers of voicing the arguments 'relied on by every heresy hunter since Socrates drank the hemlock.'" While complimenting Coe's "able argument," a local reporter noted how he "adroitly avoided the real point at issue here," the malevolence of the foreign-controlled Communist Party.[12]

The Birmingham *News* correctly predicted that the fate of the Jacksonville ordinance would be repeated in the case pending in that city as well. Two weeks later Coe argued successfully against Birmingham in federal district court. "What we have is a wave of hysteria," he told Judge Seybourne Lynne. By passing such ordinances "we are rushing headlong into Fascism because we are afraid of Communism." City councils might later decide that Mormons, Jews, or Socialists were undesirable, and use this method to "convict them of treason without a fair trial. . . . I am not arguing the case of Sam Hall, but of the American people." While it might be lawful to exclude a CPUSA member from a sensitive government post, no American could be imprisoned or executed simply because he held certain beliefs, even for "the malignant mental state of being communist" or "even if [his beliefs] extend to the overthrow of the government." Afterwards William Patterson, CRC execu-

---

11. *Trainor* v. *Cannon*, in Box 35, Folder 27, and *Hall* v. *City of Birmingham*, in Box 35, Folder 26, both in Coe Papers.

12. *Florida Times-Union* (Jacksonville), October 10, 1950, 17.

tive secretary, thanked Coe profusely for his "splendid services" and for submitting only a "minimum charge." The ACLU's New York director also congratulated Coe, asked for a copy of the Alabama decision, and pledged help if the city appealed.[13]

The Birmingham case was more interesting, and certainly better known, than Jacksonville's case. Called the "Bull Connor" ordinance, the legislation in question had been created and used as a campaign issue by then city commissioner (future police chief) Eugene Connor. A former "union-buster" for Birmingham's steel companies, Connor hated Communists, perhaps because the party had pushed for integration of Alabama unions. A local newspaper called Sam Hall, on whose behalf the CRC pursued the case, "The City's Top Commie." Long identified by the Birmingham police, he publicly acknowledged his employment as a full-time Communist Party worker.[14]

Born and raised in Anniston, Alabama, and active in Methodist youth groups as a young man, Hall briefly considered the church as a vocation. After attending college, however, he joined the staff of the Anniston *Star* as a writer and later editor. Basically an idealistic intellectual discouraged over the depression and opposed to racial segregation, Hall joined the Communist Party in the late 1930s. He served in the Navy during World War II, and for a brief period after the war he chaired the Alabama Committee for Human Welfare, an SCHW affiliate. The party trained him as an organizer and sent him first to North Carolina, where he met and married another Communist worker, then back to Birmingham in 1947. Hall wrote articles for the Communist-supported *Southern News Almanac* and the *Daily Worker* and headed the small Communist Party in Alabama in the late 1940s. Seeking to improve the party's public image and attract unionists to its cause, he never hid his political affiliation and even ran advertisements in Birmingham newspapers defending the party's right to exist.[15]

13. Birmingham *News*, editorial, October 5, 1950, in Box 35, Folder 26, William Patterson to J. M. Coe, August 5, 1950, in Box 2, Folder 19, George Soll to Coe, October 30, 1950, in Box 35, Folder 26, and Coe to Rebecca Standfield, August 26, 1950, in Box 2, Folder 29, all in Coe Papers; Security Information: John Moreno Coe, October 26, 1951, p. 35, Section 2, Coe FBI File.

14. Birmingham *News*, October 16, 1950, in Box 35, Folder 26, Coe Papers.

15. Robin D. G. Kelley, *Hammer and Hoe: Alabama Communists During the Great Depression* (Chapel Hill, 1990), 196, 218, 223–24; Thompson interview.

According to Sylvia (Hall) Thompson, his trouble began the day after the Korean War started in June, 1950. Birmingham's "red squad" arrested Hall for vagrancy as the couple sought to obtain signatures for the Stockholm Peace Petition.[16] Whatever means of support he might have, read the indictment, were "disreputable." Hall found a Birmingham lawyer to arrange his bond, and the next day the Halls left for New York to attend meetings there. Driving through northern Alabama, they heard on the car radio of the anti-Communist ordinance's passage and surmised that they would be arrested and jailed if they returned to Birmingham for the vagrancy trial.[17]

As soon as he reached New York, Hall consulted William Patterson of the CRC, who contacted John Coe. Hall did not return to Birmingham until the constitutionality of the ordinance had been successfully challenged in federal court. After Coe won the case against the ordinance and litigated the vagrancy charge using Hall's deposition taken in New York, the couple returned just long enough to pick up their belongings, entrust the sale of their house to friends, and permanently depart Alabama.[18]

Coe returned home to see a copycat ordinance passed by the Pensacola city council, an act repeated in Miami, Macon, and various other cities across the nation. He also faced a rash of harassing telephone calls, dismissal from the Kiwanis Club, and the dissolution of his partnership. He had long been the subject of an FBI investigation, and though a bureau informant had concluded in 1947 that "He may be a liberal, but I have never heard of him being a radical or a communist," Coe's CRC activity naturally escalated FBI surveillance. Agents were hard-pressed to reconcile his obvious prosperity (they appraised his home at $65,000) and deep southern roots with his professional and political associations. The 1951 report on Coe in the FBI's NLG files contains a long explanation of his family's "excellent reputation and

16. Concerned primarily with international control of atomic weapons, this petition was originally adopted by a "World Peace Congress" at Stockholm in March, 1950. HUAC denounced it as a defense of Communist aggression in Korea and named the Peace Information Center and its successor, the American Peace Crusade, as the petition's American sponsors. U.S. Congress, House Un-American Activities Committee, *Report on the Communist "Peace" Offensive: A Campaign to Disarm and Defeat the United States,* 82nd Cong., 1st Sess., April 25, 1951, H. Rept. 378.

17. Thompson interview.

18. Ibid.

high standing in the community," and describes him as a "brilliant and keen thinker" who "uses big words and complex language but does it correctly." But the accolade in no way prevented continued FBI surveillance or listing his name as a "prominent person" in the "Special Section of the Security Index." The bureau planned to apprehend and hold such persons if a war broke out.[19]

Smeared by half-truths, innuendo, rumor mills, and gossipy right-wing publications, opponents of state-sponsored anti-Communism endured continued public insults once they were identified by the FBI and disclosed to other government bodies. Some Pensacolans firmly believed local gossip about John Coe's disloyalty and membership in the Communist Party. And even after Durr resigned the controversial NLG presidency, he suffered through a terrible year largely as a result of right-wing publicity connecting him to Communist causes. Cliff and Virginia Durr found that the Red scare thrived as well in western as in eastern or southern soil.

In mid-1950, concluding that his Washington law practice would never be able to support his family, Cliff Durr accepted a job in the insurance and investments division of the National Farmers Union (NFU) at its home offices in Denver. The position would be half-time, and he planned to continue his current cases and speak or teach when the opportunity arose. Aubrey Williams' employment as an NFU organizer after he left Washington probably influenced Coe's decision. A liberal organization, the NFU had taken a strong stand in opposition to the loyalty order.[20]

The sojourn in Denver, from midsummer 1950 to spring 1951, turned into a distressing period for the Durrs. Cliff suffered from serious back problems and underwent major surgery that left him incapacitated for almost a year after leaving Colorado. In addition, the two endured the stings of anti-Communism in another decisive episode. As Durr settled into his Denver job, Virginia ingenuously signed a petition sponsored by the American Peace Crusade indicating her disapproval of widening the Korean War beyond the Yalu River. Discovered by the conservative Denver *Post,* the petition, also

19. Pensacola *News-Journal,* August 8, 1950, p. 1; Harold Tannen to J. M. Coe, September 7, 1950, in Box 35, Folder 27, Coe Papers; Horne, *Communist Front,* 82; Memorandums, October 13, September 28, 1950, Section 2, Coe FBI File.

20. Salmond, *Conscience of a Lawyer,* 145.

signed by James Dombrowski, Paul Robeson, Linus Pauling, W. E. B. Du Bois, and Harry Bridges, became evidence incriminating the wife of the union's lawyer. The publicity upset the NFU board, which had recently suffered accusations of Communist infiltration from other quarters. When the board insisted that Virginia Durr publicly recant, issued an ultimatum to Cliff Durr, and prepared a mea culpa for her to sign, he resigned his position.[21]

The barbs aimed at Virginia Durr's pacifism by the Denver *Post* surely sprang as much from the reputation Cliff Durr brought with him to the West as from her indiscretion. Back in Washington, conservative congressmen continued to harass him. Just before his move to Denver, when he was still president of the NLG, a California representative read into the *Congressional Record* the testimony of HUAC informant and former party member Paul Crouch, who said he knew Durr to be a Communist because he saw him "at a secret national conference in New York of top members of the Communist Party and the Communist underground." Congressmen denounced Durr on the floor of the House of Representatives for his NLG activities, his interest in SCHW, his participation in a 1949 Bill of Rights Conference sponsored by the CRC, and his attendance at the 1948 conference of World Intellectuals for Peace in Wrocław, Poland. Like the "liberal" label, "peace" and "rights" had become suspicious words in conservative circles.[22]

After the move to Denver, Republican senator Styles Bridges attacked Durr on the floor of the U.S. Senate in a speech entitled "Communist Invasion of Agriculture." The speech censured Durr as the leader of the "subversive" NLG, a follower of Henry Wallace, a lawyer who advised his clients to take the Fifth Amendment, and an employee of a "communist front" organization, the NFU. Durr's letter to Bridges answering these charges affirmed his membership in the NLG, though he had recently given up the presidency. He pointed out that though it was under attack by HUAC and the FBI because

---

21. Letters concerning Durr's tenure with the NFU are found in Box 1, Folder 12, through Box 2, Folder 3, C. J. Durr Papers. See also Salmond, *Conscience of a Lawyer,* 144–52, and Barnard, ed., *Outside the Magic Circle,* 233–38.

22. *Congressional Record,* 81st Cong., 1st Sess., 3912–13; C. J. Durr to Hon. John S. Wood, March 23, 1950, in Box 2, Folder 1, C. J. Durr Papers. The One World Committee sponsoring the Durrs' trip to Poland was established in memory of Wendell Willkie, 1944 Republican presidential candidate, whose optimism about the postwar world would surely have diminished had he lived to experience the cold war years.

it had the audacity to oppose both, the guild was *"not* on the Attorney General's list." He conceded "without apology" his "admiration and respect" for Wallace, who had served his country well and "still has the courage to say what he thinks," but insisted Bridges had "considerably exaggerate[d] my own part in the Wallace campaign." As for his work as an attorney, Durr willingly acknowledged advising clients to refuse to state whether they were Communists. He reasoned that since the Constitution guaranteed accused citizens the right to counsel, and American lawyers took an oath to defend the unpopular to the best of their abilities, he had a duty to advise the accused of their constitutional rights.[23]

Only a few weeks before this Senate attack, and three days before the outbreak of the Korean War, the first edition of *Red Channels* listed Durr's name along with 151 other suspected Communists in the radio and television industries. This virulently anti-Communist blacklisting publication ruined the careers of many actors, directors, and producers during the 1950s. A letter to Patrick Malin of the ACLU written from Durr's hospital bed expressed amazement at the wild charges aimed at him. He denied being either a Fascist or a Communist, and certainly had not "contributed $4,790.00 per year or any other amounts to the cost of destroying American business and/or the American way of life." Durr acknowledged having written and spoken on many radio programs "in opposition to our trend toward a government by fear," but he had never "infiltrated the airwaves" with Communist propaganda, nor had he any ownership in a radio station or even a client who was an applicant for a radio license whom he might influence.[24]

Not long before he left Denver, Durr delivered the Palm Sunday sermon at the First Unitarian Church, pastored by the one good friend he had made in Denver, Rudy Gilbert. The talk, called "Trial by Terror," was one of several essays he wrote over the years connecting biblical themes and First Amendment issues. He described the events leading to Jesus' crucifixion with a lawyer's eye for detail, pointing out how the "climate of fear and hate," a disinterested, opportunistic officialdom, and the pettiness and hypocrisy of

23. C. J. Durr to Honorable Styles Bridges, September 27, 1950, in Box 2, Folder 2, C. J. Durr Papers.

24. C. J. Durr to Patrick M. Malin, October 30, 1950, ibid. For *Red Channels* see Caute, *Great Fear,* 521–23.

the scribes and Pharisees affected the outcome of the trial. Our emphasis on the "supernatural elements" of Jesus' death and resurrection, he said, has obscured a "very significant aspect of the whole affair. . . . Here was a typical civil liberties case with the issue of freedom of speech, opinion, and worship, and of 'due process of law' directly involved." Jesus was charged and found guilty of treason (that is, of calling himself "The King of the Jews," an affront to the Roman emperor, Tiberius). In response he brought up issues such as freedom of speech ("I spake openly . . . why asketh thou me?"), demanded the evidence ("Why smiteth thou me?"), and steadfastly "refuse[d] to 'confess' his guilt to any crime." The sermon demonstrates Durr's piety as well as his civil libertarianism. No matter how difficult the path he trod, he always blamed men, not God, for the injustice in the world. His faith remained a source of sustenance and consolation.[25]

Durr reported the sad saga of the NFU misadventure in a long, moving letter to his friend at Princeton, Hugh Wilson. The house had been put up for sale, he said, and the family was leaving "the wide open spaces where men are men." Unsure what lay ahead, with his back still mending, he wanted to find a small farm and then slowly begin a law practice. He knew he would need to keep some of his opinions to himself while he developed a southern clientele. "But I don't know whether it will work," he wrote. How could he "keep quiet and pretend I don't believe any more" in social justice and civil liberties? He worried that the Communists might be "the only ones left with the guts—or fanaticism, if that is the more appropriate word—to stand up openly for the things we all say under our breath that we are for." Durr grieved over the corruption and conformity that seemed to sicken the nation and stifle freedom of speech and action, North and South. Those who understood the current oppressive atmosphere must save "the seed corn of decency . . . or there won't be any for replanting" when the American people came to their senses. It would be very hard for him to remain a philosophical, innocent bystander in Montgomery.[26]

He returned to the accepting arms of his extended family discouraged,

25. "Trial by Terror," March 18, 1951, in Box 9, Folder 5, Dombrowski Papers. The sermon was reprinted by Aubrey Williams' magazine, *Southern Farm and Home,* and by the *Churchman,* an independent journal of the Episcopal Church, in 1960.

26. C. J. Durr to Hugh Wilson, March 4, 1951, in Box 2, Folder 3, C. J. Durr Papers.

financially drained, and in terrible physical shape. It would be a year before he began a full-time law practice, a year of rehabilitation and readjustment to the slower-paced life of a small southern city. His friend Aubrey Williams, in need of liberal companionship, welcomed him warmly.[27] Few other Montgomerians understood his ideas and opinions, which seemed, as Coe remarked of his own around the same time, "exotic" if not "screwy."

In June, 1952, just a couple of months after he finally opened a Montgomery office, Durr declined with regret Beanie Baldwin's offer of a case involving the dwindling Progressive Party. He wanted to make a place for himself in Montgomery, and becoming absorbed once again in highly visible liberal causes would impede his acceptance in this conservative environment. "I believe in time I can be helpful here, and I am throwing in my lot with this part of the country." To another correspondent he explained that he needed to get his law practice going and realized there was "no middle ground"; for better or worse, the time had come to leave the old battles behind and become an Alabama lawyer. Thankful to be home, Durr wanted to relax and savor the place he loved best. He and Virginia were "at last beginning to feel at home again," he said, "beginning to talk like unreconstructed rebels." Still, he added an important qualifier: "But we haven't yet become Dixiecrats."[28]

Luckily for Durr he had the legal business of the Durr Drug Company, the family concern headed by his brother, to help to pay the rent. In the months before officially opening his office he "eased back into practice," he wrote Rudy Gilbert in Denver, by helping the Alabama Service Commission in a case against Southern Bell. He thought the telephone rate case important because it provided an avenue through which he could gradually reenter his "old field of training and experience." Durr did not acquire other corporate business, however, and quickly developed a general practice handling cases not much different from Coe's or Smith's early local work, that is, taking whatever cases came his way. He even applied for work as a labor arbitrator through his friend Alton Lawrence of the Union of Mine, Mill and Smelter Workers, but as far as can be ascertained from his papers, nothing came of the application. About a year after he began the practice, a group of interstate

27. Aubrey Williams to C. J. Durr, March 7, 1951, ibid.

28. C. J. Durr to C. B. Baldwin, June 4, 1952, to Saul, June 5, 1952, in Box 12, Folder 2, and to Houston Waring, January 31, 1952, in Box 2, Folder 4, all ibid.

truckers who felt they had been swindled by their employer, the Baggett Trucking Company of Birmingham, came to him for help in filing damage claims against the firm. This large and very intricate case held the promise of future reward, but in the beginning it simply required a great deal of demanding work, work that would not finance this year's college tuition or next week's grocery bill. The years 1952 and 1953 were lean ones for the Durrs, a time of retrenchment and retreat from public life.[29]

Nevertheless, a few gaps appeared in the discreet facade of the family on Montgomery's Felder Avenue. Cliff Durr's speech to the women of the First Presbyterian Church in September, 1951, asked the question "Is Our Church Christian?"; and he made every effort to introduce challenging ideas along with the Bible study in his once-a-month Sunday school lesson. Along with John Coe and a host of others, he signed a petition to abolish HUAC in 1952, and he wrote a letter to the editor of the Washington *Post* condemning the Supreme Court's refusal, in *Dennis* v. *U.S.*,[30] to overturn contempt charges against the Communist Foley Square lawyers. A letter to the editor of the Montgomery *Advertiser* denounced Alabama's "little McCarran Act." In a second missive to the *Advertiser* he pretended to be Alexis de Tocqueville commenting on the terrible changes in the United States since his last visit, finding it, as had the paper's editor in a piece of which Durr essentially approved, "sterilized by dread." The tongue-in-cheek letter has an air of sadness and cynicism that provides a hint to Durr's state of mind in the early 1950s. Above all it is evidence that he suffered the sting of ostracism in Montgomery, not only from racists who labeled him a traitor, but also from those who trusted his patriotism but still feared to be associated with him. Despite all his attempts to become a part of the community, he was, he said, "an alien" among his own people.[31]

Durr could no more retire from his convictions than he could drop his

29. C. J. Durr to Rudy Gilbert, January 25, 1952, in Box 2, Folder 4, to Alton Lawrence, January 28, 1953, to William S. Pierce, March 26, 1953, to Bob Silverstein, October 13, 1953, in Box 2, Folder 5, *Bynum, Roe, et al.* v. *Baggett Transportation,* in Box 40, Folder 5, through in Box 41, Folder 7, all ibid. See also Salmond, *Conscience of a Lawyer,* 155–57.

30. 341 U.S. 494 (1951).

31. "Is Our Church Christian?" September 24, 1951, in Box 14, Folder 2, newsprint copy, petition to abolish HUAC, Washington *Post,* March 16, 1952, in Box 12, Folder 9, and Montgomery *Advertiser,* August 31, 1952, in Box 2, Folder 4, all in C. J. Durr Papers.

refined southern accent. When he addressed a Montgomery men's service club, a discussion group he joined at the public library, or a speech class at the University of Alabama, his civil libertarianism always surfaced.[32] Nevertheless, during the first few years back in Montgomery he tried to keep a low profile and cultivate his small-town law practice without offending bench, bar, or prospective clients.

Coe, on the other hand, continued to risk his reputation, and perhaps to limit his own local effectiveness, through his involvement with the CRC. "Comes now Willie McGee," read his petition to Chief Justice Fred M. Vinson in March, 1951, "a man . . . about to be executed without ever having had an opportunity to have a hearing on substantial issues of fact as to a null and void conviction obtained by the knowing and conscious use of perjured evidence by the prosecution, and through denial of the equal protection of the law to Negro persons against whom the state of Mississippi uses the death penalty for rape."[33] Perhaps the most celebrated of all CRC causes, the Willie McGee case attracted the national and international press, engendered sympathy and contributions from all parts of the United States and Europe, and caused near hysteria in Mississippi. There were rallies and marches in Chicago, Detroit, Louisville, New Orleans, and New York, petitions to Congress and the president, and contributions from labor unions, church groups, and local chapters of the NAACP and the ACLU. Despite their lack of enthusiasm in litigating the case, McGee's early defense lawyers "were almost disbarred, . . . virtually ruined economically," and one of them was beaten on the courthouse steps. Coe participated only in the final stages of the ordeal.[34]

The state charged McGee in 1945 with rape of a white Laurel, Mississippi, housewife with whom, according to local wags and later testimony, he had a long-term sexual relationship. When his mother asked him why he confessed to the crime, considering the contradictory and extenuating circumstances surrounding the accusation, he answered, "I signed to be living when you got

32. Montgomery *Advertiser,* "Government Secrecy Assailed by Former RFC Executive," October 10, 1952, in Box 12, Folder 2, "The Confessions of a Bureaucrat," speech before the Unity Club, October 14, 1952, and "Remarks," Department of Speech, University of Alabama, n.d., in Box 14, Folder 2, all ibid.

33. *McGee* v. *Jones,* in Box 36, Folder 24, Coe Papers.

34. Horne, *Communist Front,* 78–93, quote on 80; *McGee* v. *State,* 47 So. 2d 155, 339 U.S. 958 (1950).

here." Eyewitnesses placed him in another part of town at the time the woman's husband alleged the rape took place; unfortunately, they were all black. Although townspeople knew of his relationship with the woman, it was never revealed during his trials. The case reached the U.S. Supreme Court four times, twice being remanded to Hinds County for retrial. One Mississippi Supreme Court justice who signed a temporary stay of execution said that he believed McGee to be innocent, but out of fear he refused to write a dissenting opinion when his court heard the case.[35]

The case had all the elements of southern drama: rape of a southern white woman by a young black man, an aroused local populace, and interference in southern justice by Communists and other outside agitators. Surely John Coe's value to the CRC increased because he could not be labeled an "outside agitator," but he was one of very few CRC lawyers who lived in the South, and his position as a southern turncoat in no way endeared him to Mississippi's Governor Fielding Wright, Senator Eastland, or to the FBI, which followed the McGee case closely. Anne Braden became a member of a "white women's delegation" that traveled to Mississippi in 1951 under CRC sponsorship to protest McGee's inability to get a fair trial. She remembered meeting John Coe at the Jackson jail, where local officials briefly detained the women for disturbing the peace. After visiting McGee, Coe encouraged the incarcerated protestors and offered them legal advice.[36]

Coe and fellow CRC attorney Bella Abzug of New York entered the case in January, 1951, after the U.S. Supreme Court refused to review the case for a third time. When the Supreme Court of Mississippi set the execution date for March 20, Abzug and Coe appealed to the federal district court for another stay. They based their appeal on several grounds: a confession they believed to be forced by physical violence, but null in any case because McGee faced certain lynching had he told the truth; perjured trial testimony; and denial of equal protection of the law, that is, of federally guaranteed civil rights, because Mississippi executed only black men for rape. After the federal district court in Mississippi denied a full hearing, the CRC team flew to New Orleans to appeal to the Fifth Circuit on the same grounds, and thence to Washington

---

35. Horne, *Communist Front*, 78–97, quote on 79; *McGee v. Jones*, in Box 36, Folder 24, Coe Papers.

36. Braden interview; Horne, *Communist Front*, 96.

with the petition for Vinson. After exhausting all other avenues they appealed to Governor Wright, who denied clemency. On May 8, 1951, the state of Mississippi executed McGee, as was its macabre custom, in the Laurel courtroom where the case began.[37]

A picture of John Coe and Bella Abzug on the steps of the Mississippi state capitol building appeared in many southern newspapers, including the Pensacola *News Journal,* and in *Life* magazine, which captioned it "Willie's Lawyers, Bella Abzug, John Coe, Imported from New York, Florida." The day after the execution, Coe wrote to Abzug that he had "thought of poor Willie [yesterday]—a poor human being sacrificed on the altar of brutality and intransigence of the 'master race.'" He and Abzug had disagreed on a final procedure aimed at saving McGee's life, a suit against Mississippi officials under the civil rights statutes which she took to federal court for the CRC. Stetson Kennedy, who followed CRC cases carefully and frequently made suggestions, had pressed the action on the CRC. Coe thought it ill-advised, futile, and redundant, "somewhat analogous to bringing an action for malicious prosecution after a defendant has been convicted."[38] Coe's concern that Abzug did not understand his reservations about this last-ditch legal maneuver seems to have been unfounded. She assured Coe that she had great respect for his judgment and declared that their association had been "a very constructive experience. . . . My contact with you," she wrote, "was a rich thing from which I gained much inspiration and courage."[39] Their friendship continued long after the demise of the CRC, supported by sporadic correspondence and conversations at NLG meetings.

Coe's next CRC case, though not as sensational, also had the attributes of an early 1950s drama. Roosevelt Ward, a "black red" originally from New Orleans, moved to New York to work as administrative secretary of a Communist organization, the Labor Youth League. His draft board accused him of failing to leave them a forwarding address. Although they had his work address, they contacted first his mother in New Orleans and then a New York home address from which he had moved. When finally found and notified,

37. *McGee* v. *Jones,* in Box 36, Folder 24, Coe Papers.

38. J. M. Coe to Bella Abzug, April 8, May 9, June 13, 1951, Stetson Kennedy to Coe, April 19, 1951, Pensacola *News-Journal,* May 8, 1951, p. 1, and *Life,* May 21, 1951, p. 44, all ibid.

39. Bella Abzug to J. M. Coe, June 20, 1951, ibid.

he reported for service, but contrary to its normal practice, the draft board refused to accept his excuse and instituted a suit. At the height of the Korean War, and with anti-Communism a commonplace theme in the Louisiana legislature, no known Communist could be allowed to go unprosecuted.

At the CRC's request, Coe associated in this case with a young black attorney from New Orleans, Alvin Jones. Twelve years later, Jones would become Ben Smith's law partner. When they lost before a federal district jury and Judge J. Skelly Wright sentenced Ward to three years for draft evasion, Coe wrote William Patterson that the jurors "obviously lied in the voir dire, because no sane jury could have brought this verdict." The Supreme Court finally reversed the verdict, noting that "the record does not support the charge that . . . there was a deliberate purpose on the part of petitioner not to comply with the Selective Service Act or the regulation issued thereunder." Having been admitted to practice before the bar of the U.S. Supreme Court in December, 1952, Coe argued this case on May 12, 1953, his first appearance before the full high court panel.[40]

Several differences between Patterson and Coe demonstrating their cultural and political biases are illuminated in their correspondence. Coe asked in the beginning if it would not be better for him to take the case as an individual, rather than as a CRC lawyer. He hoped that the "cracked brained decisions" made by the CRC Bail Fund during the Foley Square trials could be thereby avoided. "If we can present [Ward] merely as a persecuted human being, without all the political heat incident to a political trial," he wrote, "we might get an acquittal from the jury." In his next letter he praised Alvin Jones but stated his disagreement with the young black lawyer about attacking the federal grand jury's indictment because only a token number of blacks served on southern federal jury panels. "I don't want to take the position that judge, jury and all are against us until it is thrust upon us." He thought they should make this "an ordinary criminal case." It could not win sympathetic publicity like the McGee case, he said, because "the race question which arises in rape cases is not so conspicuously present." He feared that "too much propaganda . . . [would] imperil Mr. Ward's chance of acquittal."[41]

40. *Ward* v. *United States,* 344 U.S. 924 (1953); Celinni, ed., *Digest of Communism,* 216–17; W. L. Patterson to J. M. Coe, July 17, 1951, Coe to Patterson, July 18, August 1, 1951, and November 20, 1952, in Box 37, Folder 35, Coe Papers.

41. J. M. Coe to W. L. Patterson, July 18, August 1, 1951, in Box 37, Folder 35, Coe Papers.

As Coe saw it, the CRC's first job was to protect Ward. He wanted to win, and insisted that Patterson make this clear to the CRC members in New Orleans, "because this question always arises." During his visits to New Orleans to appeal CRC cases in the Fifth Circuit, Coe had been introduced to some zealous and judgmental local CRC members. Their leader was a Dillard University English professor named Oakley Johnson, at whose home Coe met his Birmingham client, Sam Hall, for the first time in 1951. According to later testimony in a Senate Internal Security Subcommittee hearing, Hall had become the party's district organizer in New Orleans.[42]

Patterson assured Coe he would tell the New Orleans group that protecting Ward took precedence over any propaganda benefits accruing from the case. Regardless, he agreed with Jones on the question of black representation on the grand jury. "I think no opportunity should be missed where the Negro people could be shown the effort made by high places to freeze them in a secondary category." He also chastised Coe's "stenographer" for using a small "n" when typing the word "Negro," because "such a thing is offensive to the Negro people." And he added that he did not believe this to be "an ordinary criminal case," but a highly political matter. Those associated with such cases have obligation to make such injustices known to "Negro youth in particular," he wrote to Coe.[43]

A local cause Coe championed around the same time turned out less successfully. He took the cases of three black Pensacolans who wished to study at the local vocational school. Two of the applicants were veterans certified by the Veterans Administration for courses in cabinetmaking and auto mechanics, the other a young woman who wished to become a practical

42. J. M. Coe to W. L. Patterson, August 1, 1951, ibid.; J. M. Coe to Mynelle Cook, March 20, 1954, in Box 3, Folder 22, ibid.; for Sam Hall see U.S. Congress, Senate Committee on the Judiciary, Subcommittee to Investigate the Administration of the Internal Security Act and Other Internal Security Laws, *Scope of Soviet Activity in the United States,* Part 12, Hearings April 5–6, 1956 (New Orleans), 84th Cong., 2nd Sess., 710 [hereinafter cited as New Orleans SISS Hearings, 1956].

43. W. L. Patterson to J. M. Coe, August 2, 1951, in Box 37, Folder 35, Coe Papers. Coe's reply to this letter admits that the use of the small "n" was his fault, since he typed the letter himself: "The automatic habits of a lifetime are hard to break, but let me assure you that they were accompanied by no actual thought of disrespect." Coe to Patterson, September 3, 1951, ibid.

nurse. After the local court refused to overturn the county superintendent's judgment that they were unqualified, and as the school board hurried to ready plans for a "separate but equal" facility, Coe appealed the case to the Florida Supreme Court.

During his preparation for this presentation, Coe considered asking for a federal injunction against the school board "to put the heat under them" and asked South Carolina attorney Harold Boulware for a copy of his complaint in *Briggs* v. *Elliott* to use as a guide. "The relief therein granted is exactly what I want," he wrote, "and it is conceivable that I might break segregation, as I am dealing with adults and not children, and may come within the exception suggested on that ground in that opinion." But his hopefulness about the significance of the case was not rewarded. The state supreme court affirmed the superintendent's right to determine eligibility, causing both the case and plans for a separate black vocational school in Escambia County eventually to be dropped, though not without considerable publicity in the local press. When FBI agents asked some Pensacola attorneys for their opinions of Coe a couple of months later, all thought that except for his "activities in behalf of draft dodgers and colored persons, which they read about in the newspapers," he was probably not involved in Communist activities. "According to them," reported the bureau, "he is quietly pursuing his law practice and is still a dangerous adversary in the courtroom."[44]

Around the time Coe was visiting New Orleans to argue CRC cases in the Fifth Circuit, Ben Smith opened the doors of his first law practice on Baronne Street. Their friendship blossomed later, but Smith, as a fellow southern NLG member and Progressive Party leader, may have met Coe and certainly heard about Coe's exploits during this period. Smith himself became involved in a New Orleans civil liberties case of some note in 1953, and his client, Dr. Robert Hodes of the Tulane Medical School, probably knew Coe's CRC host Oakley Johnson well. The FBI identified Hodes as "either a past or a present member of the Professional Group of the Communist Party in New Orleans," listed Smith among those who attended "meetings held in the [Hodes] home" in 1953, and said Smith agreed "with the political views advanced by

44. Pensacola *News-Journal,* August 22, 29, 1951, Coe to Harold R. Boulware, November 29, 1951, and Brief, *State of Florida ex rel. Rankin* v. *Dan J. Anderson et al.,* all in Box 38, Folder 5, ibid.; Report, October 2, 1951, p. 3, Section 2, Coe FBI File.

[Hodes]." At one of these meetings, an informant reported, Smith had called the Louisiana Communist Control Bill "a bad piece of legislation" and discussed a recent Supreme Court decision "concerning the legal consequences of pleading the Fifth Amendment."[45]

Despite his interest in such highly charged political matters, Smith probably took whatever honest work came into his office at that point. The 1953 "Lawyers' Referral List" of the NLG described his specialties as "labor relations, title and abstract, and collections." Searching titles in real estate cases, a field for which he seems unsuited, must have been an offshoot of family business, either that of his own family or his wife's relatives. His legal work began with occasional business from his new father-in-law's large and successful engineering company, but the bulk of his work involved personal injury and labor union–related cases. Quite early on, his contact with Herman Wright through the NLG brought him a recommendation to the Maritime Union local in New Orleans, and through this work he also developed a relationship with the predominantly black Packinghouse Workers, eventually his best union clients. These connections, his membership in the NLG, and his friendship with another leftist Tulane professor, Mitchell Franklin, presumably led Robert Hodes to choose Smith as an advocate.[46]

Smith represented Hodes, a tenured professor of neurophysiology and experimental neurology dismissed for "creating friction in the Department of Psychiatry and Neurology," at hearings arranged at the insistence of the American Association of University Professors (AAUP). Hodes was considered an "outstanding scientist," but he was unpopular personally and suspect politically. Since the university cited neither "incompetency" nor "moral turpitude," offenses recognized by the AAUP as valid grounds for dismissal, as the basis for the firing, the association asked that the matter be formally reviewed by the board of administrators of Tulane University. In his brief for Dr. Hodes, Smith noted that only "insubordinate and incompetent technicians" had accused Hodes. He thus concluded that the charges were simply Tulane's "immoral and disreputable attempt" not only to rid itself of a ten-

45. Report, July 20, 1954, p. 10, Smith FBI File. The author is reasonably sure that the name blacked out in her copy of this FBI report is "Hodes"; thus the brackets here.

46. Jones interview; National Lawyers Guild, "Lawyers Referral List, 1953," in Box 92, NLG Papers, King Center; Wright interview.

ured professor "with unpopular political views," but to discard "its very strength and virtue . . . academic freedom and scholarship, things which have made it what it is."[47] The case differed from academic cases handled by Cliff Durr because Durr's clients encountered HUAC before facing dismissal, but this hearing was an internal university matter, and the dismissal provoked the hearing. Smith attempted, at least, to define the issue as academic freedom rather than subversion.

Nevertheless, it remained essentially a political investigation. Hodes's accusers or Tulane officials were supplied with information by the same government investigators collecting data on Smith. Hodes and his wife, Jane, enlisted in integrationist causes and belonged to several left-wing groups, likely including the Communist Party. They had sponsored a meeting of faculty members in 1951 to hear a presentation from a representative of the China Welfare Appeal, a group soliciting aid for mainland China and listed as subversive by the attorney general. They also outspokenly criticized the Korean War. In addition, Hodes had publicly embarrassed both the university and his colleagues in the medical school. He encouraged black scientists to attend an American Physiology Association meeting in New Orleans and then challenged Tulane's segregated cafeteria, which refused to feed the visiting scholars.[48]

Hodes himself claimed the charges against him to be "a subterfuge" designed to hide the political nature of his opposition. Testimony supported Hodes's claim that his political views were an important factor in his inability to "fit in" with his department, if an uncooperative personality was indeed the primary reason for the dismissal. One colleague testified that "Dr. Hodes' unpopular social and political views" left him with the impression that Hodes

47. B. E. Smith, "Before a Committee of the Board of Administrators of Tulane University, February–April, 1953, In the Matter of Dr. Robert Hodes and Tulane University, Brief for Dr. Hodes," in Box 92, NLG Papers, King Center; David R. Holmes, *Stalking the Academic Communist: Intellectual Freedom and the Firing of Alex Novikoff* (Hanover, N.H., 1989), 106–107; Schrecker, *No Ivory Tower*, 141–44.

48. Schrecker, *No Ivory Tower*, 242; Lionel S. Lewis, *Cold War on Campus: A Study of the Politics of Organizational Control* (New Brunswick, N.J., 1988), 55–57; see also New Orleans SISS Hearings, 1956, pp. 168, 171.

"was in danger of dismissal at any time." The meeting concerning China relief was termed "treasonous" by Hodes's immediate superior.[49]

Some of the testimony, like the accusation that Hodes pointedly "described and extolled the work of the RUSSIAN physiologist, Pavlov," had an almost comic-opera quality. In his statement, Hodes related that "Dr. Heath [the department head] said I should ignore the problems facing Negroes and concentrate on curing schizophrenia. That would help the Negro people more." Hodes said he had been told that Tulane, in the midst of a fund-raising campaign, feared his radical ideas would affect the giving of some wealthy alumni. In any case, the medical school dean and department chairman used somewhat arbitrary means to discourage and then dismiss Hodes. The hearing also revealed a confusing sequence of events through which university officials attempted to vindicate themselves or, from the point of view of Hodes's supporters, camouflage the petty or political motives for his firing.[50]

In an article written years later, Anne Braden blamed Hodes's troubles on Senator Eastland's plans to bring SISS to New Orleans to hunt for "subversives." "Tulane was frightened," she maintained.[51] Eastland's investigation of SCEF, however, remained unannounced until January, 1954, almost a year after the Hodes hearing, and a connection between the two events seems doubtful. Yet it is true that by early 1953 Louisiana and Crescent City officials had joined the anti-Communist crusade enthusiastically. Local grand juries had been questioning Communists and "fellow travelers" in New Orleans' unions and schools intermittently since 1949. The South was no exception to the national movement against left-wing teachers. Oakley Johnson, whose early 1930s radicalism caused his dismissal from his first teaching job at City College of New York, lost his New Orleans position at Dillard in 1951 because of his politics. The University of Florida discharged political scientist John Reynolds, a Progressive Party associate of John Coe, when he invoked

49. Lewis, *Cold War on Campus,* 55, 57.

50. Ibid.; Jane Hodes, "A Note on Robert Hodes," in presentation booklet and catalogue for "The Robert Hodes Memorial Collection, Learning Materials in Neurophysiology," Meharry Medical Library, in Box 9, Folder 22, Dombrowski Papers, quotes on 349 and 351.

51. Anne Braden, "One Who Fought Back," *Daily World,* September 7, 1978, ibid.

the Fifth Amendment before HUAC in 1953. After even the university's AAUP chapter refused to support him, Reynolds gave up the effort to regain his post, "feeling that my cause was hopeless."[52]

In spite of the AAUP's involvement, Smith's carefully prepared brief and spirited representation of Hodes failed to bring the professor's reinstatement. After the board upheld the administration's actions, a civil suit for monetary damages would have been futile. Like Cliff Durr's academic clients and other scholars caught in the Red scare, Hodes could not find a teaching job in the United States and worked abroad from 1953 until 1959, first in England, then, appropriately, in China. He returned to the United States in 1959 to a professorship in physiology at Mt. Sinai School of Medicine in New York. In the early 1960s he formed a scientist's committee to help upgrade opportunities for blacks in his profession, enthusiastically supported his son's participation in civil rights activities in Mississippi, and actively opposed the war in Vietnam. For a brief period his liberal son, Bill, worked in Ben Smith's law office in New Orleans. After Hodes's death in 1966 his family donated "The Robert Hodes Memorial Collection of Learning Materials in Neurophysiology" to the medical library at Meharry, one of the nation's top black medical schools.[53]

Perhaps the dismissal of Hodes anticipated the storm that would blow into New Orleans with SISS in 1954, as Anne Braden suggested, but a significant dissimilarity exists between the targets of the two hearings. Robert Hodes, a native of New Jersey and a Ph.D. graduate of Harvard, typified the kind of outsider who might be expected to harbor eccentric or disloyal ideas. But native southern subversives—"insiders" who should have known better than to oppose southern segregation laws—were Senator Eastland's primary targets. Whether these southerners were actually Communists remained, in the final analysis, a matter of little consequence to defenders of white supremacy. Eastland suggested to Judiciary Committee chairman William Jenner that SISS investigate SCEF just a few months before an important congressional election. The hearings would remind white southerners of the necessity for solidarity behind the Stars and Bars.

52. Horne, *Communist Front*, 63; Schrecker, *No Ivory Tower*, 65, 317.

53. Presentation booklet, "The Robert Hodes Memorial Collection," in Box 9, Folder 22, Dombrowski Papers; Barnwell interview.

In fact, the presence of many active, well-organized Communists working covertly to bring integration to southern institutions was simply a useful fiction in 1954. If nothing else, the extremely weak southern support for Henry Wallace's presidential bid in 1948, a cause ardently promoted by the party, should provide a clue to the numbers of southern left-wing radicals. By the early 1950s, as Robin Kelley pointed out in his study of Communism in Alabama, "the Alabama CP and most of its auxiliary organizations ceased to exist" in the wake of Red-baiting and loss of the popular front base that had validated party activity in earlier decades. The entire CPUSA had less than five thousand members by the late 1950s, a large percentage of them government informants. Numbers fell precipitously after a disastrous 1956 convention endorsed Soviet policies blindly, including the invasion of Hungary. The civil rights movement probably eventually inherited and absorbed many CPUSA defectors, particularly southern leftists. But most black integrationists, like Martin Luther King, Jr., followed the NAACP lead in the 1950s and avoided political radicalism. And white radicalism, under attack since the early 1940s, remained at most a vulnerable, marginalized force in southern politics and society.[54]

Nonetheless, for many archsegregationists, including most southerners in Congress, Communism and integrationism became indivisible. In the waning days of the reign of *Plessy* v. *Ferguson,* southern conservatives girded for battle against the Supreme Court's advances on segregation. Often congressmen, senators, and their counterparts on the state level opportunistically depicted changes threatening "the southern way of life" as the work of southern Communists and their dishonorable collaborators, foreign and domestic. Certainly lawyers supporting such criminals and apostates as Willie McGee and Robert Hodes fell into several proscribed categories. Civil libertarians, pacifists, integrationists, Communists, and the Soviet Union, portrayed as the fomenter of all black discontent and agitation for social equality, gained equal billing as enemies of "100% Americanism." To carry the fiction of widespread southern subversion to its obvious conclusion, only the "neobourbons" and their compliant allies could save the South—and the country—from Armageddon.

54. Kelley, *Hammer and Hoe,* 227–28; Branch, *Parting the Waters,* 122–23, 129.

CHAPTER FIVE

Congressional Offensive, 1954:
The SCEF Investigation and
Its Echoes

The hearings called by Senator Jenner's Senate Internal Security Subcommittee to investigate subversion in the Southern Conference Educational Fund occurred three months after the Supreme Court heard concluding arguments in the prolonged *Brown* case but two months before the May 17, 1954, decree. By early that year it had become clear to close observers, including SISS member James Eastland, that the five final questions framed by the Court for attorneys contesting *Brown* v. *Board of Education* indicated the direction of its reasoning away from "separate but equal."

Nonetheless, other parts of the federal government seemed determined to resist revision of postwar conservatism, even at the slow pace required by the judicial branch. McCarthy became an embarrassment to the Republican Senate and the administration, but the Communist Control Act, the Robert Oppenheimer case, and the army-McCarthy hearings still progressed. On the foreign-policy front the Eisenhower administration sent American dollars to support failing French forces at Dien Bien Phu, assisted the recently restored shah of Iran, and readied a similar CIA coup against the elected but leftist government of Guatemala.

Contradictory messages from Washington buffeted and beguiled the South. On the one hand, the Supreme Court and a new generation of assertive black Americans warned white southerners that their time-honored social structure had been built on antidemocratic doctrine intentionally perpetuated through state-sponsored segregation, a wrong overripe for remedy. Some understood this instinctively, but guilt exposed is humiliating and breeds indignation and defensiveness among otherwise rational men and women. Southerners who felt no remorse displayed anger, truculence, and fear.

On the other hand, outside the federal judiciary and a small band of congressional liberals, little enthusiasm for social change existed in the national government. The Eisenhower administration, as Michal Belknap has shown, "would not accept responsibility for preserving order in the South" and, when it came, all but ignored the unanimous *Brown* v. *Board of Education* decision until faced with an unavoidable threat to civil order in 1957.[1] The conservative Republicanism of the president and others in his administration surely undergirded their bias toward avoiding conflict with state powers. But the popular president's indifference encouraged critics of the Court and disheartened its supporters.

As the administration concentrated on defeating Communism and stimulating capitalism around the world, the Republican Congress did its best, though with little success, to dismantle the New Deal. Even as McCarthy's personal influence waned, leaders in both the legislative and executive branches scorned old-style liberals and quarantined left-wing activists. The Congress became, in effect, an important center of resistance to the liberal activism of the Court. Among the most grateful beneficiaries of this climate were conservative southern congressmen, Eastland being only the most extreme example. They conveyed the federal government's complacency to their constituents and capitalized on the national mood to secure support for or acquiescence in a political agenda based on defiance and recalcitrance.

After Carl and Anne Braden sold their house in a white Louisville, Kentucky, neighborhood to a black couple in May, 1954, they faced indictment under Kentucky's "little Smith Act" for conspiring to overthrow the commonwealth's government. HUAC sent witnesses south to document the Bradens' subversion.[2] The Highlander Folk School came under increasing pressure from anti-Communist, segregationist, and antiunion newspapers and legislators in 1953 and 1954. A congressman from Tennessee, Pat Sutton, launched a particularly ruthless attack in which he unearthed numerous right-wing complaints and allegations about the school, impugning the names of just about every Highlander associate, contributor, or board member, including Myles Horton, Jim Dombrowski, Aubrey Williams, Mrs. Roosevelt, Frank Graham, and some prominent labor leaders. In a rambling six-page letter sent to several Tennessee newspapers, he called Highlander's founders

---

1. Michal R. Belknap, *Federal Law and Southern Order: Racial Violence and Constitutional Conflict in the Post-Brown South* (Athens, Ga., 1987), 27.

2. *Kentucky* v. *Braden,* 291 SW 2d 843 (1954).

"stooges" and SCHW a "communist front organization." Sutton's documentation came from the 1949 HUAC testimony of Paul Crouch, a witness who would become familiar to participants in the SCEF hearings in New Orleans.[3]

As rumors of the Supreme Court's inclinations circulated, Governor Herman Talmadge submitted a "private school plan" to the Georgia legislature, and Mississippi lawmakers passed a series of acts designed to ensure continued segregation just in case it was declared illegal. SCEF gained some prominence in late 1953 through a nationwide television and radio debate captioned "Segregation in the Public Schools" between its president, Aubrey Williams, and Governor Talmadge and by publicizing a poll of southern educators concerning the possibility of integrated schools. In an article reporting on the poll, the Atlanta *Journal* carefully pointed to the left-wing ties of former SCEF board members Louis Burnham and Clark Foreman. The article also criticized SCEF's objections to the "regional education plan" recently formulated by southern governors to evade integration of graduate schools. Two weeks before the hearings opened in New Orleans, Benjamin Mays, widely respected president of Morehouse College and a longtime supporter of SCHW and SCEF, resigned from the SCEF board of directors. Jim Dombrowski mourned the loss and blamed it on Senator Eastland and SISS.[4]

Surprisingly, McCarthy's decline seemed to breathe new life into SISS and HUAC, which had languished in his shadow for three years. Republican lawmakers, aided by the indefatigably anti-Communist vice-president, Richard Nixon, made anti-Communism the central issue of 1954 congressional campaigns. Though Democrats that year gained a slight majority in both houses, the ruling alliance of conservative Republicans and southern Democrats maintained control in Congress. After the army hearings and McCarthy's censure, however, inquiries into subversion in the federal government had run their course. The anti-Communist committees began to

3. Pat Sutton, M.C., to Myles Horton, December 1, 1953, in Box 2, Folder 5, C. J. Durr Papers.

4. Bartley, *Rise of Massive Resistance*, 54–56; Debate, "Segregation and the Public Schools," October 12, 1953, in Box 23, Folder 19, Carl and Anne Braden Papers, Archives Division, State Historical Society of Wisconsin, Madison [hereinafter cited as Braden Papers]; Atlanta *Journal*, October 11, 1953, in Box 2, Folder 5, C. J. Durr Papers; J. A. Dombrowski to Benjamin Mays, March 5, 1954, in Box 16, Folder 9, Dombrowski Papers.

concentrate on regional Communism and nongovernmental institutions and organizations deemed to be infiltrated by Communists.[5]

Naturally SCEF, with its suspected ancestry and colorful mixture of radicalism and integrationism, became an early target of the hunt for southern subversives. Senator Eastland framed his intentions in historical terms. He asked the committee's first friendly witness on March 18, 1954, "Is it your contention that the Southern Conference for Human Welfare was the agency of the Communist Party that penetrated the Southern States?" He repeatedly probed the relationship between SCHW, subject of the apparently incriminating 1944 HUAC report, and SCEF.[6] With the benefit of hindsight, the appearance of Coe, Durr, and Smith as advocates for the southerners under subpoena in New Orleans also seems to be a natural development. Rare among southern lawyers, by 1954 each of them had acquired some expertise in the peculiar art of confronting the machinery of anti-Communism.

With the possible exception of Miami lawyer Leo Sheiner and Miami contractor Max Schlafrock, John Coe's client, none of those called to testify in the SCEF hearings was or had ever been a Communist. Schlafrock and Sheiner, who both testified on the first day of the hearings, faced simultaneous investigations by an ambitious Dade County anti-Communist, State's Attorney George A. Brautigam. Both men had apparently either joined the party or been sympathetic associates of the Communist group in Miami in the 1930s or 1940s; they had supported Wallace in 1948 and remained active in leftist causes. Schlafrock came to the United States from Poland in 1921 and migrated to Miami in 1933, where he developed a successful building business. On Coe's advice he refused on Fifth Amendment grounds to answer any of the Eastland committee's questions about his personal and political associations, including Florida Communists such as Coe's Jacksonville client Alexander Trainor, SCEF, SCHW, the CRC, or his union membership.[7]

Schlafrock may have become peripherally involved in SCHW through Leo

5. Goodman, *Committee,* 345, 364–98.

6. U.S. Congress, Senate Committee on the Judiciary, Subcommittee to Investigate the Administration of the Internal Security Act and Other Internal Security Laws, *Hearings on Subversive Influence in Southern Conference Educational Fund Inc.* (New Orleans), 83rd Cong., 2nd Sess., March 18, 19, 20, 1954, p. 2 [hereinafter cited as SCEF Hearings, 1954].

7. Miami *Herald,* n.d. [March, 1954], in Box 47, Folder 35, Coe Papers; SCEF Hearings, 1954, pp. 6–11.

Sheiner, former chairman of the Southern Conference's south Florida committee and a SCEF board member from 1948 to at least 1950. Sheiner opened a Florida law practice in 1946, and the following year, representing SCHW, he helped to organize an important Winter Park meeting and subsequent campaign against the Matthews white primary bill, an attempt to abrogate *Smith* v. *Allwright*. Daniel C. Whitsett, a minister from the Alabama–West Florida Conference of the Methodist Church, chaired this conference, which brought together many liberal and moderate clergymen, educators, and unionists black and white. Jim Dombrowski, Sheiner, Mary McLeod Bethune, Ocala First Methodist Church pastor George Foster, Rollins College president Edwin L. Clarke, representatives of the AFL and the CIO, and Harry T. Moore, the NAACP leader killed in a 1951 north Florida bombing, all spoke and helped to plan the campaign against the bill.[8] About a year after this conference, Sheiner worked closely with party leader John Coe while serving as finance committee chairman of the Progressive Party in Florida.

Acting as his own attorney in New Orleans, Sheiner issued a prepared statement to the press denying the committee's accusations. On the stand he answered questions about his educational and employment history and told Eastland of his membership in the National Lawyers Guild but denied being a Communist. Then he refused to answer questions about SCHW, SCEF, or his past political associations, standing on "the First, the Fourth, Fifth, Sixth, Eighth, Ninth, and Tenth Amendments." He infuriated Senator Eastland by aggressively debating with the chair. At one point during his statement of grounds for refusal Eastland said: "Keep your mouth shut. You will take orders from me. I know Communist tactics. I am not going to let you take over this hearing." Later he told Sheiner only a guilty man would "slink behind the Fifth Amendment. . . . You're a big-time communist and I know it."[9]

Besides John Coe and the subpoenaed Leo Sheiner, the nongovernment lawyers present at these hearings were Benjamin Smith, representing SCEF

8. "Conference to Defend Democracy in Florida," Congregational-Christian Church, Winter Park, Florida, March 22, 1947, and Minutes of the Board of Representatives, SCHW, May 22, 1948, both in Box 17, Folder 3, Dombrowski Papers.

9. SCEF Hearings, 1954, pp. 23–29; quotes from Pensacola *News-Journal*, March 19, 1954, pp. 1, 20.

and its executive director, James Dombrowski; Clifford Durr, for Myles Horton of Highlander and SCEF president Aubrey Williams; and John P. Kohn, an old friend of the Durrs from Montgomery. Feeling that a husband should not be his wife's advocate, Kohn had volunteered to represent Virginia Durr despite his conservative bent. Unfortunately, while the lawyers certainly planned their clients' strategy outside the hearing room, they could only observe and whisper advice during the proceedings.

The committee's rules were arbitrary and the decisions of the chairman sacrosanct, with no statements or objections allowed. Investigatory reports could not be examined or verified, and witnesses, often unknown until they appeared to testify, faced almost no chance of cross-examination by unfriendly counsel. Because of the accusatory nature of the proceedings and the reasonable expectation that contempt or perjury charges might ensue, lawyers accustomed to zealous defense of their clients fiercely resented the absence of due process. Traditional lawyers like John Kohn as well as activist civil libertarians like Coe, Durr, and Smith found the situation disgraceful, insulting, at times almost unendurable.

Their protestations proved futile. Eastland answered twenty-seven-year-old Ben Smith's queries about procedure abruptly and, as he had with Sheiner, insinuated the possibility of a subversive motive behind the young lawyer's challenge. When asked about the rules of procedure he answered, "I will announce them when I desire. Proceed." Smith objected to the chair's refusal to read written objections to the committee's jurisdiction; Eastland overruled him with "I know the jurisdiction of this committee." Smith asked, in lieu of the right of cross-examination, if he could at least have a copy of the record. The chair sneered, "You are a fine lawyer." Smith replied that he was "profoundly shocked"; Eastland stated his disinterest in the lawyer's concerns. "I know these kinds of tactics," he replied. "I know the sources from which they come and you are not going to take this hearing over."[10]

Franklin Roosevelt's description of congressional anti-Communist hearings as a "sordid procedure," John Coe wrote to a friend, "was a masterpiece of understatement." Cliff Durr had experienced service before congressional committees in his private Washington practice in 1949 and 1950. Surely none of those encounters could have been as unnerving as seeing his wife and close

10. SCEF Hearings, 1954, pp. 5–144, quotes on 5, 31, and 43.

friends stretched on Eastland's rack. He, too, repeatedly asked for legal structure and for the right to challenge the committee's witnesses. In the end,
desperate to be heard, he became a witness himself.[11]

Attorneys and investigators employed by congressional committees, abetted by informants who provided the basis of their interrogations, became the
prevailing legal authorities in these proceedings, overshadowing impotent
defense lawyers. Attorney Richard Arens enjoyed a long and amazing career
hunting Communists, first as counsel for SISS and later as HUAC's main
lawyer. An ultraconservative Senate staffer even before his term at SISS, as
counsel to the McCarran Subcommittee on Immigration he had engineered
the defeat of Emanuel Celler's bill to allow 25,000 German Jews into the
United States in 1949. He joined the fanatical Anti-Communist Christian
Crusade organized by Benjamin Swartz, and such groups as the American
Legion and the Daughters of the American Revolution heralded him as a great
patriot. Arens twice led the questioning of witnesses in New Orleans and later
guided similar sessions in Charlotte and Atlanta as well. He often employed
a signature exhortation: "Stand up like a red-blooded American!"[12]

In New Orleans, professional informants John Butler and Paul Crouch
turned out to be even more troublesome than their champion, Mr. Arens.
Butler said he joined the Communist Party in Birmingham in the early 1940s,
while a member of the "communist dominated" Mine, Mill and Smelter
Workers Union. He called union president Alton Lawrence, an old friend of
the Durrs who had once worked for SCHW, a member of the Communist
Party. Butler apparently left the party after the union expelled him for em-
bezzlement.[13]

Crouch, one of the most frequently used government witnesses during the
McCarthy period, would likely have long since been exposed as a pathological
liar had he been answerable to opposing attorneys' cross-examination. In
1925, to excuse mutinous letters exposed during his army court-martial for
offenses against the military code, Crouch had revealed his "habit of writing
letters to my friends and imaginary persons, sometimes to kings and other
foreign persons, in which I place myself in an imaginary position." Though

11. J. M. Coe to Mynelle, March 20, 1954, in Box 3, Folder 22, Coe Papers.
12. Caute, *Great Fear,* 93.
13. SCEF Hearings, 1954, pp. 96–97; Adams, *James Dombrowski,* 228–29.

the court sentenced him to forty years at hard labor, the government freed him from Alcatraz after only three, ostensibly as a result of a campaign orchestrated by the Communist Party. After his release he briefly attended school in Moscow, but the Soviets found his behavior so strange that they sent him home after two or three months. A rural Baptist minister's son from North Carolina, Crouch became a party organizer in the South in the 1930s and was one of the six Communists (out of twelve hundred delegates) at the founding meeting of SCHW in 1938. During the war his Communist comrades relieved him of party duties, first in the South, then in his new home in California.[14]

In 1949 and 1950 Crouch emerged as a professional ex-Communist in California, Hawaii, and Florida, where he denounced Leo Sheiner as part of a "'secret plot' to go underground and stage an uprising after the Red Army landed." Employed as a "consultant" by the Immigration and Naturalization Service (a part of the Justice Department) in 1951, he lived rent-free in Hawaii in a house provided by a Chinese Nationalist archbishop. He traveled to hearings and consultations at the government's behest and headed the "Federation of Former Communists." This organization tried to improve the status and the compensation of ex-Communist informants, a sad cadre upon whom congressional anti-Communist committees had become dependent. Crouch particularly relished stories about Soviet invasion plans and efforts to infiltrate the American military, which he said he had learned about as an adviser to top Russian military figures. One of his reports had provided justification for the army-McCarthy hearings getting under way in Washington as he assumed the stand in New Orleans.[15]

John Salmond gauges the high value Eastland placed on the SCEF hearings by Crouch's presence there as a witness, probably a fair judgment. Eastland found him ideal as an expert on southern Communists and obviously admired his credentials and his proficiency as a witness. Yet in the end Crouch's testimony in New Orleans, combined with his other perjuries, so discredited him that he never again found employment as a federal witness. Like McCarthy, his time in the limelight was brief, and his descent as rapid and

14. Cedric Belfrage, *The American Inquisition, 1945–1960* (New York, 1973), 16, 22–23, 45, 108, quote on 16.

15. Caute, *Great Fear*, 126–28.

ignominious as his rise to prominence. After the SCEF hearings, attacks in the press, especially a series of articles by Stewart and Joseph Alsop, forced the attorney general to investigate him. He died at the end of 1955, abandoned by the politicians who had made him a star.[16]

After their testimony against Schlafrock and Sheiner, Crouch and Butler took the stand to denounce Ben Smith's client, Jim Dombrowski. Crouch claimed that he had ridden from Miami to Winter Park[17] with Dombrowski for the 1947 meeting organized by Sheiner and the Florida SCHW to fight the white primary bill. Dombrowski entertained him en route singing the "Internationale." Dombrowski had been "chosen by the party" to be active in SCHW, Crouch maintained, but SCEF's director always refused to admit to being under Communist discipline because "he could serve the revolutionary movement better under the Socialist label than he could under the Communist label." On his part, Dombrowski vaguely remembered meeting Crouch once in Miami and the Winter Park meeting, but could not recall the automobile trip or the subversive singing. He found it heartwarming, however, that someone liked his voice. At Emory, he said, "I managed the glee club but they wouldn't let me sing." When Crouch asserted that he had overheard Sheiner and Dombrowski discussing proposed "hideouts" for Communist leaders at a meeting, Dombrowski countered with "That is a lie, sir."[18]

The balance of Dombrowski's testimony answered questioning by Arens and Eastland about SCHW, the integrationist purposes of SCEF, and liberal statements and petitions sponsored by Dombrowski or these groups. The committee asked him to confirm or deny his relationship with long lists of persons and organizations, both black and white, Communist and non-Communist. After enduring relentless interrogation from two until five on the afternoon of the first day of the hearings, he resumed the stand briefly the next day to reiterate a point made at the beginning of his testimony: he would not produce the names of SCEF's contributors.[19]

16. Ibid.; Alsop columns, n.d. [1954], in Box 12, Folder 3, C. J. Durr Papers; Salmond, *Conscience of a Lawyer*, 161.

17. Crouch actually called the trip's destination Winter Haven, not Winter Park. SCEF Hearings, 1954, p. 48.

18. SCEF Hearings, 1954, pp. 40–52, quotes on 49, 51, and 52.

19. Ibid., 52–80.

On the previous day Dombrowski had based his refusal on the First and Fourth Amendments, that is, on his right to free speech, belief, and association and on the constitutional protection against unreasonable searches and seizures. He had also invoked the Fifth Amendment, "but only that clause which states that no person shall be deprived of liberty or property without due process of law." He took this course because he felt an obligation "in times of hysteria such as this" to SCEF's supporters, who might misunderstand his motives if he invoked protections against self-incrimination. Nevertheless, he did not disparage anyone who took refuge in the Fifth Amendment. "On the contrary," he believed witnesses had a perfect right to claim all the protections of the Constitution. But even without its use, he believed he had both a right and a duty to protect the list of SCEF's backers. At the end of Dombrowski's ordeal, Smith tried to place in the record a second list of objections to the subcommittee and its subpoenas. Eastland promptly overruled them all and finally allowed Dombrowski to stand down.[20]

After reading into the record a long quotation about fellow travelers carrying on the work of the Soviet conspiracy, Arens called Virginia Durr to the stand. John Kohn immediately stated his objections to the committee's "fishing expedition." It violated Durr's First Amendment rights, he contended, and the committee had no authority without a quorum, Eastland being the only senator present. Nevertheless, his client would not "in any way, shape or form" invoke the Fifth Amendment. Kohn asked that she be allowed to make a statement; Eastland refused. Might he, as her counsel, read the statement? "No, sir," replied the chair. Through a long barrage of questions, Virginia Durr either took refuge in silence or replied "I stand mute." When Arens announced the recall of Paul Crouch, Kohn asked for the right to cross-examine. Since Durr was in contempt, replied Eastland, her counsel had no rights before the committee. But, insisted Kohn, "We are still before the tribunal." When he asked the chair to note in record that "this witness is an ex-convict," Eastland and attorney Arens both became irate. "Wait just a minute, please. Sit down. That is self-serving," Eastland replied. Arens suggested that the "record show reprimand of this counsel."[21]

After Crouch's testimony accusing Virginia Durr of conspiring with Com-

---

20. Ibid., 30–83, quotes on 41.
21. Ibid., 84–90, quotes on 85, 86, and 90.

munists to influence Eleanor Roosevelt and plotting "to exploit her relationship as a sister-in-law of a Justice of the Supreme Court in the interest of the World Communist conspiracy and in the interest of overthrowing our government," Kohn's anger turned cold. His protests, nonetheless, hit a stone wall. He had "placed his client in contempt of the Senate of the United States," said Eastland, and could not raise any objections to the testimony: "You have nothing to do here." John Butler resumed the witness stand to testify regarding an allegedly subversive dinner conversation between the Durrs and Alton Lawrence, whom he identified as the Communist who "introduced me to the party." Without comment the confounded Kohn finally asked, "Are we excused?" and he and Virginia yielded the microphone to Cliff Durr and SCEF president Aubrey Williams.[22]

Williams' testimony was divided into two parts by the statements of the two informants. Eastland treated him with civility during the opening questions, perhaps aware that both Williams and his counsel still had some important contacts in Washington, notably the majority leader of the Senate, Lyndon Johnson. Williams and Virginia Durr had contacted friends from New Deal days after the subpoenas were issued, and Johnson, according to most reports, was instrumental in discouraging other senators from accompanying Eastland to New Orleans. Though they had never been friendly, Eastland and Williams had known each other for twenty years. Williams testified about his New Deal service, his connections to the National Farmers Union, Highlander, and the Southern Negro Youth Congress, and his SCHW and SCEF experience. He said that he had dissociated himself from the CRC and the Stockholm Peace Petition after initial participation, and that he had never been a Communist.[23]

Butler returned to continue the story of his relationship to union leader Lawrence, whom he swore introduced him to Aubrey Williams as "Comrade Williams . . . who is a party member." He also insisted that Williams often met with Rob Hall, Communist Party leader in Alabama in the early 1940s. Infuriated, Williams challenged Butler to repeat his story for newsmen outside

22. Ibid., 90–99, quotes on 93, 95, and 99.
23. John Salmond, *A Southern Rebel: The Life and Times of Aubrey Willis Williams, 1890–1965* (Chapel Hill, 1983), 232–36; Barnard, ed., *Outside the Magic Circle*, 256–57; SCEF Hearings, 1954, pp. 104–16.

the hearing room, so he could be sued for libel. Butler never accepted the invitation. When Crouch resumed the stand to reinforce Butler's story about Rob Hall, who allegedly told him Williams "was a secret member of the Communist Party," the hearings took a surprising turn.[24]

Durr, as had Coe, Smith, and Kohn, asked for the right to cross-examine Crouch. Surely his colleagues were incredulous when Eastland consented to Durr's request. On his part, Crouch seemed to almost enjoy the ordeal. The examination gave him a chance to pour out the story of his sordid background in shocking detail, for Durr led him slowly through his army court-martial, his time in the Soviet Union, and his party schooling. Durr aimed for the admission that Crouch had been "trained in deception," then encouraged him to make specific statements about his claims that Dombrowski, Williams, and Horton were Communists. Many of Crouch's answers were long-winded speeches, much of his testimony equivocal. "Let me say right here that the Chair thinks [Crouch] knows what he is talking about," interjected Eastland; "the FBI has gotten some very valuable information from this man and has confidence in what he says." Crouch had already testified about knowing Dombrowski and Sheiner as Communists in 1947, yet he said he had left the party in 1942. Miami party head Charles Smolikoff forced him to rejoin in 1947, he said, but in the intervening years he had lived in fear of being "liquidated by the International Soviet conspiracy" because he knew too much.[25]

Did he go to the FBI to report his fears between 1942 and 1947, asked Durr? Not until December of 1947, when he decided the Soviets would soon conquer the world and drop atomic bombs on the United States, replied the witness, and since then he had "devoted approximately 5,000 hours to giving the FBI information." He had broad knowledge, he said, of "the Communist access to information on the atomic bombs." Crouch reported two sources of income since 1947: the *Dade County News* in Miami, where, Durr pointed out, he had recently been involved in a case in which a libel judgment was obtained by an airline employee he accused of subversion, and the Justice Department, which paid his salary as an informant.[26]

24. SCEF Hearings, 1954, pp. 116–21, quotes on 117 and 121.
25. Ibid., 121–30, quotes on 124, 129 and 130.
26. Ibid., 130–33, quotes on 130.

When Durr asked Crouch to "prove" that he was no longer a Communist, Arens interrupted to ask, "Mr. Crouch, is Mr. Durr a Communist?" Perhaps Durr was no longer a party member, Crouch replied, but "yes, sir" he was a Communist at one time. The crowd in the courtroom snickered at this characterization of the gentlemanly southern lawyer at the bar, and Eastland moved to strike the testimony since Durr was not an official of SCEF, the subject of the investigation. But Durr dug in: "His testimony is on the record. Let's leave it under oath." As Durr directed the witness back to Williams, Crouch eventually took refuge in the statement that he had no personal knowledge of Williams as a Communist, but had accepted Rob Hall's word. He simply surmised that since that Williams' "public activities always coincided with the party line," and because Highlander founder Don West, whom he knew to be a Communist, had written for Williams' magazine *Southern Farm and Home,* Williams must be a party member. Arens questioned Williams again about his relationship with Hall and Lawrence, and Eastland prodded Williams to admit that SCEF was simply a continuation of SCHW, carefully referring to HUAC's 1947 assertion that Earl Browder had called SCHW the southern conduit for the CPUSA. When the committee finally released his friend and client, Durr reopened the subject of his own "subversion" with Crouch.[27]

Crouch tendered ambiguous and apparently unrehearsed testimony about Durr's alleged Communism. Again he named Alabama Communist Rob Hall as the person who identified Durr to him as a party member. He also claimed he had attended secret Communist Party meetings in New York with Durr, William Z. Foster, Earl Browder, Henry Winston, Eugene Dennis, and other top party officials five or six times between 1938 and 1941. He thought these meetings coincided with Durr's term on the FCC. Durr tried to pin him down, since his FCC service did not begin until 1941, but Crouch could not recall exactly when, exactly where, or exactly how many of the meetings he attended. He remembered being told to send copies of the Communist magazine *New South* to Durr as a "reliable comrade who would see that this was given personally to Justice Black." The informer reported that he had lost touch with Durr between 1941 and 1949, when by chance he recognized Durr at a HUAC hearing and quickly advised committee investigators of the previous

27. Ibid., 133–39, quotes on 133.

association. It was this happenstance, buttressed by FBI reports during his NLG and NFU years, that had inspired congressional censures of Durr in 1950 and 1951.[28]

Finally, in order to make a statement in rebuttal, Durr himself took the oath as a witness. Paul Crouch lied about seeing him at party meetings between 1938 and 1941, he said: "I have never been a member of the Communist Party." He had never considered it, and never would. Durr's declaration that "One or the other of us . . . should be indicted for perjury" capped his dismissal of Crouch's veracity.[29]

When Arens immediately began questioning Durr about his presidency of the NLG, Ben Smith stepped in to declare himself to be acting as witness Durr's lawyer. Durr claimed to be "very proud" of his guild association and of the NLG's fight against the methods of the FBI and congressional committees, and said he had opposed HUAC even before his guild membership. Arens asked about his friendship with Joseph Gelders, an Alabama leftist and one of the founders of SCHW. Durr had known Gelders as a student at the University of Alabama and described him as "a very fine person" who had remained an acquaintance until his death. Yes, he had attended the Wrocław conference in 1948 and the Bill of Rights Conference at the Waldorf sponsored by the CRC and others the next year, "and anything I can do toward alleviating world tensions I will do." When pressed for names of members of the One World Award Committee who made the trip to Poland, however, he decided to take the same position his wife had chosen, to "invoke all the provisions of the Constitution . . . which protect me in my rights . . . all except the self-incrimination clause." He would give straightforward answers to questions about himself, but he refused to take the chance of incriminating others or, on the other hand, to take refuge in the Fifth Amendment as though he had some guilty secret to hide.[30]

The next morning Durr resumed the stand to answer questions about his relationship with the liberal NFU. The committee then called a final witness, Californian Richard English, to testify that the NFU (which had at one time

28. Ibid., 139–44, quote on 142; for Durr's denunciation by Congress see Chapter 4 of this text.

29. SCEF Hearings, 1954, p. 144.

30. Ibid., 145–48.

employed both Williams and Durr and maintained a close relationship with Highlander as well) had been under Communist control until the early 1950s. But before Crouch took the stand for a last time or English was announced, Smith stood to request that as Durr's lawyer he be allowed to cross-examine Crouch. Eastland accused him of making a speech and rejected his appeal.[31]

After Durr had received the right to cross-examine, he asked several times that the other attorneys be allowed the same privilege. Eastland refused on the grounds that "people who are in contempt of this committee are not going to be permitted to ask questions." His reasoning appeared a little muddy. Williams, like Dombrowski, had declined to turn over the names of SCEF's contributors, though without explanation Eastland and Arens did not insist that Williams state his grounds for noncompliance with the committee's *subpoena duces tecum*. Why was Dombrowski "in contempt" but not Williams? Why was Williams' lawyer alone allowed to cross-examine Crouch? Sheiner and Schlafrock, while they refused to testify after initial disclosure of biographical data, had done so on the constitutionally accepted grounds of Fifth Amendment privilege. Eastland might disdain these witnesses, but they had not perjured themselves and it is doubtful that they could have been the subjects of legal contempt proceedings. No such charge had ever been upheld by the Supreme Court. Though they all denied Communist Party membership, only Virginia and Cliff Durr and Jim Dombrowski had refused both to answer some of the committee's questions and to invoke the privilege against self-incrimination. Myles Horton never had a chance to state his objections.[32]

Horton's testimony, the briefest heard in three days of hearings, began with his description of Highlander. When he started a statement about his reasons for not wanting to answer a question about Dombrowski, Eastland cut him off at midsentence. Horton argued with the chairman—"Won't you listen to an American talk?"—and Eastland ordered federal marshals to escort

---

31. Ibid., 148–50, 157–59.

32. Ibid., 135, 137, 150, quote on 137. See Goodman, *Committee,* 351–52; Caute, *Great Fear,* 147–52; Victor Rabinowitz, *Unrepentant Leftist: A Lawyer's Memoir* (Urbana, Ill., 1996), 117–30; and esp. Carl Beck, *Contempt of Congress: A Study of Prosecutions Initiated by the Committee on Un-American Activities, 1945–1957* (1959; rpr. New York, 1974), Appendix B, 217–40, for the First and Fifth Amendments and contempt citations.

him from the room. As they led him out, Horton shouted, "They're treating me like a criminal!" "We are not," the chairman maintained, "going to have any self-serving declarations."[33]

Arens asked Crouch to return to the stand to "clean up a couple of items." The informant's final testimony amplified and expanded his previous statements. He talked about conspiratorial southern Communists who were personal friends of President and Mrs. Roosevelt and accused Virginia Durr of being fully cognizant of a clandestine alliance active in the South in the 1930s and 1940s. She had been important because of her relationship to Justice Black, he said for the third or fourth time.[34]

Surely politics provided the clue to Eastland's motives. When he ran successfully for reelection the following fall, the Supreme Court and its "New Deal liberal" champions, not his Mississippi opponent, became the focus of his campaign. The hearings provided publicity and propaganda linking the integrationist Supreme Court and the New Deal to a "communist-inspired" nexus of southern liberals. In the aftermath of the hearings, Cliff Durr wrote to NLG lawyer Frank Donner that "the motivation for the affair was obvious." Eastland, worried about a strong opponent in his upcoming reelection campaign, challenged SCEF in order to "whip up the white supremacy issue." The really amusing thing, Durr concluded, was that attorney Arens, a conservative Republican, had tried to stress an anti–Democratic Party "twenty years of treason" theme, which occasionally resulted in some "rather amusing conflicts between Eastland and his counsel." The Republicans were worried about black votes in states outside the South, Durr surmised, a concern that had no significance for Eastland's campaign in Mississippi.[35]

After Eastland returned to Washington from his fact-finding mission, SISS's "report" found no substantive difference between the supposedly subversive defunct SCHW and its heir, SCEF, and recommended that the Subversive Activities Control Board (SACB) list SCEF. Yet, probably because the Durrs and Williams still had important friends in the government, the SACB never acted on the report and Eastland's threats of contempt citations never

33. SCEF Hearings, 1954, pp. 150–51; quotes in New York *Times,* Sunday, March 21, 1954, pp. 1, 31.
34. SCEF Hearings, 1954, pp. 151–55, quote on 151.
35. C. J. Durr to Frank Donner, October 28, 1954, in Box 2, Folder 7, C. J. Durr Papers.

materialized. Despite the power of the southern conservative block in Congress, Eastland was not the Senate's best or most respected negotiator. In addition, most senators probably recognized that Eastland's political goals had been fulfilled simply by holding the hearings.[36]

The editor of the St. Petersburg *Times* defended the Durrs and Williams as decent and honorable southern liberals who had been the objects of a "character lynching." He called Eastland "ultra-conservative even among southern Democrats" and asked for his censure by other Democratic senators. The Mississippi senator's attempts to label southern liberals Communists amounted to "political opportunism" just like that practiced by McCarthy. "Responsible southern Senators cannot pass the buck," he wrote, but must reproach Eastland just as responsible Republicans were speaking out against McCarthy. But Eastland's southern Senate colleagues would never have permitted the exposure of his motives at such a critical hour in southern history, regardless of the political credit Republicans accrued by purging themselves of McCarthy later in 1954. After the hearings Eastland planned to pursue the Durrs and Williams again, and he asked the FBI for Alabama informants to testify against them. But Lyndon Johnson, Lister Hill, and other influential friends of the Durrs and Williams quietly discouraged an investigation planned for Birmingham or Montgomery later that year, a great blessing for the Montgomery liberals, whose lives in Alabama were sufficiently disrupted by the New Orleans experience.[37]

Durr wound up in a New Orleans Hospital with a mild heart attack after lunging at Crouch as the hearings dispersed and crying, "You dirty dog! I'll kill you for lying about my wife!" The incident resulted in a week of hospitalization; widely reported in the press, it brought many letters of encouragement and sympathy for Durr's position. Newspapers in Montgomery, Washington, and New York also generally supported the Durrs and Williams while harshly criticizing Eastland.[38]

36. SCEF Hearings, 1954, "Report," v–viii.

37. St. Petersburg *Times,* Tuesday, March 23, 1954, p. 6; Memos, R. R. Roach to A. H. Belmont, May 7, 1958, and G. A. Nease to Mr. Tolson, May 19, 1958, Smith FBI File; Virginia Van der Veer Hamilton, *Lister Hill: Statesman from the South* (Chapel Hill, 1987), 211.

38. *Alabama Journal* (Birmingham), March 19, 22, 25, 1954, New York *Times,* March 21, 1954, pp. 1, 31, Washington *Evening Star,* March 20, 1954, pp. 1, 3, Washington *Post,* March

Though the New Orleans papers sensationalized the hearings, they published so many long pages of revealing testimony that Dombrowski thought the public persecution might actually have gained SCEF adherents among southern liberals. Thirty-two prominent black southerners signed an open letter to Senator Jenner protesting the unfairness of the attack on SCEF, and a biracial group including both Eleanor Roosevelt and Mary McLeod Bethune dispatched another letter of protest. The second letter was sponsored first by Ethel Clyde, a New York left-wing philanthropist and longtime SCEF backer. Mrs. Clyde attended the hearings and generously provided hotel accommodations and meals for the SCEF board members called to New Orleans. SCEF contributions trebled in the first half of 1954, and the size of its board increased in May, when John Coe's official relationship as a SCEF board member began.[39]

For the south Florida participants, however, harassment persisted in the press, with attempts made almost immediately to deprive them of professional prerogatives. Damon Runyon, Jr., with the help of a reconstructed ex-Communist named Al Spears, authored a long series of irresponsible, inflammatory articles for the Miami *News*. Runyon called the First Unitarian Church of Miami a "communist cell" and the progressive Jewish Cultural Center of Miami Beach a "nest of reds." In his stories he listed members of these religious organizations as well as persons who had been members of the Lincoln Brigade, the Progressive Party, the CRC, or the NLG. Runyon identified John Coe and Miami attorney Louis Glick as part of "a legal clique with a record of representing Communists"—which, of course, they were.[40]

21, 1954, p. 1, *I. F. Stone's Weekly,* March 29, 1954, and many letters of sympathy and support written to the Durrs in the wake of the hearings, all in Box 2, Folder 6, C. J. Durr Papers.

39. Front-page and inside stories about the hearings appeared in all three New Orleans papers, the *Times-Picayune, States,* and *Item,* March 18–21, 1954; *Arkansas State Press,* March 26, 1954, Jim Dombrowski for SCEF to "Dear Friend," n.d., in Box 23, Folder 19, Braden Papers; "Minutes of the Board of Directors, Southern Conference Educational Fund, Butler Street YMCA, Atlanta," May 8, 1954, in Box 48, Folder 16, Coe Papers. Mrs. Clyde was heir to the Clyde Steamship Company fortune. See Barnard, ed., *Outside the Magic Circle,* 257–68, 264–66.

40. Miami *Herald,* n.d. [March, 1954], in Box 47, Folder 35, Miami *News,* June 21, 1954, and n.d. (three articles), in Box 48, Folder 12, and "Plan for Victory Against the McCarthy-Brownell Witchhunt in Florida," attached to letter, Mynelle to J. M. Coe, September 1, 1954, in Box 2, Folder 22, all in Coe Papers.

The Dade County grand jury hearings continued relentlessly. In one action, State's Attorney Brautigam moved to institute disbarment proceedings against Leo Sheiner based on his refusal to answer Eastland's questions. In another, he began contempt proceedings against several other leftists, including Max Schlafrock, who had taken the Fifth Amendment in federal grand jury hearings even before the Eastland proceeding. Coe became immediately involved in the latter case and eventually the primary litigator in the former.

Sheiner's ordeal began with the Eastland hearings and continued until the Florida bar readmitted him in 1959, by which time he had left Miami to practice in his native New York. The Florida attorney general based his case not only on Sheiner's use of the Fifth Amendment in New Orleans but on his alleged association with the NLG, the CRC, SCEF, and the Communist Party—all, according to his briefs, "organizations advocating and teaching the theory of forceful overthrow of the Constitutional form of government of the United States of America." One difficulty with the allegation that Sheiner had belonged to the Communist Party was its primary source, an informant named Joseph Mazzei, whose testimony in federal courts proved to be as trustworthy as that of Paul Crouch. Chief Justice Earl Warren warned that Mazzei "poisoned the well" of evidence with his frequent perjury and, after causing an important case to be retried in 1956, should never again be accepted as a federal witness. With Mazzei discredited and his testimony stricken, the circuit court on third hearing of the case dismissed the disbarment action, and in 1958 Coe convinced the Florida Supreme Court to reject a state appeal.[41]

By 1958 the Tallahassee court had heard the Sheiner case four times, remanding it to the circuit jurisdiction for retrial three times. Both the Florida Bar Association and the ABA wrote amicus briefs opposing Sheiner's reinstatement. The Anti-Communist Committee of the ABA took the firm position in this case as in others that "attorneys who seek protection of the Fifth Amendment are not qualified to retain their licenses" and urged the court to disbar Sheiner as a precedent for cases elsewhere. The NLG and the ACLU supported the four decisions of Florida's high court, maintaining, as did the

41. *Sheiner* v. *Florida* 82 So. 2d 657, 662 (Fla. 1955, 1957); quote in *State of Florida* v. *Leo Sheiner,* "Judgement and Opinion," Circuit Court of the Eleventh Circuit of Florida, Dade County, April 5, 1957, p. 2, in Box 53, Folder 45, Coe Papers; Caute, *Great Fear,* 222.

court, that being a lawyer did not abrogate Sheiner's constitutional right to exercise Fifth Amendment protections against self-incrimination and that the state had not proved that Sheiner had violated the bar's code of ethics.[42]

"Invoking the Fifth Amendment may or may not imply good character," read the decision, "neither does it prove guilt." The only "evidence" incriminating Sheiner, besides his use of the Fifth Amendment, was testimony from the SCEF hearings about "activities that took place seven years before this proceeding was brought." The court noted that "before the Congressional Committee, appellant was denied the right of confrontation and cross-examination." Cross-examination of the two witnesses who testified against Sheiner—Paul Crouch in New Orleans and Joseph Mazzei before a Florida panel—would have been a delight for his attorney, John Coe.[43]

After the final state supreme court argument, Louis Jepeway, the Miami attorney associated with Coe in this case, wrote to Sheiner that "John Coe was simply magnificent . . . at the completion of his presentation those present—and a number of lawyers were present—almost broke out into applause." As in the Benemovsky case, Coe took great pride in winning *Sheiner* v. *State,* which proved to be critical litigation. The United States attorney general refused to take action to bring about federal disbarments until state and local courts had acted, and after Sheiner's first victory in the Florida Supreme Court, Herbert O'Conor of the ABA reported that his committee's efforts to disbar radical lawyers in other states had been stymied.[44]

State's Attorney Brautigam fought mightily for Sheiner's disbarment and for the conviction of Charles Smolikoff and Michael Shantzek, Coe's clients indicted for contempt after the grand jury hearings. The cases of these two men were joined with those of New Orleans witness Schlafrock, ten other Jewish Miamians, and one Cuban American for the appeal. Paul Crouch visited Tallahassee to give a deposition to Assistant Attorney General Ellis Rubin denouncing most of the defendants, but Smolikoff had already been

42. *Sheiner* v. *Florida;* Baily, "The Case of the NLG," in *Beyond the Hiss Case,* ed. Theoharis, 159.

43. *Sheiner* v. *Florida;* Baily, "The Case of the NLG," in *Beyond the Hiss Case,* ed. Theoharis, 159; Ginger and Tobin, eds., *NLG,* 145.

44. Baily, "The Case of the NLG," in *Beyond the Hiss Case,* ed. Theoharis, 159; Louis M. Jepeway to Leo Sheiner, September 4, 1958, in Box 53, Folder 41, Coe Papers.

identified as a Communist organizer on several occasions, including the 1948 Miami HUAC hearings, and Shantzek had recently been the subject of several Runyon attacks. Publicity had been the natural result of his refusal, in June, to take a loyalty oath demanded by co-workers in the Painters Union.[45]

Coe and his fellow lawyers again succeeded in their appeal. Though the justices explained in lengthy opinions their reluctance to rule against the state, the supreme court discharged the petitioners on legal grounds. Coe said "the court really dished out a poisonous analysis of the situation to show its purity and unwillingness to decide as it did," but he thought maybe the excesses of the decision's language might help "in future proceedings to test the constitutional validity of Chapter 876," Florida's "little Smith Act."[46]

Yet a month later, Coe appeared reluctant to become involved in such a suit because, upon careful reading of the decision and Chapter 876, he saw little chance of success. Nevertheless, having committed himself to the cause, he associated with Frank Donner of the New York firm of Donner, Kinoy and Perlin to seek a federal injunction against Florida's antisubversive laws. When the federal district judge ruled against him in December, 1954, and Donner urged an appeal, Coe refused to go forward with the case. The judge "had done exactly what I myself would ultimately have done if I had been on the bench," he said. Ever the pragmatist, he had no interest in continuing what seemed to him a pointless effort, and the case was eventually dropped.[47] During the time that their appeal remained under advisement in federal court, some of these defendants answered subpoenas of HUAC, which convened in Miami November 29 through December 1, 1954. Smolikoff, like Leah Benemovsky in 1948, had been sent to jail when he invoked Fifth Amendment protections before the Dade County grand jury. HUAC's appearance boded no good for him, and he fled to a safe haven in Mexico; but several of Coe's

45. "Plan for Victory Against McCarthy-Brownell Witchhunt in Florida," attached to letter, Mynelle to Mr. Coe, September 1, 1954, in Box 2, Folder 22, Miami *News,* June 21, 1954, in Box 48, Folder 12, and Miami *News,* n.d. [November, 1954], in Box 49, Folder 9, all in Coe Papers.

46. "In the Supreme Court of Florida, June Term, 1954, *State ex rel. Phil Feldman et al., Petitioners* v. *Thomas J. Kelly, Respondent,* Opinion," J. M. Coe to Louis Glick, November 22, 1954, in Box 48, Folder 12, ibid.

47. J. M. Coe to Frank Donner, November 23, December 16, 26, 1954, January 4, 1955 [misdated 1954], in Box 9, Folder 49, ibid.

other Miami acquaintances, among them Shantzek and Schlafrock, testified at these hearings.[48]

On a more personal level, the fallout from the SCEF hearings affected the Durr, Coe, and Smith families. After his hospitalization in New Orleans, Cliff Durr was advised to rest, so the family spent the summer in New England at the invitation of friends. When they returned to Montgomery, his practice, never thriving, dropped off considerably. Most people did not really believe that they were Communists, Virginia Durr said, but prospective clients rejected a lawyer touched by such unfavorable publicity. The Durrs' three daughters still at home in 1954 endured many unkindnesses meted out by children, teachers, and parents.[49] Coe's five children were older, his oldest son having recently become his law partner and the youngest just entering medical school, but they also felt the sting of rumor and ostracism as a result of local publicity surrounding the hearings. Not a new experience, such irritations had followed them at least since the 1948 campaign. The Coe children faced an environment in which their father's views were usually misunderstood and often ridiculed.[50]

Ben Smith's first child, only two years old in 1954, probably experienced little fallout from the SCEF hearings, but Smith's brother, a young air force officer stationed in Seattle, Washington, did. Air force intelligence officers interrogated Patrick Smith twice during the mid-1950s, asking questions about his politics. Unaware of his brother's activities and frightened and confused by the questioning, he asked his commanding officer to make sure no black marks remained on his permanent service record. Finally a full colonel questioned him about Ben Smith and accepted his word that he was not "mixed up" in his brother's radical politics.[51] The FBI redoubled its efforts

48. U.S. Congress, House Un-American Activities Committee, *Investigation of Communist Activities in the State of Florida,* Part I and Part II (Miami), 83rd Cong., 2nd Sess., November 30–December 1, 1954 [hereinafter cited as Florida HUAC Hearings, 1954]; Eric Tscheschlok, "'So Goes the Negro': Race and Labor in Miami, 1940–63," *Florida Historical Quarterly,* LXXVI (Summer, 1997), 63, 67; Raymond H. Mohl, "'South of the South': Jews, Blacks, and the Civil Rights Movement in Miami, 1945–1960," forthcoming in the *Journal of American Ethnic History* (1998).

49. Barnard, ed., *Outside the Magic Circle,* 269–70.

50. Coe-Grubbs interview.

51. Smith interview.

to gather information on participants in the wake of the southern congressional investigations.

As a result of the publicity SCEF received during the congressional hearings, a young editor of the New Orleans Chamber of Commerce "News Bulletin" lost his job. Ben Smith's client, Robert Barnes, refused to resign from SCEF or to discontinue his association with Jim Dombrowski when told that the chamber of commerce considered the connection "inimical to his relations with the public." Not having a contract, Barnes could not sue to recapture the position. But upon being denied unemployment compensation because, according to the Louisiana Labor Department, "he was guilty of misconduct to his employment," he sued the state and the chamber of commerce. Smith won a memorable judgment for his client. In his statement, the Louisiana district court judge, L. H. Yarrut, said that SCHW, SCEF, or Dombrowski had never been "judicially charged or proved to be Communistic. . . . The substance of the evidence against Dr. Dombrowski is that he neither condemned nor excluded Communists from any of his organizations. The gravamen of the evidence against the Fund and its members is that they aggressively espouse integration of the races."[52] Kinder and closer to the truth than most evaluations the organization received, Judge Yarrut's statement endured as a rare exculpation for SCEF.

Nevertheless, as the civil rights struggle developed, SCEF not only suffered denunciation from segregationists but increasing isolation from the mainstream of the integration movement it passionately espoused. Eastland's persecution may have, as Dombrowski at first believed, attracted some new followers, but it failed to improve the organization's image among liberals of the vital center, black or white.

In mid-1956 SCEF was excluded from a Washington conference of civil rights leaders who announced to the press that the meeting included "only those organizations whose Americanism was above suspicion." In response to this slight, SCEF president Aubrey Williams composed a long letter to black labor leader A. Philip Randolph, explaining the precarious position

52. *Robert D. Barnes* v. *Administrator, Division of Unemployment Security, Department of Labor, State of Louisiana, and the Chamber of Commerce of the New Orleans Area, Inc. (Employer)*, Civil District Court for the Parish of New Orleans, Division "C," No. 347-562, Docket No. 5, *Judgment*, in Box 3, Folder 58, Coe Papers.

occupied by white southerners who espoused black equality. Other white southerners labeled them "communists" long ago, and "that is the Southerner's definition of the word communist." Dies and Eastland committee propaganda could expect success among southern conservatives, but he grieved that "they succeeded with the national leaders of the CIO and Afofl and the NAACP also." Eastland's whole idea was to destroy the effectiveness of white liberals in the South by naming them traitors. SCEF expected more understanding from like-minded liberals in the North.[53]

In the mid-1950s the NAACP and its lawyers remained the primary force behind civil rights change, and SCEF, in spite of its militancy and radical reputation, was the NAACP's most zealous southern support group. Thus rejection by the NAACP not only wounded SCEF but undermined its very reason for being. The perplexing estrangement of SCEF from the NAACP is well illustrated by a series of letters between Professor Albert Barnett of the Candler School of Theology of Emory University, a SCEF board member, and the NAACP's Roy Wilkins, chairman of the Leadership Conference on Civil Rights (LCCR). SCEF sought membership in this coordinating group in 1957, but Wilkins and his subordinates, obviously avoiding the real issue of SCEF's notoriety, first refused it entrance to LCCR on spurious grounds, then declined to answer SCEF's letters asking for an explanation. And although Williams' letter to Randolph the year before had indicated that southern black leaders, unlike their northern counterparts, appreciated maligned white liberals, southern civil rights organizations also became concerned about appearances and dodged controversial left-wing sympathizers. As the southern movement took fire in the late 1950s, Martin Luther King, Jr., cautiously advised fledgling Southern Christian Leadership Conference organizer Bob Moses to stay away from projects sponsored by SCEF in order to keep the movement free of the stain of Communism.[54]

Congressional hearings and state-sponsored anti-Communism devastated

---

53. Aubrey Williams to A. Philip Randolph, July 10, 1956, in Box 3, Folder 60, ibid.

54. Ibid.; Albert E. Barnett, "SCEF Committee on Relationships with Other Agencies, 1956–1957," to Roy Wilkins, December 4, 1956, Wilkins to Barnett, February 4, 1957, Anne Braden to Wilkins, n.d. [March, 1957], John A. Morell to Braden, April 3, 1957, and Barnett to Morell, April 10, 1957, all in Box 23, Folder 1, Braden Papers. Martin Luther King, Jr., always maintained friendly personal relations with SCEF. See Branch, *Parting the Waters*, 328.

the fragment of popular front liberalism remaining in the South, and the persecution of such leftists increased as the civil rights movement developed. The New Orleans *Item* ran a series of six half-page articles in 1957 titled "What Is SCEF?" which, according to Dombrowski, never addressed SCEF's purpose or programs but, relying on the testimony of "former convicts" like Crouch and Butler, used "the words Communist, Communism, Communist Front, Fellow Traveler, etc., 105 times."[55]

Again in New Orleans in 1956 and 1957 and in Miami, Charlotte, Memphis, and Atlanta, SISS and HUAC investigators tried to connect SCEF to the Communist Party. Anti-Communism exploded in the South as the civil rights movement developed, but at the same time single-minded civil rights leaders sought to divorce themselves from superfluous controversy by rejecting suspicious allies. Discrimination and isolation hounded not only black integrationists and the few authentic southern Communists or former Communists of both races. It also followed the scattering of white southerners who distrusted cold war militarism, feared the suppression of dissent, and extolled an old-fashioned liberalism rooted in the openness and idealism of the New Deal era.

55. "The New Orleans *Item's* Report on SCEF," in Box 16, Folder 10, Dombrowski Papers.

CHAPTER SIX

After *Brown:*

Congressional Anti-Communism and

Southern "Sedition," 1954–1961

Because the CPUSA had advocated civil rights for black southerners at least since it led the fight for the Scottsboro defendants in the early 1930s, and since many Communists had supported Henry Wallace's refusal to speak before segregated southern audiences in 1948, identification of integrationists with the Communist Party made sense to many southerners. In addition, most southern politicians found it logical, convincing, and profitable to combine Red-baiting with race-baiting. Anti-Communism had gripped the whole nation in the early 1950s; white supremacists had many allies, even after McCarthy's censure, in equating nonconformity with political radicalism.

After the *Brown* decision, the search for southern subversives intensified. The mandate to end segregation encountered and animated southern anti-Communism at high tide. State and federal grand juries reinstituted investigations connecting local Communists to integrationism in both Miami and New Orleans in 1954. Mississippi, Louisiana, Florida, Virginia, Georgia, and Arkansas all established or strengthened antiradical laws and investigatory committees of their legislatures in that year or soon after. They held hearings to identify and officially label integrationists and their organizations both criminal and subversive. Called by such misnomers as "Education Commission" (Georgia), "Sovereignty Commissions" (Mississippi and Arkansas), or committees to investigate "Offenses Against the Administration of Justice" (Virginia) or on "Constitutional Government" (Alabama, which established its committee late, in 1963), these groups had identical purposes. Many—perhaps even most—white southerners accepted the proposition that Communists guided, or at the very least infiltrated, the integration movement for their own sinister purposes. Some believed that by proving this they could turn back the clock.[1]

Federal hearings blessed these similar regional efforts with the sanction of the federal government. Despite the decline of anti-Communism as a national political issue after 1954, confrontations between southern liberals and federal anti-Communists, especially SISS and HUAC, accelerated. Hearings conducted outside the South also sometimes focused on southern groups, and federal investigators and their ubiquitous informants eagerly aided the proliferating local grand juries and state anti-Communist committees. Congressional inquiries into southern subversion climaxed in 1958 with HUAC hearings in Atlanta involving SCEF staff member and Coe client Carl Braden. As a result Braden faced trial and finally imprisonment for contempt of Congress in 1961. He and Frank Wilkinson, his co-defendant, became the last persons jailed for contempt of the House Un-American Activities Committee.

The scope of federally sponsored anti-Communism in the South has sometimes been underestimated. House or Senate committees held hearings in the South eight times. Excepting an early foray into Florida in 1948, these proceedings all occurred between 1954 and 1958. After the Democrats regained control of Congress in November, 1954, James Eastland was named permanent chairman of SISS. Over the protests of the NAACP and liberals all over the country, he became head of the full Senate Judiciary Committee in 1957.[2]

Although the SCEF hearings chaired by Eastland in New Orleans have received by far the most scholarly attention, the crusade John Salmond called the "Great Southern Commie Hunt"[3] had many other manifestations. The SISS "report" containing the committee's vituperative conclusions about the

---

1. Celinni, ed., *Digest of Communism*, 455; "Notes from Research in Nashville," Box 50, Folder 11, Braden Papers.

2. "An Appeal to Senators of the 85th Congress from the National Association for the Advancement of Colored People Urging That Senator Eastland Not Be Seated on the Senate Judiciary Committee," March 1, 1957, and "Eastland Heads Judiciary over Douglas' Opposition," *Fairmont Times* (UP), January 10, 1957, in Box 23, Folder 2, ibid.

3. John A. Salmond, "'The Great Southern Commie Hunt': Aubrey Williams, the Southern Conference Educational Fund, and the Internal Security Subcommittee," *South Atlantic Quarterly*, LXXVII (Autumn, 1978), 433–52. This early article, a balanced account of the 1954 proceedings in New Orleans, contends that there were "no further investigations and nothing was done about their report" (452).

hearings and SCEF's subversion was used repeatedly as holy writ by federal and state investigators hounding white integrationists. And despite Eastland's cancellation—after pressure from Lyndon Johnson and other friends of Aubrey Williams and the Durrs—of announced hearings in Birmingham, he accomplished similar purposes in other locations. Mississippi's energetic senior senator brought his panel back to the Crescent City just two years later, in the midst of the Montgomery bus boycott, and took it to Memphis in 1957, not long after Eisenhower sent troops to restore order in nearby Little Rock. In addition to the southern forays of the Senate's anti-Communist committee, the House committee investigated Communism in Miami in 1948 and 1954, Charlotte in 1956, New Orleans in 1957, and Atlanta in 1958. John Coe's client Leah Benemovsky first faced a grand jury probe and contempt indictment as a result of HUAC's 1948 visit to Miami. While ostensibly designed to investigate such local subversion, the southern hearings often overlapped in confusing ways. For instance, HUAC subpoenaed North Carolina suspects to Miami in 1954; and New Orleanians unavailable when the committee visited that city in 1956 were rounded up for the Memphis hearings in 1957, which in spite of their venue centered more on Kentucky than Tennessee affairs.

In other parts of the country, HUAC and SISS often centered anti-Communist investigations on liberal churchmen, dissident university professors, or left-wing unionists. Unrepentant New Dealers joined suspected Communists, fellow travelers, and former Communists on committee witness stands. The seven investigations conducted in the South between 1954 and 1958 often ferreted out similar game to support their antiliberal objectives. But the southern hearings also echoed distinctively regional themes and finally ended where they began, in a determined attempt to bolster southern resistance and brand white integrationists as traitors. Although Communists or former Communists were witnesses (often friendly witnesses) in all southern hearings, in most cases they were part of a sideshow that did not obscure the main event. SISS staff members applauded the identification of a genuine black Communist in New Orleans, but they worked just as diligently at branding non-Communist black integrationists dupes of a movement infiltrated or led by the CPUSA. The party's clever rhetoric and agitation, according to this view, brought a few blacks into the party and fooled many others into going along. This attitude, which pervades the committee transcripts, was accepted as reasonable by most committee lawyers, including many who were not southerners. White integrationists were presumed to be disloyal Americans, and black witnesses faced patronizing, condescending, or contemptuous federal examiners. Disparagement of the manifestly anti-Communist NAACP often capped these efforts.

Other congressional committee goals in the South included collecting evidence for the prosecution of Junius Scales, the North Carolina Communist whose Smith Act case paralleled the congressional hearings from Miami in 1954 to Atlanta in 1958; ferreting out subversion in southern unions, especially integrated unions; and gathering testimony to support pending bills, especially those designed to squelch Supreme Court civil libertarianism. Anti-alien propaganda also made very good politics in the changing South. Senator Eastland ran successfully for reelection just after the SCEF hearings in 1954 and in succeeding years, with campaign rhetoric focused squarely on the Supreme Court and its "communist-inspired" liberal champions.

Many of John Coe's political allies in the late 1940s were members of Miami's vital left-wing community, which included a substantial number of party sympathizers. Henry Wallace received more votes there than in any other part of the South, and many Progressives were also members of the Civil Rights Congress, which maintained an active chapter in Miami from 1948 until 1951. Communist organizers worked in several Florida unions. But by 1954 the Florida party had dwindled and, in words taken from Junius Scales's autobiography, "was full of aged northern Jewish retirees scarcely suited for much activity." In late 1954, members of this group—most from the Miami or Tampa areas—and a variety of other witnesses received subpoenas from HUAC. Testimony gathered from the men and women summoned to Miami confirms Scales's assessment of the local organization.[4]

The 1954 HUAC hearings in Miami, chaired by Harold H. Velde of Illinois, began typically with several former members of the once active Communist Party in south Florida. The chairman acknowledged that "as a result of the 1948 [HUAC] hearings the Communist Party in Miami was dealt a serious blow," and announced that he sought the "hard core of dedicated revolu-

4. Brown, "Pensacola Progressive," 13, 22; Mohl, "South of the South"; Junius Irving Scales and Richard Nickson, *Cause at Heart: A Former Communist Remembers* (Athens, Ga., 1987), 249.

tionaries" left in the area in order to deliver "a death blow to communism in the great State of Florida and the southeastern area of these United States." In addition to summoning Miami witnesses, the committee inquired into Communism in Tampa, especially in the Cigar Workers Union, and in Jacksonville. Several black ex-Communists, primarily members of the Dade County Laundry Workers Union, testified as friendly witnesses that the Communist Party practiced segregation and had not delivered on its promise to help southern blacks. This theme reappeared sixteen months later when HUAC investigated North Carolina Communists.[5]

Only ten days before the Miami hearings, a federal grand jury had indicted Junius Scales for violating the membership clause of the Smith Act. As a result, the committee actually began its inquiry into North Carolina subversion at the Miami hearings. Scales, son of a prominent southern family, had participated in the North Carolina branch of the SCHW and, more important, led public Communist Party meetings in Chapel Hill in the mid-1940s. After "going underground" in the 1950s, he was responsible for party activities in Virginia, Tennessee, and northern Mississippi. Two witnesses at the Miami hearings described Scales's activities in detail and named many other southern party members. One former North Carolinian, in 1954 a University of Miami drama professor, denied party membership but acknowledged meeting Scales as a member of a study and discussion group in Chapel Hill. Another, brought to Miami by HUAC from his home in Durham, claimed a long and close relationship with Scales. The second witness was Ralph Long, a young man with an extensive history of mental problems and alcoholism. He had been dropped from the party in 1948, then volunteered for FBI duty. Scales contended that Long "had been taken either from the gutter or from the jail to perform."[6]

Besides extensive testimony about Scales and Communist organizations and their influence, Long also affirmed that "the party exploits the Negro" in North Carolina. He named many other southern party members, including Coe's client Sam Hall, and related Communist plans for taking over such organizations as SCHW. His lengthy testimony, rambling and detailed, re-

5. Florida HUAC Hearings, 1954, pp. 7287–89, quotes on 7288.

6. Ibid., 7325–72; Scales and Nickson, *Cause at Heart*, see esp. 237–40, quote on 237; Buhle, Buhle, and Georgakas, eds., *Encyclopedia of the American Left*, 676–77.

mained unchallenged and unverified. Four years later, in Atlanta, a beleaguered witness said Long had been "convicted about 20 or 30 times of drunkenness and disorderly conduct in Chapel Hill," an accusation verified by David Caute, who says the government witness was "tried twenty times for public drunkenness and once for assault and battery" between 1949 and 1954. Nevertheless, his testimony seems to have been accepted as credible. Both segregationists eager to discourage southern iconoclasts and federal prosecutors seeking to convict Junius Scales relied heavily on Long's evidence, citing this transcript repeatedly.[7]

Ralph Long rated mention several times, but was not called to testify, when HUAC continued its investigation of subversion in North Carolina at meetings in Charlotte in March, 1956. Junius Scales again became a primary target of the committee. His district court conviction had been upheld by the Fourth Circuit, and the case was within days of being granted its first Supreme Court review.[8] The Charlotte hearings centered on testimony of several North Carolina ex-Communists, two of whom were also witnesses for the prosecution in Scales's trials. One of these was Ralph Clontz, who had enlisted with the FBI before he joined Scales's Carolina Communists in 1948. Another young man, Charles Childs, explained his indoctrination and training as a Communist under Scales guidance.[9]

With the help of attorney Richard Arens, late of SISS and now counsel for HUAC, the attending congressmen also inquired into Communism in black colleges, unions, and leftist alliances such as the National Negro Labor Council. Several of those subpoenaed were teachers in black colleges or active members of the North Carolina NAACP. Arens and the chairman, Representative Edwin E. Willis of Louisiana, pressed their informants to demonstrate a relationship between the NAACP and the Communist Party. A black ex-Communist testified that he and a friend had been told by Junius Scales to

---

7. Florida HUAC Hearings, 1954, pp. 7325–72, quote on 7359; U.S. Congress, House Un-American Activities Committee, *Communist Infiltration in the South, Hearings Before the Committee on Un-American Activities* (Atlanta), 85th Cong., 2nd Sess., July 29, 30, 31, 1958, p. 2651 [hereinafter cited as Atlanta HUAC Hearings, 1958]; Caute, *Great Fear,* 548.

8. *Scales* v. *U.S.,* 367 U.S. 203 (1961).

9. U.S. Congress, House Un-American Activities Committee, *Investigation of Communist Activities in the North Carolina Area* (Charlotte), 84th Cong., 2nd Sess., March 12, 13, 14, 1956, see esp. 3506–56.

attend an NAACP meeting in Durham "as Communists, separate and apart from the NAACP, but to aid NAACP activity." In a turnaround from the usual depiction of blacks as dupes of white subversives, Clontz accused Nathaniel Bond, a language professor who headed the "North Carolina Conference of Youth Councils and College Chapters of the NAACP" of hiding "behind his supposed connection to the NAACP" while he ran the party, with Scales and others as front men. But Clontz also reported that unsuspecting black ministers often allowed closet Communists to use their buildings "through the misapprehension that they are helping the cause of justice."[10]

The time was ripe for such a correlation. Attacks on the NAACP and its allies, groups such as the CIO, the Urban League, and the National Council of Churches, had become irrational but at the same time officially sanctioned in the southern states. In May, 1955, the Supreme Court ordered these states to conform to the 1954 desegregation decision, directing them to undo segregation in public education "with all deliberate speed." A few weeks later the national NAACP urged its branches to file petitions asking local school boards to obey the directive. Across the South, legislative committees formed and legislators passed bills to combat subversion, many openly aimed at the NAACP. Five states enacted laws requiring the NAACP to register as a subversive organization and list its members and contributors. In January, 1956, the Chicago *Tribune* quoted Eastland as saying that organizations supporting the NAACP ran the gamut "from the blood red of the Communist Party to the almost equal red of the National Council of Churches of Christ in the USA." On March 12, 1956, the day HUAC hearings opened in North Carolina, 80 percent of the members of Congress representing the states of the former Confederacy signed a document that became known as the "Southern Manifesto," a direct challenge to *Brown* encouraging states to resist compliance. Among southern senators only Lyndon Johnson, Albert Gore, and Estes Kefauver refused to sign.[11]

In the two years since the SCEF hearings in New Orleans, the South had become an armed camp. White reactions to the NAACP petitions for support of *Brown* were an important element in the germination of the ardently right-

10. Ibid., quotes on 3641 and 3552.

11. Notes on Chicago *Tribune* article, in Box 15, Folder 4, Dombrowski Papers; Bartley, *Rise of Massive Resistance*, 116, 121, 211–36.

wing White Citizens' Council movement. An NAACP petition went to the Montgomery County Board of Education in August, 1955, and three months later, on December 1, NAACP secretary Rosa Parks decided to defy Montgomery's bus segregation ordinance. In February, as the Stars and Bars waved and the band played "Dixie," Senator Eastland told a huge Montgomery crowd at a White Citizens' Council rally to "organize and be militant." That same month, riots broke out in nearby Tuscaloosa when Autherine Lucy attempted to integrate the university. In the face of this determined white resistance, the Montgomery bus boycott struggled along and inspired black southerners to take enforcement of *Brown* into their own hands.[12]

Because Rosa Parks's courage sparked the groundswell that generated the grassroots civil rights movement, Cliff Durr became the southern movement's first white attorney. With the NAACP's local lawyer out of town, E. D. Nixon, the Montgomery NAACP leader, called Durr for legal advice when Parks was arrested. Nixon asked for his help in negotiating with city police and arranging her bail.

The segregationist extremism Durr sensed around him, combined with his earlier experience in New Orleans, seemed to have freed him from the reticence about public involvement in liberal causes he felt upon first returning to the South. This changed attitude is evident in a letter Durr wrote to Joseph Welsh in mid-1954 to congratulate him on his much-publicized defense of the young attorney Fred Fisher. McCarthy had accused Fisher because he once belonged to the NLG. Durr praised Welsh's stand against character assassination, but took offense at the Boston lawyer's passive endorsement of McCarthy's characterization of the liberal lawyers association. "I believe," said the former guild president, "that in its stand against the proscription of individuals for their beliefs and their associations, [the NLG] was defending basic American principles." "Welcome back" to the battle for civil liberties, Clark Foreman wrote to Durr about the same time. In the year since the SCEF hearings scared away most of his paying clients, Durr had been busy. But as his "secretary," Virginia Durr, wrote to a friend, their clients were "mostly all poor—Cliff is taking their cases up on appeal and I am doing the record."[13]

12. Bartley, *Rise of Massive Resistance,* 82–107, quote on 106.

13. Clark Foreman to C. J. Durr, March 21, 1954, Durr to Edward Condon, April 4, 1955, in Box 2, Folder 8, and Durr to Joseph Welsh, June 10, 1954, in Box 2, Folder 7, all in C. J. Durr Papers.

Durr had been involved in earlier consultations about proposed lawsuits to invalidate Montgomery's bus ordinance, and both Durrs knew and liked Rosa Parks. He had no second thoughts about acting as her attorney in the early hours after her arrest. Fred Gray, one of the two black lawyers in Montgomery, became the attorney of record in both the original Parks case and in *Browder* v. *Gayle*,[14] the federal case challenging the legality of bus segregation. NAACP attorney Gray catapulted to national acclaim because of *Browder* and became one of the stalwarts among movement lawyers. In 1956, however, he was twenty-six years old, only two years out of law school. The year before he had asked and received Durr's advice and assistance in two cases, one a damage suit brought by a black man against a white motorist, the other the first case against Montgomery's municipal bus lines, that of teenager Claudette Colvin. Though Gray wanted to appeal the Colvin case, Durr and E. D. Nixon prevailed upon him to wait for a more suitable defendant. Rosa Parks's case was the perfect substitute for a Colvin appeal. Durr insisted that he played a very small part in *Browder* v. *Gayle*, but both Nixon and Virginia Durr attributed to him the idea of bringing the precedent-setting federal suit against bus segregation. Answering a query from a researcher in 1973, Fred Gray said that Durr's help was invaluable, not only in preparing the many documents needed for the case but in formulating litigation strategy, and that his time was contributed to the cause "gratis."[15]

Leonard Boudin and Corliss Lamont of the Emergency Civil Liberties Committee both wrote to Durr during the winter of 1956 offering money to help with the defense of Parks, the many black boycotters arrested for loitering or vagrancy, and the eighty-nine members of the Montgomery Improvement Association indicted in February for "conspiring to boycott." Martin Luther King, Jr., was the only member of the last group ever brought to trial. Durr agreed to apply ECLC money as needed for court costs. When Boudin offered him a retainer to become an ECLC "assistant counsel" in the South, however, he declined, perhaps for the same reason he stayed in the background during

14. 142 F. Supp. 707 (1956).

15. Branch, *Parting the Waters,* 122–23, 129; Barnard, ed., *Outside the Magic Circle,* 280; Salmond, *Conscience of a Lawyer,* 171–79; J. Mills Thornton III, "Challenge and Response in the Montgomery Bus Boycott of 1955–1956," *Alabama Review,* XXXIII (June, 1980), 163–235; Fred Gray to Bryce Rucker, January 30, 1973, in Box 5, Folder 1, C. J. Durr Papers.

the boycott litigation. "The Negroes seem to have effective leadership of their own," he wrote, "and they want to keep it that way, as their own show." He would do his part by trying to influence the white community and standing ready to help Gray and other black lawyers when needed. But he feared taking the ECLC's money would "destroy what little effectiveness I have," because white courts and juries would resent his formal association with northern organizations known to support integration and suspected as opponents of anti-Communism.[16]

Durr handled another controversial case involving both integration and anti-Communism during the boycott period, that of writers Dorothy and Alfred Maund. Alfred Maund, a longtime left-wing activist and friend of SCEF, wrote primarily for the *Nation,* but a syndicate sometimes sold his articles to labor and leftist publications. He also worked as "make up editor" for the *Nation* in Montgomery, that magazine being printed by Pointer Press, Aubrey Williams' business. Maund's troubles began when Montgomery *Advertiser* reporter Joe Abzell uncovered Maund's exposé of the Montgomery White Citizens' Council, "How the Present Day KKK Took Over Montgomery," in the *Daily Worker* and reprinted the article in the *Advertiser, Worker* byline and all.[17]

The employment of Maund's wife as editor of the *Craig Field Courier,* a paper printed by Williams' press for the air force base in Selma, seriously complicated the matter. As a result of this confusing series of circumstances, when the *Advertiser* accused Alfred Maund of being a Communist, Dorothy Maund lost her job at Craig Air Force Base and Aubrey Williams lost an important client. She sued the reporter and the newspaper, in the end to no avail. The Montgomery judge who tried the case, himself a columnist for the *Advertiser,* refused to recuse himself despite Durr's impressive complaint. To say the least, the case was well covered in the local press, but for Durr, Williams, and the Maunds it became a very discouraging affair.[18]

Meanwhile, in April, 1955, Ben Smith encountered the Durrs' old nemesis, Senator Eastland, on a flight between Houston and New Orleans. Somehow

16. Corliss Lamont to C. J. Durr, February 2, 1956, Leonard Boudin to Durr, March 31, 1956, and Durr to Lamont and Boudin, April 12, 1956, all in Box 38, Folder 1, C. J. Durr Papers.
17. *Alfred and Dorothy Maund* v. *Joe Abzell et al.,* in Box 42, Folders 1 through 4, ibid.
18. Ibid.

Eastland and Smith managed to sit next to each other, and they drank whiskey and told southern stories all the way to New Orleans, finishing up like old pals with a couple of parting drinks in the New Orleans airport. Smith wrote to the Durrs about the encounter. Eastland said "he had a great deal of respect for Aubrey, but he thought the rest of us were a bunch of fools. . . . He was especially scornful and frustrated at Virginia and kept calling her 'that woman.'" In a friendly reply, Cliff Durr acknowledged his apprehension about people like McCarthy and Eastland but said that he was "much more concerned about the Brownells and the Dulleses." "The problem is not the out and out stinkers, but the 'respectables' who let them get by with it all for fear that their immaculate linen might get splattered. Then too, the 'respectables' are not above using the stinkers when it suits their purposes." His discussion of such "respectable" folk may be a clue to his feelings about old friends and genteel acquaintances in Montgomery. He expected much more in the way of support and understanding than they delivered.[19]

In spite of Durr's refusal of retainers from Lamont and Boudin, his cases, clients, and beliefs inevitably branded him with the mark of the Yankee sympathizer not completely unlike that visited on his grandfather Judkins after he supported the Republican Roosevelt in the election of 1901. The resulting ostracism made life very difficult for a man whose emotional attachment to Alabama and its people struggled against his intellectual resolve to uphold the Constitution and moral precepts. And rejection came not just from locals, but infected some former Washington colleagues as well. An old friend from New Deal days ("quite a liberal," Durr wrote, "as well as a successful businessman") showed up during the bus boycott and expressed his admiration for the Durrs' civil rights stand. However, he declined to hire Cliff for his Montgomery business because he needed "someone who stood better with the courts"; he ended up employing "the town's best white supremacist lawyer." "This type of incident," Durr complained, "happened time after time." Nevertheless, by the late 1950s Durr seemed to have come to terms with his predicament.[20]

19. B. E. Smith to C. J. Durr, April 4, 1955, in Box 2, Folder 8, ibid.; Durr to Smith, April 11, 1955, in Box 1, Folder 5, Virginia Durr Papers, LPR No. 28, Alabama Department of Archives and History, Montgomery.

20. Clifford Durr, Draft of Autobiography, Chapter 9, "Damned Liberals," 1, Box 17, Folder 12, C. J. Durr Papers.

This coming to terms with being a southern dissident, an outsider, proved more difficult for Ben Smith, a younger and less philosophical man. In the early years of his practice, Smith seemed to believe that he could satisfy both parts of his nature, the outgoing, fun-loving southerner and the serious, left-liberal labor lawyer who wanted change. But southern labor lawyers, especially those who, like Smith or Herman Wright, represented leftist unions, had to accept the stigma of identification with "alien" organizations as part and parcel of their chosen field. New Orleans, with its diverse ethnic mix, organized waterfront, and large sugar refineries, was more cosmopolitan on the surface than traditional Montgomery, but Smith's representation of both the predominantly black United Packinghouse Workers and the recently investigated SCEF assured him a reputation as a nonconformist in the local bar and community. Yet slowly, even as Smith became aware of the personal and professional problems inherent in his public identification as a "radical," he seemed more determined and committed to progressive ideas and societal change.[21]

During the summer and fall of 1955, Smith litigated a series of cases arising from a six-month-long strike against Colonial and Godchaux Sugar companies. This highly publicized strike resulted in charges of contempt against both national and local UPWA leaders. They allegedly ignored a federal injunction against picketing for twenty-four hours, then looked the other way while "non-union" wives and daughters replaced union members, continuing the activity despite the court order. Violence on both sides and the companies' refusal to rehire all striking workers, even after a settlement was reached on economic issues, complicated this strike. Walter B. Hamlin, the special judge appointed in the case, cited the national union officials in addition to local officers, alleging that the UPWA local had acted in collusion with the Chicago-based international union in "fomenting this violence." Many local picketers were black, advisers sent by the national union mostly white. The anti-union New Orleans newspapers ran pictures of black and white women holding "Don't be a Scab" signs and published many accounts of union lawlessness. In the end, the strike itself resulted in wage increases for the refinery workers, but the union lost its fight against the contempt charges.[22]

21. Jones and Massimini interviews.
22. *Colonial Sugars* v. *Arceneaux et al.,* in Box 2, Folders 1 through 4, Benjamin E. Smith

Judge Hamlin's motion adding the names of union leaders, or as he called them, "these Chicago people," to the contempt citation underscored local anxiety about liberal outsiders. He did not characterize armed Pinkerton agents hired by refinery managers as outsiders in the dispute, but strike consultants from the union's headquarters seemed both alien and un-American. Company attorneys made it clear to Hamlin that they believed the trouble resulted from the subversive influence of the leftist international union. The judge's only legal recourse, since the northern unionists had committed no crimes, was to cite them for contempt because they had been in New Orleans at the time the local organization allegedly ignored the court's injunction.[23]

Less than three years later, an innovative Louisiana law provided a formula Hamlin might have used to sever the local unit's ties to its international union. This 1958 legislation touched all liberal, leftist, or integrationist organizations mentioned in congressional or loyalty board reports, including Smith's Maritime Union and Packinghouse Workers clients. Eventually it would be used against SCEF, as well. Jim Dombrowski and Aubrey Williams asked John Coe and Cliff Durr to comment on the bill after it passed the Louisiana house. Durr called the legislation vague, unconstitutional, and "a disgraceful business, an outrage and affront to the South."[24] As an active member of the ACLU of Louisiana, Smith lobbied hard against Act 260 in Baton Rouge. The law prohibited groups "engaged in social, educational or political activities in the state of Louisiana" from association with any national group mentioned unfavorably in HUAC reports or listed by the attorney general. Louisiana courts were instructed to accept HUAC's word as "prima facie evidence" that such organizations were affiliated with the Communist Party.[25]

Even before the enactment of this law, the state found the means to expose and censure heretics and alien ideas. William M. "Willie" Rainach, the chairman of the Louisiana legislature's joint committee on segregation, also

Papers, Archives Division, State Historical Society of Wisconsin, Madison [hereinafter cited as Smith Papers]; New Orleans *Times-Picayune,* June 23, July 1, 7, 8, 13, 14, 15, 30, August 6, September 12, 14, October 1, 1955.

23. New Orleans *Times-Picayune,* July 14, 1955, p. 1.

24. C. J. Durr to James Dombrowski, June 24, 1958, in Box 3, Folder 86, Coe Papers.

25. "For Immediate Release," October, 1958, news release from the Louisiana Civil Liberties Union, in Box 4, ACLU-Collection No. 661, University Archives, Howard-Tilton Memorial Library, Tulane University, New Orleans.

served as president of the state's White Citizens' Councils. One writer described him as a sort of latter-day Bilbo, "a young man with slick black hair and a long upper lip . . . wearing a broad necktie emblazoned with a Confederate flag . . . who addressed a microphone with gestures appropriate to mass meetings." He had been organizing resistance to "outside agitators" since a few days after the *Brown* decision. A vote against his reactionary bills, Rainach said, would invite "carpet-baggers, scalawags and the National Association for the Advancement of the [*sic*] Colored People" to meddle in Louisiana's business. One bill provided for the expulsion of children who advocated violent overthrow of Louisiana's segregated schools; a Rainach-sponsored constitutional amendment removed state funding from any system that considered compliance with *Brown*.[26]

In April, 1956, one month after southerners in Congress issued the "Southern Manifesto," the Orleans Parish School Board responded to federal district court judge J. Skelly Wright's desegregation order by reiterating its plan to "use every legal and honorable means of maintaining segregation." A few weeks later, Senator Eastland met Ben Smith again during the repeat performance of SISS in New Orleans. The second Senate subcommittee hearings were followed less than a year later by HUAC hearings in New Orleans. As if to capitalize on the two federal probes, the Rainach committee held its own hearings later in 1957, employing the very same professional informants, furnished gratis by HUAC and SISS. The state hearings concluded not only that racial unrest in the South stemmed from Communist activity but that the NAACP was "nothing more than a vehicle of the Communist Party, in which the Communists are colonizing for the purpose of inciting racial rebellion in the South." Further, "in the insane confusion" of race war, this conspiracy planned "to seize power and take over the reins of government in the United States."[27]

Many of the leftists investigated at the two congressional committee gatherings in New Orleans in 1956 and 1957 were once part of the group of Communist professionals of which Oakley Johnson and Robert Hodes had

26. Bartley, *Rise of Massive Resistance,* 74–75; Peter R. Teachout, "Louisiana Underlaw," in *Southern Justice,* ed. Friedman, 64; Caute, *Great Fear,* 71.

27. Louisa Dalcher, "A Time of Worry in 'The City Care Forgot,'" *Reporter,* March 8, 1956, pp. 17–20, quote on 17; Bartley, *Rise of Massive Resistance,* 187.

been prominent members. Some of them were natives, and all had long been under scrutiny by local and state officials. Most others questioned were unionists, especially former members of the Maritime Union, which had purged Communists in the early 1950s, the Longshoremen, the Packinghouse Workers, and the Food, Tobacco, Agricultural and Allied Workers, a group expelled by the CIO in 1949. The last group was also well represented in the North Carolina and Atlanta hearings.

The 1956 SISS hearings in New Orleans highlighted Communist plans for infiltrating churches and other institutions. Ben Smith represented Winifred Feise, an assistant school librarian and an officer in the PTA of Jefferson Parish. She answered procedural questions but on her attorney's advice "took the fifth" in matters relating to her political associations. Not long after the two committees finished their interrogations in New Orleans, the state indicted Feise and her husband, Richard, along with Judy and Grady Jenkins and Hunter Pitts O'Dell, under Louisiana's criminal anarchy and subversive activity laws.[28]

O'Dell, usually called Jack, became the unseen star of these SISS hearings. O'Dell epitomized the evil Eastland sought. A well-educated "black red," he had been expelled from the National Maritime Union for circulating a peace petition in the midst of the union's anti-Communist purge in 1950. This was probably the same Stockholm Peace Petition that caused trouble for Sam and Sylvia Hall in Birmingham.[29] According to testimony at the hearing, he had recently replaced the party leader assigned to New Orleans as district organizer after the death of Sam Hall in 1951. While the committee could not locate him, it possessed, through the good offices of the New Orleans police, his confiscated library. The 175 books and articles included everything from materials authored by Stalin, Lenin, Gus Hall, and W. E. B. Du Bois to proposals for penetrating the NAACP, black and white churches, the Demo-

---

28. New Orleans SISS Hearings, 1956, pp. 610–22, 669–70; *State* v. *Jenkins* (236 La 300, 107 So. 2d 648). The Jenkins case became a cause célèbre with leftists and a frequent topic for the *Daily Worker;* Oakley Johnson wrote to John Coe from New York asking for assistance for his friends, and Coe made two contributions. After a federal court decision nullified the Louisiana laws, the defendants prevailed. See Oakley Johnson to J. M. Coe, April 23, 1957, September 12, 1958, Coe to Johnson, April 25, 1957, in Box 3, Folder 66, and Johnson to Coe, December 25, 1958, in Box 3, Folder 80, all in Coe Papers.

29. Branch, *Parting the Waters,* 573–74.

cratic Party, and black civic and voters leagues. Police found lists of SCEF's contributors, copies of the *Southern Patriot,* various articles on "The Negro Question," several union agreements involving the Longshoremen and the Packinghouse Workers, and enough copies of the *Worker* to indicate their purpose to be distribution rather than personal use. The SISS investigator carefully listed every title for the committee's benefit and then entered each into the record.[30]

O'Dell remained at large when HUAC, led by Congressman Edwin Willis of Louisiana, followed SISS to New Orleans in 1957. Nevertheless, a New Orleans Police Department intelligence agent based his expert report on Communist activities and methods in the South on a study of O'Dell's library. While world domination was still the ultimate objective of the party, the agent said, to make their program regionally "palatable" the party's southern program included "high flown language about struggling and improving people and whatnot." He gave examples of these insidious pledges from O'Dell's papers:

> Secure the right to vote for every person, Negro and white,
>   18-year-olds and over.
> Restore and uphold academic freedom.
> Abolish practice of loyalty testing and thought control.
> Cut the size of and introduce democratic reforms into the
>   State Militia, the national guard, and the police force.

"That," responded committee counsel Richard Arens, "is what we call the Aesopian language of the Communists."[31]

On the second day of these hearings, two ex-Communist informants testified. One, a black seaman and native of New Orleans, told about Communism in the maritime unions. In response, a HUAC member called him "a credit to his race." The second witness, Dr. William Sorum, a New Orleans psychiatrist, said he belonged to the Communist Party from 1945 until 1952.

30. New Orleans SISS Hearings, 1956, pp. 672–94.

31. U.S. Congress, House Un-American Activities Committee, *Investigation of Communist Activities in the New Orleans, La., Area* (New Orleans), 85th Cong., 1st Sess., February 14, 15, 1957, pp. 105–18, quotes on 110.

Having been involved in what Arens called "the notorious Willie McGee case," Sorum described at some length the party's activities in connection with McGee's defense. He identified Robert and Jane Hodes, two other Tulane doctors, and several other local professionals as party members. Although he thought most members of SCEF were not Communists, he believed the organization to be "controlled by Communists." They might have been skeptical about the testimony of some witnesses, but New Orleanians widely accepted the evidence offered by Tulane graduate Sorum. Thirty-four years later, when asked why he rejected another attorney's assertion that his partner Ben Smith had been a Communist, lawyer Bruce Waltzer remarked that "his name wasn't even mentioned by Dr. Sorum."[32]

Although Smith was never a member of the Communist Party, his uninhibited liberalism led him to involvement with the National Lawyers Guild during the most difficult decade in its history, in the midst of U.S. attorney general Brownell's determined drive to label it subversive. Perhaps for Smith and for John Coe, membership in the guild simply represented a way to find sympathetic lawyers who supported and respected their work. Neither man had the wide liberal contacts outside the South that Cliff Durr developed during his New Deal years. Associations formed in the 1930s and 1940s sustained Durr in Montgomery, not only with contributions supporting his civil rights cases but through warm friendships strengthened by letters, visits, and offers of short lecture and seminar stints. Several of his old colleagues remained active in NLG work. Regardless, by the mid-1950s Durr had allowed his guild membership to lapse, but Smith and Coe both served as officers and regularly attended guild conventions.

In February, 1957, just as Leo Sheiner's case was remanded to the Florida circuit court for the third time, John Coe became the NLG's president, a position he held until September, 1960. This long tenure enabled him to travel extensively as the guild's envoy, and he sometimes combined guild trips with SCEF missions, speaking in the North and West for both organizations. Coe enjoyed this role, especially when it brought him contact with like-minded liberals whom he respected and whose esteem he valued. The guild had been under intense pressure from the FBI since Durr's term of leadership ended in 1950, and had been involved in the prolonged lawsuit against the attorney

32. Ibid., 131–76, quotes on 149, 165, and 169; Waltzer interview.

general since 1953. The government finally dropped its effort to place the guild on the Subversive Activities Control Board list in 1958. The NLG board celebrated this victory by launching drives that increased membership moderately during Coe's term, though numbers never approached the almost four thousand lawyers on the rolls when Durr assumed the presidency.[33]

Traveling to California in September, 1957, Coe combined progressive rhetoric with fund-raising and recruiting at large dinner meetings in Los Angeles and San Francisco. Later he recalled doing "pretty well at both" and declared that he and his wife were captivated by the beauty of the West. In a Los Angeles speech entitled "The Receding Tide of Thought Control," Coe urged lawyers to rebuild a strong civil libertarian "welfare state" with the vision of New Deal planners. He warned against the "warfare state" of cold warriors and witch-hunters but praised McCarthy's censure, the Geneva summit meeting, and especially the *Brown* decision. Acknowledging that "in the demonology of the Southland the national office of the N.A.A.C.P. has superseded the Kremlin as the chief abode of Deviltry," he still felt that the Supreme Court's "insistence upon equality and fair dealing amongst races" would promote change and bring the South back to constitutional principles. "Hypocrisy is the mother of virtue," he concluded, "and if we preach high principles long enough, they will infiltrate our practice." Liberals, even southern liberals, had powerful allies and room for hope.[34]

Though he recognized anti-Communism as a segregationist device, Coe believed that McCarthyism had abated by 1957. In a letter to an old Progressive friend in Orlando he spoke of the difference between his experiences in the Sheiner case and the Alexander Trainor and Sam Hall cases seven years before. In Birmingham he had been shunned as if stricken with "the plague,

33. New York *Times,* February 24, September 15, 1957, *National Guardian,* March 4, 1957, Press Release, "Attorney General Drops Proceeding Against National Lawyers Guild," September 12, 1958, all in Box 58, NLG Papers, King Center; "Report by Executive Secretary on Organization: Report of Membership," January 18, 1960, in Box 3, Folder 98, Coe Papers; Baily, "The Case of the NLG," in *Beyond the Hiss Case,* ed. Theoharis, 175, n. 92. In the late 1980s a revitalized guild reported "over 5,000" members participating in "200 local chapters and 30 national committees." "Law and the Struggle for Social Justice: Profiles of Members of the National Lawyers Guild," NLG National Membership Committee pamphlet, n.d.

34. J. M. Coe to E. B. Collette, October 30, 1957, in Box 3, Folder 63, unidentified clippings and speech (Los Angeles, 1957), in Box 55, Folder 42, Coe Papers.

so far as treatment or association went." He remembered how Trainor's wife feared to enter the courthouse to speak to him because of a Jacksonville ordinance forbidding "persons of leftist conviction 'to meet in any room or private place.'" But in the Sheiner case, Coe marveled at the camaraderie between opposing lawyers in the courtroom and even the public sympathy expressed for his client. He assured his friend that he did not mean to imply that "all's right with the world," but he thought things were slowly improving for the traditional targets of the witch-hunt. He wrote to Stetson Kennedy in Europe that though there was still a good deal of sound and fury about Communism, "the public is not at all excited" anymore.[35]

Coe's optimism stemmed largely from a series of decisions of the Warren Supreme Court upholding civil libertarian principles, decrees that frustrated state and congressional anti-Communists and the FBI in 1957. "It is a great pleasure after so many years in the dog house," he wrote, "for a liberal to feel that he has the Supreme Court of the United States as the champion of the principles which he loves, and the court in the last two terms has truly been such."[36] For example, in the *Yates* case the Court overturned a group of California Smith Act convictions, making it clear that advocacy without the threat of some future illegal action could not be prosecuted. The *Nelson* case made state sedition laws untenable because of the primacy of the federal Smith Act; the *Jencks* decision required that FBI reports be opened to the scrutiny of the accused; *Sweezy* banned government investigation of beliefs and affiliations; *Watkins* dismissed contempt charges against a Fifth Amendment defendant; and *Slochower* reinstated a teacher dismissed by a loyalty board. Two 1957 decisions, *Konigsberg* and *Schware*, reversed cases in which admission to the bar had been denied on political grounds; and in 1959, about a year after Leo Sheiner's victory in Florida, the justices finally reversed the disbarment of the lawyers cited for contempt in the 1949 Smith Act trial. Finally, in 1958 the high court set aside the $100,000 fine levied against the NAACP of Alabama because that allegedly subversive organization's leaders refused to disclose its membership lists.[37]

---

35. J. M. Coe to Bertha Davis, March 17, 1957, in Box 3, Folder 64, and to Stetson Kennedy, June 22, 1957, in Box 3, Folder 67, ibid.

36. J. M. Coe to E. B. Collette, October 30, 1957, ibid.

37. *Yates v. U.S.*, 354 U.S. 298; *Pennsylvania v. Nelson*, 350 U.S. 497; *Jencks v. U.S.*, 353

Conservative congressmen struck back against this spurt of judicial liberalism, and southern legislators naturally assumed leadership roles in the fight to subdue the Court. Southern antipathy toward Supreme Court activism did not begin with the 1957 and 1958 decisions, of course, but they provided a way for southerners to join forces with northern anti-Communists "under the banner of states' rights." Georgia congressman James Davis called the *Nelson* decision "a brazen attack on the sovereignty of all the States." Representative Howard Smith of Virginia, whose namesake Smith Act had actually been strengthened by *Nelson,* offered a bill that would have made that act, or any similar federal law, null if states legislated in the same field. In an anti-Communist frenzy, congressmen introduced about 175 anti–civil liberties bills in 1957 and 1958, most of them aimed at the Supreme Court. Though only one eventually passed both houses, some votes were close and hotly contested. The bill that passed limited the access to FBI files granted through the *Jencks* decision. Durr wrote an impassioned letter to Senator Lister Hill beseeching him to oppose this legislation and expressed disappointment when a chastened Supreme Court upheld the new law in 1959.[38]

Guild members and other civil libertarians mounted a strong fight against the most wide-ranging of these anti-Court actions. The Jenner Bill (S. 2646) would have deprived the Supreme Court of appellate jurisdiction in five areas: contempt of Congress, federal employees' security programs, antisubversive laws of the states, antisubversive rules of school boards, and admission of lawyers to practice in state courts. The NAACP, convinced that the bill would

---

U.S. 657; *Sweezy* v. *New Hampshire,* 354 U.S. 234; *Watkins* v. *U.S.,* 354 U.S. 178; *Slochower* v. *Board of Education of New York City,* 350 U.S. 551; *Konigsberg* v. *State Bar of California,* 353 U.S. 252; *Schware* v. *Bd. of Examiners of New Mexico,* 353 U.S. 232; *NAACP* v. *Alabama,* 357 U.S. 449; *Bar of the City of New York* v. *Isserman,* 271 F.2d 784, 785. See also Ginger and Tobin, eds., *NLG,* 152–58; Jonathan D. Casper, *Lawyers Before the Warren Court: Civil Liberties and Civil Rights, 1957–66* (Urbana, Ill., 1972), 19–34; Edwin S. Newman, *Civil Liberties and Civil Rights* (Legal Almanac Series No. 13) (Dobbs Ferry, N.Y., 1979), 36–40. Because the Court ruled only on membership disclosure and not on parts of the Alabama registration law yet untried in state courts, Alabama barred the NAACP until the Court issued a fourth order in October, 1964. See also Michael Meltsner, "Southern Appellate Courts: A Dead End," in *Southern Justice,* ed. Friedman, 141–45.

38. Caute, *Great Fear,* 156–58, quotes on 156; C. J. Durr to Lister Hill, June 7, 1957, in Box 38, Folder 1, C. J. Durr Papers.

have given states the right to prohibit its Legal Defense and Education Fund lawyers from handling civil rights litigation, lobbied zealously for its defeat. Ben Smith, the member of the NLG's national executive board who knew Senator Eastland best, arrived in Washington in March, 1958, to present the guild's resolution against the Jenner measure to Eastland's committee. "The bill is obnoxious because it interferes with the independence of the judiciary and with our Constitutional system of separation of powers," Smith told the committee. "The real purpose of the bill is to discipline the Supreme Court because they have been upholding civil liberties."[39]

Coe wrote to his senators and Durr to the editor of the New York *Times* urging the bill's defeat, and in a delightful exchange of telegrams, Aubrey Williams and Lyndon Johnson argued over the possibility that the bill might pass. "What in heaven's name has gotten into you," railed SCEF's president, afraid he would be jailed for opposing state segregation laws if the bill passed. Johnson wired the anxious Williams on August 21 to "take the advice of an old friend and keep your shirt on. The Senate in my judgement is not going to do anything that will end up by throwing innocent people in jail." That same day, Johnson delivered on his assurances. The Senate killed the Jenner Bill by a vote of forty-one to forty. The other Texas senator and six border state senators voted with Johnson; the remainder of southern senators who voted supported the bill. Several other anti-Court measures passed in the House but lost in the Senate the same week that S. 2646 went down to defeat, largely on account of the political skill and determination of the majority leader.[40]

Smith's Washington visit to testify before SISS came five months after he attended that committee's hearings investigating "Communism in the Mid-South" in Memphis. At these hearings he represented two physics teachers who had been students in Atlanta at the time Highlander founder Don West taught at Oglethorpe University. Richard Stauverman attended Georgia Tech

---

39. Press Release: "Lawyers Guild Opposes Curb on Supreme Court Powers," March 3, 1958, in Box 55, Folder 42, Coe Papers.

40. J. M. Coe to George Smathers, May 7, 1958, in Box 3, Folder 86, ibid.; C. J. Durr to Editor, New York *Times,* March 20, 1958, in Box 2, Folder 9, C. J. Durr Papers; Notes and typed copies of telegrams, Aubrey [Williams] to Lyndon [Johnson] and Lyndon to Aubrey, August 20, 21, 1958, in Box 51, Folder 3, Braden Papers.

and had two Emory degrees, and Philip J. Lorenz earned a B.S. degree from Oglethorpe in 1949 and an M.S. from Vanderbilt in 1952. Then employed at different colleges in the Midwest, both men had previously taught at LeMoyne College, a black institution in Memphis, and the committee believed both to have been Communists there and in Atlanta. They took the Fifth Amendment when asked about associations with West and other known party members, except that Lorenz admitted to knowing West slightly on the Oglethorpe campus. The committee intimated that Lorenz got Stauverman his job at LeMoyne on orders from the Communist Party but introduced no evidence to substantiate the charge.[41]

Committee counsel J. G. Sourwine called Ben Smith a Communist lawyer because he regularly turned up at SISS hearings. He questioned Lorenz at some length about why he and Stauverman both employed this controversial lawyer from New Orleans, where neither resided. Lorenz answered that after his subpoena arrived he discussed hiring a lawyer with his friend, who had already employed Smith on the advice of another acquaintance. Nothing came of this line of questioning, but it was typical of the treatment lawyers representing alleged subversives received from SISS and HUAC and demonstrates the committees' general interest in progressive lawyers. Eastland had thrown lawyer Philip Wittenberg out of the room when he refused on First Amendment grounds to attest to his anti-Communism at the second SISS session in New Orleans in 1956. Smith, on the other hand, had told the committee at that time that he was "not now a communist, I have never been one, and I do not believe in communism." John Coe's FBI file further accents the offensive against lawyers. According to one memo, a month after the Memphis hearings HUAC tried to organize "hearings regarding lawyers with communist backgrounds" and planned to subpoena Coe. "We should assist the Committee" with this effort "in any way we can," and "I suggest a memo to [the attorney general] re: Coe's background," commented Assistant Director A. H. Belmont in a handwritten note in the memo's margin. "DeLoach should talk to Arens to make sure they go ahead with this hearing." A further note in another hand

41. U.S. Congress, Senate Committee on the Judiciary, Subcommittee to Investigate the Administration of the Internal Security Act and Other Internal Security Laws, *Communism in the Mid-South* (Memphis), 85th Cong., 1st Sess., October 28, 29, 1957, pp. 25–31, 44–52 [hereinafter cited as Mid-South Hearings, 1957].

says Belmont's requests were "handled 11-14-58." About the same time, SISS prepared a dossier on Coe and about seventy other lawyers for use at its own hearings, which would "go fully into the lawyer question."[42]

In Memphis the senators subsequently called several other witnesses, including two friendly ex-Communists, to testify about the movement in Tennessee. Both the young teachers had left their Memphis positions, but the *Commercial Appeal* carefully listed other local witnesses' names and addresses, then in later editions told how they lost jobs as a result of the publicity surrounding the subpoenas. They also called Grace Lorch of Little Rock, a woman with a history of participation in left-wing causes. Lorch had gained local notoriety about a month before by instinctively protecting a black girl trying to dodge rocks and bats on the long walk into Central High School. Jenner and Eastland made it clear that her subpoena was in no way related to that well-publicized incident: "This committee is not interested in integration in any sense of the word."[43] She had been called because "you are trying to hide the fact that you are a communist." Producing a letter Lorch wrote to a Nashville newspaper in 1953 opposing the Rosenberg execution, they claimed to have "information" connecting her "with Junius Scales, the southern regional director of the Communist Party."[44]

Regardless of the senators' energetic offensive, however, Lorch's testimony, like the appearances of Don West and Smith's clients, was largely superfluous, inflating proceedings that began with two specific missions. The

42. Ibid., 55–62; New Orleans SISS Hearings, 1956, pp. 712–13; Memorandum for Mr. Belmont, November 12, 1958, p. 2, and "Correlation Summary," March 20, 1962, p. 14, Section 5, Coe FBI File.

43. Mid-South Hearings, 1957, p. 80; Memphis *Commercial Appeal*, October 25–31, 1957 (p. 1 for each issue). Bartley made a cogent comment on the senators' disavowal of interest in desegregation in Memphis. The hearing, he says, definitely contributed "to a general atmosphere that linked patriotism with the status quo." *Rise of Massive Resistance*, 188.

44. Mid-South Hearings, 1957, pp. 79–81. In 1954 Lorch's husband, Lee, lost his job as mathematics chair at Fisk University after refusing to answer HUAC questions in Dayton, Ohio, on First Amendment grounds and enrolling their child in a black Nashville school. Earlier denied tenure at City College of New York and Penn State because of civil rights work, he found employment after Fisk at a small black college in Little Rock. Jim Dombrowski stayed with the Lorches when visiting there to signal his appreciation of the dangerous position they had taken in the community. Grace Lorch's subpoena killed the Little Rock job, and Lee Lorch eventually settled at a Canadian university. Schrecker, *No Ivory Tower*, 290–91; Braden interview.

presence of Kentucky's attorney general and the commonwealth attorney from Louisville revealed the committee's real purposes in Memphis. The Kentuckians came to Memphis to denounce SCEF's new field secretary, Carl Braden, recently released from prison after *Pennsylvania* v. *Nelson* invalidated state sedition laws. Anthony Dunbar maintained that these hearings were "staged" so that Kentucky could "rehash the case made, but ultimately lost in the courts, against Carl Braden and SCEF."[45] Although the committee did not subpoena Braden, like the evasive Jack O'Dell in New Orleans his presence overshadowed the hearings. The Kentucky officials also appeared to engender support for the Jenner Bill, then pending in Congress.

A. Scott Hamilton, a well-connected[46] rising local politician then running for reelection in Louisville, had prosecuted Anne and Carl Braden in their 1955 sedition trial and reaped wide acclaim from Carl Braden's conviction. The *Nelson* decision prompted Braden's release by the Kentucky Supreme Court after he served only eight months of a fifteen-year sentence. Through Hamilton and other witnesses, the government began building a case against Carl Braden in Memphis which culminated in his contempt citation in Atlanta nine months later. Testimony about the Braden sedition case also bolstered the Jenner Bill's specific provisions banning high court review of state anti-subversive laws. The Memphis hearings immediately preceded the introduction of Senator Jenner's anti–Supreme Court bill.[47]

Indianan Jenner presided on the committee's first day in Memphis in the absence of SISS chairman Eastland, who appeared late but in time to confront Ben Smith. Jenner's first witness, Attorney General Jo M. Ferguson of Kentucky, affirmed that the offending U.S. Supreme Court decision had rendered his state's law against advocacy of sedition and criminal syndicalism "inoperative." He spoke at length about Kentucky's abiding interest in sedition laws since Thomas Jefferson's Kentucky Resolutions in 1798. As Justice Stanley Reed, formerly from Kentucky, had written in his dissent to *Pennsylvania* v. *Nelson*, Ferguson avowed that the state still held to its Jeffersonian tradition. Validating the subcommittee's mandate to research proposed leg-

45. Dunbar, *Against the Grain*, 247.

46. Hamilton's father was a federal district judge in Kentucky, and he mentioned during the hearings his family's close friendship with former chief justice Fred Vinson.

47. *Kentucky* v. *Braden*, 291 SW 2d 843; Mid-South Hearings, 1957, pp. 1–22.

islation and confirming its analysis of the pending Jenner Bill, he asked SISS to pass laws to restore to the states the power to control their own subversives.[48]

When Scott Hamilton took the stand, he discussed not only the need for federal legislation but also the Braden sedition case and the subversive literature Louisville police had confiscated from the Braden home. He described a mass of impounded left-wing materials, including a few tracts and essays written by American Communist Party leaders. Interpreting letters he said were written on Communist Party letterhead, he hammered home themes familiar to followers of southern anti-Communism. Communists tried to "play up . . . to the colored people and miners" but "between themselves" referred to "miners as hillbillies and to the Negroes as niggers, and all that sort of thing. . . . So that I would say that they are not sincere in trying to help anybody, for that matter." He told the committee that Braden had headed the Progressive Party in Kentucky in 1948 and said he had in his possession a letter from Carl and Anne Braden announcing their recent employment as field secretaries for SCEF. Hamilton contended, as he had during Braden's trial, that Communists looking for publicity, not segregationists seeking to enforce conformity, had blown up the house Anne and Carl Braden sold to a black couple in 1954.[49]

Louisville native Alberta Ahearn, an FBI undercover agent from 1948 to 1954, assumed the stand to affirm Hamilton's statement and thus to reemphasize the outrage of Braden's release as a result of *Nelson*. A last-minute witness in Carl Braden's sedition trial, Ahearn's testimony had persuaded an undecided jury to convict him in spite of his sworn testimony that he had never been a Communist. The Bradens, she testified, recruited her and put her in charge of the Louisville chapter of the American Peace Crusade (APC). She witnessed to the APC's opposition to the Korean War, the H-bomb, and McCarthyism, its support of trade with Red China, and its close association with the American Council for Soviet-American Friendship, long prominent on the SACB list. The party had asked her to join the Negro Labor Council and church groups, through which she surreptitiously disseminated APC literature. Ahearn professed membership in a "militant church group" that

48. Mid-South Hearings, 1957, pp. 2–6.
49. Ibid., 6–22, quote on 13.

promoted integration and an "interracial hospital group" dedicated to securing entrance of blacks into city hospitals. She belonged to Louisville's International Harvester plant's Farm Equipment Workers Union, which must have been Communist-controlled because it employed Anne and Carl Braden as publicity agents. Though herself never a member, she thought Anne Braden chaired the "overall city group" of representatives of Communist Party cells in Louisville. Later employed by HUAC to impeach Carl Braden in Atlanta, this paid informant remained the only person who ever swore to personal knowledge that he or his wife belonged to the Communist Party.[50]

Just nine months after this SISS inquiry in Memphis, the House committee continued the government's pursuit of Braden at its own hearings in Atlanta. HUAC subpoenaed both Bradens in July, 1958, but postponed Anne Braden's appearance because of her family responsibilities. Nevertheless, because her recent book about the Louisville case, *The Wall Between,* criticized "expert witnesses" supplied by HUAC who had helped prosecutor Hamilton convict her husband, she probably sparked the committee's renewed interest. HUAC's participation in the Kentucky trial motivated the Bradens to become active in the Emergency Civil Liberties Committee, an organization singlemindedly devoted to First Amendment rights and conspicuously involved in the movement to abolish HUAC and SISS. A sympathetic article in the *Christian Century* suggested that the book and the couple's involvement with ECLC, combined with their recent affiliation with SCEF, provoked their subpoenas.[51]

Representatives Francis E. Walter of Pennsylvania, Edwin E. Willis of Louisiana, William M. Tuck of Virginia, and Donald L. Jackson of California accompanied Chief Counsel Arens and his staff to Atlanta. Perhaps for the benefit of Willis, who had directed HUAC proceedings in New Orleans and Charlotte, the committee questioned former New Orleanian Jack O'Dell on the second day of the hearings. Now working as the manager of an insurance company in Montgomery, O'Dell arrived in Atlanta accompanied by Orzell Billingsley, Jr., one of only three black lawyers in Birmingham in 1958. O'Dell probably did not take much of Billingsley's advice. Though he employed the

---

50. Ibid., 35–41, quotes on 39; *I. F. Stone's Weekly,* March 6, 1961, p. 1.

51. Anne Braden, *The Wall Between* (New York, 1958); Howard Schomer, "Two Defenders of Freedom," *Christian Century,* December 6, 1961, pp. 1465–66.

Fifth Amendment in answer to most questions, he could not resist lecturing Arens about the true meaning of subversion and the crimes visited upon black Americans since slavery.[52]

The committee also interviewed five North Carolinians connected to the Food, Tobacco, Agricultural, and Allied Workers Union, some of whom had been identified in previous testimony as associates of Junius Scales. Joseph Forer, a well-known NLG member from the District of Columbia bar, represented this group of five former textile workers. Forer had been defending radicals since Cliff Durr's days in Washington and had helped to write the NLG's report on the FBI in 1950. He also represented a Virginia couple living in the district of Congressman (and former governor) William Tuck; their subpoenas resulted from informant Ralph Long's accusations four years earlier in Miami. The couple refused to answer questions about their political associations, called their accuser a known malefactor, and claimed integrationism to be their only crime.[53]

The first witness at these hearings, Armando Penha, since 1950 an FBI mole in the Communist Party, denounced the seven mentioned above and many other southerners as Communists. Penha had belonged to the Communist Party's National Textile Commission, which had as its primary objective the infiltration and "colonization" of the textile industry, especially in the South. Much of his testimony centered around Junius Scales's activities and associates. In September, 1957, almost two years after Scales lost his first appeal, the Supreme Court had ordered a new trial under the recently decided *Jencks* rule. As Penha implicated him in Atlanta, a three-judge panel of the Fourth Circuit considered Scales's second appeal.[54]

---

52. Atlanta HUAC Hearings, 1958, pp. 2605, 2712–21. William A. Rusher, assistant SISS counsel in New Orleans, says O'Dell resigned from SCLC in 1962, "by mutual agreement" with Martin Luther King, Jr., when it was revealed in the press that he was a Communist. *Special Counsel* (New Rochelle, N.Y.: 1968), 55–60. For a fuller account of O'Dell's employment by the SCLC and the FBI's role in King's decision to dismiss him, see David J. Garrow, *The FBI and Martin Luther King, Jr.* (1981; rpr. New York, 1983), and Branch, *Parting the Waters*, esp. 574–75, 850–51, and 904.

53. Atlanta HUAC Hearings, 1958, pp. 2648–63, 2688–2709, 2721–25.

54. Ibid., 2614–36. A good synopsis of the Scales case is found in Lucius J. and Twiley W. Barker, *Freedom, Courts, Politics: Studies in Civil Liberties* (Englewood Cliffs, N.J., 1972), 95–125.

Penha also remembered Georgia teacher, preacher, and farmer Don West as an active party member. Subpoenaed, West sat in on the first day of the Atlanta hearings but never testified. The Atlanta *Constitution*'s editor commented that West had been "an enthusiastic communist in the 30's," but since "has taken the Fifth Amendment so many times count has been lost."[55]

The heyday of Atlanta Communism was certainly long past; the AFL-CIO's regional director in Atlanta commented as the hearings began that "We haven't seen any [Communists] in years." Nevertheless, the committee called John Hester, who worked with West for a short time selling vegetables, to answer to his alleged subversion by association. Perhaps this former Georgia resident's appearance justified hearings held in the state. The only other Georgian to address the committee, Governor Marvin Griffin, appeared and welcomed HUAC warmly during its opening session. Committee interrogators made one local connection when they used a surveillance photograph to show how the Atlanta Red Cross had been hoodwinked into allowing a "Communist organization"—SCEF's board—the use of its headquarters for a meeting in 1957. *Journal* writer Shannon concluded that "the hearings did not produce one bona fide Communist—or even a Fifth Amendment Communist—now in residence in the state." The dearth of local participants may account for the story related by Carl Braden that, according to Atlanta *Constitution* publisher Ralph McGill, the newspaper "got not one letter approving or even commenting on the Committee's doings in Atlanta." This is surprising considering the large amount of space relegated to the hearings by both the *Constitution* and the Atlanta *Journal*.[56]

Penha finally led the committee to the relationship of Communists to the southern integration movement by identifying two editors of the Louisville-based *Southern Newsletter*. After testifying that their publication reached 2,100 subscribers, 85 percent of whom were southern whites, both men refused to discuss their financial backers or their relationship with Anne and Carl Braden, editors of SCEF's editorially similar *Southern Patriot*. One of

55. Atlanta HUAC Hearings, 1958, p. 2662; Atlanta *Constitution*, July 29, 1958, p. 4.

56. Atlanta HUAC Hearings, 1958, pp. 2608, 2663–65, 2677; Atlanta *Constitution,* July 29, 1958, pp. 1, 4; Atlanta *Journal,* August 3, 1958, Sec. C, p. 3; Carl Braden to J. M. Coe, December 20, 1958, in Box 60, Folder 18, Coe Papers; front-page and inside stories appear in both the *Constitution* and the *Journal* from July 27 through August 1, 1958.

the men had written articles for Don West's magazine, the *Southerner,* but like the Bradens he professed to be a Socialist who had never belonged to the Communist Party.[57]

At the beginning of the second day of the Atlanta hearings, Carl Braden appeared accompanied by attorneys John Coe and C. Ewbank Tucker of Louisville. Newspaper stories noted that Tucker, a bishop of the African Methodist Episcopal Church, wore clerical attire and a large gold cross. Like Coe, Tucker served on SCEF's board. Braden identified himself as a "worker in the integration movement in the South." Now employed by SCEF, before the sedition trial and the harassment that followed he had been a newspaper man with the Louisville *Courier-Journal.* He outlined his work history and described his college education as two years of study for the Catholic priesthood, though he now belonged to the Episcopal Church.[58]

But Braden would not catalog his politics or his colleagues. Arens went to great lengths to lay the proper groundwork, insisting that the committee's questions related to security laws under consideration by HUAC. He insisted that though he did not want "to probe any private beliefs," the government had a right to investigate Communism, "a Godless, atheistic conspiracy which is sweeping the world and which ultimately threatens, and will threaten, the integrity of this Nation." If he could not question witnesses about the existence of Communism within its borders, then "God help this country." "Are you saying," Braden queried his accuser, "that integration is communism, like they do in Louisiana?" Arens called Braden a Communist "masquerading behind a facade of humanitarianism" and making an "emotional appeal to certain segments of our society." Braden insisted that "integration is what you are investigating." He refused to answer questions concerning his ideas or associations, basing his noncompliance "on the First Amendment and on the grounds that the question[s have] no possible pertinency to any legislation," regardless of Arens' claims to the contrary. Since the First Amendment precluded any legislation by Congress in the area of speech or associations, Braden repudiated the committee's attempts to investigate in these areas.[59]

The committee's characterization of an open letter signed by more than

57. Atlanta HUAC Hearings, 1958, pp. 2629–48.
58. Ibid., 2667–68, quote on 2667; Atlanta *Journal,* July 30, 1958, p. 16.
59. Atlanta HUAC Hearings, 1958, pp. 2667–71, quotes on 2669, 2670, and 2671.

two hundred southern black leaders and delivered to Congress in early July supported Braden's view that HUAC targeted integrationists. The letter asked the House to reconsider sending HUAC to Atlanta unless it would come "to help us defend against those subversives who oppose the Supreme Court, our federal policy of civil rights for all, and our American ideals of equality and brotherhood." It accused HUAC of "spreading terror among our white citizens," making it nearly impossible for civil rights advocates to find allies. "Southerners, white and Negro, who strive today for full democracy must work at best against tremendous odds. They need the support of every agency of the Federal Government. It is unthinkable that they should instead be harassed by committees of the United States Congress." Representative Jackson of California commented that "the letter was prepared by a communist" since it appeared on the letterhead of "a communist organization" and some signers were probably duped into adding their names. Printed on SCEF stationary, it ran as an advertisement in the Washington *Post* and *Times-Herald* on July 31, though the Atlanta *Journal-Constitution* refused to accept it. Signer Austin T. Walden, an Atlanta attorney, said the *Constitution* feared a libel suit because the letter referred to recent racial unrest in Dawson, Georgia, and mentioned both Senator Eastland and the House committee unfavorably.[60]

Frank Wilkinson, a civil liberties activist from California, came to Atlanta at SCEF's invitation to observe the hearings. HUAC agents discovered his plans and handed him a last-minute subpoena as he checked into the room he shared with Jim Dombrowski at the Biltmore Hotel. Arens called Wilkinson "an agent of the Communist Party as an arm of the international Communist Conspiracy sent into Atlanta for the purpose of engaging in conspiratorial activities." Appearing without counsel, he answered every question unequivocally: "As a matter of conscience and personal responsibility, I refuse to answer any questions of this committee." Wilkinson's posture recalled Virginia Durr's "I stand mute" in New Orleans, and complemented Braden's more didactic expositions.[61]

Braden also neither invoked the Fifth Amendment nor answered the

60. Ibid., 2672–75, quotes on 2674 and 2675; "Memo from James Dombrowski re: Open Letter Supporting Carl Braden," August 9, 1958, in Box 51, Folder 3, Braden Papers.

61. Atlanta HUAC Hearings, 1958, pp. 2681–88, quotes on 2687, 2681.

committee's probes. On principle he did not answer questions about his associations, even to deny party membership, a truth that might have rescued him from considerable future distress. A straightforward response to the committee's questions could have saved him from a prolonged contempt case and eventually a year in federal prison. In spite of testimony against him by a paid informant, a sustainable perjury indictment seemed unlikely. On the other hand, refusal to testify on Fifth rather than First Amendment grounds would have been constitutionally protected and almost certainly upheld by the Supreme Court in the unlikely event of a contempt citation.

Though he respected Braden's integrity, John Coe took exception to this suicidal path, wishing to save his client from a contempt citation. Some other liberals agreed. For example, longtime SCEF board member Albert Barnett of Emory University wrote the Bradens that he supported Carl as a friend and ally in the integration movement but could not accept his First Amendment objection to HUAC. Braden's refusal to cooperate was based on his belief, in the first place, that the committee had no right to exist, and secondly that his racial views, rather than his politics, had provoked his subpoena. He believed that anti-Communism, at least in southern guise, had become a sham completely unrelated to espionage or any threat to national security. In a statement issued after the House of Representatives voted to cite him for contempt, Braden said he could not cooperate because that might indicate that he supported the committee. "It is to cooperate with evil. I could not in good conscience do this."[62]

A few months earlier, Coe had believed he would face a similar decision. In February, 1958, J. B. Matthews, a Hearst columnist and ex-Communist who called himself the former "Director of Research for the House Committee on un-American Activities," informed the Florida Legislative Investigating Committee of Coe's left-wing activities and offices in great detail. The informant held up a long list of petitions and letters Coe had signed, and discussed both his current presidency of the NLG and his SCEF connections. That evening the Pensacola newspaper reported Coe's alleged affiliation with twenty-four Communist-front organizations. Coe wrote Jim Dombrowski

62. J. M. Coe to James Dombrowski, March 8, 1958, in Box 48, Folder 16, Coe Papers; Anne Braden to Frank Wilkinson, December 29, 1958, in Box 51, Folder 6, Braden Papers; *Southern Patriot,* September, 1958, p. 3.

that if called to Tallahassee he, like Braden, would not take the Fifth, and that he would "not name names (for I have none to name)." But he would answer all the committee's questions candidly and could "of course answer the $64.00 question 'No.'" He wanted to "make my appearance a sounding board for a just, free and decent view of political liberty and desegregation." Though Coe hated HUAC, he would not have chosen Braden's path.[63]

Before the Atlanta hearings, Coe and Braden were all but unacquainted. Coe's appearance as Braden's lawyer there resulted from his SCEF board position and friendship with Dombrowski. Not surprisingly, after the hearings and Braden's indictment, misunderstandings arose surrounding the choice of counsel for the ensuing contempt case.

HUAC had issued its subpoena while Braden vacationed in Rhode Island at the home of Harvey O'Connor, president of the ECLC. Even before the hearings, O'Connor offered legal help if a contempt citation should arise, and ECLC counsel Leonard Boudin, a well-known expert in civil liberties law, agreed to represent Braden without fee. Braden, an ECLC member who knew Boudin's reputation, seemed very pleased with the arrangement. The case would be about freedom of conscience, and the ECLC embraced the First Amendment as its first priority.

Jim Dombrowski, on the other hand, felt strongly that SCEF's field secretary should have southern counsel. He feared that Braden's identification with ECLC, a northern-based civil liberties organization, would undercut SCEF's position as an all-southern civil rights alliance. Dombrowski recommended John Coe as chief counsel, but Braden balked at turning down ECLC's offer. Coe himself saw no point in joining the case as an assistant simply because he was a southerner. Boudin would do a fine job. But Dombrowski would not relent. A long and complicated exchange of letters finally resulted in joint counsel, with Boudin and Coe in charge. Bishop Tucker,

63. J. M. Coe to James Dombrowski, March 8, 1958, in Box 48, Folder 16, Coe Papers; Anne Braden to Frank Wilkinson, December 29, 1958, in Box 51, Folder 6, Braden Papers; SAC, Jacksonville, to Director, FBI, February 27, 1958, p. 1, and Report, January 1, 1962, p. 6, Section 5, Coe FBI File; Transcript of Testimony (document 2 of 2), Florida Legislative Investigating Committee Papers, Series 1486, Carton 5, February 9, 1961, Florida Department of Archives and History, Department of State, Tallahassee [hereinafter cited as Fla. Leg. Investigating Committee Papers]. Testimony for 1958 is quoted beginning on a page numbered 24; the pages of this transcript are misnumbered or unnumbered.

Boudin's partner Victor Rabinowitz, and later NAACP lawyer Conrad Lynn assisted but remained relatively inactive in preparing the case. Coe agreed to take primary responsibility for the contempt trial and Boudin for the appeal, though in practice the two men worked well together on all aspects of the litigation. Boudin ostensibly participated as an individual, not as a representative of the ECLC, and all the lawyers served without fee.[64]

Nevertheless, disagreements between client and counsel continued unabated until the case was finally lost in the Supreme Court. Braden wanted to direct his own defense, and both lawyers, while they always respected him, at times found him difficult to work with. Braden's attitude toward his case was similar to that of the CRC's Patterson toward Roosevelt Ward's trial, though their political roots differed. Both men, hard-nosed propagandists, looked for the widest audience and the most lasting effect, and they determined to stand on principle regardless of the costs.

At one point Coe, lamenting Braden's desire to rewrite the Supreme Court brief, wrote to Boudin:

> I recognize the justice of Carl's criticism of legal thinking from the standpoint of a revolutionist; but you may fight with the pen when it is impossible to draw the sword, and you must recognize the limits of your weapons, "Yea though it were pain and grief to me."

A revision of the same brief brought this sharp response from Braden:

> From my viewpoint, [this brief] might just as well not have been written. . . . *Do not try to convince the judges of my political purity.* Try to convince them that it is wrong for the Un-American Committee or any other inquisitorial body

---

64. Anne [Braden] to Aubrey [Williams] and Jim [Dombrowski], August 16, 1958, and n.d., Aubrey to Carl [Braden], n.d., Anne to Clark Foresman, September 4, 1958, and Carl to Jim, September 20, 1958, all in Box 51, Folder 6, Braden Papers; Carl Braden to J. M. Coe, September 6, 30, 1958, Jim to Carl and Anne, September 17, 1958, Leonard Boudin to Coe, October 1, 1958, Coe to Carl Braden, September 22, October 4, 1958, and Coe to Boudin, October 4, 1958, all in Box 60, Folder 18, Coe Papers.

to question *anybody* about *any* political beliefs or associations. That is what *I* am fighting about, and I hope it is what
my lawyers are fighting about. (Emphasis in original)

Braden and his lawyers exchanged correspondence of this nature throughout
the trial, and both Boudin and Coe remained perplexed by his refusal to
cooperate with their strategies to win his freedom. "I appreciate all that you
say about the German left compromising with Nazism," Coe wrote in response to one Braden lecture, "I would never advocate it." Nevertheless,
pragmatic lawyer Coe would also "not advocate pissing in the eye of a court
from which I was hoping for a helpful decision." Coe maintained that their
disagreements resulted from their different missions, one the lawyer's charge
to do his best for his client, the other the propagandist. The latter could not
compromise without weakening his position, but lawyers must work "within
the limits of possible accomplishment." Great political battles could not be
won in court, he told Braden; they simply could not be as inflexible in court
as Braden must be in public.[65]

Coe even found himself at odds with his old friend and frequent corre-
spondent Aubrey Williams as the first trial approached. Coe felt that Braden
had stated his case completely at the hearings and should not take the stand.
Instead, Williams and Jim Dombrowski should testify to the purposes of
SCEF and Braden's employment. On the other hand, Cliff Durr advised
Williams to refuse Coe's request. Durr felt, Williams wrote to Dombrowski,
that "one slip of memory by you or me in the testimony we give in Atlanta
from that we gave in New Orleans and we would be in the soup. They are
after you and they are after me." Dombrowski's lawyer, Ben Smith, agreed
with Durr, and though Williams and Dombrowski observed the trial they did
not testify. Coe graciously bowed to his colleagues' decision. As Braden
wished, he based his trial brief solely on constitutional objections to the
committee's jurisdiction. Both Braden and Frank Wilkinson, represented by
the ACLU's general counsel from New York, Rowland Watts, were found
guilty of contempt by a federal district court jury in Atlanta. In January, 1959,
the judge released them on bail pending an appeal.[66]

65. J. M. Coe to Leonard Boudin, September 12, 1960, Carl Braden to Boudin, October 29,
1960, and Coe to Braden, November 7, 1960, all in Box 60, Folder 18, Coe Papers.

66. J. M. Coe to Leonard Boudin, January 3, 1959 [misdated 1958], Aubrey Williams to

Boudin and Coe filed an appeal brief in the Fifth Circuit Court. They contended that HUAC's questions regarding both the letter endorsed by southern black leaders and another letter the Bradens circulated opposing HUAC chairman Walter's bill to revive state sedition laws "reveal its firm determination to interfere with the basic rights of petition, association, and belief." Richard Arens, the brief continued, admitted that SCEF employed Braden to support integration but "claimed the right to question whether [SCEF] had a 'proper motive.'" This improper probing could serve no "legislative purpose," but was simply an "effrontery." The Constitution guaranteed citizens the right to oppose, and sign petitions against, proposed legislative actions.[67]

Nevertheless, a three-judge panel in New Orleans refused to reverse the conviction, and the full court declined to hear the case. Coe and Boudin appealed to the Supreme Court. There, on November 17, 1960, the lawyers split the argument. At one point Justice Black objected to discussion about whether Braden had been a Communist when he wrote the letter opposing the Walter bill: "Doesn't a communist have a right to oppose a bill?" But Justice Frankfurter, upset about the tenor of the questions, asked Coe if he thought "the fact that a man has petitioned Congress immunizes him from questions about his exercise of the right of petition." Coe later reported that he stirred up a "hell of a hassle" when he stated his position that in "noncommercial lobbying" citizens could not be restrained in contacting their public officials. Several NLG lawyers observing the argument judged that Boudin and Coe had the better of the case.[68]

But they were mistaken. The Court divided along lines taken in many civil liberties cases by 1959 and 1960, five to four upholding conviction in both the Braden and Wilkinson cases. About three months after this decision, handed down February 27, 1961, Junius Scales's case finally met a similar end. In December, 1958, the Supreme Court had granted his petition for

---

Jim Dombrowski, January 9, 1959, Williams to Coe, January 10, 1959, Coe to Williams, January 12, 1959, *Afro-American,* January 31, 1959, p. 5, and Louisville *Defender,* February 5, 1959, p. 1, all ibid.

67. "News from Southern Conference Educational Fund, Inc.," August 12, 1959, ibid.

68. Louisville *Courier-Journal,* November 18, 1960, and J. M. Coe to Carl Braden, November 18, 1960, ibid.

certiorari. His attorneys (led by former general, Nuremberg prosecutor, and FCC counsel Telford Taylor) and the ACLU and NLG in amicus briefs to the Court contended that the Smith Act clause under which Scales had been convicted violated the First Amendment right of free association. But the Court ultimately sustained Scales's conviction and, on the same day, sustained the Subversive Activities Control Act, in each case over dissents by Justices Warren, Black, Brennan, and Douglas. When it allowed Scales to go to jail for party membership alone, Justice Douglas argued, the Court made "a sharp break with traditional concepts of First Amendment rights." He lamented the majority decision as sad confirmation of "Mark Twain's lighthearted comment that 'It is by the goodness of God that in our country we have those three unspeakably precious things: freedom of speech, freedom of conscience, and the prudence never to practice either of them.'" The Court had upheld guilt by association twenty years after Martin Dies's tenure at HUAC.[69]

In *Braden* v. *U.S.,* the majority, though they confirmed that congressional investigations often curtail freedoms guaranteed by the Bill of Rights, said in effect that these committees had a mandate to investigate subversion that made this abridgment of rights sometimes necessary. The four dissenters— Warren, Brennan, Black, and Douglas—rejected the position that Americans must choose between First Amendment freedoms and national security. In the words of Justice Black, if the government gave HUAC authority to question every American labeled Communist, "no legislative committee, state or federal, will have trouble finding cause to subpoena all persons anywhere who take a public stand for or against segregation." The majority opinion, he protested, did not address the question of whether, in the process of hunting subversion, the committees sometimes persecuted innocent nonconformists.[70]

Carl Braden and Frank Wilkinson served a year in federal prison because they insisted that the First Amendment protected their right to remain silent when questioned about beliefs and associations. Braden always believed that he was prosecuted because of his integrationist activities, not his radical

69. *Scales* v. *U.S.;* Barker, *Freedom, Courts, Politics,* 95–125. John F. Kennedy pardoned Scales on December 24, 1962.

70. *U.S.* v. *Braden,* 2 U.S.C. 192 (1961); "Supreme Court of the United States, No. 54— October Term, 1960, *Carl Braden* v. *U.S.,*" February 27, 1961, Dissent of Justice Black, 4–5, in Box 61, Folder 1, Coe Papers.

politics, and surely he would not have found himself in court the first time but for his devotion to racial equality. Whether or not the Supreme Court considered this point important to the case brought by the House of Representatives, the Court's liberal activism had been tempered considerably since the major 1957 cases that so cheered civil libertarians.

The world seemed to be changing at the beginning of the new decade. When the high court finally adjudicated Braden's case, anti-Communism had lost its attraction for all but the most recalcitrant national politicians, and the young Kennedy administration displayed a fresh image of liberalism and hopefulness. But nongovernmental anti-Communist groups like the John Birch Society and the Minutemen proliferated in the hinterlands, and anti-Communism remained a mainstay of southern state-sponsored segregationism until the mid-1960s. Efforts of right-wing organizations to undermine the federal institution responsible for the *Brown* decision found fertile ground in the South, as "Impeach Earl Warren" billboards sprouted throughout the region. Citing such bitterly divided decisions as *Braden, Wilkinson,* and *Scales,* Senator Eastland, during a filibuster against a Kennedy administration bill to outlaw literacy tests, said that whenever he has the chance the chief justice "decides for the communists."[71]

Between the SCEF hearings in New Orleans and Atlanta fell the critical formative years of the civil rights movement. The movement fueled the anti-Communist rhetoric of the leaders of massive resistance, from local politicians to federal legislators. For southerners caught in the net of congressional anti-Communist committees in the late 1950s, the threat of punishment and social isolation remained very real. The apostasy targeted by SISS and HUAC in the South may have been integrationism, but this purpose was securely robed in the American flag.

71. New York *Times,* April 2, 1961, May 3, 1962.

CHAPTER SEVEN

"Radicals" and "Respectables": The Cold War Against "Outside Agitators," 1958–1963

Coe, Durr, and Smith enlisted naturally in the quickening southern civil rights movement after the Montgomery bus boycott. In retrospect it seems as if all the experience of the two older men (Durr was sixty-one in 1960, Coe sixty-four) had prepared them to advise the young lawyers who faced the constitutional battles of the 1960s; and though only thirty-three in 1960, Smith had much more experience in civil rights and civil liberties matters than most of his southern contemporaries. For these lawyers and others like them, no great chasm separated civil liberties and civil rights cases. The contest simply continued, an endless stream of challenges to the Constitution acknowledged by an expanding arsenal of legal rejoinders and remedies.

Even after congressional hearings probing southern subversion ended, federally sustained anti-Communism plagued controversial lawyers. At a Christmas gathering in 1959, as the Braden case awaited Supreme Court review and Coe prepared for a last year as head of the NLG, several members of his family reported FBI interrogations concerning his loyalty. The relatives themselves had been cleared of wrongdoing, Coe wrote Carl Braden, because the investigators were "vigorously assured, by a well meaning but not too truthful source, that members of my family, related both by blood and marriage, strongly disagree with my politico-social views." He asked the *Southern Patriot,* preparing an article on him for its January, 1960, issue, to say that only his wife shared his ideas.[1]

In addition to his relationship with Braden, Coe's leadership of the National Lawyers Guild doubtless created these dilemmas for his family. Despite

---

1. J. M. Coe to Carl Braden, December 31, 1959, in Box 60, Folder 18, and Braden to Coe, January 1, 1960, in Box 3, Folder 106, Coe Papers.

the attorney general's abandonment of the case against the organization in 1958, the FBI continued to hound the guild. John Satterfield, a prominent Mississippi attorney and president-elect of the ABA, indicated to J. Edgar Hoover at a meeting in March, 1960, that "he wanted to expel from the ABA any attorney who continued to be associated with the NLG." He asked the director for information to assist with this undertaking. In response, a high-ranking bureau official personally delivered to Satterfield a twenty-five-page memorandum, including the old HUAC reports on the guild and photographs taken by FBI agents at the 1958 NLG convention. Not surprisingly, during Satterfield's presidency Cliff Durr finally severed formal ties with the ABA.[2]

Durr remained convinced that civil rights abuses resulted directly from the American people's inability to accept and live up to the promise of the First Amendment. Just after Eisenhower used federal troops to enforce *Brown* in Little Rock, Durr wrote to Drew Pearson, "We are so scared of saying what we think that we seem to have stopped thinking entirely and I am not just talking about the South. . . . I hope it won't take four years of Dickie Nixon to bring us to our senses." Three years later, with a Democrat safely ensconced in the White House, he was still angry about the cowardice of liberals, North and South. The South's inability to change evidenced only "a slightly different symptom of the national disease. Somehow the disease itself seems to be the only acceptable evidence of good health. Those who don't have it are sent to quarantine." From Durr's perspective, national politics had not changed much from the days of Harry Truman. "GOD SAVE US!" he wrote to newspaperman Ray Jenkins, "from the 'liberals' as well as the righteous and the patriotic (super patriots)."[3]

But of the three lawyers, Durr was the most moderate politically. Though he despised ADA-inspired "anti-Communist" liberalism, in classic terms he was an authentic American liberal, an open-minded progressive reformer who espoused democracy, regulated capitalism, and equal opportunity. He en-

2. Ginger and Tobin, eds., *NLG*, 190; C. J. Durr to Claude E. Hamilton, July 24, 1964, in Box 3, Folder 9, C. J. Durr Papers. In 1962, Satterfield advised Governor Ross Barnett to defy the Fifth Circuit Court order to admit James Meredith to the University of Mississippi. See Jack Bass, *Unlikely Heroes* (Tuscaloosa, 1981), 187.

3. C. J. Durr to Drew Pearson, October 18, 31, 1957, in Box 38, Folder 1, to Prof. Dallas Smythe, May 5, 1960, in Box 3, Folder 2, and to Ray Jenkins, February 2, 1961, in Box 3, Folder 4, all in C. J. Durr Papers.

dured stoically, but never appreciated, being called "left wing." Nevertheless, evidence indicates that elements of the federal bureaucracy and the national press continued to consider him such. For instance, in 1960 three British students came to see the Durrs after visiting with their controversial British-born friend Jessica Mitford in California. Commonwealth scholars, the graduate students had studied at the University of California at Berkeley. One of the young men had been held briefly along with a large group of protesting students who tried to get into a HUAC hearing in California, though charges were dropped. Government agents followed the three across the country, and the FBI maintained constant watch outside the Durrs' house during their visit in Montgomery.[4]

After the students left the country, the Washington *Post* reported that they had stopped in Alabama to get advice from "Clifford Durr, former president of the left wing National Lawyers Guild." This method of identifying him, Durr wrote to the reporter, seemed mystifying. Why not say he had been with the RFC, the DPC, the FCC, "or, for that matter, a Deacon in the Presbyterian Church, a life long Democrat or a Grandpa?" He did not mind being remembered as NLG president, or even being labeled "left wing," but he objected to the article's overall "impression that on his arrival in Alabama [Oxford student] Cassen was again inadvertently thrown in with a 'radical.'"[5]

Nevertheless, Durr was enough of a southern iconoclast to be infuriated by the Alabama bar's rationalizations about "the law of the case" as opposed to "the law of the land," the tedious legal dogma of retreat from the implications of the *Brown* decision. He hated the propensity of the South's leading lawyers for "cussing the courts" and avoiding the obvious meanings of the Fourteenth Amendment. Contrary to local opinion, Durr believed that the Supreme Court and "outside agitators" were not the South's problem. Her distress issued from the many wary southerners who knew better but refused to speak out for justice.[6]

---

4. Memorandum for the Files, Re: English Students—Christopher Bacon, Cambridge, Robert Cassen, Oxford, Caroline Mitchell, Cambridge, with attached clipping, Washington *Post*, n.d., in Box 45, Folder 9, ibid.

5. Ibid., C. J. Durr to Daniel Greenberg, Washington *Post*, September 7, 1960, in Box 3, Folder 3, ibid.

6. C. J. Durr, "The Law of the Case," n.d. (this paper was written in response to a speech

During the McCarthy era he had worried more about the "respectables" than the "stinkers." As the 1960s began, "the spectacle of [southern] decency retreating into expedience under the pressure of fear" offended him. The danger that jobs and social position might be lost kindled this fear in "decent" southerners, Durr told a northern supporter. "Above all" they dreaded "the loneliness that is the price for non-conformity," a loneliness he understood very well. His own heresy, for example, had led to his removal from leadership of a Sunday school class at the First Presbyterian Church in 1957. To an old friend from Oxford days he wrote in 1960 of trying "to do what I can . . . to salvage bits and pieces of the law from the not too cold war of the Confederacy against the 'outside agitators.'" The effort was making him poor and unpopular. In 1961 he lamented that the new black lawyers had become heroes in their own communities, while white liberal lawyers suffered isolation and failure.[7]

A great deal of Durr's frustration stemmed from his professional life. His reputation as a liberal and integrationist made it difficult to secure profitable cases in Montgomery. Business and professional men did not seek him out. His day-to-day practice, with a few important exceptions, also brought little intellectual satisfaction. He accepted small criminal cases with graciousness and a sense of duty and purpose, but he was not, at heart, a small-town general practice lawyer. Most of his clients were "impecunious Negroes who have far more legal problems than money for legal fees," he complained. Though many "northern 'liberal' friends of former days assure Virginia and me of their deep admiration [they] refer any legal business they might have to more respectable white supremacist lawyers." Writing a decade later, Birmingham attorney Charles Morgan agreed, saying northern liberals often commended civil rights lawyers but "sent their paying clients' law business to Ivy League law school classmates who had joined the South's leading

---

given by the president of the Alabama Bar Association on July 17, 1958), in Box 14, Folder 3, ibid.

7. C. J. Durr to Editor, Montgomery *Advertiser,* March 1, 1960, in Box 3, Folder 2, to John A. V. Davies, M.D., May 5, 1960, to Dr. Ralph Harlow, December 9, 1960, in Box 3, Folder 3, and undated, untitled letter signed by Durr and found in file titled "*Nesmith* v. *Alford*—May–Dec 1961" (though this case is not mentioned in the letter), in Box 43, Folder 8, all ibid.

segregationist firms." Durr retained a few old clients and his family's business, but the number of cases of police violence and harassment to be handled dismayed and depressed him. As he litigated against the local law enforcement establishment or helped with cases arising from early civil rights activities, his practice seemed to have the threadbare flavor of a legal aid society.[8]

Often Durr simply wanted to escape both his practice and the suffocating intellectual atmosphere of segregated Montgomery. In the spring of 1958 he went gladly to lecture at Sarah Lawrence College and Princeton, and after returning he once again began to investigate the possibility of finding work as a teacher. He wrote to Professor Jay Murphy at the University of Alabama Law School asking for advice about finding an academic position. As in the past this inquiry proved futile, but Durr continued over the next few years to treasure occasional stints as a part-time professor at Sarah Lawrence, Rutgers, Yale, and several other colleges, including two happy trips to speak at seminars in England. The invitations to England were tendered in response to the Durrs' frequent hospitality to Harkness fellows, outstanding young English students similar to American Rhodes scholars.[9]

At home the Durrs became more and more identified with the civil rights movement, and they often found themselves acting as surrogate parents to "SNCC kids" who, like the English visitors, spent "R & R" time at the Durr farm in Wetumpka. The new decade began with demonstrations spreading throughout the South in the wake of sit-ins staged in early February in Greensboro, North Carolina, and the subsequent formation of the Student Non-Violent Coordinating Committee (SNCC). Within weeks of the Greensboro protests, students at Montgomery's all-black Alabama State College staged a sit-in at the snack bar of the Montgomery County courthouse, beginning a

8. Untitled, undated Durr letter, in Box 43, Folder 8, and C. J. Durr to Irving Brant, *Northwest Review,* March 3, 1963, in Box 3, Folder 8—for cases against the city police see the cases of Rufus Horne (1958), in Box 42, Folder 9, Bessie Mae Prince (1959–61), in Box 43, Folders 1 and 2, Henry Jackson (1960), in Box 45, Folder 8, Mack London (1961), in Box 46, Folder 1, and Caesar Davis (1961), in Box 46, Folder 3, all ibid.; Charles Morgan, *One Man, One Voice* (New York, 1979), 21.

9. C. J. Durr to Professor Jay Murphy, June 16, 1958, in Box 2, Folder 9, and to Professor Dallas Smythe, May 24, 1960, in Box 3, Folder 2, both in C. J. Durr Papers; Ann Durr Lyon to author, October 20, 1996.

series of civil rights demonstrations that lasted through the first week in March.[10]

Three weeks later, Montgomery officials arrested a group of black and white students who continued a prolonged academic discussion about race relations by sharing lunch in a black-owned restaurant. The Montgomery city council had repealed ordinances prohibiting interracial dining, but police detained the group for "disorderly conduct" because, after the arrival of several patrol cars, the police commissioner, the chief of police, three reporters, and television cameras, a crowd of black Montgomerians gathered across the street from the restaurant. Police entered the café and took moving pictures of the integrated luncheon before sending the participants to the city jail.[11]

Traveling through the South on a field trip with their dean and sociology professor, his wife, and their small child, the ten detained white students attended McMurray College, a small Methodist school in Illinois. An editor of the *Alabama Journal* called them "an Illinois sociologist and his 10 amateur exhibitionist students." The group had been to Little Rock, New Orleans, Jackson, and Vicksburg before Montgomery. According to the *Journal*'s editorial they "made a bee-line for Hodding Carter, Aubrey Williams, Clifford Durr and other unrepresentative citizens who are wholly unorthodox in their views about race mixing." The college contacted Cliff Durr after their arrests and asked him to represent them. Four black students from Montgomery, including two who had been expelled by the Alabama Board of Education for participation in the recent sit-ins, two black ministers, leaders of the Montgomery Improvement Association, and one visiting white theological student from Boston were arrested at the café with the McMurray group. Lawyers Fred Gray, Solomon S. Seay, Jr. (son of one of the arrested ministers), and Charles Langford represented these local defendants.[12]

10. Ann Durr Lyon to author, October 20, 1996; Solomon S. Seay, Sr., *I Was There by the Grace of God* (Montgomery, 1990), 219–21.

11. Briefs, transcripts, letters, and notes concerning *City of Montgomery* v. *Richard A. Nesmith et al.* and *Nesmith et al.* v. *Alford et al.* are found in Boxes 43, Folder 5, through Box 45, and in Boxes 53 and 54, C. J. Durr Papers.

12. Seay, *I Was There*, 222–23; *Alabama Journal*, articles, April 1, 4, 1960, editorial, April 4, 1960, in Box 43, Folder 4, and C. J. Durr to editor, April 7, 1960, in Box 45, Folder 6, all in C. J. Durr Papers.

The McMurray students spent a night in jail. Durr could arrange bail only for the distressed professor, Richard A. Nesmith, and his wife, whose little girl had been taken by county authorities during the afternoon. After a frantic evening, the Durrs located the two-year-old child in a foster home; the county finally released her to the Nesmiths late that night. The next morning a recorder's court magistrate found the couple, the local ministers, and the students guilty of disturbing the peace. After the college arranged bond, Nesmith and his entourage returned to their Illinois campus. When they came back to Montgomery for a trial in state circuit court in May, a jury acquitted the students and Mrs. Nesmith but fined the dean $100 plus court costs, obviously a compromise verdict. Adding injury to insult, because the clerk's office had closed its doors for the night the judge refused to accept bond. Since Durr could not file a formal appeal until the next day, Dean Nesmith spent the night in jail. Fred Gray and Durr immediately filed joint appeals for all of those arrested. The Court of Appeals of Alabama reversed the circuit court decision on technical grounds related to the arrest procedure, but never considered the merits of the case.[13]

Durr decided "something [should] be done to slow down the police and also to stop the use of such statutes as disorderly conduct, vagrancy, and the like for substitutes for the old segregation ordinances." He initiated *Nesmith* v. *Sullivan,* the civil suit that became *Nesmith* v. *Alford,* to recover damages from the police commissioner, the chief of police, and three other Montgomery police officers. It charged malicious prosecution, unlawful arrest, and violation of the plaintiffs' civil rights.[14]

Durr faced "three sets of lawyers," he told Nesmith in a letter seeking authorization to engage Ben Smith to assist him with the fight in federal courts. One defendant's attorney, John Kohn, had represented Virginia Durr in New Orleans. Kohn, however, had become a key adviser and speechwriter for Alabama governor George Wallace; before the Nesmith litigation ended

13. Montgomery *Advertiser,* April 2, 1960, Sec. A, p. 6, *Alabama Journal,* April 27, May 10, 11, 14, 1960, in Box 45, Folder 6, and Montgomery *Advertiser,* May 11, 1960, p. 1, in Box 43, Folder 4, all in C. J. Durr Papers.

14. *Nesmith* v. *Alford,* 318 F.2d 110 (1963), *cert. denied,* 375 U.S. 975 (1963); unidentified transcript, Cliff Durr interview by "Henrietta," quote on "Tape 1, Page 7–8," in Box 45, Folder 7 [hereinafter cited as "Henrietta Transcript"], and Durr to George Eddy, June 15, 1961, in Box 44, Folder 3, both in C. J. Durr Papers.

he would be one of the architects of Wallace's schoolhouse-door "statement and proclamation" against the federal order to admit black students to the University of Alabama. Against such formidable opposition, Durr thought he needed help from Smith, his "old friend," whom he believed to be "a very fine lawyer" and who had more experience in preparing damage suits for the federal courts. The two men worked together through a jury trial before Alabama district judge Frank Johnson and the appeal in New Orleans before a three-judge panel of the Fifth Circuit Court composed of Judges Richard Rives, John R. Brown, and Benjamin F. Cameron. Although the suit failed in federal district court before an Alabama jury, over a strong Cameron dissent Rives and Brown sent the case back to Johnson's court in 1963 with instructions for a directed verdict in the Nesmiths' favor. Donations from the NAACP Inc. Fund, the ACLU, and the ECLC's Bill of Rights Fund supported the Fifth Circuit appeal.[15]

According to Judge Brown's majority opinion, only the amount of damages still required determination by a district court jury. "Liberty is at an end," he wrote, when police, without warrants, arrest citizens behaving peacefully and legally simply because they offend some members of the community. "When that day comes, freedom of the press, freedom of assembly, speech, and freedom of religion will all be imperiled." The opinion was everything Durr had hoped for, a great moral victory.[16]

After the Supreme Court denied the defendants' petition for certiorari, John Kohn approached Durr with an offer to settle rather than retry the case. Ben Smith declared his willingness to undertake a new trial, but Durr recommended that the Nesmiths accept Kohn's offer. The parties resolved the matter out of court for little more than costs. Durr felt that his clients might

15. C. J. Durr to Richard Nesmith, August 1, 1961, in Box 44, Folder 3, C. J. Durr Papers; *Nesmith v. Alford;* Dan T. Carter, *The Politics of Rage: George Wallace, the Origins of the New Conservatism, and the Transformation of American Politics* (New York, 1995), 145–49. For information on financial support for the case see esp. C. J. Durr to B. E. Smith, March 9, 1962, and Jack Greenberg to Durr, February 20, 1962, in Box 44, Folder 4, Durr to Corliss Lamont, January 9, 1962, and to Mel Wulf, January 8, 1962, in Box 44, Folder 5, and also letters to contributors in Box 44, Folder 6, all in C. J. Durr Papers.

16. *Nesmith v. Alford.* For a good description of the litigation see Durr's article, "A Field Trip to Montgomery, Alabama," in *Southern Justice,* ed. Friedman, which quotes this paragraph on page 56.

not even recover out-of-pocket expenses in another trial before an Alabama jury. "Unless there is a tremendous change in the climate of opinion . . . there is no use kidding ourselves about the prospects of getting more than nominal damages," he wrote Smith, "but the case may have some further educational value as well as a deterrent effect on police irresponsibility." The victory took four years and brought no profit to the attorneys, but Durr believed that it helped to temper the behavior of the city's police, especially during the 1965 Selma march.[17]

During the four years of the McMurray litigation, the civil rights movement matured and both Smith and Durr became involved in many other similar matters. As preparations began for the first federal complaint in *Nesmith* v. *Alford,* Durr litigated a civil liberties case connected to the "freedom rides" that electrified the South in May, 1961. Jessica Mitford, visiting the Durrs when the integrated buses arrived at the Greyhound station in Montgomery, witnessed not only the intimidation and beatings there but the mass meetings that night at which Martin Luther King, Jr., and Ralph David Abernathy spoke while a malevolent crowd and state police surrounded First Baptist Church. Unfortunately, Mitford parked the Durrs' car near the church, and the crowd overturned and burned it during the disturbance. In the turmoil that morning Mitford had encountered Fred and Anna Gach, whom she later introduced to Cliff Durr.[18]

Though not involved in the freedom rides or other civil rights activities, Fred Gach, an ex-paratrooper and student at Auburn University, and his wife, Anna, a Linotype operator for the Montgomery *Advertiser,* happened upon the violence taking place near the bus station. As the scene seemed to settle down they moved nearer to investigate. The couple found themselves confronted by three white men, one holding a baseball bat, beating a young black man lying in the street. Appalled and frightened, Anna Gach began to call for the police while Fred Gach tried to intervene. A crowd gathered, including three armed Montgomery policemen who refused to become part of the melee. Finally the Alabama state police commissioner happened by and, brandishing

17. *Nesmith* v. *Alford;* C. J. Durr to B. E. Smith, January 8, 1964, in Box 45, Folder 4, C. J. Durr Papers.

18. C. J. Durr to George Eddy, June 15, 1961, in Box 44, Folder 3, C. J. Durr Papers; Barnard, ed., *Outside the Magic Circle,* 298–301.

his weapon, ordered the attackers to back off. Unfortunately, after the commissioner disappeared the crowd again turned on the Gachs, who in the end were detained by local police, the first arrests of that terrible day.[19]

Straightaway the recorder's court found the couple guilty of disorderly conduct and resisting arrest and fined them $150 each. When the bail bondsman discovered they had been convicted for defending a black man during the freedom ride disturbances, he refused to make bond. New residents without contacts in Montgomery, the Gachs spent the day in jail before her sister in Selma could arrange their bail. In the ensuing jury trial Durr said, "I took as my text the story of the good Samaritan." The trial received a good deal of publicity and generated financial assistance not only from Mitford and her husband, NLG lawyer Robert Truehaft, but from Jim Dombrowski and SCEF. Although "the jury couldn't bring themselves to an acquittal," they reduced Fred Gach's fine to $50 and Anna's to $25. Durr wanted to appeal the convictions, but Mrs. Gach had already lost her job at the *Advertiser* as a result of the case and could not bear the possibility of spending more time in jail. The couple left Alabama and dropped the case.[20]

The day-to-day practices of Coe, Durr, and Smith differed a great deal in the late 1950s and early 1960s, in spite of similarities in the issues they faced and rare shared cases like *Nesmith*. Durr's struggling general practice always centered in Montgomery, where the Durrs assisted civil rights workers from near and far. When called upon, he advised younger lawyers and made his law library available to the movement. Smith, though his firm handled a great variety of cases, operated primarily as a New Orleans labor lawyer until NLG-sponsored civil rights responsibilities overtook his practice in 1962 and 1963. Coe had his work as guild president until 1961 and, through the Braden case, a deepening involvement with SCEF and its causes in other parts of the South. Travel as a representative of these organizations afforded him the kind of respite and sympathetic companionship Durr found in his teaching stints, though in Coe's case at greater sacrifice in income.

19. Barnard, ed., *Outside the Magic Circle*, 300–301; *City of Montgomery* v. *Fred and Anna Gach*, in Box 46, Folder 4, C. J. Durr Papers.

20. *City of Montgomery* v. *Fred and Anna Gach*; "Henrietta Transcript," "Tape 2, Side 2, Page 7" to "Tape 2, Side 1, Page 12," quotes on "Tape 2, Side 1, Page 11," in Box 45, Folder 7, C. J. Durr Papers; Salmond, *Conscience of a Lawyer*, 188.

Coe spent a great deal of time speaking for the guild and SCEF in places as far-flung as Boston, Philadelphia, and Los Angeles. In March, 1960, he addressed SCEF's annual New York fund-raising party at the Delmonico Hotel, a reception hosted by Eleanor Roosevelt. The final NLG convention of his presidency took place in September. The lawyers' resolutions at that meeting reflected the guild's twenty-year-plus popular front stance, advocating bills mandating integration in housing and expanded voting rights in the South and opposing both capital punishment and the Smith Act. Coe received numerous accolades from NLG members who appreciated his faithful service. After the convention the guild's executive secretary wrote about Coe's "enthusiasm, warmth, and extraordinary eloquence [which] contributed to the very maintenance of the Guild as an organization." In addition to SCEF and NLG activities, until illness slowed Coe down in 1961 he also continued to be a very busy trial lawyer in north Florida and a "poor man's lawyer," as well.[21]

Ben Smith embarked on one of the busiest periods of his career in the late 1950s. When Orleans Parish district attorney Richard Dowling took office, he asked Smith and his good friend and fellow Louisiana Civil Liberties Union board member Leonard Dreyfus to join the department's staff. The liberal New Orleans official also appointed Earl Amedee as the first black assistant district attorney in the city's history "to handle cases involving Negroes."[22]

The FBI noted these appointments in a May 7, 1958, internal memo reporting Senator Eastland's interest in the matter and his "opinion some of these individuals have bad backgrounds and may be communistically inclined. [He] desired a check on the names." A response stated that Smith's name had been "on the security index from August 12, 1954 to June 7, 1955," when it was "removed therefrom due to lack of positive information placing him in the CP." Despite two further inconclusive checks, after Smith denied party membership under oath in the 1956 SISS hearings and appeared as

21. J. M. Coe to Jim Dombrowski, January 8, 1960, in Box 3, Folder 108, Howard Melish to Coe, March 3, 1960, and David Scribner to Coe, September 6, 1960, in Box 3, Folder 117, all in Coe Papers; Dombrowski to Coe, January 13, 1960, Microfilm No. 306, Reel 4, Braden Papers; *New York Guild Lawyer*, XVIV (May, 1960), 1, and (September, 1960), 1, in Box 90, NLG Papers, King Center.

22. New Orleans *Times-Picayune*, April 24, 1958, p. 1.

counsel before the committee again in 1957, the FBI continued to compile information on him. His presence and speech at an NLG convention were noted in November, 1958. Another memo, from G. A. Nease to Clyde Tolson, Hoover's assistant and roommate, reported the bureau's "problems" with 150Eastland, who had asked a Justice Department official to "disclose an informant" who would witness against Smith. Since there were "relatively few Party members in the South," Nease worried that disclosing one name would probably mean other informants would be uncovered. Most would lose their jobs if they were exposed as Communists, so they would have to admit to being FBI informants. This had been explained to Eastland before, the official reported, when the senator had requested names for hearings in Montgomery. (Surely this was a reference to Eastland's original plan to follow up the 1954 SCEF hearings by persecuting the Durrs and Aubrey Williams in their hometown.) In the past the FBI had maintained a close but "informal" relationship with the senator. Nease carefully explained to Eastland that because he had "formalized this request" by going to a Justice Department official, "it placed our previous cooperation, which was informal . . . in jeopardy and it placed the Bureau in a most embarrassing position." While the FBI completed yet another long, repetitious report listing Smith's activities, Nease recommended that the matter be "referred to the Domestic Intelligence Division" and that "within a reasonable time I call the Senator and advise him that we cannot help him in this matter."[23]

Despite these probes, Smith served as an assistant district attorney from 1958 until 1960. Following local custom, he retained his private clients as well. Smith worked with Coe on several administrative matters for SCEF during the time he was in the district attorney's office, and he remained an active labor lawyer, representing Maritime Union members, Longshoremen, and Packinghouse Workers in both organizational and personal injury matters. The Maritime Union retained him for its New Orleans local, and he served the Packinghouse Workers as regional attorney in southern Louisiana.[24]

23. Memos, R. R. Roach to A. H. Belmont, May 7, 1958, and G. A. Nease to Mr. Tolson, May 19, 1958, Smith FBI File; SAC (100-16805), SA Milton R. Kaack, November 4, 1958, in FBI files for New Orleans chapter, National Lawyers Guild (copies, gift of Mary E. Howell, attorney).

24. Wright interview.

In late 1959 Smith fired off a series of letters on UPWA's behalf indicating his willingness to file a civil rights action against New Orleans Public Service. This company operated the buses that transported workers to the American Sugar Refinery in St. Bernard Parish from their homes in Orleans Parish. In addition to the bus company, Smith's letters went to St. Bernard's law enforcement officials, including Leander Perez, the notorious and powerful district attorney for Louisiana's Twenty-Fifth Judicial Circuit. Officers boarded the buses as they entered St. Bernard Parish and required passengers to segregate themselves by race, in defiance of a recent order from federal district judge J. Skelly Wright. The sheriff, indicating that his deputies were not involved, replied that the trouble must be originating with officers assigned to the office of District Attorney Perez. Smith suggested that the union carefully document the misconduct over a period of weeks to create a written list of abuses before filing for remedy under the civil rights statutes. SCEF's successful challenge to Louisiana's bus segregation laws had led to Judge Wright's decision in 1958, and Smith believed that a lawsuit against Perez could succeed in federal court.[25]

Employment by the district attorney in Orleans Parish apparently did not restrict Smith's authority to bring suit as a private attorney against his superior's counterpart in a nearby district. Nor did it prohibit his participation in the NLG or SCEF; he continued to be active in both while serving in parish government. In October, 1960, for example, he begged off from a SCEF board meeting at Fisk University in Nashville because he had asked his good friend NLG vice-president Herman Wright to come from Houston to address a group of thirty New Orleans lawyers about "a professional question."[26]

Smith litigated another controversial case during this period as an attorney for the Louisiana Civil Liberties Union. In May, 1960, Shreveport police

25. B. E. Smith to New Orleans Public Service, Inc., and to Dr. Nicholas B. Trist, Sheriff, October 2, 1959 (copies of both letters sent to Leander Perez and others), Trist to Smith, October 6, 1959, and Smith to President and Executive Board, UPWA, October 19, 1959, in Box 49, Folder 2, A. P. Tureaud Papers, Amistad Research Center, New Orleans [hereinafter cited as Tureaud Papers]. The Twenty-Fifth Judicial Circuit included St. Bernard and Plaquemines, Perez's home parish. For Judge Wright's decision see *Morrison* v. *Davis,* 252 F.2d 102 (1958), *cert. denied* 78 S.Ct. 108.

26. B. E. Smith to Jim Dombrowski, October 13, 1960, Microfilm No. 306, Reel 5, Braden Papers.

arrested Ashton Jones, a white itinerant minister en route from California to Georgia, and a judge sentenced him to eight months in jail for "disturbing the peace and vagrancy." A pacifist and integrationist, Jones attended a black church, ate lunch at a black-owned café, and then faced arrest as he left town with the word "brotherhood" painted on the side of his van. With supplemental funds from ECLC and SCEF, Smith appealed Jones's case to federal courts on both First and Fourteenth Amendment grounds, finally obtaining his release in 1961.[27]

Almost simultaneously, Smith handled a countersuit for five black picketers arrested by state police in New Orleans while protesting the hiring practices of Puglia Market. The defendants in this suit included nine state policemen, the owner of the market, and an investigator for the Louisiana State Sovereignty Commission, the legislative body charged with upholding Louisiana's expanding antisubversive legislation. The picketers had been charged under recent statutes deviously designed to squelch civil rights activity, according to Smith's complaint. He characterized the arrest as a "conspiracy" between the state police, businessman Puglia, and agents of the Sovereignty Commission. In this matter, as in his brush with Perez, Smith tempted fate.[28]

The employment of Bruce Waltzer as his clerk in 1959 enabled Smith to sustain his private cases while working in the district attorney's office. Waltzer, a bright, liberal Tulane law student who had served with the U.S. Army Counter-Intelligence Corps in Europe, remained with Smith after he resigned the parish post in October, 1960. Not long after Waltzer's admission

27. B. E. Smith to John R. Downes, October 3, 1960, to Booker Powell, November, 1961, unidentified clipping, and page from trial transcript, Reel 5, Microfilm No. 360, all ibid.; Shreveport *Journal,* March 31, 1961, p. 1, in Box 3, Folder 5, C. J. Durr Papers. Southern police arrested Jones, a graduate of Emory University, several times, most famously after he and two young black friends attempted to worship in Atlanta's First Baptist Church in 1963. He was sentenced to twelve months at hard labor plus six months in Fulton County jail. In May, 1965, sixty-eight-year-old Jones went on a hunger strike in jail. SCEF issued an "action memo" asking people to write to the Georgia Pardons and Parole Board urging his release. By that time the church, the Atlanta newspapers, and the Fulton County attorney all favored his release, and the church had opened its doors to all. See the *Southern Patriot,* November, 1963, p. 7; and "Action Memo Re: The Reverend Ashton B. Jones," May 19, 1965, in Box 48, Folder 16, Coe Papers.

28. *Margaret M. Thomas et al.* v. *Joseph R. Capaci et al.,* in Box 3, Folder 13, Smith Papers.

to the bar in 1961, the two men formed a partnership that lasted until 1967. While they agreed on many contemporary issues and both worked primarily as litigators, Waltzer and Smith differed in temperament and background. Smith cultivated clients and causes; Waltzer became the firm administrator and caretaker, attempting, sometimes in vain, to keep his partner's extravagances in check. "I very much idolized him and I felt what we were doing was right," he said in 1990, but "you could have an everyday relationship with him and never really get to know him." Born and raised in Brooklyn, Waltzer shared a common background with the civil liberties lawyers of New York who dominated the NLG until the 1960s, but he had a hard time understanding Ben Smith.[29]

Some of Smith's southern friends and family also had a hard time understanding his ideas and activities in late 1960. Three months after resigning as assistant district attorney, he accompanied a group of liberal lawyers, including John Coe, on a trip to Cuba at the invitation of the lawyers association in Havana. A Havana newspaper called Smith the "North American attorney for the Sugar Workers Union of New Orleans, Louisiana" and reported he spoke of "a lively interest" in Cuba "for some time." An informant told the FBI that Smith had interviewed Fidel Castro and believed he was "helping the poor people of Cuba." In a note thanking his hosts, Coe called Cuba "a new order which . . . gives promise to be the finest in the hemisphere, and a brilliant example not only to the other Latin American countries but to my own." Smith and Coe joined about one thousand "invitados" from all over the world in a celebration of the second anniversary of Castro's socialist revolution. Wined, dined, and treated to long Castro speeches, they also toured new housing projects and reorganized sugar plantations.[30]

When the returning lawyers arrived in Miami on January 2, 1961, hostile newspaper reporters greeted them with the news that the United States had broken diplomatic relations with Cuba. The Pensacola *News-Journal,* however, ran several articles about Coe's trip which he thought basically fair.

29. Waltzer interview.

30. Report, July 24, 1962, pp. 3–4, Smith FBI File. The best descriptions of this trip are long letters written by Coe the week after his return from Cuba: J. M. Coe to Ann Fagan Ginger, January 7, 1961, in Box 3, Folder 119, to *Colegio de Abogados de la Havana* and Wick and Judy Coe, January 7, 1961, and to Sis, January 8, 1961, in Box 65, Folder 9, all in Coe Papers.

Then a series of letters debating his patriotism appeared. Coe told one correspondent that the newspapers published his own statements "honestly and properly, with the result that a large blast of scurrility descended on me and mine. I can stand it, but mine it hurts." Letters to the editor included a defensive rejoinder from Evalyn Coe containing suspicious hints of her husband's writing style.[31]

A few weeks later, speculation arose again that Coe would be called before Florida's Legislative Investigating Committee probing "communism in the integration movement." Coe stated publicly that he would be glad to answer questions at any time. SCEF appeared in the local news as prominently as had Coe's trip to Cuba after the Florida committee issued a subpoena to Carl Braden, then speaking and organizing for SCEF in Florida while awaiting the Supreme Court's opinion in his contempt case. Coe dispensed another statement to the newspaper in which he defended both his representation of Braden and his membership in SCEF and the NLG. He assured the press of his willingness to state under oath that he was not and had never been a member of the Communist Party.[32]

Field secretary Braden came to Pensacola to discuss the Florida legislative hearing. Coe learned with some distress that, except for stating his name, Braden did not plan to answer any of the committee's questions. The strategy appeared even more likely to bring contempt charges than his behavior toward HUAC in 1958. Complaining of "the lawyer's mind at work," Braden told Dombrowski he and Coe had cleared the air but had not come to an understanding. Coe assured SCEF's executive director that he would accompany Braden and "preach at his funeral," though he strongly disagreed with the strategy.[33]

Later he sent Braden a long explanation of his objections. Rebuffed again, Coe reversed his earlier decision, deciding that since his advice had been

31. Pensacola *News-Journal*, January 6, 22, 1961, p. 1; Miami *News*, January 5, 1961, and J. M. Coe to Mr. and Mrs. E. B. Collette, January 21, 1961, in Box 4, Folder 2, Coe Papers.

32. Daytona *Morning Journal*, January 26, 1961, p. 1, and SCEF News Release, "Carl Braden to Friends in Florida," n.d., in Box 65, Folder 13, Coe Papers; Pensacola *News-Journal*, February 13, 1961, p. 1.

33. J. M. Coe to Jim Dombrowski, January 30, 1961, and Carl Braden to Coe, February 4, 1961, in Box 65, Folder 13, Coe Papers; Braden to Dombrowski, January 30, 1961, in Box 51, Folder 8, Braden Papers.

rejected "I might as well stay home." A young black attorney and new SCEF board member from Norfolk, Len Holt, attended the Tallahassee hearings with Braden on February 9, 1961. The Florida investigating committee, ready for Coe and surprised by Holt's appearance, discussed the absent attorney anyway, listing his subversive connections. Forewarned by Braden's repeated statements that he would resist their questions on First Amendment grounds, they refused to swear him in unless he changed his mind. When he did not, they proceeded to read into their record a litany of old reports and testimony about SCEF and Braden, beginning with the 1954 testimony of Alberta Ahearn in Louisville.[34]

After the U.S. Supreme Court rejected Braden's appeal of the contempt conviction in late February and he entered federal prison, the Florida committee dropped its efforts against him. Coe was amazed that Braden got off so lightly. A year later, declining with regret an invitation to speak at a New York celebration after Braden's release, he ventured that Braden had "confused his enemies through a reckless disregard of their power, where they have been accustomed to see people cringe before them." Regardless of their disagreements, he considered Braden a singularly brave man.[35]

Since Braden's Florida appearance and the defeat of his federal appeal occurred at the same time, they provoked a rush of articles and speculation about Coe, SCEF, and the NLG in Pensacola newspapers. The publicity accompanying the Braden cases and the Cuba trip took their toll on Coe, who became acutely aware of the strains his activities brought to his practice and his family. Tired and perhaps sensing that he was overextended, Coe decided to cut down on outside activities; the Pensacola practice would come first at this stage in his life. He tried to explain his motives to Jim Dombrowski: "Ever since I got damned and cussed at the time of the Korean War . . . and subsequently suffered more of the same about integration, communism, etc.," people in town had been predicting that he would lose his practice. He had fooled them all and succeeded, "but I have done it the hard way, by diligence, volume, and really excellent technical legal work. . . . Pride drives me to it,"

34. Coe to Braden, February 6, 1961, in Box 65, Folder 13, Coe Papers; Transcript of Testimony, Fla. Leg. Investigating Committee Papers, Carton 5, February 9, 1961 (1 of 2), pp. 12–20 [?] ff. and (2 of 2) pp. 24 [?] ff.

35. J. M. Coe to Howard Melish, December 12, 1961, in Box 48, Folder 16, Coe Papers.

he wrote, "and I expect to continue until matters of health, or possibly really vigorous persecution, drive me out." He was determined to continue at the local bar, no matter what. Quite uncharacteristically, he admitted to Dombrowski some limits to his capacity for work. He thought he must reduce the amount of time he gave to SCEF and other causes not directly related to the local cases handled by "Coe and Coe" in Pensacola.[36]

About a month after writing this letter, Coe entered Emory hospital in Atlanta to have a lung tumor removed and suffered a small stroke while in the hospital. In June, 1961, when Ben Smith asked him to speak at an NLG function in New Orleans honoring the NAACP lawyers who had won the long and complicated New Orleans Parish desegregation case,[37] Coe replied that he was under doctor's orders to stay at home until the following September. The tumor turned out to be benign, but recovery from the surgical procedure and the effects of the stroke had left him incapacitated. A few weeks later he apologized to the guild for sending a "reduced amount" of dues, being temporarily unable to practice law.[38]

Nonetheless, a year later John Coe appeared ready to return full-time to his practice and progressive activities, attending NLG conventions and SCEF board meetings and again defending Carl Braden. The difficulties that prompted *Gray* v. *Alabama*[39] began with mass demonstrations involving several different civil rights groups in the small town of Talladega, Alabama. Many students from the local black college went to jail, and several suffered beatings by police or local segregationists. The Talladega Circuit Court issued a temporary injunction prohibiting civil rights activity by a long list of defendants. In addition to Braden, the injunction cited the Student Action Committee and faculty of Talladega College, SNCC, the Congress of Racial Equality (CORE), SNCC field secretary Robert Zellner (a young friend of the Durrs), Joanne Grant (a reporter for the *National Guardian*), and Norman C. Jimerson of Birmingham, a white American Baptist minister and executive

36. Pensacola *News-Journal*, February 10, 11, 12, 13, 1961; J. M. Coe to Jim Dombrowski, April 26, 1961, in Box 4, Folder 3, Coe Papers (also in Reel 4, Microfilm No. 4, Braden Papers).

37. *Bush* v. *Orleans Parish School Board*, 138 F. Supp. 337.

38. J. M. Coe to B. E. Smith, June 8, 1961, in Box 48, Folder 16, and Coe to the NLG, July 7, 1961, in Box 4, Folder 9, both in Coe Papers.

39. 185 So. 2d 125.

director of the Alabama Council on Human Relations, an affiliate of the Southern Regional Council. Lawyers included Victor Rabinowitz of New York, defending Ms. Grant; Charles Morgan, from Birmingham, for Mr. Jimerson;[40] and Arthur Shores of Birmingham, Bishop Ewbank Tucker of Louisville, and Charles Conley of Montgomery, who represented Talladega faculty, the NAACP, and young members of SNCC and CORE.[41]

Throughout the hearings in Talladega, Coe and Braden continued familiar friendly disagreements about how such a case should be managed. It was a difficult business taking a great deal of his time, Coe told Dombrowski, but he knew he needed to be in Talladega when Braden went on the stand, because he feared Braden would take a "theatrical" position. This would simply "play into the hands of the state," which was trying to create "a great anti-Communist Roman holiday out of a trial that has nothing to do with such matters." Like the Nesmith case, this matter turned around after most of the defendants joined in a countersuit against local and state officials. Though *Gray v. Alabama* defied final settlement until a successful second appeal to the Alabama Supreme Court in 1965, the state simplified the case by dismissing its charges against most of the out-of-state defendants, including Braden, in February, 1963.[42]

Publicity from such cases continued to separate John Coe from childhood friends and professional colleagues in Pensacola as he grew older, but in times of stress he, like Cliff Durr, found a great deal of solace and support in his

40. Morgan would later gain notoriety as the white man who, after four little girls were killed in Birmingham's Sixteenth Avenue Baptist Church in 1963, answered the question "Who threw that bomb?" with a resounding "We all did it" in a speech to a downtown business club. The Talladega case helped to launch his distinguished career as a civil rights and civil liberties lawyer in the South, most of it as head of ACLU offices in Atlanta and Washington. See his autobiography, *One Man, One Voice,* 16–17.

41. Pittsburgh *Courier,* June 23, 1962, SCEF News Release, June 20, 1962, *Alabama ex rel. Gallion* v. *Gray* and *Gray* v. *Alabama,* 1962–1965, entries 55.18 and 63.2, all in Civil Liberties Docket Notebooks, Meiklejohn Civil Liberties Institute, Berkeley, California; Victor Rabinowitz to Ann Wood (Ginger), September 20, 1962, and to George W. Crockett and Ernest Goodman, October 15, 1962, in Box 32, Folder 5, Ann Fagan Ginger Papers, National Lawyers Guild Papers, Meiklejohn Institute [hereinafter cited as NLG Papers, Meiklejohn Institute].

42. *Alabama* v. *Johnson* (Talladega), 173 So. 2d 824 (1963); J. M. Coe to Jim Dombrowski, January 12, 1963, Microfilm No. 360, Reel 4, Braden Papers; see also Rabinowitz, *Unrepentant Leftist,* 271–73.

marriage. Though never an activist like Virginia Durr, Evalyn Coe quietly encouraged her controversial husband and learned to endure his notoriety. She often attended NLG meetings in New York and accompanied her husband to Cuba.[43] Much younger and even less politically involved than Evalyn Coe, Ben Smith's wife, Lillian, often became upset over the publicity engendered by her husband's activism and by his apparently cavalier attitude about its effect on their families and social life.

Smith's trip to Cuba particularly disturbed and embarrassed her. He arrived back at the New Orleans airport resplendent in a new beard and Che Guevara–style fatigues, expressing enthusiasm about the miracle in Cuba to all who would listen, including attendant cameramen from the New Orleans newspapers. Lillian Smith later told her daughter that she would have left him to hire a cab for the ride home had he not already recognized her in the crowd. During the Cuban missile crisis the following year, daughter Penny recalled, the family "felt strange" because everybody knew her father thought Castro was "just doing fine."[44]

Around this time, the New York firm of Boudin and Rabinowitz, which handled the Cuban government's business in the United States and had organized the trip to Cuba, retained Smith to look out for Cuban interests in the port of New Orleans. "Representation of Cuba in the U.S. courts was a very risky business in 1961 and 1962," according to Rabinowitz, but it "did not seem to bother Ben in the slightest" that the cause was very unpopular. He remembered one very complex New Orleans case which Smith "handled quite expertly. . . . I think he took great joy in battling the well-financed shipping companies which were seeking to recover a substantial judgement from Cuba—a judgement they never did succeed in collecting."[45]

In the light of the Cuban venture, it is interesting that Smith and Waltzer's most famous early client was not a leftist but a right-wing fanatic named George Lincoln Rockwell. Supported by the Louisiana Civil Liberties Union and the national ACLU, the firm defended the American "Führer" and other members of the American Nazi Party after their arrest in New Orleans for picketing the film *Exodus* and then an NAACP rally. Although Smith's win-

43. Coe-Grubbs interview.
44. Jones interview.
45. Letter, Victor Rabinowitz to author, September 22, 1992.

ning arguments convinced the appellate court to reverse their convictions, the clients refused to acknowledge the value of their attorneys' civil libertarianism. Rockwell warned Waltzer he would be "the first to go" when the virulently anti-Semitic American Nazi Party came to power.[46]

At about the time the Rockwell case was won, perhaps to celebrate being rid of these offensive clients, Smith employed Marjorie Hamilton, who became the first black secretary in New Orleans' central business district. When he hired her, Smith lost his lease. The firm received an ultimatum—fire Hamilton or move—and they had a very hard time finding new quarters. She worked as his secretary for the next ten years.[47]

As the firm dealt with the Rockwell matter, Smith accepted Durr's invitation to join the Nesmith case. Durr applauded such advocacy, citing *Rockwell* to liberal contributors as an example of his young associate's civil libertarianism. During the years of the Nesmith litigation, Smith visited in the Durrs' home several times. Like many others, he considered them wise counselors and gracious hosts. He frequently consulted Durr on legal matters other than the Nesmith case, including SCEF's problems. He asked both Coe and Durr for advice when, as SCEF's treasurer, he worked out a procedure through which SCEF could arrange bond for SNCC members arrested in sit-ins and picketing actions. He and Jim Dombrowski enlisted Durr to address a "Conference on Freedom and the First Amendment" sponsored by SCEF on October 27, 1961, in Chapel Hill, North Carolina. Speakers included representatives of the NAACP and SNCC, as well as academic civil libertarians and civil rights lawyers. Smith spoke on "The History of the Senate Subcommittee on Internal Security"; Durr's topic was "What Are Some of the Moral Issues Involved in Legislative Inquisitions?"[48]

The next spring, however, when Smith spoke at a conference sponsored

46. *Louisiana* v. *Rockwell,* Appellate Division, Criminal District Court, Orleans Parish, May 31, 1961, May 28, 1962, see Civil Liberties Docket Notebooks, entry 58.21, Meiklejohn Civil Liberties Institute; Waltzer interview.

47. Marjorie Hamilton, interview by author, tape recording, New Orleans, September 5, 1990.

48. B. E. Smith to Jim Dombrowski, July 5, 1962, in Box 4, Folder 15, Coe Papers; "A Conference on Freedom and the First Amendment," in Box 41, Folder 6, NLG Papers, Meiklejohn Institute (also in Box 3, Folder 2, C. J. Durr Papers).

by SCEF, SNCC, and the Alabama Christian Movement for Human Rights at which several of those listed in the Chapel Hill program appeared, Durr did not participate. This "Conference on the Deep South: Ways and Means to Integration" met at a black Methodist church in Birmingham in April, 1962. "Bull" Connor sent undercover photographers to snap pictures of suspicious participants, among them Myles Horton, Robert Moses, Hosea Williams, Fred Shuttlesworth, James Foreman, Carl Braden, Ella Baker, and NLG lawyers Leonard Holt of Virginia and Irving Rosenfield of California. The Birmingham meeting centered on basic problems of the civil rights movement: how to organize, how to get publicity, and how to use and combat the legal system. Waltzer attended with Smith, who spoke on "Protecting our right to speak and establishing civil liberties." Just a few weeks later, lawyers Rosenfield, Holt, and Victor Rabinowitz conducted workshops at a SNCC conference held on the Atlanta University campus, and Detroit NLG leader Ernest Goodman spoke on legal matters before a Southern Christian Leadership Conference meeting in Virginia.[49]

Smith, Waltzer, Rabinowitz, Goodman, Holt, and Rosenfield attended the SCEF, SNCC, and SCLC meetings as representatives of a new NLG civil rights committee formed at the convention held in Detroit in February, 1962. At this gathering the guild had honored six southerners for their efforts against segregation: two white lawyers, Ben Smith and John Coe, and four black lawyers, Len Holt and E. A. Dawley of Norfolk, Alexander P. Tureaud of New Orleans, and Ernest D. Jackson, Sr., of Jacksonville. The guild asked Durr to take part in this convention, but he declined.[50]

Coe addressed the more than five hundred people present at the convention's final banquet, but Holt spoke at the luncheon for the six honorees. Holt described his law firm's subpoenas from the Virginia Committee on Offenses Against the Administration of Justice. This committee of the state legislature demanded the firm's records in four civil rights cases. Ernest Goodman

49. "Conference on the Deep South," in Box 86, Folder 16, Braden Papers; Irving Rosenfield, "Report on Guild Committee Participation at Two Conferences in the South," in Box 4, Folder 4, NLG Papers, Meiklejohn Institute; *New York Guild Lawyer*, XX (May, 1962), 1, 4–5, in Box 90, NLG Papers, King Center.

50. Ginger and Tobin, eds., *NLG*, 187; Aryay Lenske to C. J. Durr, December 12, 1961, in Box 3, Folder 6, C. J. Durr Papers.

thought Holt's "impassioned plea for help" and his call for the lawyers to stand and join in singing the movement anthem, "We Shall Overcome," inspired many guild members to join the movement in the South. "Most of us left convinced," said Goodman, "that 'This is *our* struggle.'" Holt's emphasis on "the fighting qualities and activities of lawyers in the South and the need for more lawyers to go there and participate in the movement directly" led the convention to draft a resolution calling for the organization of the Committee to Assist Southern Lawyers.[51]

The Committee to Assist Southern Lawyers (CASL) integrated its leadership, with Goodman and his partner George Crockett as co-chairs and Ben Smith and Len Holt as co-secretaries. In 1964 Goodman accepted the presidency of the guild and Smith and Crockett became co-chairs of CASL. At the convention's suggestion, CASL launched two initiatives immediately. First, they approached lawyers associations for help in increasing the number of lawyers representing civil rights workers arrested in the South; and second, they began designing a conference to provide professional education for civil rights attorneys. At the Detroit meeting, thirty NLG lawyers signed a list pledging to spend at least forty hours during the next year assisting southern civil rights lawyers. Within a few weeks after the convention, the number of volunteers had increased to eighty-five. Jim Dombrowski's biographer, Frank Adams, calls CASL a joint SCEF-NLG venture, and Dombrowski had encouraged CASL activists Smith and Holt, both SCEF board members, to find a way to render legal assistance in the South. Both spoke about the plan at SCEF-sponsored meetings. SCEF's ongoing relationship to the lawyers' project, however, stemmed from Dombrowski's commitment to locate bond money for SNCC activists, CASL's primary clients. The administration of CASL and its conferences was left to the NLG.[52]

Several northern NLG lawyers, among them Rabinowitz, Arthur Kinoy, and William Kunstler, had already worked on sit-in, picketing, and freedom rider cases. But no organized group of attorneys other than the overburdened NAACP Inc. Fund and, periodically, the Justice Department supported the

51. Ginger and Tobin, eds., *NLG*, 187–88.

52. *New York Guild Lawyer*, XX, no. 1 (January, 1962), 6, no. 3 (March–April, 1962), 1, and no. 4 (May, 1962), 1, in Box 90, NLG Papers, King Center; Adams, *James Dombrowski*, 257.

rare, lonely, and sometimes inadequately trained civil rights lawyers of the South. Crockett immediately informed SNCC headquarters in Atlanta of CASL's plans. SNCC, then an interracial committee of student activists organizing voting rights and desegregation drives in the Deep South, greeted Crockett's news with rejoicing. "Outside Atlanta, I know of no southern city that has more than three lawyers who will take civil rights cases," wrote one SNCC field secretary, and those who would were often poorly prepared for this work. "In short, gentlemen, the need for all types of legal aid in the South is great, both for lawyers and for their clients."[53]

In May, Smith and Crockett met in Washington with the ABA's Committee on the Bill of Rights to discuss legal representation in the South. Smith outlined the problems, dwelling especially on the "pitifully small" number of lawyers willing to accept controversial cases, and Crockett discussed CASL's plans. The ABA committee "seemed to agree that the paramount task faced by their organization would be that of interesting and moving the leadership of their affiliated Bar Associations in the southern states." The chairman reminded the NLG lawyers that back in 1953, addressing Smith Act prosecutions, the ABA had passed a resolution urging bar members to face up to the responsibility to provide legal assistance to unpopular clients. Smith and Crockett left the meeting hoping that the ABA's August convention would reemphasize and strengthen this old and heretofore often-ineffective resolution with special emphasis on civil rights workers.[54]

CASL also contacted the National Bar Association to secure its help in planning a conference to be held in Atlanta on November 30 and December 1. The two groups sponsored the meeting in cooperation with the SCLC, and Martin Luther King, Jr., spoke at its Saturday evening banquet. King's attorney, NBA member Donald Hollowell, accepted the position as general conference chairman. Hollowell and Leroy Johnson, Georgia's first black state

53. Ernest Goodman and George Crockett to Student Non-Violent Coordinating Committee, Atlanta, April 27, 1962, with copy of letter attached from "field secretary," May 4, 1962, in Box 17, Folder 27, Series 4, Student Non-Violent Coordinating Committee Papers, Martin Luther King Library and Archives, Atlanta [hereinafter cited as SNCC Papers].

54. *New York Guild Lawyer*, XX, no. 5 (July–August, 1962), 4, in Box 90, NLG Papers, King Center.

senator since Reconstruction, held parties in their homes for the participants. About sixty lawyers attended the conference, mostly either southern black attorneys or northern whites. The meeting, held at the Waluhaje Hotel, was billed as "an historic integrated conference," but as far as can be ascertained, only three white southerners came: Ben Smith of New Orleans, Herman Wright of Houston, and William Higgs of Jackson. Higgs, a young man who came to prominence in 1959 as the lawyer for white Mississippians protesting assignment of public funds to White Citizens' Councils, also acted as the original local counsel in both the freedom rider cases and James Meredith's suit to enter the University of Mississippi. He "described the isolation experienced by the southern white lawyer who takes racially controversial cases." Within a year of his Atlanta speech, Higgs would be hounded out of Mississippi for good.[55]

Seminars instructed the lawyers in both civil rights and negligence law, "to make it possible for more attorneys to accept civil rights cases by making their practices more lucrative in other areas of the law." Before adjourning, conference leaders proposed another meeting with a similar purpose. Ben Smith, who loved to show off his hometown to his friends, began to envision the first integrated bar meeting in Louisiana since Reconstruction.[56]

Most New Orleanians, however, were not prepared for an integrated meeting of liberal and leftist lawyers. NAACP Inc. Fund lawyers who litigated *Bush v. Orleans Parish School Board* from 1952 until 1960 faced, according to Jack Bass, "the most furious legal assault of any state against the supremacy clause of the constitution." This offensive continued even after the ultimate enforcement of Judge J. Skelly Wright's 1956 desegregation decision in 1961. The inauguration of a "liberal" Democratic administration in Washington that supported Judge Wright only strengthened the resolve of Louisiana segregationists and increased their suspicion of outsiders and nonconformists. A

55. *New York Guild Lawyer*, XX, no. 9 (December, 1962), 6, in Box 90, and "Resolution of the National Executive Board of the National Lawyers Guild: Conviction of William Higgs," in Box 92, both ibid.; William Moses Kunstler, *Deep in My Heart* (New York, 1966), 154–69; and Clayborne Carson, *In Struggle: SNCC and the Black Awakening of the 1960s* (Cambridge, Mass., 1981), 86.

56. *New York Guild Lawyer*, XX, no. 9 (December, 1962), 1–6, in Box 90, NLG Papers, King Center.

deep-seated paranoia infected the power structure, the press, and many people of white New Orleans in the wake of the desegregation cases.[57]

In 1961 the New Orleans Chamber of Commerce sponsored an "Anti-Communism School," with speakers and a collection of films, tapes, and literature from fervently right-wing Harding College in Searcy, Arkansas. The influence of the week-long meeting was extended by its heavy and sympathetic coverage in the local press. The Americanism Committee of the chamber then organized a sort of lending library of anti-Communist materials, which were used by civic groups and by high schools in a required six-week course in anti-Communism. In addition, the committee met twice a month to consider and take action to combat the Communist menace. Along with similar groups in other parts of the state, it pressed state officials to pass sedition laws proscribing groups that opposed anti-Communism or advanced other aberrant ideas.[58]

Measures to combat integration through the ruse of anti-Communism dominated the legislature in Baton Rouge. The Louisiana Committee on Un-American Activities, "empowered to study, investigate and expose enemies of the state," elected as its chairman Representative James Pfister of New Orleans, a legislator whose opposition to integration and Communism was above question. The attorney for Pfister's committee, Jack N. Rogers, prepared two bills enacted by the legislature in 1962, the Subversive Activities and Communist Control Law and the Communist Propaganda Control Act. New Orleans attorney Jack Peebles called the new laws unusual because of "their breadth and their penalties." The statutes identified the "Communist Party" as any group that could be "construed by prosecution officials to parallel or coincide with 'in any manner' any of the objectives, immediate or long range," of the vaguely defined "international communist conspiracy." Like similar statutes in Mississippi and earlier Louisiana laws sponsored by Willie Rainach, these acts accepted as proof of subversion "citation" or "identification" of an organization by a committee or subcommittee of the Congress. Tailor-made to ensnare Louisiana-based SCEF, the legislation could be useful in harassing any suspect civil rights, labor, civil liberties, antiwar, or human welfare group working in the state. Most of the new

57. Bass, *Unlikely Heroes*, 112–35.
58. Peebles, "Subversion and SCEF," 47–48.

organizations using nonviolent civil disobedience against segregation were obviously not parts of the Communist Party, however, and some of them had not yet been tested in the fire of congressional investigation. Therefore, the Pfister-Rogers statutes also named as "subversive" any organization using "unlawful means" to "change the Constitutional form of government of the State of Louisiana."[59]

Smith's identification with Cuba, leftist unions, and SCEF certainly already qualified him in local eyes as the agent of alien conspiracies recognized by congressional anti-Communists. Despite the liability involved, in April, 1962, Smith and Waltzer litigated a case for SNCC and CORE involving the integration of the student cafeteria at Tulane University. That same month Smith defended Ronnie Moore, chairman of CORE in Baton Rouge, on the charge of using a loudspeaker illegally at a large rally at Southern University. Smith introduced an affidavit claiming that the Baton Rouge courtroom remained segregated in defiance of federal law, but the judge refused to hear his motions. In 1962 and 1963 his firm handled several important Packinghouse Workers cases and successfully appealed a well-publicized case involving a large judgment against Cuba. At the request of Leonard Boudin, he also arbitrated a settlement between Loyola University and the controversial folk singer Joan Baez, who missed a concert there on account of a last-minute illness in early 1963.[60]

More and more, however, Ben Smith's practice revolved around the NLG's Committee to Assist Southern Lawyers and cases arising out of SNCC's burgeoning voter education and registration drives in Mississippi. The Smith-Waltzer firm, now with a new associate, Jack Peebles, became the point of entry for NLG lawyers coming to help Bob Moses and his SNCC compatriots in Mississippi. At the end of 1963, CASL reported, fifty-nine lawyers had assisted the movement through local trial work, argument in appellate courts, preparation of documents, consultation with southern lawyers, or participation in educational conferences. CASL had held two two-day conferences

---

59. Ibid., 48–50.

60. *Clark v. Tulane,* in Box 1, Folder 13, United Packinghouse Workers of America Cases, in Box 3, Folders 15, 16, 17, and 18, and *Smith v. Baez,* in Box 3, Folder 11, all in Smith Papers; Report, July 24, 1962, p. 3, Smith FBI File; *Republic of Cuba* v. *Mayan Lines, S.A.,* 145 So. 2d 679 (1962); New Orleans *States-Item,* March 22, 1962, p. 28.

in both the South and the North, supported the publication of a handbook for civil rights lawyers, and sponsored a summer program through which northern law students interned in the offices of southern civil rights lawyers.[61]

CASL's leadership took pride in these accomplishments but expressed disappointment with the result of its efforts to influence the ABA. An ABA recommendation issued after the association's August, 1963, meeting, the NLG lawyers believed, "misinterprets or fails to understand the nature of the problems in the South." Counseling that "the settlement of the critical racial problems at hand must be made around a conference table and cannot be made on the streets," the ABA encouraged its members to be the agents of improved communication between the races as members of biracial committees and counselors to local officials. The ABA report centered on the maintenance of law and order, condemning with equal weight lawbreaking local officials who disregarded due process or federal civil rights law and lawbreaking civil rights demonstrators who tested discriminatory local and state statutes. CASL leaders saw this pronouncement as naive and unrealistic, a failure of the ABA "to deal with its own responsibility as a bar association. . . . It is hypocritical to urge Negroes to curtail their demonstrations and to rely on judicial proceedings to secure their rights" when neither lawyers nor judges in the South were committed to enforcing "federal constitutional rights." CASL urged ABA lawyers to join in taking "practical steps" to reform the administration of justice in the South and help overthrow the "illegal, unconstitutional system of segregation." Until those goals were accomplished, no lawyer or bar association could "lecture Negroes about law and order and the duty of citizens to follow the judicial process."[62]

Centrist liberals noticed the activities of CASL in 1962 and 1963. President Kennedy called prominent members of the American bar to the White House in the summer of 1963, asking them to find ways to provide appropriate legal assistance to civil rights workers. The following winter the Lawyers Committee for Civil Rights under Law (or simply the "President's Committee")

61. "Report of the Committee to Assist Southern Lawyers to the National Executive Board," November 8, 1963, in Box 32, Folder 6, NLG Papers, Meiklejohn Institute.

62. Ibid.; "American Bar Association Special Committee on Civil Rights and Racial Unrest, Recommendations of the Board of Governors Adopted by the House of Delegates," August, 1963—No. 39, ibid.

announced that it would draft lawyers for work in Mississippi that summer. At the meeting in New Orleans called to inaugurate this committee, former ABA president Satterfield hotly defended Mississippi lawyers, protesting that they saw a great deal of difference between "representing individuals in unpopular causes and representing paid agitators" who just came to Mississippi to get arrested. Mississippi lawyers could not accept civil rights "agitators" as clients, Satterfield said, because representing them would be tantamount to sanctioning the alien organizations that sent them into the state and supported them. He failed to comment on prosecutions of native Mississippians involved in civil rights activities. Other members of the Mississippi bar, however, embraced the President's Committee because their plan "seemed to reflect an effort to undermine the legal monopoly that the left-wing Lawyers Guild has had so far in the Mississippi civil rights movement." Sherwood Wise, the president-elect of the Mississippi Bar Association, told organizers that they would do Mississippi "a great favor" if they would simply "keep these zealots off our necks."[63]

A third legal committee, the Lawyers Constitutional Defense Committee (LCDC), formed at about the same time with support from diverse liberal organizations including the American Jewish Congress and the American Jewish Committee, the National Council of Churches, CORE, the ACLU, the AFL, the NAACP, and SNCC. Spearheaded by Melvin Wulf, legal director of the ACLU, and Robert F. Drinan, S.J., dean of Boston College Law School, this effort reflected the same civil rights viewpoints as CASL. But according to some sources, its anti-Communist or cold war liberal members hoped to use the LCDC to push the guild out of Mississippi. Robert Spike of the National Council of Churches, AFL counsel Joseph Rauh, and Jack Greenberg of the NAACP strenuously objected to association with guild lawyers.[64]

63. New York *Times,* February 8, 1964, p. 1.

64. Robert F. Drinan to prospective lawyers (and attached description and application blank for Lawyers Constitutional Defense Committee), ca. June, 1964, in Box 3, Folder 11, Jack Greenberg to Robert Moses, April 7, 1964, and Robert W. Spike to Moses, April 17, 1964, in Box 3, Folder 4, all in Hunter Morey Papers, Archives Division, State Historical Society of Wisconsin [hereinafter cited as Morey Papers]. For general discussions of the tensions between movement lawyers in 1963 and 1964 see Richard Cummings, *The Pied Piper: Allard K. Lowenstein and the Liberal Dream* (New York, 1985), 246–54, and John Dittmer, *Local People: The Struggle for Civil Rights in Mississippi* (Urbana, Ill., 1994), 229–34.

SNCC leaders in Mississippi paid little attention to the LCDC's attitude, but it continued to be a problem for the Mississippi legal effort through 1964 and 1965. Ben Smith, an active ACLU attorney as well as an officer of the guild, helped to bridge the gap between the two groups. He and Melvin Wulf cooperated throughout the time CASL worked in Mississippi. Although CASL led the first efforts to bring volunteer lawyers to work short stints in Mississippi, by the summer of 1964 three outside legal groups had opened offices in Jackson.

CASL asked both Cliff Durr and John Coe about taking summer interns during the summer of 1963, but neither man accepted the offer. With both *Nesmith* v. *Alford* and *Gray* v. *Alabama* nearing completion, the older lawyers began cutting back on their practices and planning easy summers. The last important civil rights case Durr accepted involved Bob Zellner, a young man the Durrs befriended while he was a student at Huntington, the local Methodist college in Montgomery.

Police arrested Zellner, who had become SNCC's first white field secretary in 1961, for vagrancy while he visited friends at his alma mater in January, 1963. When insufficient evidence was found to sustain that accusation, they indicted him on a "false pretenses" charge. The second charge resulted from a "bounced" check he used to pay for a camera, though sufficient funds later appeared in his account. Durr believed his criminal law experience insufficient to handle the felony charge, which could have resulted in a ten-year sentence, and SNCC approved his association with Birmingham lawyer Charles Morgan for the trial. SCEF agreed to help with legal costs, and the lawyers won Zellner's acquittal in April.[65]

Durr traveled to several schools in the summer of 1963, lecturing at Sarah Lawrence, Amherst, Washington University, and on an invitation from an old friend from FCC days, the University of Saskatchewan. In October, NLG

65. *John Robert Zellner* v. *William F. Thetford et al.*, in Box 46, Folder 5, and *Alabama Journal*, February 18, 1963, Sec. D, p. 1, in Box 12, Folder 3, both in C. J. Durr Papers; James R. Foreman to Ernest Goodman, February 18, 1963, in Box 17, Folder 27, Series 4, SNCC Papers; Robert Zellner to Jim Dombrowski, April 18, 1963, in Box 21, Folder 1, Braden Papers. Zellner lived with the Durrs for about a year while police stood vigil outside. When Zellner's grandmother died in Mobile, Montgomery police cars became a part of the funeral procession. See Durr to Irving Brant, March 20, 1963, in Box 3, Folder 8, C. J. Durr Papers.

president Benjamin Dreyfus entertained the Durrs at a reception in San Francisco and Cliff spoke at a Unitarian forum in Los Angeles. Closer to home, he addressed both a Unitarian congregation and a meeting of the Alabama Council on Human Relations in Birmingham. He also planned a series of lectures to be given at the London School of Economics, Oxford, and Cambridge, part of a very successful trip to England in early 1964.[66]

In a move reminiscent of his attempts in 1948 to help the Democratic Party remove Dixiecrats from the Alabama ballot, Durr fought hard, if unsuccessfully, in 1964 to replace an unpledged "Wallacite" list of Alabama Democratic electors with a slate pledged to Lyndon Johnson and the national Democratic Party. Johnson had become very unpopular in Alabama, and Barry Goldwater was revered because he had opposed the Civil Rights Act. Durr defended Johnson in a debate sponsored by a Montgomery discussion group of which he was a longtime member. Calling Goldwater "an Arizona Carpetbagger dressed in gray," he accused George Wallace of leading the South back to the Tilden-Hayes Compromise of 1876: "Every time the North shouts 'Nigger' the South lets it get the upper hand and the result is more economic colonialism." While a "real two party system" might benefit Alabama, "I would find it hard to go along with the Republican Party even if I could swallow Barry Goldwater." The so-called "southern patriots" had taken away his right to vote for "a good Southern Democrat. . . . I think I will just pass this election by, as I did the one in 1948." When a Goldwater partisan replaced Durr's LBJ bumper sticker with one promoting Goldwater, he fired off a long letter to the editor of the *Alabama Journal*. Goldwater conservatives, he said, believed Communists had taken over the country because the Democratic Party was supposedly liberal, by which they meant Socialist, and which they understood to be the same as being Communist. He ended the epistle with the plaint, "Have we all gone crazy?"[67]

Durr escaped Montgomery politics by spending a good deal of time in the country, building a house on land he had inherited at Wetumpka, the part of his grandfather's farm he called "Pea Level." Frustrated by southern politics

66. Speeches, 1963–1964, in Box 14, Folders 5 and 6, C. J. Durr Papers.
67. Forum Club, "Goldwater v. Johnson," October 22, 1964, in Box 14, Folder 6, and C. J. Durr to Editor, *Alabama Journal,* October 6, 1964, in Box 3, Folder 9, both ibid.

and his difficult practice, he thought more and more about retirement. After inheriting a moderate sum of money, he felt secure enough in 1962 to begin making plans to close the law practice permanently in 1964.[68]

Although not ready to quit the practice of law, John Coe also began slowing down. He thought it was time for him to resign from SCEF's board, he wrote Jim Dombrowski in June, "not from change of mind or heart, but from weariness." The world was changing. At one time he felt he must fight with SCEF because he was needed, but today the Supreme Court, the president, and even the business community appeared to see racial change as necessary. The civil rights movement, especially the new black lawyers who so impressed him at Talladega, had shown his contribution to be less essential than it had been in the past. When Dombrowski asked him to allow his name to remain on the letterhead, though SCEF would not expect him to come to meetings or take an active part, Coe agreed.[69]

Still, just a month later he acceded to SCEF's request that he join Ben Smith in a mission to Washington to testify before the House Judiciary Committee, then considering the 1964 Civil Rights Bill. Coe's testimony related to opening public accommodations and improving local judicial systems in the South. He asked the congressmen to consider provisions for supervision of local officials and even of southern federal judges during the administration of the new law. Dombrowski thought "your testimony was splendid" and issued a press release praising Coe, the "chairman of SCEF's legal committee," Smith, SCEF's treasurer, and their successful trip to Washington.[70]

Even as their professional lives ebbed, Coe and Durr stood firmly with Ben Smith and the small body of white southerners who eschewed gradualism and faced southern race problems squarely. While Durr appropriately resisted classification as a "left-winger" and on the other hand Coe and Smith lauded budding socialism in Cuba, from their communities' viewpoints they differed very little. Regardless of their variant political outlooks, all made commit-

68. Salmond, *Conscience of a Lawyer*, 193–95.

69. J. M. Coe to Jim Dombrowski, June 6, 1963, in Box 48, Folder 16, Coe Papers.

70. "Testimony Before the Judiciary Committee," July 29, 1963, and Dombrowski to Coe and SCEF Press Release, August 8, 1963, in Box 73, Folder 29, Coe Papers; Telegram, Emanuel Celler to Fred Shuttlesworth, July 29, 1963, and Coe to Dombrowski, August 2, 1963, Microfilm No. 306, Reel 4, Braden Papers.

ments, publicly and privately, to the idea that southern segregation and dis-franchisement should end. Smith, entering a frenetic but very productive period, would give the civil rights movement his most mature and dedicated legal efforts. None of these southerners became one of the "respectables" Cliff Durr often denigrated in his letters; none hid his light under a bushel or dodged perceived responsibilities. In the era of massive resistance, southern contemporaries branded them "radical" lawyers.

If radicalism means trying to get at the root or center of problems, all three men fit that dictionary definition. They looked for solutions—straightfor-ward, practical, lawful answers—to the region's dilemmas, not rationaliza-tions or excuses. In the fall of 1963, Ben Smith's radicalism, and that of the organizations he championed, once more stood at the center of a firestorm in New Orleans and Washington. SCEF and Smith became targets of both Representative Pfister and Senator Eastland, who had pursued the organiza-tion, and the man, for nearly ten years. Both legislators considered Smith to be not a problem solver but a seditious extremist, a troublemaker, and a southern turncoat.

CHAPTER EIGHT

"*They* Were the Real Subversives":
The *Dombrowski* Case and the
Mississippi Crusade, 1963–1965

In May, 1963, children marched in Birmingham and Martin Luther King, Jr., wrote the letter from the Birmingham jail that became sacred script for the civil rights movement. In August, King led the Washington march and proclaimed his dream, capturing the world's imagination and legitimizing the movement for still-hesitating northern liberals. These two documents—seeking equal treatment under existing constitutional law and dreaming the American dream for all American children—placed the civil rights movement solidly in the liberal mainstream and increased the vulnerability of urban southerners like the negotiating businessmen of Birmingham and Atlanta.

Outside the limelight, in places like Albany, Georgia, Selma, Alabama, and the Mississippi and Louisiana Deltas, determined but less celebrated volunteers worked with smaller resources and an even more inflexible rural establishment, attempting to revolutionize the southern electorate. The nature of the volunteers—young, educated, and idealistic; the nature of the projected electorate—poor, dominated, and barely educated; and the nature of their opposition—official, brutal, and doctrinal, almost guaranteed that this part of the movement would become disorderly, radicalized, and involved on a daily basis with the criminal justice system. Voting rights and due process cases quickly overwhelmed the three black lawyers willing to defend civil rights workers in Mississippi. By early summer, 1964, according to Hunter Morey, legal coordinator for the voter registration drives, eighteen lawyers had come to help in Mississippi—two from the NAACP, nine from the Lawyers Constitutional Defense Committee, and seven from the NLG. Ben Smith and others from the NLG's Committee to Assist Southern Lawyers were deeply absorbed and very busy in Mississippi by mid-1963.[1]

Smith escaped almost weekly trips from New Orleans to Mississippi for a short time in the summer of 1963 to attend the March on Washington with his friend Albert D'Orlando, a New Orleans Unitarian pastor. After his return he organized a second CASL conference for New Orleans, advertised, like the first meeting in Atlanta, as a "Civil Rights and Negligence Workshop-Seminar." He enlisted Leonard Dreyfus, head of the Louisiana Civil Liberties Union, and Revis Ortigue, president of the Louis A. Martinet Society, New Orleans' black bar association, as cosponsors. Together they recruited panelists such as Donald Hollowell and C. B. King of Georgia, Arthur Kinoy, William Kunstler, and CORE's Carl Rachlin of New York, Herman Wright of Texas, John Conyers and Supreme Court justice Otis Smith of Michigan, and Peter Hall and Oscar Adams of Alabama. This diverse group would be the first to integrate the rooms, restaurants, and swimming pool of the Hilton Airport Inn in New Orleans.[2]

On September 30, 1963, four days before the groundbreaking conference began, Representative James Pfister's Joint Legislative Committee on Un-American Activities met in executive session in Baton Rouge. Committee counsel Jack Rogers recommended that the committee ask the New Orleans police to implement "Project 50," the committee's code name for a plan to seize SCEF records. New Orleans law enforcement officers renamed Project 50 "Operation Tip-Top." The legislators appointed a subcommittee consist-

1. "Report—COFO Legal Coordinator," June 6, 1964, in Box 3, Folder 1, Morey Papers. For discussions of the three young black Mississippi lawyers—Carsie Hall, Jack Young, and Jess Brown—and of problems arising from the sparsity of civil rights lawyers in Mississippi, see Oppenheim, "Abdication of the Southern Bar," in *Southern Justice*, ed. Friedman, 127–35; "The Problem of Legal Aid in Mississippi," March 12, 1964, "Summary of R. Hunter Morey . . . Before the Lawyers' Committee for Civil Rights Under Law," March 3, 1964, in Box 3, Folder 1, and "Memorandum Re: Legal Counsel for Summer Project," John Due to Jack Greenberg, Jack Pratt, Ben Smith, Carl Rachlin, Marion Wright, Bob Moses et al., April 2, 1964, in Box 3, Folder 4, both in Morey Papers.

2. Albert D'Orlando, interview by author, tape recording, New Orleans, September 5, 1990; Pamphlet, "A Workshop-Seminar for Lawyers on Civil Rights and Negligence Law," October 4, 5, 6, 1963, in Box 4, Folder 25, Coe Papers; *Guild Lawyer,* February, 1964, in Box 90, NLG Papers, King Center.

ing of the chairman and two other members to be "on call" in New Orleans on October 4 and 5, in case they were needed by local investigators. The strategy for this new assault on SCEF had taken shape the preceding summer, when the Louisiana officials consulted with J. G. Sourwine, now chief counsel for the Senate Internal Security Subcommittee and the emissary of Senator Eastland. Eastland had been waiting for an opportunity to peruse SCEF's contributor lists since Jim Dombrowski and Aubrey Williams rebuffed SISS's attempt to examine records in 1954. Both Louisiana's governor and New Orleans' mayor endorsed the legislature's plan to assist Mississippi's persistent senator.[3]

A series of circumstances and recent events led Senator Eastland and the Louisiana officials to rekindle their long dispute with SCEF at this time. Aware of SCEF treasurer Smith's connection to the NLG's CASL, they intended the offensive to coincide with the lawyers' meeting at the Hilton. Plans for a massive voter registration drive in Mississippi in the summer of 1964 had already been announced, and the well-publicized CASL conference included seminars on the lawyer's role in direct-action techniques and in combating the abuse of state power. Intimidation of lawyers preparing to challenge the Mississippi establishment provided an added benefit of persecuting SCEF. Thus Operation Tip-Top involved more than a simple police action to further an ongoing investigation of SCEF. In the words of two attorneys close to the case, it afforded a way to effect "severe intimidation of the growing southern civil rights movement . . . particularly the white collaborators," and became a "part of an all-out effort to apply the weapons of the Cold War to the Freedom Movement all over the South."[4]

Some writers find the roots of the Louisiana committee's 1963 offensive in segregationist response to the SCEF conference held in Birmingham in April, 1962, the meeting at which Ben Smith and several other NLG attorneys led workshops and various civil rights leaders discussed strategy. Though the

3. "Minutes of Committee Meeting of September 30, 1963," Joint Legislative Committee on Un-American Activities, issued October 1, 1963, in Box 24, Folder 4, Braden Papers; Peebles, "Subversion and SCEF," 51.

4. "A Workshop-Seminar for Lawyers on Civil Rights and Negligence Law," in Box 4, Folder 25, Coe Papers; quotes from Peebles, "Reminiscences," 8, and Kinoy, *Rights on Trial*, 221.

path to this conclusion may be circuitous, it is clearly reasonable. The inter-
vening fifteen months had brought turmoil in the South. In June, 1962,
Governor George Wallace ostentatiously but unsuccessfully threatened ad-
mission of two black students by "standing in the schoolhouse door" in
Tuscaloosa; in October, riots greeted James Meredith in Oxford, Mississippi.
The following June, just after the pivotal demonstrations in Birmingham,
Medgar Evers died, and in August, King spoke at the Lincoln Memorial.
According to Taylor Branch, "758 racial demonstrations and 14,733 arrests
in 186 American cities" took place in the summer of 1963 alone.[5]

In September, two weeks before the New Orleans CASL conference and
SCEF raids and only a few weeks after the March on Washington, four little
girls died after the bombing of a black church in Birmingham. Within days
Birmingham lawyer Charles Morgan delivered his dramatic speech denouncing moderate southerners, and all over the country reverberations from the
bombing caused Americans to rethink their opinions about southerners who
defended segregation. Both King and Attorney General Robert Kennedy
spoke out forcefully on television, King specifically blaming Governor Wallace for creating an atmosphere in which such a crime would be tolerated.[6]

Wallace responded on the *Today* show on September 27, contending that
"the people of Alabama bear no blame for this, these murders," but that
culpability lay with the Supreme Court, the Kennedy administration, and
"outside agitators." He showed the audience police surveillance photographs
of the Bradens and Dombrowski at the 1962 meeting in Birmingham, accusing
them of subversion and citing as evidence reports of the New Orleans SISS
hearings in 1954 and the Atlanta HUAC hearings in 1958. Wallace, noted
Irwin Kilbaner, "dragged in the red menace." In his press conference on
October 5, legislative counsel Rogers claimed that the Louisiana committee
had been so impressed by Wallace's statements that it decided, after the show
aired, to carry out the raids.[7]

---

5. Branch, *Parting the Waters,* 825.

6. Adams, *James Dombrowski,* 267; Irwin Kilbaner, *Conscience of a Troubled South: The
Southern Conference Educational Fund, 1946–1966* (Brooklyn, 1989), 200–201.

7. Kilbaner, *Conscience of a Troubled South,* 200–201. John Coe accused Wallace of slander
and demanded equal time for a SCEF reply; J. M. Coe to President, NBC, September 28, 1963,
in Box 48, Folder 16, Coe Papers.

Since SISS counsel Sourwine's deposition in the ensuing federal case revealed exploratory discussions between Senator Eastland and the Pfister committee several weeks before the Birmingham bombing, the Wallace interview certainly was not the only catalyst for the raids and arrests.[8] Like the integrated CASL conference and SCEF's association with SNCC, however, it seems to have been an encouraging factor. Supported by authoritative intelligence from Bull Connor's police department, SISS, and HUAC, Wallace helped to set the stage for yet another official move against SCEF. This time the needs of a state rather than a congressional investigating committee ostensibly inspired the assault.

Wallace's assessment of SCEF as responsible for the September church bombings in Alabama may seem preposterous, but right-wing hate groups carefully fostered such ideas during this period. They disseminated malignant materials to sympathizers all over the country, and especially to segregationist groups in the South. One such document, a "confidential" report from an unidentified source called "Councilor Research," appeared after the assassination of President John F. Kennedy the following November. Echoing Wallace, this report implicated SCEF in the Birmingham church bombings and also in a 1962 plot to kill Kennedy in New Orleans. In both cases they supposed SCEF to be motivated by a desire "to create hatred toward Southern whites and suspicion toward southern whites and so-called 'hate groups.'" The document suggested a connection between SCEF and Lee Harvey Oswald, called Virginia Durr "a major decision maker" in the "Dombrowski Communist apparatus in New Orleans," traced Cliff Durr's descent from collaborators of Reconstruction days, and named Dombrowski's lawyer (John Coe?) and his treasurer (Ben Smith) Communists and agents of Castro. "Councilor Research" claimed SCEF received funds from Communist spies and "kinsmen of Senator Herbert Lehman," a descendant of the Durr family's Civil War–era partners in the drug business in Alabama. A vicious piece, it surpassed even publications such as *Red Channels,* which hounded the Durrs in the early 1950s.[9]

The Louisiana investigators probably found more substantial "evidence"

8. Peebles, "Subversion and SCEF," 105, n. 25.
9. "Confidential—from Councilor Research," n.d., in Box 11, Folder 15, Dombrowski Papers.

in SCEF's expanding relationship with SNCC. SCEF made a valuable contribution to SNCC by finding "the money to bail a lot of these kids out of jail," Smith said in a radio interview just after the raids. "We don't charge anything for that," though "it's awful hard to find that kind of money." Both SISS and the Louisiana committee also followed SCEF funding of former Huntingdon student Bob Zellner as SNCC's representative to students on white college campuses. Recently freed from Alabama justice after the Montgomery trial in which Cliff Durr and Charles Morgan undertook his defense, Zellner had also been jailed in Georgia, Mississippi, and Louisiana. In 1961 he was beaten during a SNCC "pray-in" in McComb, Mississippi, and in 1962 he took part in the Talladega demonstrations with Carl Braden. Between Zellner's incarcerations for these offenses, Ben Smith assisted him when, with SNCC chairman Charles McDew, he faced "criminal anarchy" charges for visiting a fellow civil rights worker jailed in Baton Rouge.[10]

New Orleans Parish Criminal District Court issued search warrants for the homes and offices of James Dombrowski, Ben Smith, and Bruce Waltzer on October 2. The Dombrowski and Smith warrants cited their association with SCEF, "an identified communist front and a subversive organization" under Louisiana law. The warrants included Waltzer as Smith's law partner and a member of the allegedly subversive NLG, though he had no official connection to SCEF. Louisiana officials employed about one hundred policemen and jail trustees for five raids on October 4. They stripped the SCEF office clean of its files, books, and even pictures, loading seventy-three cartons of materials onto a moving van, including signed photographs of Eleanor Roosevelt and Mary McLeod Bethune, framed letters from Franklin Roosevelt and Albert Einstein, and a portfolio of Dombrowski's own paintings. Most important, the "investigators" took all of SCEF's corporate records and letters, including the 8,000-name contributor list and the 10,000-name *Southern Patriot* mailing list. At the offices of Smith and Waltzer, officers waved revolvers at a protesting part-time secretary and ransacked the firm's files. They were unable to locate many papers pertaining to SCEF, but some

10. Carson, *In Struggle,* 68; Kilbaner, *Conscience of a Troubled South,* 186–89; "Conversation Carte Blanche," WDSU Radio, New Orleans, October 31, 1963, pp. 20–21, transcript provided by former WDSU news reporter Jim Kemp, in possession of author [hereinafter cited as WDSU radio transcript].

impounded files concerned cases of the Louisiana Civil Liberties Union, which Smith served as legal committee chairman.[11]

Even more traumatic were the raids on the homes of the three men. At the Dombrowski house, officers threatened to shoot the leashed family dog. Waltzer's young German-Jewish wife said the day evoked memories of her years as a child under Hitler. No SCEF or NLG materials could be located in Waltzer's personal belongings, but the policemen confiscated Hebrew Bibles, a tape in German made by Mrs. Waltzer's father, and the mailing list of the New Orleans Council for Peaceful Alternatives, a group that supported the test ban treaty. They also discovered CIA papers revealing Waltzer's top-secret clearance during his years in Europe and photographed both the family's private telephone directory and Mrs. Waltzer's current university textbooks.[12]

Penny Smith Jones wrote an account of this day when her young life shattered. As the school bus deposited her in front of the Smith home that afternoon, a crowd gathered on the lawn alerted her to trouble inside. Upon entering, she discovered the french doors across the back of the house axed open because the frightened young woman staying with her three-year-old brother at first denied the policemen entrance. They would not permit her, and now refused to allow Penny, use of the telephone to contact friends or family. When Lillian Smith arrived at home, she, her children, and her maid remained under house arrest, forbidden to contact other family members or friends. Held downstairs in the kitchen, Mrs. Smith endured separation from her children kept in an upstairs sitting room. Until long after nightfall, they listened to policemen "tearing the house apart":

> The police opened every closet, every drawer, and removed
> every cushion and bolster in the house. They crawled under

11. Search Warrants, in Box 11, Folder 15, and handwritten notes by James Dombrowski titled "The Argosy and the Agony of the *Records*," in Box 16, Folder 11, both in Dombrowski Papers (also in Box 24, Folder 9, Braden Papers); "List of property belonging to Dr. James A. Dombrowski, etc.," in Box 24, Folder 9, Braden Papers; State of Louisiana, Parish of Orleans: Statement of Anne Ford, secretary to Smith and Waltzer, in Box 41, Folder 6, NLG Papers, Meiklejohn Institute.

12. "The Argosy and the Agony of the *Records*," in Box 16, Folder 11, Dombrowski Papers; WDSU radio transcript, 10–14.

the beds. They pulled every book . . . down from the shelves and flipped the pages and held them by their spines and shook them [looking for] "subversive material." . . . I remember two of them pulling down [and suspecting] C. Vann Woodward's *History of the New South.* . . . I could hear the officers ransacking my parents' bedroom. . . . They broke into [my mother's locked] closets, destroying all the mirrored doors. Nothing of my mother's most personal possessions was respected. . . . My father's closet . . . [and] my brother's room and my room were searched. [The policemen made] a variety of snide remarks to the effect that our kind could be pretty well treated with impunity.

Committee lawyer Jack Rogers personally supervised the raids, visiting each location to decide what should be appropriated from materials collected in piles by police and trustees. At the Smith home he actually participated in the search, carefully perusing the Smiths' personal papers and bank books. About nine that evening the police began to leave and allowed the Smiths' friends Leonard and Rhoda Dreyfus to enter the house. The family then learned of the jailing of Smith, Waltzer, and Dombrowski, lead stories on the evening news.[13]

Later Penny asked her father about the television stories—was he really a Communist who was going to jail for thirty years? He replied that the charges were false and that he would prove that fact in court. For the eleven-year-old child the story ended on an even sadder note: after her father's release on bond, her mother, pushed to the limits of her endurance, asked him to move out of their home. The next day they told Penny of their plans to divorce, and Smith settled into bachelor quarters in the French Quarter.[14]

Police had arrested Dombrowski at his office and whisked him away to jail. They apprehended Smith in the Hilton parking lot, leaving the conference after a telephone call alerted him that his client Dombrowski needed help, and seized Waltzer at home, where he had hurried to comfort his terrified

13. Penny Smith Jones, "The Raids," unpublished document in possession of author, quotes on 1 and 2; WDSU radio transcript, 5–6, 14.
14. Jones, "The Raids."

wife. When Smith arrived at the jail, a relieved Dombrowski thought that his lawyer had come to orchestrate his release until, in amazement, he discovered that Smith was also a prisoner. After several local judges claimed to be "unavailable," the lawyers' young associate Jack Peebles arranged bond for the three men on the night of October 4 through the good offices of Louisiana district judge Bernard J. Cocke, an acquaintance of Ben Smith since his days in the district attorney's office.[15]

The next day Smith returned to the CASL meeting to deliver a stirring address, a speech about the relationship of civil liberties and constitutional government to the civil rights movement. He planned to lay bare "the political character" of the SCEF raids and arrests by exposing the state antisubversive acts as segregationist subterfuge and proving their unconstitutionality. "We cannot de-segregate a witch-hunting society—we cannot integrate a silent and fearful nation—we cannot provide equal rights that have any meaning to citizens of a police state," he warned. The "wider aspects" of civil rights work were laid bare by these persecutions. The Louisiana subversive statutes devised "a breed of official devils" outside constitutional protections. "Where then is the world of our Constitution, where free men seek the truth?" he asked. "Where is the public opinion state envisioned by the creators of our Bill of Rights?"

On the other hand, the only reason he could see for the antisubversive legislation of Louisiana, "which has about as many communists as Greenland has trees," was that most Louisianans considered any white person who worked for civil rights a traitor. Sounding like Cliff Durr or John Coe in letters to liberal friends, Smith despaired that the region had bred "a society of cowards" in which "any policy except that of the ostrich" was dangerous. His recent experiences in the Mississippi Delta seemed to flavor his remarks as he challenged the lawyers with a flourishing conclusion. "As long as we are separate—as long as we fear—as long as we countenance terror—as long as we seek to isolate ourselves from common problems . . . so long will we suffer." In the segregated South, "even the possibility that persons of different race might share common problems is an anathema. . . . How long, oh

---

15. Waltzer and Peebles interviews; "The Argosy and the Agony of the Records," in Box 16, Folder 11, Dombrowski Papers; "Fact Sheets on the Raid and Arrests," in Box 23, Folder 3, Braden Papers.

Jerusalem! I say . . . the fruit is within our grasp—smite the serpent and strive again for the land of our fathers, where men live in dignity." Unfailingly idealistic despite many disappointments, Smith looked for the day when lingering ills like poverty and poor educational opportunities would be solved by a united, democratic South.[16]

While Smith delivered his speech, committee counsel Rogers held a press conference in Baton Rouge. Reporters asked if the committee had coordinated the SCEF raid with the FBI. No, said Rogers, because while the committee had "complete confidence" in J. Edgar Hoover, they remained unsure about Hoover's boss, Robert Kennedy. Kennedy might have divulged the information to "his friend, Martin Luther King," a confidant of Fred Shuttlesworth and Ella Baker. Baker had recently resigned from her position as executive director of the Southern Christian Leadership Conference and joined the SCEF staff in New Orleans. Shuttlesworth, King's codirector during the recent Birmingham demonstrations, became president of SCEF's board after Aubrey Williams' retirement in 1963. He told reporters at his new church in Cincinnati that the raids were "just a part of a campaign by our three most backward states (Alabama, Mississippi, and Louisiana) to stop the freedom movement" and "push the country back again to the age of McCarthyism." King himself denounced the raids as another attempt by "hard core racists" to equate the struggle for civil rights in the South with Communism. A few local groups, such as the Louisiana Civil Liberties Union, the New Orleans chapter of the AAUP, the Rabbinical Council of New Orleans, Albert D'Orlando's Unitarian congregation, and a black Baptist church, also voiced strenuous objections.[17]

Two weeks passed after the arrests without action from the district attorney's office. Smith's clients, especially the labor unions he represented, worried about the safety of confidential legal documents in his files and questioned the wisdom of continuing his services. Smith himself wondered why the bar association had not protested the way policemen "went through my private

16. Speech given by Benjamin Smith at Hilton Airport Inn, New Orleans, October 5, 1963, gift of Corinne Barnwell.

17. New Orleans *Times-Picayune*, October 6, 1963, pp. 1, 23, and October 7, 1963, p. 22; New Orleans *States-Item*, October 8, 1963, p. 21; Adams, *James Dombrowski*, 260.

files that have all kinds of confidential information in them" and took "files related to commercial transactions," especially a group of mortgages. The lawyers became anxious to reassure their clients and resume normal business. Finally, Smith, Waltzer, and Dombrowski filed a motion for a preliminary hearing.[18]

The case began in promising fashion when Judge Cocke formally freed the men, finding insufficient evidence of subversion to hold them for trial. Later even District Attorney Jim Garrison admitted "as an individual" that he feared that the committee had overstepped its bounds ordering the arrests. There was little danger, he thought, that "the attorneys in this case, for instance, were about to leave town," and the information about SCEF was not "so new as to require immediate physical arrests." On another level, however, the defendants found the hearing unsatisfactory. Cocke based his ruling on the state's refusal to produce the confiscated documents. The material, the state asserted, appeared "mountainous" and they needed more time for assessment. The next day Representative Pfister revealed that he, attorney Rogers, and the seized records had been subpoenaed to appear before SISS in Washington on Tuesday, October 29.[19]

After Pfister reported that the records, held by the state police, would soon be turned over to the Eastland committee, attorneys for SCEF, Smith, and Waltzer immediately asked for a federal court injunction to prevent removal of the records from the state. On Sunday, October 27, Colonel Thomas Burbank, head of the state police, guaranteed to federal district judge Robert A. Ainsworth the security of the materials in his headquarters in Baton Rouge. He agreed to a hearing at 9:00 A.M. the following morning to discuss the matter. The next morning, state authorities notified the judge that they would be unable to be present until noon. When they appeared they announced that the records were in the hands of J. G. Sourwine, having been spirited across the border to Mississippi. The state produced a letter from Sourwine dated October 25 which had commissioned Burbank temporary custodian of the documents for SISS, and a telegram dated 11:23 P.M. on October 27 ordering removal of the papers from Baton Rouge to the county clerk in Woodville.

18. WDSU radio transcript, 7; Peebles, "Subversion and SCEF," 61–65.
19. WDSU radio transcript, 56; Peebles, "Subversion and SCEF," 61–65, quote on 65.

Senator Eastland now possessed SCEF's records, rendering Judge Ainsworth's hearing moot.[20]

Two weeks later, Pfister's committee held an open hearing in New Orleans and then presented photostats of some of SCEF's records to the grand jury for New Orleans Parish. Citing the state antisubversive laws, Judge Malcolm V. O'Hara directed the grand jury to decide if enough evidence existed to indict the three men for criminal conspiracy. Since indictments were almost inevitable, lawyers for SCEF and the besieged attorneys, led by William Kunstler and Arthur Kinoy, decided to sue for relief in federal court. They aimed not only to test the constitutionality of the Louisiana anti-Communist laws but to circumvent the doctrine of abstention, under which access to the federal court system could be denied until the state trial and appellate processes had been exhausted. The abstention rule, a treasured doctrine of states fighting to retain segregation, often created long waits, financial stress, and prolonged incarceration for civil rights appellants seeking relief in the courts.[21]

After the lawyers filed their motion in the Fifth Circuit Court, Judge John Minor Wisdom issued a temporary restraining order prohibiting any state indictment until a federal three-judge panel heard the challenge to the state's antisubversive laws. Judge Wisdom's order, noted Arthur Kinoy, encouraged civil rights workers all over the South, signaling that a respected federal judge shared SCEF's lawyers' view of the Louisiana anti-Communist statutes. As he prepared to argue before the three-judge Fifth Circuit panel on December 9, Kinoy felt he had been "cast by history into a strange role," that of challenging a part of the American legal system that had abandoned the most basic constitutional principles lawyers and judges were sworn to uphold. Although Louisiana officials "branded" civil rights advocates "subversive to America," he emphasized, "*they* were the real subversives" (emphasis in original).[22]

On January 19, 1964, the three-judge panel ruled against Kinoy and the

20. Peebles, "Subversion and SCEF," 65–67; see also Kinoy, *Rights on Trial,* 219–22, and Adams, *James Dombrowski,* 269–70.

21. Peebles, "Subversion and SCEF," 67–69; Bradley R. Brewer, "*Dombrowski v. Pfister:* Federal Injunctions Against State Prosecutions in Civil Rights Cases—A New Trend in Federal-State Judicial Relations," *Fordham Law Review,* XXXIV (October, 1965), 71–106, esp. 73 and 76–77.

22. Kinoy, *Rights on Trial,* 228.

New Orleans lawyers working with him in the case. Over Wisdom's dissent, conservative district court judges E. Gordon West and Frank B. Ellis judged the doctrine of abstention appropriate, called the Louisiana statutes constitutional on their face, and refused to hear arguments on whether the laws had been illegally applied. Perhaps realizing the strength of his opposing arguments, Judge Wisdom suggested that Kinoy and Smith take a copy of his dissent with them when they flew to Washington the next day. It would buttress their arguments for an emergency continuation of the stay against state indictments.[23]

The Supreme Court's refusal to continue Judge Wisdom's initial stay provoked grand jury indictments of Dombrowski, Smith, and Waltzer, though District Attorney Garrison agreed to delay prosecutions until the Supreme Court acted on their appeal. Louisiana charged Smith with membership in two Communist organizations, the NLG and SCEF, and with "participating in the management" of SCEF and failing to register his membership with the state. Dombrowski faced indictment on the last two counts and Waltzer on the first. Smith faced possible penalties of thirty years hard labor or $30,000, Dombrowski twenty years or $20,000, and Waltzer ten years or $10,000. During the anxious two-year period under indictment, the lawyers "attempted to continue to earn a living and carry on some semblance of organized civil rights activities" in the face of criminal indictments and the persistent publicity generated by Pfister's committee.[24]

Though rejecting the immediate stay, the Supreme Court accepted the case on appeal. The arguments advanced in Wisdom's brilliant twenty-seven-page dissent formed the basis of the appellants' ultimate victory in *Dombrowski v. Pfister*. The majority in the Fifth Circuit decision had called the main concern of the case "the State's right of self-preservation." "No one questions this right," Wisdom declared, but he saw this as a spurious issue in this instance. "The main issue is whether the State is abusing its legislative power and criminal processes: whether the State, under the pretext of protecting itself against subversion, has harassed and humiliated the plaintiffs and is about to prosecute them solely because their activities in promoting civil rights for Negroes conflict with the State's steel-hard policy of segregation. They

23. Ibid., 230–32.
24. Peebles, "Subversion and SCEF," 72–75, quotes on 72 and 74.

ask the federal court to defend their federally protected rights." Wisdom explored the meaning of federalism, evoking James Madison's warnings about the dangers of the abuse of political power by the states, and examined southerners' historic interpretation of the "mystical, emotion-laden" words "states' rights," which conjured up "visions of the hearth and defense of the homeland and carry the sound of trumpets and the beat of drums. . . . [T]he crowning glory of American federalism is not States' Rights," he wrote in words strong enough to send a thrill through the most cynical civil liberties lawyer. "It is the protection the United States Constitution gives to the private citizen against *all* wrongful governmental invasion of fundamental rights and freedoms" (emphasis in original).[25]

A detailed analysis of the three-judge court's jurisdiction and the constitutionality of the Louisiana laws in question followed the opening section of the opinion. In both cases Wisdom disagreed profoundly with Judges Ellis and West. He quoted Judge Richard Rives's words from the New Orleans schools decision, lamenting that "once again, as in *Bush* v. *Orleans Parish School Board*, the State has 'marshalled the full force of its criminal law to enforce its social philosophy through the policeman's club.'" The responsibility of judging whether the state had abrogated federally guaranteed rights and liberties in order to maintain segregation rested with the federal district court, he said, and "this court should get on with its work."[26]

The Supreme Court heard the case almost exactly a year later. Kinoy spoke for SCEF, and Leon Hubert, a Tulane law professor and old friend, represented Smith and Waltzer; State Attorney John Jackson joined Jack Rogers for Louisiana. Kinoy and Hubert centered on the unconstitutionality of the state antisubversive statutes and "the critical question of whether there was federal power to intervene and enjoin" state courts. When Kinoy accused the state of raiding SCEF to test the waters, with an eye toward persecution of other civil rights organizations as "subversive" if this assault proved successful, Rogers admitted to this design. Later State Attorney Jackson stumbled, responding with clumsy uncertainty when asked for Louisiana's definition of

---

25. United States District Court, Eastern District of Louisiana, New Orleans Division, Civil Action No. 14,019, Division B, *James A. Dombrowski et al.* v. *James H. Pfister et al.*, "Wisdom, Dissenting," in Box 24, Folder 5, Braden Papers.

26. Ibid.

subversion. But despite apparent weaknesses on the state's part, Dombrowski felt pessimistic about the case. Smith, however, was characteristically optimistic as he left Washington, encouraged by the tenor of some of the justices' questions.[27]

The Court issued a decision against the state April 26, 1965, by a vote of five to two. Justices Black and Stewart did not participate, and Harlan and Clark dissented, primarily on the issue of abstention. Justice Brennan's majority opinion held the Louisiana laws to be unconstitutional and ordered the federal district court to enjoin the state court to issue a decree taking that ruling into consideration. States have a duty to uphold constitutional rights and to restrain "overzealous prosecutors," said the Court, and if malicious politicians misused the state courts, the federal courts must act. According to Brennan, the federal courts must condemn any state action that had "a chilling effect upon the exercise of First Amendment rights." The decision required that the government return the confiscated records at once.[28]

As for the doctrine of abstention, commented law professor Michael E. Tigar in the *Yale Law Review*, "the court did not tarry long, for deference to a state court by waiting for it to construe a statute in the first instance is silly when the statute is unconstitutional on any reading." Another legal scholar wrote that "in *Dombrowski* v. *Pfister,* the Supreme Court was clearly concerned with providing practical and realistic protection for fundamental constitutional rights . . . [and with] the problem of injustice resulting from delay in the judicial process." The Court found the remedy for both in the federal court injunction against state prosecutions in which citizens' federally protected rights are threatened. For the next few years the *Dombrowski* ruling would be "a powerful weapon in protecting the day to day struggles of the Freedom Movement," as civil rights lawyers sought to defend their clients against state prosecutions for picketing, demonstrating, or other matters touched by civil liberties law. "The Supreme Court of the United States," gloated Kinoy, "had kicked Louisiana and Jim Eastland right in the teeth!"[29]

27. Kinoy, *Rights of Trial,* 276–80, quote on 278; Adams, *James Dombrowski,* 274–75.

28. *Dombrowski* v. *Pfister,* 380 U.S. 499 (1965).

29. Michael E. Tigar, "Whose Rights? What Danger?" reprinted from *Yale Law Review,* XCIV, in Ginger and Tobin, eds., *NLG,* 222; Brewer, "*Dombrowski* v. *Pfister,*" 103; Kinoy, *Rights on Trial,* 283–85. The "loophole" in the doctrine of abstention provided by *Dombrowski*

James Pfister's committee had continued to harass SCEF and the lawyers during the two years following the raids. The Joint Legislative Committee followed up its November, 1963, hearings in New Orleans with more hearings on SCEF's activities in April, 1964, and January, 1965, concluding each time that SCEF was indeed a "communist front." Smith and Waltzer, asserted one report, had chosen the "Communist Party's top attorneys" as their defense lawyers. The committee even enlisted testimony from Dr. William Sorum, the former Communist who had been a hero of the 1957 HUAC hearings in New Orleans. Altering his evidence slightly from that earlier testimony, Sorum told the legislators that for many years SCEF had been "simply a tool and a 'front' for the Communist Conspiracy." Furthermore, the committee found "quite conclusive" evidence that the civil rights movement, including Martin Luther King, Jr.'s, SCLC, "has been grossly and solidly infiltrated by the Communist Party," and saw SNCC as "substantially under the control of the Communist Party through the influence of the Southern Conference Educational Fund and the Communists who manage it." Soon after the death of President Kennedy, the committee had made a disgraceful attempt to link Lee Harvey Oswald to SCEF, suggesting that the Louisiana legislators may have been in touch with organizations like "Councilor Research."[30]

Ben Smith, Bruce Waltzer, and their law partners surely felt personally vindicated when the New Orleans Parish Criminal District Court required the state to issue a statement exonerating them and James Dombrowski. Though Pfister was no longer committee chairman, the court ordered him to write a long explanation of the raids and arrests and to conclude publicly that upon reconsideration "we find . . . no basis for the charges" that the arrested men "are guilty of any un-American activities." Because "harm to the reputations of Dombrowski, Smith and Waltzer may unfortunately have resulted," this public clarification was being issued. The court had ruled that the arrests, searches, and seizures were "instigated without probable cause."

---

was substantially closed in 1971 by *Young* v. *Harris*. See Kermit L. Hall, ed., *The Oxford Companion to the Supreme Court* (New York, 1992), 232.

30. Joint Legislative Committee on Un-American Activities, *Activities of the Southern Conference Educational Fund, Inc., in Louisiana,* Report No. 4, November 19, 1963, Report No. 5, April 13, 1964, and Report No. 6, January 19, 1965, quotes from Report No. 4, p. 121, Report No. 5, pp. 124–25, and Report No. 6, p. 105.

Further, at the court's request the ABA "investigated the activities of Benjamin E. Smith and Bruce Waltzer, and their connection with Southern Conference Educational Fund, and exonerated them from charges of being communists."[31]

During 1963 and 1964, Smith, Waltzer, and Jack Peebles spent more and more of their time in Mississippi. Another partner, Alvin Jones, joined the firm largely to handle business during their absences. The addition of Jones, the attorney who had assisted John Coe in the Roosevelt Ward Civil Rights Congress case twelve years before, made the firm the first integrated law firm in New Orleans, perhaps the first of its kind in the Deep South. Later in 1964, Peebles also became a partner. Regardless of the difficulties with their paying clients, the offices of Smith, Waltzer, Jones, and Peebles remained busy in the year after the arrests. In the spring and summer of 1964 the firm became "a civil rights clearing house." National Lawyers Guild volunteers, headed for short stints in Mississippi, "stopped by for refresher courses regarding the problems they would encounter in Eastland's home state." Like other out-of-state attorneys, the members of Smith's firm worked in Mississippi without fee.[32]

"In March, 1964, while the FBI indexed the names listed in the SCEF files" seized by Eastland, one writer comments, "the Guild accepted an invitation from Bob Moses and SNCC to open an office in Jackson." SNCC consistently refused to distinguish friends from enemies based on the recommendations of conservatives or anti-Communist liberals. Moses, voter registration director for the Council of Federated Organizations (COFO), an umbrella alliance created in 1962 to administer funds of the Voter Education Project (VEP) in Mississippi, gladly accepted the NLG's assistance. Moses and his colleagues faced terror and risked their lives daily; during the period of his leadership, SNCC workers were likely to welcome any steadfast allies who served willingly in the trenches. In addition, they generally felt more comfortable with guild politics than with those of other lawyers, including the stalwarts representing the NAACP Inc. Fund. From their risky rural enclaves, SNCC workers sometimes criticized the more sedate centrist liberalism of the SCLC and NAACP.[33]

31. Apology of James E. Pfister, n.d., in Box 11, Folder 15, Dombrowski Papers.
32. Peebles, "Subversion and SCEF," 74–75; Waltzer interview.
33. Kenneth O'Reilly, *"Racial Matters": The FBI's Secret File on Black America, 1960–*

After the raids, Ben Smith threw himself into the work in Mississippi, becoming involved in cases all over the state in the spring and summer of 1964. In New Orleans, Smith's partner noted, "we handled seaman's claims and workmen's compensation claims, and Ben still represented his labor unions. But the thrust of our practice became the Mississippi Freedom Summer. . . . [W]e went into over-drive." This was COFO's "Mississippi Summer," when hundreds of students came to participate in voter registration projects. Mississippi filled her jails, and guild lawyers found plenty of work. A good deal of CASL's work, and the work of the Smith firm, centered in the delta town of Greenwood in LeFlore, one of the counties targeted by SNCC for voter registration organizing.[34]

Many of the cases were similar. Police arrested groups of prospective voters or supportive protestors for violations of a picketing law or disturbing the peace as they stood in line or picketed a courthouse claiming unfair discrimination in the application of registration rules or requirements. Lawyers arranged bail if possible, then represented the picketers in court. The lawyers routinely consolidated these cases so that a long list of persons arrested for the same offense could be tried together. Usually the attorneys filed motions in state and federal courts to have the cases "removed" to federal jurisdiction.

The removal device changed the nature of legal work in Mississippi during "Freedom Summer." It circumvented local justice and the doctrine of abstention but at the same time placed liberal lawyers like Ben Smith before stubborn defenders of the southern establishment like W. Harold Cox, chief judge of the federal court for the Southern District of Mississippi, or his older and more refined but similarly unsympathetic fellow judge, Sidney C. Mize. Mize had been appointed by Roosevelt in 1937; the ABA told the Kennedy administration it found Cox "exceptionally well qualified" for the federal judiciary in 1961. But the *Yale Law Review* called Judge Cox "leaden-footed" in his

---

1972 (New York, 1989), 181–85, quote on 181; Branch, *Parting the Waters,* 557–58; Carson, *In Struggle,* 107, 137, 182; Cummings, *Pied Piper,* 246; Dittmer, *Local People,* 230–36.

34. Peebles, "Reminiscences," 56. There are many good sources for "Freedom Summer"; the best comprehensive recent accounts are Dittmer's *Local People* and Charles M. Payne's *I've Got the Light of Freedom: The Organizing Tradition and the Mississippi Freedom Struggle* (Berkeley, 1995).

disposition of civil rights cases, and both judges made every effort to impede the removal process.[35]

The removal statute in question, passed by the Reconstruction Congress in 1866 to prevent capricious state prosecutions of freedmen, had been "unearthed from the dead past by a brilliant young lawyer named William Higgs" during freedom rider cases in 1961. In practice, removal involved filing motions with both state and federal courts, actions charging that the state initiated prosecutions after defendants attempted to assert federally protected rights and then refused to guarantee the civil rights of the accused. Though federal district judges sometimes tried to prevent removal motions, once filed, the district court's action on the petitions could be appealed to the circuit court in New Orleans.[36]

Hunter Morey, COFO's "legal director," described the work of Ben Smith and others in a letter to Arthur Kinoy in April, 1964. He reported on a case that began in Greenwood in March, when police arrested fourteen picketers at the LeFlore County courthouse. First, Jack Peebles filed a petition for removal. Morey said Howard Moore, a young black lawyer and SNCC member from Atlanta, had been with Peebles in Greenwood "as the major attorney," but then Ben Smith came in "as THE Attorney." Smith, accompanied by Mel Wulf of the ACLU, "filed a habeas corpus in Greenville [in federal district court]." Four protestors arranged their own release, but "the other 10 got out on bond money gotten up by Ben Smith." Smith was also "handling the Hattiesburg cases which are quite similar." In fact, both these cases grew out of "Freedom Days" organized in several Mississippi towns in the early months of 1964. Normally, COFO workers took one or two prospective voters to a registration office at a time, but on these special days large numbers were enlisted to stand in lines outside courthouses. At the same time, black and white supporters, sometimes white clergymen or similar outsiders,

35. Gerald M. Stern, "Judge William Harold Cox and the Right to Vote in Clarke County, Mississippi," in *Southern Justice,* ed. Friedman, 166. The appointment of Cox, a friend of James Eastland's from "Ole Miss" days and the son of the sheriff in Sunflower County, was an early Kennedy administration concession to the powerful Democratic senator from Mississippi. See also Bass, *Unlikely Heroes,* 164–68.

36. Kinoy, *Rights on Trial,* 191.

"set up a picket line to protest unfair practices by the circuit court" nearby. Arrests thus usually included both resident black Mississippians and alien picketers. Pleased that he had contacted the NLG about the Greenwood and Hattiesburg matters, Morey believed "Ben Smith did fabulously."[37]

He also discussed the creation of the LCDC (mislabeling it "the new Constitutional Rights Defense Committee"), which included the ACLU, CORE, the American Jewish Congress, the National Council of Churches, and the NAACP, but "definitely NOT you, Kunstler, Rabinowitz nor any Guild lawyers FOR POLITICAL REASONS." Morey had castigated the ACLU's Wulf about this, and thought Wulf "got mad, mostly as he knew he was wrong." He despaired that he would probably have to design different "Spheres of Action" for the skirmishing lawyers during the summer of 1964. Regardless of these tensions, SNCC leader Bob Moses repeatedly advised his wary center liberal allies that he would not renounce the guild.[38]

The NLG recruited more than sixty lawyers to work in Mississippi that summer, necessitating a permanent staff at its office in Jackson. In a letter to Morey in May, George Crockett outlined the guild's plans for bringing in volunteer lawyers for one- or two-week stints, stating that he and Ben Smith would be available "for the duration." Nevertheless, "it will be our policy to step in and render assistance only in those instances where no other civil rights organization operating in Mississippi is ready, willing, and able to act," he said. "We are not in competition" with the other groups of lawyers coming to Mississippi.[39]

The guild planned an orientation conference in Detroit for June 5–7 that Morey would attend. He agreed to drive a station wagon designated for use by guild lawyers back to Jackson. At about the same time, Crockett reported to Robert Moses on CASL's activities and the conference and asked for the SNCC leader's suggestions. "We are most pleased to note," he said, "the New York *Times* article of May 21" about the formation of the LCDC. "We look forward to unstinted cooperation with all organizations and individuals

37. Hunter Morey to Arthur Kinoy, April 13, 1964, in Box 3, Folder 4, Morey Papers; Dittmer, *Local People*, 219–24.

38. Hunter Morey to Arthur Kinoy, April 13, 1964, in Box 3, Folder 4, Morey Papers; Dittmer, *Local People*, 233–34.

39. George Crockett to Hunter Morey, May 19, 1964, in Box 3, Folder 4, Morey Papers.

engaged in this common struggle for democratic rights." On June 15 he wrote to the president of the Mississippi Bar Association announcing the opening of the guild's offices in Jackson "to help redress the shortage of lawyers" willing to represent civil rights workers.[40]

The Smith, Waltzer firm became involved in a great many of the CASL cases, if not in the initial stages then later in the appeals process after short-time volunteer attorneys left Mississippi. The Hattiesburg and Greenwood cases mentioned in Hunter Morey's letter to Arthur Kinoy typified these cases in content and became themselves critical tests of the removal strategy. Both cases began in the winter and spring before "Freedom Summer," and both eventually reached the Supreme Court.

Ben Smith argued *Peacock* v. *City of Greenwood*[41] before the high court in 1966, asking for a broad interpretation of the removal statute "based on the apparent intent of the Reconstruction Congress." Jack Peebles, who had handled the case in the Fifth Circuit, watched with envy and admiration as the firm's senior partner presented the case. By 1966 "even the Supreme Court knew who Ben was," he said, describing how "one or two of the justices smiled" when a relaxed Smith unbuttoned his coat as he began his "powerful" presentation. "He told the Court what things were really like in Mississippi and in the struggle for constitutional rights in the Deep South." Smith asked the Court to enlarge grounds for removal to include not only state statutes that denied protected rights but state courts' administration of justice, when constructed to accomplish a similar purpose. "We knew we were right and we would take nothing less than the whole package," said Peebles, though they had been advised by some colleagues to seek a narrow decision that might protect only the Greenwood demonstrators.[42]

Smith thought the case would determine the "general course of removal" and that the decision would be "the definitive Supreme Court pronouncement on the Mississippi Summer of 1964." But by a five to four vote, the Supreme Court refused to accept a broad Fifth Circuit ruling that could have greatly

40. "List of Guild Attorneys Participating in Mississippi Project," in Box 4, Folder 6, and George Crockett to Robert Moses, May 22, 1964, in Box 3, Folder 4, ibid.; Crockett to Edward J. Currie, June 15, 1964, in Box 4, Folder 4, NLG Papers, Meiklejohn Institute.

41. 347 F.2d 679 (1965), 384 U.S. 808 (1966).

42. Peebles, "Reminiscences," 76–77.

enlarged the jurisdiction of the federal courts and altered the relationship between states and the federal government. Removal would be sanctioned only if defendants were denied federal rights under a state law that could be declared unconstitutional "on its face," so vague or arbitrary that persons of common intelligence would doubt its constitutionality. The negative decision distressed civil liberties lawyers and limited the Fifth Circuit's ability to grant removal in Mississippi or elsewhere after 1966.[43] By that time, of course, the passage of the 1964 Civil Rights Act and the 1965 Voting Rights Act had greatly increased the arsenal of federal protections for civil rights workers and black voters. For instance, a provision in the 1964 act granted the right of appeal from remand of a case removed to federal court, thus solving a very important problem: "how to get demonstrators out of state jails and under federal protection before they were attacked by other racist prisoners."[44] But during the crucial early years of the civil rights movement, removal remained an important legal device.

The Hattiesburg case began two weeks after the first Greenwood arrests, when large groups of COFO workers, supported by visiting white ministers, waited and demonstrated outside the Forrest County courthouse and were arrested. Charged with violating an antipicketing bill passed only a week earlier by the Mississippi legislature, they faced a maximum penalty of $500 or six months in jail, or both, if found guilty of activities that "obstruct or interfere with ingress or egress" to Mississippi's public buildings. The sponsoring legislator thought his colleagues would "catch the significance of the bill without too much discussion." Described by the Jackson *Daily News* as "an emergency bill for Greenwood," the measure passed on April 2, two days after the fourteen VEP demonstrators were arrested in front of that city's courthouse.[45]

The early days of the Hattiesburg litigation illustrate the attempts by federal district judges of southern Mississippi to outmaneuver civil rights workers and their lawyers. Just as clearly, they demonstrate the sensitivity of a majority

43. B. E. Smith to Ernest Goodman, April 20, 1966, in Box 3, Folder 6, Smith Papers; *Peacock v. Greenwood.*

44. Ginger and Tobin, eds., *NLG*, 204.

45. Paul G. Chevigy, "A Busy Spring in the Magnolia State," in *Southern Justice*, ed. Friedman, 26–27.

of Fifth Circuit judges to infringements of civil liberties. On April 17, Judge Cox refused to allow filing of Smith's removal petition in the case. Instead, he ruled that a separate petition must be filed for each of the defendants in this large consolidated case and that each removal required a $500 bond. He also found Smith ineligible to practice in the federal courts of Mississippi, despite the Louisiana-licensed attorney's deposition pledging that he had made a reasonable effort to secure a Mississippi lawyer for the defendants. Though the courts of Mississippi's northern district accepted such affidavits, Judges Cox and Mize refused to allow this procedure. Cox complained to Judge Richard Rives two weeks later that Ben Smith had "wantonly represented to the court that local counsel was not available."[46]

Cox's edict infuriated Smith. "They're out to quash removal," he phoned Kinoy from Hattiesburg. In response, the two lawyers took a very unusual step, asking the circuit court to issue an "extraordinary" writ of mandamus, an order to Judge Cox to accept the removal petition. Bruce Waltzer drew up the papers overnight, and the next morning Smith, Kinoy, and Waltzer met in New Orleans with Judge Rives. That afternoon they presented their case against Judge Cox to a three-judge panel composed of Judges Rives, Griffin Bell, and Skelly Wright. Although the three judges diplomatically gave Cox fifteen days to comply before issuing the extraordinary writ, they held unanimously that the removal statute did not require bonds in criminal cases and that one petition sufficed for one case, no matter how large the list of defendants. They also made it clear that if local lawyers declined such cases, a member of the bars of the Fifth Circuit and the U.S. Supreme Court possessed adequate credentials to practice before the federal court in southern Mississippi.[47]

In letters to Smith and Rives, Cox fastened on an insignificant detail of the

---

46. New York *Times,* April 19, 1964, in Box 2, Folder 6, "Attorney's Affidavit," *Michael Lefton et al.* v. *City of Hattiesburg,* in Box 2, Folder 10, Harold Cox to B. E. Smith, April 22, 1964, in Box 2, Folder 6, and to Richard Rives, May 2, 1964, in Box 2, Folder 9, all in Smith Papers.

47. Kinoy, *Rights on Trial,* 236–41, quote on 237; Fifth Circuit Court of Appeals, No. 21, 411, *Michael Lefton et al.* v. *City of Hattiesburg* and *City of Hattiesburg* v. *Michael Lefton,* Petitions for Alternative Writ of Mandamus, filed April 16, 1964, in Box 2, Folder 10, Harold Cox to B. E. Smith, April 22, 1964, in Box 2, Folder 6, and to Richard Rives, May 2, 6, 22, 1964, in Box 2, Folder 9, all in Smith Papers; see also Bass, *Unlikely Heroes,* 158.

case, which had been mistakenly styled *Hattiesburg* v. *Lefton et al.,* although Michael Lefton was a juvenile who had been released to his parents. Cox seemed to be contending that Smith tried to trick him with this misnomer; according to policemen the judge questioned, Lefton had not even been arrested. On the contrary, Smith replied, the young man had been arrested and then released, and "there is nothing incredible about this." His petition to the court "was drawn in good faith, was not intended to deceive and was designed to call forth the protection of the Federal Statutes on behalf of persons entitled to that protection." He resented Cox's "saying that I presented an imaginary and false situation to the Federal Court. . . . My clients were in jail. There was nothing imaginary about that." The antipicketing law under which they were arrested and incarcerated, on the other hand, was certainly a smoke screen. Smith also objected to the assertion that he had "made wanton representation to you concerning the availability of local counsel." He had made every effort to find a Mississippi lawyer. Cox told the circuit court judges that his office located a Jackson lawyer, Dixon Pyles, who agreed to join the out-of-state attorneys as local counsel. "Had you not approached Mr. Pyles on our behalf," wrote Smith, "we would still not have been able to find local counsel." One of Willie McGee's first attorneys in 1948, Pyles, a veteran white trial lawyer, sometimes represented black Mississippians in racially charged criminal cases, though he had not previously defended civil rights workers.[48]

Only one other white Mississippi lawyer, Leonard Rosenthal, later stepped forward to associate himself with CASL and civil rights cases during the summer of 1964. As a result, his landlord evicted him from his office building in Jackson, and one of his relatives became so enraged at his association with civil rights attorneys that he chased the young lawyer with a shotgun. Nevertheless, Rosenthal courageously accepted a position as local attorney for the COFO Legal Advisory Committee and as associate counsel in the guild's cases, becoming responsible for signing and filing papers as a member of the Mississippi bar. By the spring of 1966 his life in Jackson had become so difficult that Smith reported to Ernest Goodman of Rosenthal's "definite plans to leave Mississippi and also to leave the practice of law."[49]

48. B. E. Smith to Harold Cox, May 4, 1964, in Box 2, Folder 6, Smith Papers. For Dixon Pyles see Horne, *Communist Front,* 76–80, 196–97.

49. "Project Mississippi—An Account of the National Lawyers Guild Program of Legal

In the Hattiesburg case, finally titled *Cameron* v. *Johnson,* CASL attorneys, with Pyles's help in the Mississippi courts, challenged the new antipicketing law. The case reached the Supreme Court twice, being remanded first because of inconsistency with the *Dombrowski* ruling. When Ben Smith and Arthur Kinoy argued the case in 1968, however, they failed to convince a majority of justices that the Mississippi antipicketing statute was unconstitutional on its face or had been selectively enforced. Nevertheless, Justice Douglas recognized the significance of the case in his strong dissent: "*Dombrowski* means precious little . . . if the presumption supporting state action is not overcome by facts such as those before us now."[50]

Despite his preoccupation with civil rights litigation, Ben Smith managed to handle a few very profitable cases in New Orleans in the mid-1960s. The firm's personal injury business multiplied in late 1964 when an explosion in the American Sugar Refinery killed several people and injured dozens more. The United Packinghouse Workers and the United Maritime Workers continued to refer cases to Smith, Waltzer, Jones, and Peebles. If the partners had centered on this business, Peebles noted, they might have "had the beginnings of . . . a very lucrative law practice." But this work failed to absorb the firm as did their civil rights activities. They would concentrate on damage cases for a while, then "head out for Mississippi again."[51]

Smith also handled pro bono cases at home in Louisiana, usually as a lawyer for the Civil Liberties Union. In 1962 he appealed the case of black death row inmate Edgar Labat, convicted as an accomplice in the rape of a white woman in 1953. Unless a jury recommended mercy, Louisiana law mandated the death penalty for rape. This long and difficult case went to the Supreme Court five times on requests for stays of execution or appeal. By the time Smith argued the case in the Fifth Circuit in 1966, Labat had been on

Assistance to Civil Rights Workers in Mississippi: Summer, 1964," and "Memo to Volunteer Lawyers from CASL, Subject: Mississippi Follow Up," n.d., in Box 4, Folder 4, NLG Papers, Meiklejohn Institute; Ginger and Tobin, eds., *NLG,* 218–19; "Report, Meeting of the Legal Advisory Committee, Council of Federated Organizations," August 26, 1964, in Box 3, Folder 5, Morey Papers; B. E. Smith to Ernest Goodman, April 20, 1964, in Box 3, Folder 6, Smith Papers.

50. *Cameron* v. *Johnson,* 262 F. Supp. 873, 381 U.S. 741 (1967); 389 U.S. 809, 390 U.S. 611 (1968).

51. Peebles, "Reminiscences," 70–71.

death row at Angola for twelve years and nine months, longer than any other person in American history. In 1957, only two months after his appointment to the bench, as one of his first official acts, Judge Wisdom had issued a stay of execution for Labat.[52]

Thirty years after one of the Scottsboro cases, *Norris* v. *Alabama,* apparently decided the issue, Smith argued that Louisiana systematically excluded blacks from the jury trying Labat and his alleged accomplice, Clifton Alton Poret. In 1966 the Fifth Circuit Court, sitting en banc for two days, heard seven cases claiming discrimination in state or federal jury selection processes. These included *Labat,* argued by Smith; *Davis* v. *Davis,* concerning Louisiana grand juries, presented by Bruce Waltzer; *Billingsley* v. *Clayton,* an Alabama case involving the father of Birmingham lawyer Orzell Billingsley, Jr., handled by Charles Morgan; and *Rabinowitz* v. *United States,* involving Victor Rabinowitz as counsel for his daughter, Joni.[53] John Coe had participated in the original *Rabinowitz* trial in Albany, Georgia, witnessing as an expert on southern juries that Joni Rabinowitz and other SNCC protestors could not get a fair trial in Georgia and should be granted a change of venue. In each of these cases the court agreed that, though the systems differed, discrimination in jury selection existed. Smith used a long statistical table to show how the Orleans Parish selection system exempting hourly or daily wage earners from jury service to spare them "financial hardship" disqualified most blacks and many fewer whites. He scrawled in large letters at the top of his handwritten notes for the hearing, "Hardship excuse is a *coverup!*" Wisdom wrote the opinion for the court's majority in the *Labat* case. The system, he said, operated to exclude "all but a token number of Negroes from the venires. . . . The system was neutral, principled, and—foolproof: No black ever sat on a grand jury or a trial jury panel in Orleans Parish." When the Supreme Court denied the petition of the state of Louisiana for a writ of certiorari, Orleans Parish was forced to reconsider jury selection and Labat and Poret won the right to another new trial.[54]

In addition to an abundance of civil rights cases, *Dombrowski* v. *Pfister,*

---

52. Bass, *Unlikely Heroes,* 46.

53. Victor Rabinowitz to J. M. Coe, September 25, 1963, in Box 4, Folder 31, Coe Papers.

54. *Labat* v. *Bennett,* 365 F.2d 698, in Box 4, Folders 1 and 4, Smith Papers; Bass, *Unlikely Heroes,* 281–83, quote on 283; Morgan, *One Man, One Vote,* 15–16.

and his New Orleans practice, Ben Smith became deeply involved toward the end of 1964 in the activities surrounding the Mississippi Freedom Democratic Challenge, an effort to remove the regular Mississippi congressional delegation and replace them with members selected through a nondiscriminatory "freedom vote" organized by COFO. The Mississippi Freedom Democratic Party (MFDP) had been represented by Joseph Rauh in its attempt to unseat the Mississippi delegation at the Democratic Party convention in August. When President Johnson, vice-president elect Humphrey, and others convinced Rauh to recommend a compromise that allowed the regulars to keep their seats, the MFDP walked out of the convention and severed its relationship with Rauh. Robert Moses and COFO called on Kinoy, Kunstler, and Smith to devise another strategy to bring attention to Mississippi's systematically exclusive election process. The lawyers met in Smith's French Quarter apartment in September, according to Kinoy, and discussed the MFDP's request while they went over the final Supreme Court brief for *Dombrowski* v. *Pfister*.[55]

The lawyers suggested that the MFDP contest the legality of Mississippi's elections in Congress itself, using as a guide a mid-nineteenth-century federal law that provided a clear-cut procedure for such a challenge. On December 4, 1964, a "notice of contest" was served on Congress by winners of another freedom vote held in five congressional districts from October 31 to November 2, just before the regular primary elections. Freedom vote winners claimed the right to be seated in place of the prospective members elected (in the absence of viable second-party opposition in the general election) in the regular Democratic Party primary elections. On opening day, members of the House of Representatives challenged the seating of Mississippi's congressmen-elect on the grounds that Mississippi deliberately disfranchised 50 percent of its potential electorate, setting in motion the procedure outlined in the 1851 statute.

After active recruiting by the NLG, more than 150 out-of-state lawyers assisted in the next step, taking depositions for forty days to establish that the challenge was based in fact. Ben Smith spoke in Los Angeles and San Francisco on January 10 and 11, encouraging lawyers there to participate, and many California volunteers answered his call. All of the attorneys paid

55. Kinoy, *Rights on Trial*, 261–62.

their own travel and living expenses, and some even brought court reporters, for interviews conducted throughout Mississippi.

They interviewed four hundred witnesses and had more than ten thousand typed pages of testimony transcribed (three thousand pages of very fine print when printed by the House of Representatives). Most of the witnesses were black citizens relating rebuffs of their attempts at registration through intimidation, violence, or economic reprisal. "It is clear," said lawyer Morton Stavis, who organized the effort along with Bruce Waltzer, "that it took enormous courage for many of the witnesses to agree to testify." The MFDP also called some adverse witnesses, such as former Mississippi governor Ross Barnett, the current attorney general and secretary of state of Mississippi, and the registrar of Forrest County. On many occasions the contestees—that is, the challenged regular Democratic Party candidates—were present or represented by their counsel, former Mississippi governor (and future Fifth Circuit judge) James P. Coleman. Ross Barnett contended, "I don't know of a single Negro who has been discriminated against—not a one."[56]

The Mississippi press and Senator Eastland, who led the fight against the challenge in the Senate, saw a Communist plot on the part of "foreign" lawyers. Ben Smith and exiled Mississippian William Higgs, who worked for the challenge in Washington, were surely the only native white southerners participating on MFDP's behalf. The lawyers who came to take depositions, Eastland complained, were a part of "an attempt to take over the state of Mississippi by the Communist Party," and the challenge constituted "a Communist planned attempt to influence the Congress of the United States." These comments came in February, 1965, about a month before SCEF and its NLG lawyers achieved vindication in the *Dombrowski* decision, and the Red-baiting rhetoric continued unabated until the House debated the challenge brief in September.[57] It should also be noted, however, that a wide variety of

56. Morton Stavis, "A Century of Struggle for Black Enfranchisement in Mississippi: From the Civil War to the Congressional Challenge of 1965—And Beyond," *Mississippi Law Journal* LVII (December, 1987), 591–676, esp. 640–65, quotes on 656 and 657; Stavis to Fred Smith, January 4, 1965, in Box 41, Folder 5, NLG Papers, Meiklejohn Institute; Waltzer interview.

57. Stavis, "Century of Struggle," quotes on 650, n. 259; Kinoy, *Rights on Trial*, 257–96, Cummings, *Pied Piper*, 258–77; George Slaff, "The Mississippi Challenge," *Nation*, May 19,

liberal groups lent their public support to the challenge, including the ACLU, SCLC, SNCC, CORE, the National Council of Churches, the ADA, and local and state units of church denominational bodies, unions, and the Democratic Party.[58]

When lawyers presented the depositions to Congress, they also tendered a new brief, asking the House, instead of immediately seating the MFDP challengers, to order a new election in Mississippi with all citizens participating. Ben Smith helped to write the new brief and attended both the subcommittee hearings and the floor debate in the House of Representatives. On September 15 the Sub-Committee on Elections, controlled by southerners, recommended that the contests be dismissed because in August the new Voting Rights Act had become law, making the challenge moot for future elections. But the Mississippi challenge, along with the more highly publicized Selma-to-Montgomery march the preceding spring, had heightened awareness of black disfranchisement, and the committee's report faced hot debate on the floor of the House. Despite the Johnson White House's opposition to the challenge, almost 40 percent of the Congress, including the majority leader and several other prominent Democrats, supported the contestants and voted to repeat the 1964 Mississippi elections. Despite its indisputable defeat, supporters of the MFDP felt that they had won a great moral victory. This effort also gave Mississippi's black population a head start in political organization, spurring the election of many black officeholders over the next few years.[59]

The frenzied pace of Ben Smith's professional activities in the mid-1960s precipitated changes in his personal life. Perhaps seeking relief from the peripatetic bachelor life he had led in the year since his divorce, he called Marjorie Hamilton from Mississippi in late 1964 to tell her that he had met the woman who would become his second wife. In March, 1965, a month before the Supreme Court decision in *Dombrowski* and in the midst of several important

---

1965, pp. 526–29. The depositions themselves are housed today in the University of Mississippi's law library.

58. "A Message from Mississippi: Help Us Unseat the 'Congressmen' We Never Voted For!" in Box 41, Folder 5, NLG Papers, Meiklejohn Institute.

59. Stavis, "Century of Struggle," 660–64.

Mississippi civil rights cases, the personal injury litigation arising from the New Orleans refinery fire, and the Mississippi challenge, he married Corinne Freeman (now Corinne Barnwell) in Washington, D.C. A serious and idealistic young woman ten years his junior, she had volunteered as a Freedom School teacher during the summer of 1964 and subsequently worked for the National Council of Churches in Mississippi.[60]

Corinne Barnwell told interesting stories about her early days with Ben Smith. On New Year's Eve in 1964, during their brief engagement, she and Smith visited the New York offices of Kunstler, Kunstler, and Kinoy on their way to see her sister at Yale. She related only half-jokingly that the northern lawyers questioned her to "check her out," to see if she was worthy to marry into their exalted circle. It made her feel a little uneasy, but ultimately they gave her their approval and agreed to attend the wedding. Another anxious time occurred only three weeks after the couple returned to New Orleans from their honeymoon in Mexico. When they hosted an integrated fundraiser for SCEF, an arriving guest told Smith and Jim Dombrowski about a New Orleans policeman outside, taking photographs of everyone who entered. Rushing out, Smith attacked the policeman and sent him packing without his film. The middle-class black people at the party, teachers and others, worried about the ramifications of the incident, and his new wife fretted over Smith's safety. But he came back to the party laughing and regaled the guests with the story. There was a definite "gutsiness" about him, Barnwell said.[61]

The "gutsy" quality showed up again in 1969. Smith and his client Lawrence J. Rouselle were attacked by two of Leander Perez's deputies in the New Orleans federal courthouse after a hearing concerning removal of the civil rights worker's trial from Plaquemines Parish to federal district court. Rouselle faced charges of assault with a deadly weapon, with Perez as his prosecutor; the state judge in Plaquemines had cited Smith for contempt when he filed the removal motion. Though outside their jurisdiction, Perez's "goons" tried to handcuff Smith and would have whisked both men off to jail in Plaquemines, according to Barnwell. Smith foiled the kidnap attempt by

60. Hamilton interview; Corinne Barnwell, interview by author, tape recording, New Orleans, April 8, 1992.

61. Barnwell interview.

banging on the judge's nearby door with his shoe and "falling in" with his assailants in tow when it opened. The federal judge, Lansing Mitchell, issued a restraining order, and the state court dismissed the contempt citation. Later Smith sued Leander Perez and the two deputies for $25,000 in damages.[62]

Corinne Barnwell also remembered going to Washington to hear Smith argue a case, probably either *Peacock* or *Cameron*. His parents and her sister came, as well, and they all felt proud of his grace and confidence as he spoke before the Supreme Court. Afterwards the clerk of the Court, a fellow southerner, came up and congratulated Smith on a job well done; and onlookers surmised that the justices admired his presentation. Barnwell described Smith as a "person of immense charm—tremendously able, energetic, and fun to be around," but lacking in common sense. Corinne and Ben Smith, committed to the same causes, might have been compatible under better circumstances. But Smith's drinking, always heavy, was a troublesome burden during the late 1960s and early 1970s, and in her view he became "temperamental and demanding" and sometimes "irresponsible" toward his wife and children. They remained married for eight years and adopted two children. Unfortunately, during their marriage his personal and legal relationship with the children of his first marriage, and with their mother, also became increasingly strained. Throughout the period, Smith's health deteriorated and his personal life continued to be a source of tension.[63]

In November, 1965, the Smiths traveled to San Francisco for the National Lawyers Guild convention. Corinne's family lived in nearby Mill Valley, and they gave a party to introduce their daughter's new husband to their friends. Smith spent most of his time, however, on guild activities. On November 12 he presented an NLG amicus brief in federal district court in San Francisco, arguing that the "Vietnam Day Committee" should be allowed to hold a parade in Oakland. Like many of his liberal and leftist friends from the civil rights movement, he gradually became involved in the antiwar cause. His contributions in Mississippi, however, prompted the guild to bestow on him its highest honor, the Franklin D. Roosevelt Award. During his acceptance speech, his wife wondered at the "rich liberal lawyers" applauding Ben Smith.

---

62. Ibid.; New Orleans *States Item*, May 1, 1969, p. 37; New Orleans *Times-Picayune*, July 11, 1969, p. 18.

63. Barnwell and Jones interviews.

Most of them, she thought, had no idea of the danger and intensity of his civil rights service and little understanding of the social and professional ostracism that dogged the career of a liberal lawyer in the Deep South. Smith loved them all, nevertheless, and was proud to be among their number. "We are lawyers in the great tradition of the bar," he said in his acceptance speech, "engaging ourselves in the human history of our era. . . . As a somewhat down-at-the-heels veteran of the courts of the Fifth Circuit, I say: Do not despair! [Revitalizing] the Fourteenth Amendment looked as distant in 1959 and 1960 as do the problems of the Peace Movement today. . . . [We] shall prevail." He believed that the progressive lawyers of his generation stood at the forefront of a "tremendous reevaluation of our basic constitutional law." Civil rights lawyers had launched this reappraisal of American civil liberties; and their mission would continue, invigorating the protest against the war in Vietnam.[64]

Smith's speech reflected changing NLG priorities. The guild would soon enter a troubled period in its history, when the popular front politics of its older members met the hyperactive, disorderly New Left of the 1960s. After a decade of tumult and division, the guild survived to become stronger in the late 1970s than at any other time since the early 1950s, another very complicated story. But in Mississippi the guild simply ran out of money and steam after the MFDP challenge, though Smith and others remained members of the COFO legal advisory committee for the following year and continued the pending appellate cases.

Smith's New Orleans law business changed as well. Jack Peebles left to enter graduate school in 1966, and Bruce Waltzer formed his own firm at the beginning of 1967. Ann Fagan Ginger thought "the Guild killed the Smith, Waltzer firm" because NLG members came in so often and used their secretarial services, telephones, and other facilities without paying for them. Bruce Waltzer tried to keep the operation financially solvent, and Smith himself undertook fund-raising activities among liberals in other parts of the country to help support the civil rights cases. But Ben Smith remained extravagant and generous to a fault, and the firm often neglected to cultivate and sustain a paying clientele. Waltzer retreated from the movement completely, not

64. B. E. Smith, "Lawyers in the Great Tradition," *Guild Practitioner,* XXIV (Fall, 1965), 96–99.

because his convictions had changed but because "I was dead broke—absolutely flat out cold. I did it after seeing a practice completely fall apart." Echoing Cliff Durr's complaints about liberals using segregationist law firms, Waltzer protested that people who came to them for help in civil rights matters took "their paying business to somebody else . . . it was a terribly hard thing."[65]

Ben Smith poured a large part of his life's energy into the struggles of the greatest social movement of his region in the twentieth century. He felt a special need to be a part of "the movement," almost as though he could heal himself in the process. A native southerner who understood the wounds slavery and segregation had inflicted on the people of the South, he became a movement lawyer gladly, energetically—almost, to use Judge Cox's word, wantonly, and at great personal cost.

But Smith brought more to the movement than southern liberal guilt about segregation. In the San Francisco speech, Smith said, "Lawyers do not make social movements, but they help to lead them and to give them an historical continuity essential to the story of a people struggling into the future."[66] As the southern movement slowed, "historical continuity" is evident as civil rights lawyers turned to defending the civil liberties of antiwar demonstrators, to women's rights, or to broad issues affecting poor or marginalized people. The ideas of the old popular front left exemplified by SCEF and the NLG's Committee to Assist Southern Lawyers persisted despite foes within the civil rights movement. Like John Coe's and Cliff Durr's, Smith's ideological roots were planted in the depression years and nourished by the anti-Communist trials of the 1940s and 1950s. Most of all, such lawyers urged vigilance against censorship of freedom of conscience and expression. Winning against southern segregation and disfranchisement was a supreme victory, but the fight to secure the blessings of liberty for all Americans continued.

65. Ann Fagan Ginger interview, August 17, 1990; Bruce Waltzer quoted in Ginger and Tobin, eds., *NLG*, 263–64.

66. Smith, "Lawyers in the Great Tradition," 97.

Epilogue and Conclusion:
"The Importance of Heresy"

When the Florida Bar Association invited John Coe to its 1967 meeting to be honored in his fiftieth year of legal practice in the state, a friend from Progressive Party days, Louis Touby, saw a notice of the celebration in the Miami newspaper and called to offer the Coes lodging. Coe replied that "through lack of enthusiasm for the 'power elite' of the bar, who are chiefly in attendance there," he had refused the invitation. Time and age failed to mellow John Coe or lessen his devotion to progressive causes. He continued to contribute money to the NLG, SCEF, SCLC, the NAACP, and Students for a Democratic Society. When asked by old friends, he lent his name as sponsor to a wide variety of liberal and leftist causes like Willard Uphaus' Citizens' Committee for Constitutional Liberties and Civil Rights Committee for Latin Americans in the United States, Oakley Johnson's Fund for Public Information, the Institute for Marxist Studies headed by Herbert Aptheker, the Committee to Abolish HUAC, which Aubrey Williams led until his death in 1965, and Julian Bond's fight for a Georgia legislative seat in 1966. He wrote letters to President Johnson and Congress in opposition to the Vietnam War beginning in early 1964, sent money to "liberal" gubernatorial candidate Robert King High in 1966, and supported Eugene McCarthy's presidential campaign in 1968.[1]

Few outlets for his ideas existed at home, but a letter to the editor of the Pensacola *News Journal* from "Mrs. John Coe," written in 1965 to voice opposition to the death penalty, had her husband's stamp, as did the earlier

1. J. M. Coe to Mr. and Mrs. Louis Touby, June 7, August 31, 1967, in Box 4, Folder 82, to Lyndon Johnson, March 3, 1964, to Eugene McCarthy, September 25, 1964, in Box 4, Folder 42, and to Ernest Goodman, July 1, 1964, in Box 65, Folder 14, all in Coe Papers. For records of contributions, 1963–70, see almost every folder in Box 4, filed alphabetically by year.

letter about Cuba. Perhaps he felt his attitudes had become so predictable that the local gentry simply discounted his own pronouncements. But whichever of the two actually wrote the letter, Evalyn Coe remained his most valued friend and sounding board. He also developed a close friendship with the minister of the small Presbyterian church near his home during the last years of his life, and he enjoyed long philosophical discussions with the young man. This sympathetic association, rare for Coe in Pensacola, brought him great satisfaction. And he did accept slightly overdue accolades at a meeting of the Pensacola Bar Association in 1968, when that group honored him during the fifty-first year of his practice.[2]

With the help of his son and law partner, Coe managed to keep his practice going, though he cut back considerably after a second stroke in 1966. In spite of doctor's orders to work only five hours a day, he wrote, "I am still practicing law, and trying cases . . . [though] there is little progressive work to do." He took pride in winning an ACLU "rape case (negro man and white woman) in which Toby Simonds [sic] . . . had gotten a new trial . . . the upshot of it was that we got him set free, so I felt that I could still do a little good." In the last few years of his life he served on several bar committees and handled pro bono cases when appointed by the court or requested by the ACLU—in 1971 alone a death row appeal, an LSD and a marijuana possession case, an ax murder, and the case of a marine who wanted conscientious objector status. A speeding ticket for driving sixty-eight miles an hour on the Pensacola Bay Bridge in late 1972 survives as one of the last documents in his legal papers. Apparently at age seventy-six he still commuted from his waterfront home across the bay to his downtown Pensacola office to practice the profession he loved.[3]

After a funeral at the Presbyterian church in Gulf Breeze, Coe was buried beside family members in a historic Pensacola cemetery on September 12,

2. Mrs. John Coe to Editor, Pensacola *News-Journal,* March 3, 1965, in Box 4, Folder 61, Aurelia Bell to J. M. Coe, July 7, 1968, in Box 4, Folder 83, both ibid.; Coe-Grubbs interview.

3. J. M. Coe to Mr. and Mrs. Louis Touby, June 7, 1967, in Box 4, Folder 82, *Donald Schneble v. L. L. Wainwright,* in Box 94, Folder 12, *State v. Ford Allen Carr,* in Box 94, Folder 25, *State v. Ellis Daryl Mott,* in Box 94, Folder 26, *State v. Jerry C. Ellis,* in Box 94, Folder 27, "Haugesay, Gregory S., Conscientious Objector," in Box 94, Folder 31, and *City of Pensacola v. John M. Coe,* in Box 93, Folder 19, all in Coe Papers. The misnamed Tobias Simon was an important Miami civil liberties lawyer and ACLU leader in the 1960s and 1970s.

1973. In its obituary the local paper called him "soft spoken but colorful" and "a crusader for progressive causes" who headed the National Lawyers Guild and the 1948 Wallace campaign in Florida. The article recalled his eloquent demands for a statewide ban on the Ku Klux Klan, the 1964 Civil Rights Act, and an end to anti-Communist investigations in Florida colleges, as well as his unrelenting opposition to the regressive state sales tax.[4]

The obituary also noted the large Coe family—five children, nineteen grandchildren, and at the time of Coe's death, nine great-grandchildren. John Coe found great satisfaction in his growing brood of grandchildren as he grew older, and he had an important impact on the lives of those he came to know well. Just before he died, his granddaughter's senior thesis at Emory University described his work, and a few years later a younger grandson wrote a paper about him for a high school English class. The grandson told about denunciations from old friends and threats from extremists but noted proudly John Coe's strength: "Grandaddy was not one to turn tail and hide when trouble began." Young James Coe judged that "most people in this [the McCarthy] era allowed the politicians their own control, just giving it up," but believed his grandfather had "the persistence and guts to do what is right at times when doing what is wrong is so easy." Unabashed hagiography, this essay is a splendid tribute to a beloved grandfather and sheds light on a relaxed and personally gratifying part of John Moreno Coe's often stressful life.[5]

Children and grandchildren also cheered and supported Cliff Durr in the late 1960s and 1970s. When they completed the house at Pea Level in 1969, the Durrs moved permanently to Wetumpka, and their extended family, including the nine children of their four daughters, visited frequently. Durr loved Pea Level the way Coe loved his bay-front dock and cast net. "I don't know how a man can hold onto his sanity these days," he wrote his friend Hugh Wilson in 1967, "unless he has a piece of land with things growing on it. While the preachers are busy intellectualizing up a new theology based on the idea that God is dead, I just come up here and see Him at work all around me just like He always has been."[6] Intermittently tormented by serious illness

---

4. Pensacola *News-Journal,* September 12, 1973, Sec. A, p. 2.

5. Coe-Grubbs interview; James M. Coe, Jr., "Grandaddy Coe," December 4, 1979, gift of James Mansfield Coe.

6. C. J. Durr to Hugh Wilson, July 13, 1967, in Box 4, Folder 4, C. J. Durr Papers.

beginning in 1966, first heart and back trouble, then prostate cancer and persistent lung problems, Durr's spirits always lifted when he came back to Pea Level.

Between 1964, when he closed the law practice, and 1969, Durr lectured and participated in academic seminars, gaining many tributes during three trips to England and numerous visits to American campuses. These pursuits remained the kind of "work" he enjoyed most. Houghton Mifflin offered him a contract for an autobiography, an endeavor never completed despite repeated attempts, and several oral history collections asked both Virginia and Cliff Durr to contribute their memories.

Invited to the White House in 1967 "for tea and to talk with Bird about making some tapes for the Johnson library," Durr wrote a long, introspective note to organize his thoughts. Though he had applauded Johnson's domestic initiatives, he believed the president's Vietnam policy was wrong and reevaluated his ideas about his old friend in that light. Durr found him "as a politician more of an operator than a statesman and as president, a commander rather than a leader." Johnson seemed not cold, but "desperately desirous of affection as well as admiration [though] insensitive to the feelings of others where his own political interests are involved and inclined to equate personal opposition with personal disloyalty to himself." But despite his feelings about Johnson during the Vietnam War crisis period, evidence that he later repaired this old friendship is found in a 1972 letter in which the former president regretted Durr's absence from a Civil Rights symposium in Austin. "A long time ago," Johnson wrote, "you taught me so much, by precept and example, about the dignity and opportunity to which each is entitled." And the Durrs remained friendly with Lady Bird Johnson, whom they both admired a great deal. A visit to the Johnson ranch was one of their last trips away from Wetumpka before Durr's death in 1975.[7]

During the middle and late 1960s the Durrs also continued to entertain a wide variety of persons, old friends and new, who came to the South as observers or participants during civil rights demonstrations. C. Vann Woodward, after staying with the Durrs during the Selma-to-Montgomery march

7. Handwritten paper, "Washington, D.C., September 25, 1967," ibid.; Lyndon B. Johnson to Mr. and Mrs. Clifford Durr, December 13, 1972, gift of Ann Durr Lyon; Salmond, *Conscience of a Lawyer*, 200.

in 1965, called Virginia "den mother of the year" in a note thanking them for their hospitality. "Probably a good idea for a historian to see at least one revolution first hand," Woodward wrote, "sobering effect."[8]

When Clark Foreman asked him to contribute an article about the march and the killing of Viola Liuzzo to *Rights,* the Emergency Civil Liberties Committee magazine, Durr returned to a favorite focus: "The problem of the South is basically one of civil liberties." White southerners feared dissent and saw conspiracy everywhere, and "black" still meant "red." Deploring the continuation of HUAC and SISS with only weak opposition from civil rights liberals in Congress, he noted that the committees persistently provided ammunition for southern segregationists like Wallace, Barnett, and Eastland. "McCarthyism" seemed entrenched, "built into the structure of government itself." He believed that "too narrow a concentration on 'civil rights'" would destroy the civil rights movement "as it did the labor movement in the 1940s and 1950s." And just as the Korean War had encouraged the growth of McCarthyism in the 1950s, he feared a reactionary surge spurred by the Vietnam War in the 1960s. "Unless our civil liberties are kept strong and preeminent," he thought "McCarthyism may reinfect the entire country." A few months later, in a letter to the editor of the *New York Times Magazine,* Durr replayed another old theme, "the abdication of leadership" by responsible southerners. "The story of the South in the past decade," he said, "has been the tragic story of the retreat of men without convictions before men without scruples."[9]

In 1966 the New York Civil Liberties Union gave Durr its Albert and Florina Lasker Award, presenting the citation with great fanfare at a banquet at the Waldorf-Astoria Hotel. The *Herald Tribune* called Virginia Durr the "easy drawling blue-eyed wife of the stooped Southern lawyer" honored at this "$10 per egghead luncheon." Characterizing Durr as "a pre–Fred Friendly fanatic for free speech down in Washington in 1948," the article quoted him reflecting "thoughtfully, as if the idea had just occurred to him

8. C. Vann Woodward to Cliff and Virginia Durr, April 8, 1965, in Box 4, Folder 1, C. J. Durr Papers.

9. C. J. Durr, "Report from Alabama: The Affair on Highway 80," *Rights,* XII (June, 1965), 7–11; C. J. Durr to Editor, *New York Times Magazine,* November 15, 1965, in Box 3, Folder 1, C. J. Durr Papers.

and he wasn't crazy about it . . . 'I've been a stranger down there among my own people.'" But he pondered that "it's not so bad. We might show the rest of the country the way before it's all over." The citation lauded his "consistent and outstanding courage and integrity in the defense of civil liberties." Afterwards the *Nation* commissioned a guest editorial about Durr's career that commended his service in government and at the bar. Called "The Conscience of a Lawyer," the title John Salmond later chose for Durr's biography, the editorial lauded what Virginia Durr called his inclination to conduct himself honorably because it "just came naturally." The writer emphasized that the accolade was both long overdue and completely unexpected by the honoree, who always believed he did nothing more "than his personal skills and integrity required of him."[10]

By the end of the 1960s, a few southern groups also recognized Durr's contributions, asking him to participate in seminars and join boards and committees at southern institutions. He chaired the golden anniversary celebration of the University of Alabama class of 1919 and belonged to the Advisory Council for Journalism and Communication at Auburn University, the Law Center Planning Committee at the University of Alabama, and the governing committee of the Alfred I. DuPont Awards Foundation, headquartered in the journalism school at Washington and Lee University. He served on the Supreme Court Bar committee that memorialized Hugo Black, and both the *Georgia Law Review* and the *Alabama Law Review* asked him to write articles about his late brother-in-law in 1972. After many years of disagreement with the Southern Regional Council's centrist liberalism, he participated on several of its panels in the late 1960s. The organization honored both Cliff and Virginia Durr as "Life Fellows" in 1973.[11]

10. "Civil Liberties Union Luncheon: The Old New Deal Clan Recalls Days of Glory," New York *Herald Tribune,* February 23, 1966, in Box 13, Folder 2, C. J. Durr Papers; *Nation,* February 21, 1966, pp. 199–200; Salmond, *Conscience of a Lawyer,* 201.

11. C. J. Durr to members of Class of 1919, December 13, 1968, in Box 4, Folder 5, *Auburn Alumnus,* April 5, 1975, in Box 13, Folder 2, Letter to the "Law Center Planning Committee of the University of Alabama," March 5, 1975, in Box 5, Folder 3, "Committee on Resolutions for the Bar of the Supreme Court of the United States to take appropriate action in memory of Justice Black," January 24, 1972, Steve Wilson, *Georgia Law Review* to Durr, February 15, 1972, and *Alabama Law Review* to Durr, January 18, 1972, in Box 4, Folder 7, O. W. Reigle to Turner Catledge, January 1, 1967, and Mrs. M. E. (Dorothy) Tilly to Durr, March 1, 1967, in Box 4,

Cliff Durr died on May 12, 1975, and was buried after graveside services in the family plot in Montgomery. Papers in London as well as New York, Washington, and several other American cities carried his obituary. The New York *Times* listed his FCC service, his refusal of reappointment because he "could not in good conscience administer the President's loyalty program," his Washington civil liberties cases in the early 1950s, and the Rosa Parks case. The *Alabama Journal* added that he had always been "a Southerner and proud of it." In London the *Times* called him a man of "principle and grit," a "radical" who "suffered in the backwash of McCarthyism."[12]

On June 12, friends held a memorial service in Washington. Durr's colleague and neighbor from New Deal days, Charles Siepmann, presided, and speakers included Claude Pepper, Abe Fortas, Thomas Emerson, I. F. Stone, Richard Rives, Jessica Mitford, and Tilla Durr Parker. Julian Bond's name appears on the program as a speaker, but last-minute problems prevented his attendance. Naturally the most personal, Tilla Parker's talk began with an old story from her father's childhood, a story about a horse, Grandfather Judkins, and learning to live with one's ghosts. "He said when ghosts aren't confronted, fear runs wild, and the result of fear running wild is that sometimes people get needlessly hurt." She described her father as "a hero" who loved life, his family, and "the network of kin which surrounded him, with exceptions here and there. . . . He loved Jesus Christ, Thomas Jefferson, Mark Twain and the truth. He loved a few good friends, the South, good food, the moon and stars, streams, trees and wild flowers, strong coffee, the dawn, telling stories, building houses, and making gardens. . . . He taught us to take another look at our ghosts. He did it and survived. He taught us that things matter. He taught us that heroes live on." Thomas Emerson's and I. F. Stone's speeches both mentioned Durr's devotion to Jefferson and civil liberties, Stone "emphasizing the twin sources of his beliefs, Jesus and Jefferson." Among those mentioned in the preceding chapters, Ben Smith, Jim Dombrowski, Leonard Boudin, Anne Braden,[13] Fred Gray, Rosa Parks, Corliss Lamont,

---

Folder 3, and SRC Address, Atlantan Hotel, March 22, 1967, in Box 14, Folder 7, all in C. J. Durr Papers; Salmond, *Conscience of a Lawyer,* 202.

12. New York *Times* and *Alabama Journal,* both May 13, 1975, *Times* (London), May 17, 1975, and a large collection of articles and obituaries from other newspapers and magazines, in Box 12, Folder 5, C. J. Durr Papers.

13. Carl Braden died on February 20, 1975.

Frank Oppenheimer, Linus Pauling, and C. Vann Woodward sponsored this event, along with more than forty other friends of Cliff Durr.[14]

In July the Alabama Bar Association's Young Lawyers Section presented a resolution honoring Durr to the bar's annual meeting, extolling his "example and inspiration to a whole new generation of Southerners." The following October his Alabama friends held a second memorial service in what would have been, during most of his professional life, an unlikely spot for a celebration of his work, the Montgomery County courthouse. Ray Jenkins, editor at the *Alabama Journal* and an old friend, praised Durr's "courage and integrity and intellectual honesty at a time when those virtues were in gravely short supply," and a representative of the local bar called him "the conscience of the bar." Fifth Circuit judge John Godbold spoke about Durr's dedication as a "poor peoples' lawyer" as well as his defense of civil liberties.[15]

Nine months after the death of Cliff Durr, Ben Smith died in New Orleans at age forty-nine. During the last ten years of his life, Smith completed litigation of several Mississippi cases and practiced civil rights and labor law in New Orleans. He also ran for political office twice, divorced a second time, spent almost a year in Philadelphia as a legal aid attorney and adjunct professor at Temple Law School, and remarried. In 1968 his firm became Smith, Scheuermann, and Jones with the additional partnership of a young woman who had graduated from the Tulane Law School in 1964. After the death of Alvin Jones in 1969 the firm remained Smith and Scheuermann until Smith left New Orleans in 1973. On returning the next year he practiced alone from an office in his home until his death in February, 1976.

DuVernay v. U.S.,[16] the case of a young black man who wanted to avoid duty in Vietnam, became the last case Smith argued before the Supreme Court; Arthur Kinoy and Morton Stavis joined his brief when this litigation reached the high court. The case had "some substantial civil rights aspects," according to Corinne Barnwell, because "the head of the United Klans of America"

14. Remarks by Virginia Foster Durr (Tilla) Parker and Program, Memorial service for Clifford J. Durr, All Souls Church, Washington, D.C., June 12, 1975, in Box 9, Folder 5, Dombrowski Papers; Salmond, *Conscience of a Lawyer*, 214.

15. "Memorial Resolution for Clifford Durr," July 18, 1975, *Alabama Journal*, October 12, 15, 1975, Montgomery *Advertiser*, October 16, 1975, all in Box 12, Folder 5, C. J. Durr Papers.

16. 394 U.S. 309 (1969).

chaired the draft board that refused to grant conscientious objector status. But both the Fifth Circuit and the Supreme Court refused to overturn the board's ruling.[17]

As his 1965 speech to the guild had indicated, Smith considered the war a terrible mistake, and he regularly counseled young men who wanted to avoid the draft. After organizing a "teach-in" at Tulane as a member of the "Committee to End the War in Vietnam," he wrote to the dean of Tulane's law school urging introduction of a constitutional law course that would cover civil liberties and civil rights matters in greater depth. Ben and Corinne Smith both carried antiwar posters at demonstrations supported by Students for a Democratic Society. He became a leader of the New Orleans Vietnam Moratorium Committee, speaking at rallies and sponsoring several visits by prominent antiwar speakers, including his friend William Kunstler, to New Orleans. In 1970 he chose "Counseling the Protester" as one of his topics as an instructor in an institute sponsored by the Young Lawyers Section of the Louisiana Bar Association. Smith also served as state chairman of the Louisiana Conference of Concerned Democrats, the state organization for Eugene McCarthy's presidential campaign, which fervently opposed the war.[18]

Though ultimately unsuccessful, the McCarthy campaign, like Ben Smith's campaign for the Louisiana legislature in the preceding year, provided a concrete way for progressives to express mounting disillusionment not only with the war but with the urban poverty and disorder of the late 1960s. After the Kerner Commission Report emphasized the widening gap between black and white Americans, Smith issued a press release for the McCarthy group asking the city to invest the New Orleans Human Relations Commission with the power to effect real change. He noted, however, that "until the war in Vietnam is over . . . the tremendous commitment of funds called for in the Kerner Report will not be possible." Smith's letter soliciting funds for his own campaign announced his plan "to furnish a cause, a candidate, and a tangible

17. Ibid.; Barnwell interview.

18. Memorandum to Curtis Gans, National Coordinator, McCarthy for President Committee, from B. E. Smith, May 5, 1968, and pamphlet, "Bridging the Gap Institute," 1970, gifts of Corinne Barnwell; Smith to Lawrence Guyot, January 25, 1966, in Box 2, Folder 9, Smith Papers; Smith to Professor Cecil Morgan, July 29, 1966, in Box 11, Folder 19, Tureaud Papers; Report, June 23, 1972, pp. 1, 13–28, Smith FBI File.

goal for those in New Orleans interested in developing New Left politics." John Coe gave him money, but like the Louisiana Conference of Concerned Democrats, his group spent more than it collected. Smith urged the McCarthy organization to send the candidate to New Orleans to speak at the Packing-house Workers' national convention in June, 1968, but McCarthy did not come, and his supporters were not represented in the Louisiana delegation to the Democratic convention.[19]

Smith refused to vote for Humphrey, probably not only on account of the vice-president's support of Johnson's Vietnam policy but remembering his "party-line" opposition to the Mississippi Freedom Democratic Party in At-lantic City. Nevertheless, after Nixon's election he told *Newsweek* corre-spondent Richard Stout, author of a book about the McCarthy campaign, that he would not join efforts to create a "New Party," because "the Demo-cratic Party is having enough trouble surviving, as it is."[20]

In 1970, Democrat Smith ran a protest primary campaign against con-gressman Hale Boggs, a longtime legislator with a solid reputation as a mod-erate southerner, centering primarily on Boggs's support of the war. In early November he called his daughter, then a student at Mary Washington College in Virginia, asking her to join him in New York for a fund-raising party arranged by northern friends of SCEF and his campaign. Actress Jane Fonda, then married to Tom Hayden and at the height of her notoriety as a left-wing activist, hosted the party. Penny Jones believed the event achieved less than its sponsors anticipated. While her father delivered a quiet plea for help in overthrowing the Democratic establishment in the South, she thought his speech was not enough of a "red-neck basher" for the assembly of well-known leftists such as the radical lawyer Florence Kennedy and lesbian writer Ti-Grace Atkinson. Tired by travel that afternoon and slowed by too much alcohol in the long cocktail period before his talk, Smith lacked some of his usual dynamism. But Jones concluded that even at the top of his form he

---

19. "Louisiana Conference of Concerned Democrats Hails Kerner Report," March 28, 1968, and Memorandum, B. E. Smith to Curtis Gans, May 5, 1968, gifts of Corinne Barnwell; "Ben Smith for the Louisiana State Legislature, Dear Friend," August 28, 1967, and J. M. Coe to Smith, September 13, 1967, in Box 4, Folder 71, Coe Papers.

20. Richard T. Stout to McCarthy Supporters, November 20, 1969, and "Answers to Mr. Stout's Questions," n.d., gifts of Corinne Barnwell.

would not have delivered what Fonda and her guests wanted. He was too folksy, too southern. "His obvious love for the South . . . his sly stories and courtroom humor left them all flat." Although "Daddy [was] long a political outsider in his own land . . . in all save politics, he was the quintessential southern man." The northern liberals at the party wanted to hear "an educated, politically correct southerner denounce and apologize for the South," but instead they got a "southern patriot" who wanted "help to right the wrongs of his troubled but much loved region." Penny felt that "they were not pleased," and thus the party probably failed as a fund-raiser.[21]

Jones's assessment of the situation may be colored by her desire to defend her father's less-than-perfect performance before a sophisticated gathering. But regardless of the party's outcome, Fonda did not scrap her relationship with Ben Smith. A couple of weeks later she came South to assist a group of twenty-five Black Panthers involved in a standoff with New Orleans police at the Desire Housing Project. She used Ben Smith's name as a credit reference when she rented four cars to spirit the Panthers out of the city; police stopped the cars and arrested their occupants. Though he was away from New Orleans on a Thanksgiving holiday during the disturbance, Smith's name became prominent in newspaper articles about the incident. Bemoaning the *Times-Picayune*'s "low standards of journalism," Smith wrote the editors that his name had simply been used as a local contact "because my wife and I are personal friends of Miss Fonda." He admitted that he had "considerable difficulty with some of the more violent rhetoric of the Panthers." Nevertheless, he felt sympathy with such groups' attempts to instill "feelings of equality and dignity in black youth . . . who are forced to live in desolate and hopeless conditions" in the ghetto housing projects. But he was not responsible for the alleged "Black Panther escape attempt." He demanded an apology from the police superintendent who had carelessly used his name when reporting on participants in the affair.[22]

Perhaps, as his former wife and his brother believe, Smith eased away from radical New Left associations in the early 1970s, seeking a more comfortable

21. Penny Smith Jones, "The Jane Fonda Party," unpublished article, gift to author, January 30, 1992.

22. New Orleans *Times-Picayune*, November 26, 1970; B. E. Smith to Editor, New Orleans *Times-Picayune*, December 10, 1970, gift of Corinne Barnwell.

place for himself among old friends and colleagues in New Orleans. But he abandoned neither his principles nor his commitment to legal activism. A member of the board and treasurer of the New Orleans Legal Assistance Corporation, he helped to steer the legal aid organization through its early years. He continued to represent ACLU clients and members of SNCC as that organization moved out of the civil rights mainstream. He also became involved in the struggle for abortion rights in Louisiana, lobbying against a package of "right-to-life" bills in the legislature and acting as attorney in a petition against Charity Hospital. This last activity helped to widen a general disagreement with his brother, Pat, and to create a break between the two men that could not be mended.[23]

Corinne instituted divorce proceedings in 1973, and by the time the divorce was final in early 1974 Ben Smith lived in Philadelphia. He moved there to be with a young woman who had been a reporter for the Philadelphia *Inquirer* in the South, but the relationship was short-lived. Penny Jones believes that "when he tried, briefly, to live outside the South near the end of his life it precipitated the crisis that killed him." In any case, Smith returned to New Orleans and married Lucy Makinson-Sanders, a New Orleans native who worked at the Tulane Medical Center. He and Lucy took a trip to Europe and visited Alaska, where he delighted in flying an airplane over the ice and snow. For about two years he practiced law again in New Orleans, and he won one large personal injury case in federal court just before his final illness. By the time Penny married in 1975 he had reestablished a polite relationship with Lillian. He gave the bride away and they shared the cost of her wedding. As Ben Smith died of pancreatitis on February 6, 1976, Lucy asked Penny to bring her mother to the hospital room. Jack Peebles, Smith's friend, former partner, and now his lawyer, also stayed close during Smith's final hospitalization.[24]

In addition to the *Times-Picayune* article, Arthur Kinoy encouraged the New York *Times* to run Smith's obituary. The *Times* noted especially his

23. Barnwell and Smith interviews; John P. Nelson to New Orleans *Times-Picayune,* May 18, 1970, Box 2, Folder 2, and to B. E. Smith, May 30, 1970, in Box 2, Folder 3, John P. Nelson Papers, Amistad Research Center, New Orleans; New Orleans *Times-Picayune,* January 23, 1973, p. 12, June 7, 1973, p. 3.

24. Barnwell, Jones, and Smith interviews; Jones, "The Jane Fonda Party."

connections to SCEF and the NLG, his Mississippi civil rights work, and his current presidency of the Center for Constitutional Rights, a busy Washington-based legal assistance organization formed by veterans of the Mississippi Democratic Challenge. On February 14 a memorial service took place at the Unitarian church in New Orleans. Penny Jones had returned to her home in Texas, illness prevented her brother's presence, and Smith's other children, both under ten years old, could not attend. But Patrick and Lee Smith came down from Ruston, and friends from the ACLU, SCEF, the NLG, and the Mississippi campaigns attended the service.[25]

Jim Dombrowski eulogized Smith, "my friend and my lawyer for more than a quarter of a century," as a civil libertarian who defended "victims of the McCarthy era" and as a "civil rights activist when the going got rough." For a while, "when there was only one black lawyer in Louisiana, A. P. Tureaud," Smith had been "the only white lawyer in Louisiana or Mississippi who would take a civil rights case." He was "one of those heroic persons willing to pay the price." At a smaller family service organized by Episcopal clergyman William Barnwell, Methodist minister and civil rights activist David Shroyer presented another eulogy. Shroyer told a beautiful story about how Smith had helped a poorly trained black lawyer realize his own capabilities and begin to have confidence in himself. He spoke of Ben Smith's generosity of spirit, declaring that "through his work in representing the poor and oppressed and the victims of injustice, through his defense of constitutional rights, Ben made large contributions to a just society."[26]

Agreeing with this assessment, in October, 1976, the Louisiana Civil Liberties Union honored Smith along with Jim Dombrowski, Virginia Durr, Ann Braden, and two leaders of the New Orleans CORE chapter, Lolis Elie and Oretha Castle Haley, at the premier showing of *The Front*, a film dealing with blacklisting in the McCarthy era. Publicity for the event described Smith as "one of the key civil rights lawyers in the South" and "a champion of the

25. New Orleans *Times-Picayune*, February 8, 1976, p. 22; New York *Times*, February 9, 1976, p. 30; Kinoy, Jones, and Smith interviews.

26. James Dombrowski, "Benjamin E. Smith Memorial Service," February 14, 1976, in Box 11, Folder 21, Dombrowski Papers. Jim Dombrowski had retired as SCEF's director in 1966, and Anne and Carl Braden moved SCEF's headquarters to Louisville. Dombrowski died in 1983. David Shroyer, "Memorial Service, Benjamin Eugene Smith," gift of Corinne Barnwell.

ACLU who always stood ready to accept important civil liberties cases, often without fee." The following December the same group instituted the "Ben Smith Civil Liberties Award," a tribute presented annually "to an individual judged to have made a significant contribution to the cause of civil liberties in Louisiana."[27]

Certainly all three men under consideration here would have qualified for such an award, for they functioned first and foremost as civil liberties lawyers. They endorsed equal application of the law, or civil rights, as an extension of their original devotion to civil liberties, the constitutionally protected individual freedoms with which government may not interfere. And in addition to changes in race relations, they advocated broad reform in southern politics and economy. As with their professional counterparts around the country, these predilections led their careers naturally from New Deal liberalism to the fight against McCarthyism, and by late 1950s to the defense of civil rights militancy.

Yet both personal and political differences separate these lives and careers. A rebel by nature and a leftist by adoption, John Coe challenged southern standards both as an integrationist and as a defender of socialist ideas, though in his later years he was sometimes cautious about the latter and protective of his law practice. He retained an excessive pride in his family, past and present. And though he had few friends at home and thrived on the accolades he garnered abroad, he loved winning cases in Pensacola best. Doing battle with local prosecutors filled him with delight. Like Coe in his enthusiastic approach to his profession, Ben Smith wrote outstanding briefs, enjoyed the rough-and-tumble of litigation and his labor union work, and highly valued the bright leftist lawyers he came to know through the NLG. Though he defied local political precepts, the gregarious Smith collected friends and enjoyed a lively, convivial life in sophisticated New Orleans. Coe and Durr, traditional southern men of their generation, lived more moderate personal lives. Writers often use words like "patrician" and "intellectual" to describe Durr, but his sense of humor, religious devotion, and love of Alabama perhaps

27. "ACLU Plans Civil Rights Honor," New Orleans *Times-Picayune,* October 20, 1976, ACLU Press Release, "HUAC Victims Honored at 'The Front,'" n.d., and Program, Louisiana Civil Liberties Union annual meeting, December 11, 1976, all in Box 8, Folder 3, Dombrowski Papers.

define him better. Only those who did not know him or hated his principled, passionate defense of civil liberties connected him to the far left. Like Smith and Coe he loved the law, but he revered its purposes more that its processes. Though devoted to his clients and diligent as an attorney, Durr's interest in the law ultimately seems more scholarly than practical.

From a regional standpoint, of course, these three stand out most clearly because of their early and unambiguous integrationism and their willingness to accept racially charged cases. As typical southern liberals they loathed state-sponsored segregation and disfranchisement. In words often used by chastened southern contemporaries, Coe, Durr, and Smith were all "ahead of their time." The leading distinction between these attorneys and their colleagues among northern so-called "radical lawyers" lies in their unrelenting "southernness," an inconvenient but chosen affliction. Lesser men might have reluctantly conformed, or left the South for good. In the 1950s and 1960s, very few southerners of any description identified themselves as civil libertarians and supported the constitutional rights of leftists or civil rights activists.

Against the background of the southern bar, the exceptionality of Coe, Durr, and Smith looms conspicuously. Being liberal members of a very conservative professional fraternity naturally increased both their sense of responsibility and their vulnerability to notice and reprisal. All three men faced federal and state harassment and local condemnation. Though none joined the Communist Party or advocated overthrow of the government, fellow lawyers often judged them reckless or disloyal when they voiced their opinions or defended despised clients. In the face of popular or professional censure, they repeatedly affirmed the ethical canon that "no fear of judicial disfavor or public unpopularity" should interfere with the independence of the bar.[28] As James Coe said of his grandfather, none was a man to "turn tail and hide when trouble began."

But even if they are compared only with other liberals of the period, the tolerance of these men for diverse opinions and their willingness to defend alleged "subversives" is unique. Their advocacy of racial equality sprang not from *Brown* v. *Board of Education* and its aftermath but from movements rooted in the 1930s like the Southern Conference for Human Welfare, Henry

---

28. Canon 15, ABA Code of Professional Responsibility, 1908. See Gleason L. Archer, *Ethical Obligations of the Lawyer* (1910; rpr. Littleton, Colo., 1981), 306.

Wallace's Progressive Party, and the civil libertarianism that found its legal expression in the NLG. They joined the movement for an integrated South from a broad, historic perspective, a liberal outlook as genuinely American as it was southern. When, as Mary McAuliffe noted, even "the majority of liberals at mid-century became reluctant to defend the rights of the least popular left-wing minority," these unusual native southerners joined forces with the "American leftists" who, in spite of cold war pressures and the domestic Red scare, "fought to defend fundamental civil liberties." They had an almost religious affection for the Bill of Rights, and might best be described as steadfast constitutionalists, American patriots who believed that the promise of the great document could be fulfilled. Routed time and time again by corrupt or devious government officials, they resolutely expected that, somehow, democracy and constitutionality would prevail. Despite bouts of despair and intermittent periods of cynicism, each man was, in his own way, an idealist.[29]

Cliff Durr wrote in a draft of his autobiography that he thought of most of his liberal contemporaries as "damned liberals," that is, they were only "liberal above the neck. A real liberal," he said, "is liberal in other parts of the anatomy, like the heart." He highlighted his longtime suspicion of centrist liberalism in a story told about one of his many visitors around the time of the Selma-to-Montgomery March. When the daughter of a northern corporate executive was arrested in Montgomery and then went on a hunger strike with other imprisoned activists, her father asked for Durr's help. Durr investigated the situation long-distance but then demurred; he had retired, he said, from the practice of law. He wrote that the request simply brought out "the mean streak in me." He suggested that the father come to Montgomery to visit both his daughter and the prosperous Montgomery firm that handled his corporation's business in Alabama. This firm, Durr explained, "owned the mayor and the police commissioner," so "if anyone could get his daughter out of jail" they "could do it." But a prominent attorney at the Montgomery firm "lit into [the father] with the most abusive tirade he had ever heard," suggesting that the offending young woman and all other such outside agitators should "rot in jail." Durr told the man he could perhaps find another white lawyer to represent the girl "if he was willing to transfer his company's

29. McAuliffe, *Crisis on the Left*, 147.

retainer to them so that they would have something to live on until they rebuilt their practice." As always, Durr wrote, despite the fact that the executive was a Quaker who "admired [his daughter's] determination," he had to be practical, considering his company's investments in the South and "the political situation." Durr thought "his reaction was typical of the problems one has from damned liberals when one tries to do his duty as a lawyer."[30]

Younger liberal lawyers often appreciated the contribution, and the uniqueness, of these men. Bella Abzug told John Coe after Willie McGee's execution that she viewed him as "a symbol of truth and honesty at a time when so little of that kind of thing prevails in either North or South, East or West." Fred Gray, whom Durr had befriended even before the Montgomery bus boycott, thanked the older lawyer for his "assistance and counsel during the early years of my practice." Twenty years later, Gray spoke of "the close working relationship that existed between the two of us and how he assisted me in developing, not only into a good lawyer, but a good civil rights lawyer." He listed Alabama NAACP cases in which Durr had collaborated as a kind of "silent partner" and adviser, among them *NAACP* v. *Alabama* and *Gomillion* v. *Lightfoot,* the landmark Tuskegee gerrymandering case. Jack Peebles, who became the chief assistant district attorney for Orleans Parish in the early 1990s, remembers Ben Smith as "one of the best cross-examiners" he ever saw and "a dynamic, charismatic character . . . a natural leader among men." Mary Howell, who worked for him as a clerk in the 1970s, enjoys regaling younger colleagues with stories about her training "by a lawyer who was indicted for sedition by the state of Louisiana because he supported integration," and remembers Smith's "keen sense of right and wrong."[31]

If only as critics, examples, and facilitators, these men served their region and the nation well. They functioned as attorneys, after all, not as politicians or movement leaders. Sometimes "movement" or "people's" lawyers over-

30. Clifford J. Durr, draft of autobiography, Chapter 9, "Damned Liberals," 1–4, Box 17, Folder 12, C. J. Durr Papers.

31. Bella Abzug to J. M. Coe, in Box 36, Folder 24, Coe Papers; Fred Gray to C. J. Durr, June 7, 1971, in Box 4, Folder 6, C. J. Durr Papers; Fred Gray, "Remarks on the Occasion of the Inaugural of the Clifford J. Durr Lecture Series, Auburn University at Montgomery," March 1, 1992, gift of Ann Durr Lyon; Peebles, "Reminiscences," 19; Mary E. Howell, telephone conversation with author, notes, September 14, 1995; *NAACP* v. *Alabama,* 357 U.S. 499 (1958); *Gomillion* v. *Lightfoot,* 364 U.S. 339 (1960).

state their influence as activist attorneys, but most analysts see legal professionals essentially as technicians and strategists, necessary but peripheral to the movements they assist. While they may purposefully embrace cases involving legal principles or employ the law as an instrument of social change, lawyers function essentially as counselors and mediators near the center of controversy. To a young lawyer who wrote asking about his life as a "poor people's lawyer," John Coe answered that the law could be a "powerful instrument" in the hands of intelligent men, with power to do good or evil. But a lawyer who wants to help the oppressed must be a fighter "affiliated with no clique" who will serve his client and his principles alone. "To be such a lawyer presupposes a deep devotion to your profession." Ben Smith personally supported SNCC's mission in Mississippi, but he remained a legal adviser and practitioner, not a movement leader. In SNCC's case he contributed his skills to help a cause he believed in; in the case of George Lincoln Rockwell he used his skills to uphold a legal principle though he hated his client's cause. But he remained an advocate rather than an agitator or revolutionary, of necessity refraining from personal participation in activities that might hinder his ability to practice law and thus dissipate his value to his clients.[32]

Unfortunately, from the point of view of the independence of the bar, anti-Communist bureaucrats and newspaper columnists did not make such careful distinctions between leftist clients and their attorneys. In the postwar period, newspapers and politicians bellowed about Russia, Communism, atomic spies, and alien influences in the South no less than in the rest of the country. Fear of espionage justified curtailment of civil liberties everywhere. In the South the cure for Communism paralleled the cure for social equality and "race mixing." Eventually the cold war and the race question became interwoven, essentially the same issue. A liberal Mississippian wrote in the *New Republic* in 1948 that "the quest for civil liberties in the South—like every other question, and perhaps the very existence of a habitable planet—lies under the shadow of the atom bomb and the future." Perhaps, the writer

---

32. John Coe to Jim Wray, June 3, 1950, in Box 2, Folder 34, Coe Papers. See the discussion of "Radical Lawyers" as "Group Advocates" and "Civil Libertarians" in Casper, *Lawyers Before the Warren Court*, 124–85. For the opposing view that "to be a surrogate of a profound social movement, one has to be a member of it also," see Kunstler, *Deep in My Heart*, 359–63.

suggested, race questions might have been solved more expeditiously had the cold war not followed World War II.[33]

The reverse, that anti-Communism might have ended sooner in the South had race not been a major component of the doctrine, is surely also true. Nevertheless, southern anti-Communism was more than an extension of white supremacy. Domestic anti-Communism allowed state and national politicians to pursue southern dissidents with a respectable weapon. It also allowed them to link arms openly with right-wing allies from other parts of the country in a public-spirited hunt for Soviet sympathizers. Those labeled traitor to their country by southern politicians, grand juries, or committees felt the insult, and the social and economic consequences, as deeply as any other Americans. Considering the remarkable homogeneity of their community within the divided southern society, ostracism for southern whites may have been even more difficult than for northerners in similar circumstances. Public debate of southerners' patriotism disgraced families and ruined careers, leaving its victims virtually homeless.

As practiced by demagogues like McCarthy, Eastland, and Pfister, the search for subversion became a sham distracting the American people from crucial postwar dilemmas, challenges including not only nuclear proliferation and militarism in the Soviet Union, but poverty, racism, and colonialism. In its dominant antialien aspect if no other, domestic anti-Communism became indivisible. Conformity, not security, was its goal. Many otherwise reasonable Americans believed that integrationist or civil libertarian groups, even the NAACP and the ACLU, had links to an international conspiracy. Organizations advocating direct action against the status quo—SCLC, CORE, SNCC, or the legal groups assisting their endeavors—appeared even more menacing. Southern politicians intent on retaining power and preserving an increasingly vulnerable establishment found anti-Communism singularly worthwhile.

Yet the Communist Party in the United States all but died in the wake of Stalinism, the cold war, American anti-Communism, and de-Stalinization during the Khrushchev years. It shrank from a postwar high, according the most generous estimates, of about 80,000 in 1945 (out of a total population of about 150 million) to about 12,000 in 1956 and 3,000 after Khrushchev denounced Stalin and invaded Hungary in 1958. By 1960 more than half of

---

33. Thomas Sancton, "Slowly Crumbling Levees," *New Republic,* March 8, 1948, p. 21.

America's Communists lived in New York, and many reports suggest that at least half of them were FBI agents. After 1945, southern states felt effects of the CPUSA primarily through early CIO activities, the legal work of the northern-based Civil Rights Congress, which died in 1956, and weak propaganda efforts on the local level by party circles like the New Orleans groups patronized by Sam Hall, Jack O'Dell, Robert Hodes, and Oakley Johnson in the early 1950s. Ineffectual enclaves existed in a few industrial or academic communities later in that decade, but both their numbers and their influence among liberals became very small. Despite recent findings that the Soviet Union continued some funding of the CPUSA until 1989, suggestions that these southern fringe groups constituted a real threat to domestic security in the late 1950s or early 1960s seem ludicrous. It is also improbable, despite J. Edgar Hoover's convictions about Martin Luther King, Jr., that prominent southern civil rights leaders developed meaningful connections to their country's foreign enemy.[34]

In a 1966 paper called "The Importance of Heresy," Cliff Durr wrote of "heretics" like himself that "our value lies not in our rightness but in our doubts and questions." Even the greatest ideas, "unchallenged, have a way of becoming flabby or hardening into stultifying myths, and our noblest faiths, unquestioned, of degenerating into dangerous superstitions."[35] Anti-Communism combined with white supremacy in the midcentury South to redefine heresy and create both "dangerous superstitions" and crippling fear. Sons of the small-town South, educated for the nation's most tradition-bound profession, yet propelled by liberal convictions to oppose accepted doctrine, these lawyers indeed became heretics. They found compatriots within a small circle that included iconoclasts Myles Horton and Jim Dombrowski (whose biography fittingly bears the subtitle "An American Heretic"). But few white southerners raised "doubts and questions" against the reactionary current. A great tide pushed aside First Amendment freedoms, rushing to enforce the national commitment to anti-Communism and the southern commitment to

---

34. Caute, *Great Fear,* 185; James T. Patterson, *America in the Twentieth Century* (New York, 1983), 321; Klehr, Haynes, and Firsov, *Secret World,* 13–14; Charles H. Martin, "Communism," in Charles Reagan Wilson and William Ferris, eds., *The Encyclopedia of Southern Culture* (Chapel Hill, 1989), 1393; Garrow, *FBI and Martin Luther King.*

35. "The Importance of Heresy," December 15, 1966, in Box 14, Folder 7, C. J. Durr Papers.

segregation. Coe, Durr, and Smith asked searching questions of their time and place, challenging both the prevailing mores of the jim crow South and the political climate of fear in the United States. As a result, anti-Communist liberals of the vital center denounced them as imprudent or naive and southern conservatives despised them as renegades.

The political education of all three men had been enriched by the left-liberalism of the depression decade, and as young men they observed not only the innovative economic experimentation of the New Deal but the anti-Fascist idealism of the war years. These were times that encouraged thinking Americans to try out new ideas. "The Great Depression first brought me to an attempt to rationalize the contradictions in our society," Coe wrote in 1963, "and I freely acknowledge that Marx showed me many things that I would not otherwise have comprehended." Smith often talked about the "public opinion state," tolerant of ideas, protective of individual human rights, and meticulous in upholding civil liberties, the Jeffersonian ideal.[36] But by the 1950s, popular front tolerance of leftist ideas lay dead and buried everywhere, and the southern establishment countenanced no insurgence.

This era of reaction, when both national and state governments used excessive power to repress nonconformists, provoked duties and reputations these men did not seek and caused them to live lives that, in other times, might have been different. The old Chinese curse, "May you live in interesting times," seems appropriate. For resolute, conscientious liberal defense lawyers, "the times" may never be easy, but times were particularly inauspicious between the end of World War II and the mid-1960s. While principles and politics led Coe, Durr, and Smith toward activism, the substance of their progressive practices and the extent of their social isolation arose directly from the troubled times in which they lived. Often in despair, yet almost instinctively, they opposed antiradicalism and abusive government with time-less constitutional arguments, grounds outlined by the founding fathers and expanded by Congress and the courts after the Civil War. Cases and issues might change, but the First Amendment did not. The freedom to criticize government, to examine new ideas and exotic ideologies, to combine and campaign against the majority view, to challenge oppressive laws or bureau-

36. J. M. Coe to Willard Uphaus, August 20, 1963, in Box 4, Folder 25, Coe Papers; Peebles interview.

cracies and expect government protection in the process—such dormant precepts haunted all three, guiding their participation in civil rights cases as clearly as their opposition to the tactics of bureaucratic anti-Communism. Indeed uncommon as southerners and as lawyers, they joined a minority of their professional contemporaries who championed liberal constitutional remedies for the compelling inequities of the American Century.

BIBLIOGRAPHY

MANUSCRIPT COLLECTIONS

Alabama Department of Archives and History, Montgomery
Durr, Clifford Judkins. Papers, LPR No. 25.
Durr, Virginia Foster. Papers, LPR No. 28.

Amistad Research Center, New Orleans
Nelson, John P. Papers.
Tureaud, A. P. Papers.

Emory University, Special Collections Department,
Robert W. Woodruff Library, Atlanta
Coe, John Moreno. Papers, Collection No. 628.

Florida Department of Archives and History,
Department of State, Tallahassee
Florida Legislative Investigating Committee Papers, Series 1486.

Georgia State University, Southern Labor Archives, Atlanta
Kennedy, Stetson. Papers.

Martin Luther King Library and Archives, Martin Luther King, Jr.,
Center for Non-Violent Social Change, Atlanta
National Lawyers Guild Papers.
Student Non-Violent Coordinating Committee Papers.

Meiklejohn Civil Liberties Institute, Berkeley, California

Civil Liberties Docket Notebooks.

National Lawyers Guild Papers.

Tulane University, Special Collections, Howard-Tilton Memorial Library, New Orleans

Louisiana Civil Liberties Union Papers.

Tulane University Archives.

State Historical Society of Wisconsin, Social Action Collection, Archives Division, Madison

Braden, Carl and Anne. Papers.

Dombrowski, James A. Papers.

Moore, Amzie. Papers.

Morey, Hunter. Papers.

Smith, Benjamin E. Papers.

INTERVIEWS BY AUTHOR

Barnwell, Corinne, New Orleans, September 6, 1990, April 8, 1992.

Beggs, E. Dixie, Pensacola, February 14, 1988.

Bell, Aurelia, Pensacola, February 14, 1988.

Braden, Anne, Louisville, August 28, 1991 (telephone).

Coe, James Mansfield, and Evalyn Coe Grubbs, Pensacola, February 13, 1988.

D'Orlando, Albert, New Orleans, September 5, 1990.

Dreyfus, Leonard, Charlottesville, Virginia, August 17, 1991 (telephone).

Durr, Virginia, Montgomery, September 23, 1991, April 21, 1993.

George, William, Atlanta, June 11, 1990.

Ginger, Ann Fagan, Berkeley, August 17, 1990 (telephone), July 31, 1992.

Hamilton, Marjorie, New Orleans, September 5, 1990.

Heebe, Frederick, New Orleans, April 7, 1992.

Hollowell, Donald, Atlanta, May 22, 1990.

Howell, Mary E., New Orleans, September 14, 1995, September 18, 1996 (telephone).

Jones, Penny Smith, Phoenix, January 30, 1992.

Kinoy, Arthur, Newark, interviewed in Atlanta, November 2, 1990.

Massimini, William A., Slidell, Louisiana, September 4, 1990, April 22, 1992 (telephone).

Maverick, Maury, Jr., San Antonio, January 6, 1992 (telephone).

Nelson, John P., Jr., New Orleans, September 5, 1990.

Peebles, Jack, New Orleans, September 4, 1990, April 7, 1992.

Scheuermann, Arthel, New Orleans, November 5, 1995.

Smith, Patrick, Ruston, Louisiana, October 1, 1991.

Stanford, Morgan, Atlanta, April 24, 1990.

Thompson, Sylvia, New York, December 18, 1991 (telephone).

Waltzer, Bruce, New Orleans, September 6, 1990.

Wright, Herman, Houston, September 11, 1991.

WRITTEN RESPONSES

Abzug, Bella, New York, August 16, 1990.

Rabinowitz, Victor, New York, September 22, October 26, 1992.

Wisdom, John Minor, New Orleans, June 5, 1991.

THESES AND DISSERTATIONS

Newberry, Anthony Lake. "Without Urgency or Ardor: The South's Middle of the Road Liberals, 1945–1960." Ph.D. dissertation, Ohio University, 1982.

Peebles, Jack. "Subversion and the Southern Conference Educational Fund." M.A. thesis, Louisiana State University at New Orleans, 1970.

Sullivan, Patricia. "Gideon's Southern Soldiers: New Deal Politics and Civil Rights Reform, 1933–1948." Ph.D. dissertation, Emory University, 1983.

White, Vilbert J. "Developing a 'School' of Civil Rights Lawyers: From the New Deal to the New Frontier." Ph.D. dissertation, Ohio State University, 1988.

FBI REPORTS RECEIVED UNDER FREEDOM OF INFORMATION ACT

John Moreno Coe, 100-358684, Sections 1–6, 551 pages, received August, 1995.

Benjamin E. Smith, 100-408581, 224 pages, received October 6, 1994.

New Orleans chapter, National Lawyers Guild, 1948–65, 21 pages, gift of Mary E. Howell, attorney, September 20, 1995.

OTHER UNPUBLISHED DOCUMENTS

Coe, James Mansfield, Jr. "Grandaddy Coe," December 4, 1979.

Jones, Penny Smith. "The Raids" and "Jane Fonda Party," 1992.

Mohl, Raymond A. "Blacks, Jews, and the Civil Rights Movement in Miami, 1945–1960." Paper presented at the annual meeting of the Southern Historical Association, Atlanta, Georgia, November, 1992. Forthcoming in the *Journal of American Ethnic History* (1998) as "'South of the South': Jews, Blacks, and the Civil Rights Movement in Miami, 1945–1960."

Peebles, Jack. "Reminiscences of the 1960s Civil Rights Movement in New Orleans and Mississippi," 1990.

PUBLISHED DOCUMENTS

Institute of Government, University of North Carolina, and Southern Regional Education Board. *Administration of Criminal Justice: A Seminar at Chapel Hill, September 10–15, 1967*. Atlanta: Southern Regional Education Board, 1967.

Joint Legislative Committee on Un-American Activities, State of Louisiana. *Activities of the Southern Conference Educational Fund, Inc., in Louisiana*. Report No. 4, November 19, 1963, Report No. 5, April 13, 1964, Report No. 6, January 19, 1965, Baton Rouge, Louisiana.

Meiklejohn Civil Liberties Institute. *Meiklejohn Institute Inventory No. 2*. "The National Lawyers Guild: An Inventory of Records, 1936–1976"; "An Index to Periodicals, 1937–1979." Compiled by Richard N. Katz, 1980.

Southern Regional Council. *The Condition of Our Rights*. N.d. (ca. 1948).

Southern Regional Council and the American Civil Liberties Union. *Southern Justice: An Indictment*. Atlanta, 1965.

Twentieth Century Fund. "Administration of Justice in the South." [Pamphlet, copyright by Twentieth Century Fund, 1967.]

U.S. Congress, House, Un-American Activities Committee. *Communist Infiltration in the South*. Hearings, July 29, 30, 31, 1958 (Atlanta). 85th Cong., 2nd Sess., 1958.

——. *Communist Legal Subversion: The Role of the Communist Lawyer.* 86th Cong., 1st Sess., 1959.

——. *Investigation of Communist Activities in the New Orleans, La., Area.* February 15, 1957 (New Orleans). 85th Cong., 1st Sess., 1957.

——. *Investigation of Communist Activities in the North Carolina Area.* March 12, 13, 14, 1956 (Charlotte). 84th Cong., 2nd Sess., 1956.

——. *Investigation of Communist Activities in the State of Florida.* Part I and Part II. November 29–December 1, 1954 (Miami). 83rd Cong., 2nd Sess., 1954.

——. *Proceedings Against Carl Braden.* January 7–August 12, 1958. 85th Cong., 2nd Sess., 1958.

——. *Report on Civil Rights Congress as a Communist Front Organization.* 80th Cong., 1st Sess., February 15, 1947, H. Rept. 575.

——. *Report on the Communist "Peace" Offensive: A Campaign to Disarm and Defeat the United States.* 82nd Cong., 1st Sess., April 25, 1951, H. Rept. 378.

——. *Report on the National Lawyers Guild—Legal Bulwark of the Communist Party.* 81st Cong., 2nd Sess., September 21, 1950, H. Rept. 3123.

——. *Report on the Southern Conference for Human Welfare.* 80th Cong., 1st Sess., June 6, 1947, H. Rept. 592.

U.S. Congress, Senate, Committee on the Judiciary, Subcommittee to Investigate the Administration of the Internal Security Act and Other Internal Security Laws. *Communism in the Mid-South.* Hearings, October 28, 29, 1957 (Memphis). 85th Cong., 1st Sess., 1957.

——. *The Communist Party in the United States—What It Is and How It Works: A Handbook for Americans.* 84th Cong., 2nd Sess., 1956, S. Doc. 117.

——. *Report for the Year 1957.* Part 12, *Legislative Problems.* 85th Cong., 2nd Sess., 1958.

——. *Scope of Soviet Activity in the United States.* Part 12, Hearings April 5 and 6, 1956 (New Orleans). 84th Cong., 2nd Sess., 1956.

——. *Southern Conference Educational Fund, Inc.* Hearings, March 18, 19, 20, 1954 (New Orleans), and Report, *Hearings on Subversive Influence in Southern Conference Educational Fund Inc.* 83rd Cong., 2nd Sess., 1954.

NEWSPAPERS AND PERIODICALS

Alabama Journal (Birmingham)
Atlanta *Constitution*
Atlanta *Journal*
Florida Times-Union (Jacksonville)
Guild Lawyer
Guild Practitioner
Montgomery *Advertiser*
Nation
New Orleans *Item*
New Orleans *States*
New Orleans *Times-Picayune*
New Republic
New York *Times*
Pensacola *News-Journal*
Southern Patriot
Washington *Post*

ARTICLES

Alexander, Milnor. "The Right to Counsel for the Politically Unpopular." *Law in Transition,* XX (1962), 19–45.

Boudin, Leonard. "The Fifth Amendment: Freedom's Bastion." *Nation,* September 29, 1951, pp. 258–60.

Braden, Anne. "A View from the Fringes." *Southern Exposure,* IX (Spring, 1981), 69–74.

Brewer, Bradley R. "*Dombrowski* v. *Pfister:* Federal Injunctions Against State Prosecutions in Civil Rights Cases—A New Trend in Federal-State Relations." *Fordham Law Review,* XXXIV (October, 1965), 71–106.

Brown, Sarah Hart. "Pensacola Progressive: John Moreno Coe and the Campaign of 1948." *Florida Historical Quarterly,* LXVIII (July, 1989), 1–26.

Celler, Emanuel. "The Supreme Court Survives a Barrage." *Reporter,* November 27, 1958, pp. 31–33.

"Conscience of a Lawyer." *Nation,* February 21, 1966, pp. 199–200.

Dalcher, Louisa. "A Time of Worry in 'The City Care Forgot.'" *Reporter,* March 8, 1956, pp. 17–20.

Durr, Clifford J. "How to Measure Loyalty." *Nation,* April 23, 1949, pp. 471–74.

———. "Hugo L. Black: A Personal Appraisal." *Georgia Law Review,* VI (1971): 1–16.

———. "The Loyalty Order's Challenge to the Constitution," *University of Chicago Law Review,* XVI (Winter, 1949), 298–306.

Frantz, Laurent. "Wilkinson, Braden, and Deutch: The Legislative Investigation Cases." *Law in Transition,* XXII (Winter, 1962), 119–226.

Gellhorn, Walter. "A Report on a Report of the House Committee on Un-American Activities." *Harvard Law Review,* LX (October, 1947), 1193–1234.

Gillmor, Daniel S. "Guilt by Gossip." *New Republic,* May 31, 1948, pp. 15–27.

Mariast, Frank L. "Federal Injunctive Relief Against State Court Proceedings: The Significance of *Dombrowski.*" *Texas Law Review,* XLVIII (February, 1970), 535–51.

Peebles, Jack. "The Dombrowski Case." *Guild Practitioner,* XXXIII, (Summer, 1976), 89–93.

Rogers, Kim Lacey. "Memory, Struggle and Power: On Interviewing Political Activists." *Oral History Review,* XV (Spring, 1987), 165–84.

———. "Organizational Experience and Personal Narrative: Stories of New Orleans's Civil Rights Leadership." *Oral History Review,* XIII (1985), 23–54.

Salmond, John. "'The Great Southern Commie Hunt': Aubrey Williams, The Southern Conference Educational Fund, and the Internal Security Subcommittee." *South Atlantic Quarterly,* LXXVII (Autumn, 1978), 433–52.

Sancton, Thomas. "Slowly Crumbling Levees." *New Republic,* March 8, 1948, pp. 18–21.

Schomer, Howard. "Two Defenders of Freedom." *Christian Century,* December 6, 1961, pp. 1465–66.

Sedler, Robert Allen. "The *Dombrowski*-Type Suit as an Effective Weapon in Social Change: Reflections from Within and Without," Parts I and II. *Kansas Law Review,* XVIII, no. 1 (January, 1970), 273–76, and no. 4 (September, 1970), 629–49.

"The Shape of Things." *Nation,* July 29, 1950, pp. 98.

Slaff, George. "The Mississippi Challenge." *Nation,* May 19, 1965, pp. 526–29.

Smitts, Steve. "Hugo Black's [1886–1971] Constitution." *Alabama Heritage,* IX (Summer, 1988), 42–55.

Stavis, Morton. "A Century of Struggle for Black Enfranchisement in Mississippi: From the Civil War to the Congressional Challenge of 1965—And Beyond." *Mississippi Law Journal,* LVII (December, 1987), 591–676.

Thornton, J. Mills, III. "Challenge and Response in the Montgomery Bus Boycott of 1955–1956." *Alabama Review,* XXXIII (June, 1980), 163–235.

Thrasher, Thomas R. "Alabama's Bus Boycott." *Reporter,* March 8, 1956, pp. 13–20.

Tscheschlok, Eric. "'So Goes the Negro': Race and Labor in Miami, 1940–63." *Florida Historical Quarterly,* LXXVI (Summer, 1997): 42–67.

Tullos, Allen, and Candace Ward. "Clifford Durr: The FCC Years, 1941–1948." *Southern Exposure,* XX (Winter, 1975), 14–22.

Wallace, Henry. "On Testifying in Washington." *New Republic,* April 26, 1948, p. 10.

———. "A Report on the New Party." *New Republic,* May 3, 1948, pp. 11–13.

Woodward, C. Vann. "From the First Reconstruction to the Second." *Harper's Magazine,* April 1965, pp. 127–33.

BOOKS

Adams, Frank. *James A. Dombrowski: An American Heretic, 1897–1983.* Knoxville, 1992.

Adams, Frank, with Myles Horton. *Unearthing the Seeds of Fire: The Idea of Highlander.* Winston-Salem, 1975.

Anastaplo, George. *The Constitutionalist: Notes on the First Amendment.* Dallas, 1971.

Archer, Gleason L. *Ethical Obligations of the Lawyer.* 1910; rpr. Littleton, Colo., 1981.

Auerbach, Jerold S. *Justice Without Law?* New York, 1983.

———. *Unequal Justice: Lawyers and Social Change in Modern America.* New York, 1976.

Barker, Lucius J., and Twiley W. Barker. *Freedom, Courts, Politics: Studies in Civil Liberties.* Englewood Cliffs, N.J., 1972.

Barnard, Hollinger F., ed. *Outside the Magic Circle: The Autobiography of Virginia Foster Durr.* Tuscaloosa, 1985.

Barnard, William D. *Dixiecrats and Democrats: Alabama Politics, 1942–1950.* Tuscaloosa, 1974.

Bartley, Numan V. *The New South, 1945–1980: The Story of the South's Modernization.* Baton Rouge, 1995.

———. *The Rise of Massive Resistance: Race and Politics in the South During the 1950s.* Baton Rouge, 1969.

Bass, Jack. *Unlikely Heroes.* Tuscaloosa, 1981.

Bass, Jack, and Walter DeVries. *The Transformation of Southern Politics: Social Change and Political Consequence Since 1945.* New York, 1976.

Bass, Jack, and Thomas E. Terrill. *The American South Comes of Age.* New York, 1986.

Beck, Carl. *Contempt of Congress: A Study of Prosecutions Initiated by the Committee on Un-American Activities, 1945–1957.* 1959; rpr. New York, 1974.

Belfrage, Cedric. *The American Inquisition, 1945–1960.* New York, 1973.

Belknap, Michal R. *Cold War Political Justice: The Smith Act, the Communist Party, and American Civil Liberties.* Westport, Conn., 1977.

———. *Federal Law and Southern Order: Racial Violence and Constitutional Conflict in the Post-Brown South.* Athens, Ga., 1987.

Bennett, David H. *The Party of Fear: The American Far Right from Nativism to the Militia Movement.* 2nd ed. New York, 1995.

Braden, Anne. *The House Un-American Activities Committee: Bulwark of Segregation.* New York, 1963.

———. *The Wall Between.* New York, 1958.

Branch, Taylor. *Parting the Waters: America in the King Years, 1954–1963.* New York, 1988.

Buhle, Mari Jo, Paul Buhle, and Dan Georgakas. *Encyclopedia of the American Left.* Urbana, Ill., 1992.

Carleton, Don E. *Red Scare! Right Wing Hysteria, Fifties Fanaticism, and Their Legacy in Texas.* Austin, 1985.

Carson, Clayborne. *In Struggle: SNCC and the Black Awakening in the 1960s.* Cambridge, Mass., 1981.

Carter, Dan T. *The Politics of Rage: George Wallace, the Origins of the New Conservatism, and the Transformation of American Politics.* New York, 1995.

———. *Scottsboro: A Tragedy of the American South.* Rev. ed. Baton Rouge, 1979.

Casper, Jonathan D. *Lawyers Before the Warren Court: Civil Liberties and Civil Rights, 1957–66.* Urbana, Ill., 1972.

Caute, David. *The Great Fear: The Anti-Communist Purge Under Truman and Ei-senhower.* New York, 1978.

Celinni, Joseph, ed. *Digest of the Public Record of Communism in the United States.* 1955; rpr. New York, 1977.

Chestnut, J. L., Jr., and Julia Cass. *Black in Selma: The Uncommon Life of J. L. Chestnut, Jr.—Politics and Power in a Small American Town.* New York, 1990.

Clecak, Peter. *Radical Paradoxes: Dilemmas of the American Left, 1945–1970.* New York, 1973.

Cummings, Richard. *The Pied Piper: Allard K. Lowenstein and the Liberal Dream.* New York, 1985.

Daniel, Pete. *Standing at the Crossroads: Southern Life in the Twentieth Century.* New York, 1986.

Dewey, Frank L. *Thomas Jefferson, Lawyer.* Charlottesville, 1986.

Diggins, John Patrick. *The Rise and Fall of the American Left.* 1973; rpr. New York, 1992.

Dittmer, John. *Local People: The Struggle for Civil Rights in Mississippi.* Urbana, Ill., 1994.

Duberman, Martin Bauml. *Paul Robeson.* New York, 1988.

Dunbar, Anthony. *Against the Grain: Southern Radicals and Prophets, 1929–1959.* Charlottesville, 1981.

Edwards, G. Franklin. *The Negro Professional Class.* Glencoe, Ill., 1959.

Egerton, John. *Speak Now Against the Day: The Generation Before the Civil Rights Movement in the South.* Chapel Hill, 1995.

Emerson, Thomas I. *Toward a General Theory of the First Amendment.* Rev. ed. New York, 1966.

Faulk, John Henry. *Fear on Trial.* Rev. ed. Austin, 1983.

Freedman, Monroe H. *Lawyers' Ethics in an Adversary System.* New York, 1975.

Freidel, Frank. *FDR and the South.* Baton Rouge, 1965.

Freyer, Tony, ed. *Justice Hugo Black and Modern America.* Tuscaloosa, 1988.

Friedman, Leon, ed. *Southern Justice.* New York, 1965.

Garrow, David J. *The FBI and Martin Luther King, Jr.* 1981; rpr. New York, 1983.

Gellhorn, Walter, ed. *The States and Subversion.* Ithaca, 1952.

Ginger, Ann Fagan. *The Relevant Lawyers: Conversations Out of Court on Their Clients, Their Practice, and Their Lifestyle.* New York, 1972.

———, ed. *Human Rights Casefinder: 1953–1969, The Warren Court Era.* Berkeley, 1972.

Ginger, Ann Fagan, and Eugene M. Tobin, eds. *The National Lawyers Guild: From Roosevelt Through Reagan*. Philadelphia, 1988.

Goldfarb, Ronald L. *The Contempt Power*. New York, 1963.

Goldfield, David R. *Black, White, and Southern: Race Relations and Southern Culture, 1940 to the Present*. Baton Rouge, 1990.

Goodman, Walter. *The Committee: The Extraordinary Career of the House Committee on Un-American Activities*. New York, 1968.

Griffith, Robert, and Athan Theoharis. *The Specter: Original Essays on the Cold War and the Origins of McCarthyism*. New York, 1974.

Hall, Kermit L., ed. *The Oxford Companion to the Supreme Court*. New York, 1992.

Hamby, Alonzo. *Beyond the New Deal: Harry S Truman and American Liberalism*. New York, 1963.

Hamilton, Virginia Van der Veer. *Lister Hill: Statesman from the South*. Chapel Hill, 1987.

Hine, Darlene. *Speak Truth to Power: The Black Professional Class in United States History*. Brooklyn, 1996.

Holmes, David R. *Stalking the Academic Communist: Intellectual Freedom and the Firing of Alex Novikoff*. Hanover, N.H., 1989.

Horne, Gerald. *Communist Front? The Civil Rights Congress, 1946–1956*. Rutherford, N.J., 1988.

Horton, Myles, with Judith Kohl and Herbert Kohl. *The Long Haul: An Autobiography*. New York, 1990.

Hurst, James Willard. *The Growth of American Law: The Lawmakers*. Boston, 1950.

Inglis, Fred. *The Cruel Peace: Everyday Life in the Cold War*. New York, 1991.

Irons, Peter H. *The Courage of Their Convictions*. New York, 1988.

———. *The New Deal Lawyers*. Princeton, 1982.

James, Marlise. *The People's Lawyers*. New York, 1973.

Johnson, Christopher H. *Maurice Sugar: Law, Labor, and the Left in Detroit, 1912–1950*. Detroit, 1988.

Kairys, David, ed. *The Politics of Law: A Progressive Critique*. New York, 1982.

Kearns, Doris. *Lyndon Johnson and the American Dream*. New York, 1976.

Kelley, Robin D. G. *Hammer and Hoe: Alabama Communists During the Great Depression*. Chapel Hill, 1990.

Kilbaner, Irwin. *Conscience of a Troubled South: The Southern Conference Educational Fund, 1946–1966*. Brooklyn, 1989.

Kinoy, Arthur. *Rights on Trial: The Odyssey of a Peoples' Lawyer*. Cambridge, Mass., 1983.

Klehr, Harvey. *The Heyday of American Communism: The Depression Decade*. New York, 1984.

Klehr, Harvey, John Earl Haynes, and Fridrikh Igorevich Firsov. *The Secret World of American Communism*. New Haven, 1995.

Kluger, Richard. *Simple Justice: The History of Brown v. Board of Education and Black America's Struggle for Equality*. New York, 1975.

Krueger, Thomas A. *And Promises to Keep: The Southern Conference for Human Welfare, 1938–1948*. Nashville, 1967.

Kunstler, William Moses. *. . . And Justice for All*. Dobbs Ferry, N.Y., 1963.

———. *The Case for Courage*. New York, 1962.

———. *Deep in My Heart*. New York, 1966.

Kutler, Stanley I. *The American Inquisition: Justice and Injustice in the Cold War*. New York, 1982.

Lamont, Corliss. *Freedom Is as Freedom Does: Civil Liberties Today*. New York, 1956.

———. *A Lifetime of Dissent*. Buffalo, 1988.

Lawson, Steven F. *Black Ballots: Voting Rights in the South, 1944–1969*. New York, 1976.

Leonard, Walter J. *Black Lawyers: Training and Results, Then and Now*. Boston, 1977.

Levenstein, Harvey A. *Communism, Anti-Communism, and the CIO*. Westport, Conn., 1981.

Lewis, Lionel S. *Cold War on Campus: A Study of the Politics of Organizational Control*. New Brunswick, N.J., 1988.

Lively, Donald E. *The Constitution and Race*. New York, 1992.

Lynn, Conrad. *There Is a Fountain: The Autobiography of a Civil Rights Lawyer*. New York, 1987.

Marshall, Ray. *Labor in the South*. Cambridge, Mass., 1967.

McAuliffe, Mary Sperling. *Crisis on the Left: Cold War Politics and America Liberals, 1947–1954*. Amherst, 1978.

McCullough, David. *Truman*. New York, 1992.

McNeil, Genna Rae. *Groundwork: Charles Hamilton Houston and the Struggle for Civil Rights*. Philadelphia, 1983.

Miller, Loren. *The Petitioners: The Story of the Supreme Court of the United States and the Negro*. New York, 1966.

Miller, Marc S., ed. *Working Lives: The Southern Exposure History of Labor in the South*. 1974; rpr. New York, 1980.

Moore, Winfred B., Jr., Joseph F. Tripp, and Lyon G. Tyler, Jr. *Developing Dixie: Modernization in a Traditional Society*. Westport, Conn., 1988.

Morgan, Charles. *One Man, One Voice*. New York, 1979.

Morgan, Richard E. *The Law and Politics of Civil Rights and Liberties*. New York, 1985.

Murray, Hugh T. *Civil Rights History-Writing and Anti-Communism: A Critique*. New York, 1975.

National Lawyers Guild Foundation. *A History of the National Lawyers Guild, 1937– 1987*. New York, 1987.

Newby, I. A. *Challenge to the Court: Social Scientists and the Defense of Segregation, 1954–1966*. Rev. ed. Baton Rouge, 1969.

Newman, Roger K. *Hugo Black: A Biography*. New York, 1994.

O'Reilly, Kenneth. *"Racial Matters": The FBI's Secret File on Black America, 1960– 1972*. New York, 1989.

Painter, Nell Irvin. *The Narrative of Hosea Hudson: His Life as a Negro Communist in the South*. New York, 1993.

Payne, Charles. *I've Got the Light of Freedom: The Organizing Tradition and the Mississippi Freedom Struggle*. Berkeley, 1995.

Peterson, Merrill D. *The Jefferson Image in the American Mind*. New York, 1960.

Posner, Richard A. *The Economics of Justice*. Cambridge, Mass., 1981.

Rabinowitz, Victor. *Unrepentant Leftist: A Lawyer's Memoir*. Urbana, Ill., 1996.

Read, Frank T., and Lucy S. McGough. *Let Them Be Judged: The Judicial Integration of the Deep South*. Metuchen, N.J., 1978.

Reed, Linda. *Simple Decency and Common Sense: The Southern Conference Movement, 1938–1963*. Bloomington, Ind., 1991.

Reed, Merl E. *Seedtime for the Modern Civil Rights Movement: The President's Committee on Fair Employment Practices, 1941–1946*. Baton Rouge, 1991.

Rogin, Michael Paul. *The Intellectuals and McCarthy: The Radical Specter*. Cambridge, Mass., 1967.

Rovere, Richard. *Senator Joe McCarthy*. New York, 1959.

Rovere, Richard, and Gene Brown, eds. *Loyalty and Security in a Democratic State*. New York, 1977.

Rumble, Wilfrid E., Jr. *American Legal Realism: Skepticism, Reform and Judicial Process*. Ithaca, 1968.

Rusher, William A. *Special Counsel*. New Rochelle, N.Y., 1968.

Salmond, John A. *The Conscience of a Lawyer: Clifford J. Durr and American Civil Liberties, 1899–1975*. Tuscaloosa, 1990.

———. *A Southern Rebel: The Life and Times of Aubrey Willis Williams, 1890–1965*. Chapel Hill, 1983.

Scales, Junius Irving, and Richard Nickson. *Cause at Heart: A Former Communist Remembers*. Athens, Ga., 1987.

Schlesinger, Arthur M., Jr. *The Vital Center: The Politics of Freedom*. Boston, 1949.

Schrecker, Ellen. *No Ivory Tower: McCarthyism and the Universities*. New York, 1986.

Seay, Solomon S., Sr. *I Was There by the Grace of God*. Montgomery, 1990.

Sheingold, Stuart A. *The Politics of Rights: Lawyers, Public Policy, and Political Change*. New Haven, 1974.

Simmons, Jerald. *Operation Abolition: The Campaign to Abolish the House Un-American Activities Committee, 1938–1975*. New York, 1986.

Sitkoff, Harvard. *A New Deal for Blacks: The Emergence of Civil Rights as a National Issue*. New York, 1978.

———. *The Struggle for Black Equality, 1954–1980*. New York, 1981.

Sosna, Morton. *In Search of the Silent South: Southern Liberals and the Race Issue*. New York, 1977.

Steinberg, Peter L. *The Great Red Menace: United States Persecution of American Communists, 1947–1952*. Westport, Conn., 1984.

Stern, Philip M. *The Oppenheimer Case: Security on Trial*. New York, 1969.

Stout, Richard T. *People*. New York, 1970.

Taper, Bernard. Gomillion Versus Lightfoot: *The Tuskegee Gerrymander Case*. New York, 1962.

Theoharis, Athan G. *Seeds of Repression: Harry S. Truman and the Origins of McCarthyism*. Chicago, 1971.

———. *Spying on Americans: Political Surveillance from Hoover to the Huston Plan*. Philadelphia, 1978.

———, ed. *Beyond the Hiss Case: The FBI, Congress, and the Cold War*. Philadelphia, 1982.

U.S. News and World Report Book. *Communism and the New Left: What They're Up To Now*. London, 1969.

Vose, Clement E. *Constitutional Change: Amendment Politics and Supreme Court Litigation Since 1900.* Lexington, Mass., 1972.

White, Gerald T. *Billions for Defense: Government Financing by the Defense Plant Corporation During World War II.* Tuscaloosa, 1980.

Wilson, Charles Reagan, and William Ferris, eds., *The Encyclopedia of Southern Culture.* Chapel Hill, 1989.

Yarborough, Tinsley. *Judge Frank Johnson and Human Rights in Alabama.* Tuscaloosa, 1981.